THE
SCHOOL
MATHEMATICS
PROJECT

REVISED
ADVANCED
MATHEMATICS

BOOK I

CAMBRIDGE UNIVERSITY PRESS

CAMBRIDGE

LONDON · NEW YORK · MELBOURNE

Published by the Syndics of the Cambridge University Press
The Pitt Building, Trumpington Street, Cambridge CB2 1RP
Bentley House, 200 Euston Road, London NW1 2DB
32 East 57th Street, New York, NY 10022, USA
296 Beaconsfield Parade, Middle Park, Melbourne 3206, Australia

ISBN: 0 521 20241 8

First published 1967
Reprinted 1970 (metricated), 1972
Revised 1973
Reprinted 1975 (twice)

Printed in Great Britain
at the
University Printing House, Cambridge
(Euan Phillips, University Printer)

THE
SCHOOL MATHEMATICS PROJECT

When the SMP was founded in 1961, its main objective was to devise radically new secondary-school mathematics courses (and corresponding GCE and CSE syllabuses) to reflect, more adequately than did the traditional syllabuses, the up-to-date nature and usages of mathematics.

This objective has now been realized. SMP *Books 1–5* form a five-year course to the O-level examination 'SMP Mathematics', *Books 3T, 4* and *5* give a three-year course to the same O-level examination (the earlier *Books T* and *T4* being now regarded as obsolete). *Advanced Mathematics Books 1–4* cover the syllabus for the A-level examination 'SMP Mathematics' and five shorter texts cover the material of the various sections of the A-level examination 'SMP Further Mathematics'. Revisions of the first two books of *Advanced Mathematics* are available as *Revised Advanced Mathematics Books 1* and *2*. There are two books for 'SMP Additional Mathematics' at O-level. All the SMP GCE examinations are available to schools through any of the Examining Boards.

Books A–H, originally designed for non-GCE streams, cover broadly the same development of mathematics as do the first few books of the O-level series. Most CSE Boards offer appropriate examinations. In practice, this series is being used very widely across all streams of comprehensive schools, and its first seven books, followed by *Books X, Y* and *Z*, provide a course leading to the SMP O-level examination. An alternative treatment of the material in *SMP Books A, B, C* and *D* is available as *SMP Cards I* and *II*.

Teachers' Guides accompany all series of books.

The SMP has produced many other texts, and teachers are encouraged to obtain each year from the Cambridge University Press, Bentley House, 200 Euston Road, London NW1 2DB, the full list of SMP books currently available. In the same way, help and advice may always be sought by teachers from the Director at the SMP Office, Westfield College, Hampstead, London NW3 7ST, from which may also be obtained the annual Reports, details of forthcoming in-service training courses and so on.

The completion of this first ten years of work forms a firm base on which the SMP will continue to develop its research into the mathematical curriculum, and is described in detail in Bryan Thwaites's *SMP: The First Ten Years*. The team of SMP writers, numbering some forty school and university mathematicians, is continually evaluating old work and preparing for new. But at the same time, the effectiveness of the SMP's future work will depend, as it always has done, on obtaining reactions from a wide variety of teachers – and also from pupils – actively concerned in the class-room. Readers of the texts can therefore send their comments to the SMP in the knowledge that they will be warmly welcomed.

The authors of the original books on whose contributions this edition is broadly based are named in *The School Mathematics Project: the first ten years*, published by Cambridge University Press.

The *Revised Advanced Mathematics Books 1* and *2* have been produced by a team consisting of

W. M. Aitken	F. M. Hall	G. Merlane
P. G. Bowie	G. S. Howlett	A. T. Rogerson
W. M. Dain	A. Hurrell	J. B. Sampson
E. A. Door	M. J. Leach	D. J. Simmons
L. E. Ellis	P. G. T. Lewis	G. D. Stagg
G. Garrett	E. McAlpine	I. C. Warburton
C. C. Goldsmith		

The general editors were C. C. Goldsmith and P. G. T. Lewis. The detailed editing and preparation for the Press was the work of C. C. Goldsmith in collaboration with P. G. Bowie, P. G. T. Lewis and A. T. Rogerson.

Many others have helped with advice and criticism, particularly the teachers and pupils who have tested the material in draft form. Their suggestions have had a major influence on the final revision.

CONTENTS

PREFACE

There are several reasons for revising *Books 1* and *2* of the S.M.P. A-level course. It is now six years since the first edition of *Book 1* was published and the accumulated experience of teaching the material over that period has naturally produced many practical suggestions for improving the order of topics and the way that some of the ideas should be presented. Further, the S.M.P. O-level books now in use, *Books 4* and *5*, were published after the first edition of *Advanced Book 1* and some adjustment in the A-level texts is required to give greater continuity both in content and method of presentation. At the same time we have set ourselves other objectives with the result that the books are quite new and not just an updated version of the first edition.

Mathematics books are notoriously difficult to read, but we have attempted to write a text which can be used, without constant supervision, by all those who wish to study mathematics at this level. The text has been written in an exploratory style, with the aim of involving the reader more actively. Where possible, the mathematics emerges from a consideration of specific problems, and it is our hope that leading exercises early in chapters and questions posed in the text will enable students to realize the context and purpose of the work and so help them to develop concepts for themselves. For those who assimilate the main ideas quickly, there is enough extra material to provide an enriched course.

With a broad syllabus, it is important that unifying ideas are fully exploited. It is for this reason that, in the S.M.P. texts, chapters on the main areas of application—mechanics, statistics and computing—have been placed among those on algebra, calculus and geometry. Some of the revision in the order of the chapters and in the order and manner of presentation of material has been made to strengthen the links between topics and to make these links more obvious.

It is envisaged that increasing numbers of schools will have computing facilities, so both text and exercises are computer-oriented where appropriate.

Chapter 1 discusses sequences and introduces a flow chart notation so that numerical methods and computing can be used in the subsequent chapters. Inductive definitions form the main connection between the two themes of this chapter; proof by induction, however, is left until later.

The next three chapters—on functions, graphs and algebraic manipulation—provide the basic ideas, experience and skills needed for the introduction to the differential calculus. An innovation in the function chapter is an extended discussion of mathematical models and their formulation.

As before, differentiation is introduced through the scale factor of a mapping, but the development from average scale factors to derivatives and then to derived functions is now more leisurely. Reinforcement and application of the calculus techniques is provided by the differentiation of circular functions, in Chapter 6, and of vectors in the Kinematics chapter. The latter introduces vectors for the first time in the A-level course.

In Chapter 8, some essential work on indices and logarithms is covered. Then Chapter 9, on sigma notation, continues the discussion of sequences begun in Chapter 1 and prepares the way for the introduction to integration in the following chapter and for the algebra associated with the calculation of means and standard deviations in Chapter 11. In that chapter, an effort is made to place the study of statistics in a practical setting and, through a few examples, to prepare the ground for the later interlinking of statistics and probability. These examples, using algebraic models, also provide new applications of integration.

Chapter 12 introduces forces and Newton's Laws. As in the kinematics chapter, the problems are largely two dimensional and vector ideas are stressed. Chapter 13 is the first of three chapters extending calculus techniques (the others in *Book 2*). The book ends with vector geometry, establishing some affine results and furthering the study of linear algebra.

All the main components of the course—algebra, trigonometry, calculus, vectors, mechanics, statistics and computing—find a place in this book (and all are developed and reinforced in *Book 2*). Compared with the first edition, there are four more chapters, but the chapters are shorter.

We anticipate that many students will use this book with only intermittent help from teachers. It is helpful to have pen and paper at hand when reading the text, and to consider fully the answers to the questions that are posed there. It is also worth noting that some of the questions in the exercises are designed to lead into the following section in the chapter.

Each chapter ends with a miscellaneous exercise (sometimes introducing new ideas that are not 'mainstream') and a summary. Revision exercises are fuller than in the first edition, and there are also revision papers. The problem papers consist of questions that demand more insight and ingenuity. Finally there are some project exercises with themes marginally outside the syllabus; these include some open-ended questions intended to stimulate creative work. Some activity of this kind is desirable, preferably on topics of the student's own choosing; the project exercises merely give some specimen starting points. Harder questions and exercises have been marked with asterisks. Concise answers to some of the exercises —usually to the odd-numbered questions—are printed at the end of the book. Full answers and a commentary are available in the companion *Hints and Answers* book.

Relevant trigonometrical, statistical and other tables, and also lists of useful definitions and formulae, are to be found in the S.M.P. *Advanced Tables*.

GLOSSARY OF SYMBOLS

SETS

$\{x : x \text{ is even}\}$	Set of described elements
$\{1, 2, 3, 4\}$	Set with listed elements
$\mathbb{N}$	The set of natural numbers $\{1, 2, 3, \ldots\}$
$\mathbb{Z}$	The set of integers $\{0, \pm 1, \pm 2, \ldots\}$
$\mathbb{Q}$	The set of rational numbers
$\mathbb{R}$	The set of real numbers
$\mathbb{R} \times \mathbb{R}$ or $\mathbb{R}^2$	The set of ordered pairs of real numbers $\{(a, b) : a, b \in \mathbb{R}\}$
$[a, b]$	The interval $\{x : a \leqslant x \leqslant b\}$

ALGEBRA

$u_1, u_2, \ldots, u_n$	Successive terms of a sequence
$\displaystyle\sum_{i=1}^{n} u_i$ or $\displaystyle\sum_{1}^{n} u_i$	Alternative notations for $u_1 + u_2 + \ldots + u_n$

LOGICAL SYMBOLS

$p \Rightarrow q$	If p, then q (p implies q)
$p \Leftrightarrow q$	p if and only if q; p is equivalent to q

FUNCTIONS

$f : x \to y$	The function f which maps x onto y
$x \overset{f}{\to} y$	x is mapped onto y by f
$f(x)$	The image of x under the function f
f^{-1}	The inverse function to f
fg	The composite function 'f operating on the result of g'; the function mapping x onto $f(g(x))$

SPECIAL FUNCTIONS

$n!$	Factorial n; the product $1 \times 2 \times 3 \times \ldots \times n$
$\sqrt{}$	The positive square root of
$\|x\|$	The modulus of x; x for $x \geqslant 0$, $-x$ for $x < 0$
$[x]$	The greatest integer less than or equal to x

CALCULUS

$\lim\limits_{x \to a}$ — The limit of ... as x tends to a

as $x \to +\infty(-\infty)$ — as x increases (decreases) indefinitely

f' — Derived function of f

$\dfrac{dy}{dx}$ or $f'(x)$ — Derivative of y, or of $f(x)$, with respect to x

$\dfrac{d^2y}{dx^2}$ or $f''(x)$ — Second derivative of y or of $f(x)$

δx — Small increment in x

δy — Consequent increment in y

$\displaystyle\int_a^b f(x)\,dx$ — Area under the graph of f over the interval $[a, b]$

$\displaystyle\int f(x)\,dx$ — Indefinite integral or primitive; any $F(x)$ such that $F'(x) = f(x)$

$\left[F(x) \right]_a^b$ — $F(b) - F(a)$

STATISTICS

$m, \bar{x}$ — Mean value of x

$f(x_i)$ — Frequency of x_i

s — Standard deviation

s_x or s_t — Standard deviation of population of x's or of t's

VECTORS AND MECHANICS

p — Magnitude of the vector $\mathbf{p}$

$\mathbf{i}, \mathbf{j}$ — Unit vectors in the x and y directions

$\mathbf{r}$ — Position vector of a particle or a point

$\dot{\mathbf{r}}, \mathbf{v}$ — Velocity of a particle

$\ddot{\mathbf{r}}, \dot{\mathbf{v}}, \mathbf{a}$ — Acceleration of a particle

m — Mass of a particle

$\mathbf{F}$ — Force acting on a particle

$\mathbf{g}$ — Acceleration due to gravity

$\mathbf{M}, \mathbf{L}, \mathbf{T}$ — Dimensions of mass, length, and time

ARROW CONVENTION IN MECHANICS

$\longrightarrow$ Velocity

$\longrightarrow\!\!\!\rightarrow$ Acceleration

$\longrightarrow\!\!\!\!\rightarrow$ Force or mass-acceleration

$-\!\!\oplus\!\!-$ Resultant force

x

UNITS

s	Seconds
m	Metres
kg	Kilograms
N	Newtons
m/s or m s^{-1}	Metres per second
m/s^2 or m s^{-2}	Metres per second per second
x^c	x radians $= 180x/\pi$ degrees

1

FLOW CHARTS AND SEQUENCES

1. INTRODUCTION

You may already have met flow charts describing real life situations such as the sequence of events in making a telephone call, or describing more mathematical processes. Such a flow chart is in Figure 1—work through it and see what the result is.

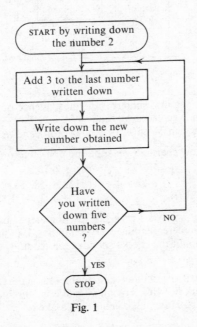

Fig. 1

If you have obeyed the instructions correctly you should have produced the first five terms of the *sequence*

$$2, 5, 8, 11, 14, 17, 20, \ldots$$

What is the eighth term in the sequence? We shall refer to this as u_8. What is u_4? What is u_6? If $u_{15} = 44$, what is u_{16}? Can you find the value of u_{30} without working through all 30 terms? How many times did you obey the 'add 3' instruction in the flow diagram before writing down u_5? How many times must we add 3 to produce u_{100}?

When using the flow chart to produce the terms of the sequence

1

2, 5, 8, ... the 5 is produced when the instructions have been obeyed once—that is, 3 has been added on once. The 8 is produced when the instructions have been obeyed twice—that is, 3 has been added on twice. To obtain u_{15}, fourteen 3's are added to the initial number 2.

$$u_{15} = 2 + 14 \times 3 = 44.$$

Exercise A

1. (a) Write down the first six terms of the sequence given by the instructions:

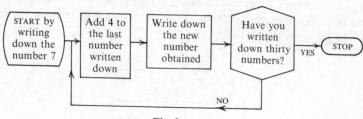

Fig. 2

(b) Write down the first six terms of the sequence obtained if 'add 4' in the second instruction is replaced by 'add -6'.

In both these sequences, give the values of u_{10} and u_{20}.

2. Write simple flow charts to generate the first 30 terms of sequences beginning

(a) $1, 3\frac{1}{2}, 6, 8\frac{1}{2}, \dots$;

(b) $4, 0, -4, -8, \dots$;

(c) $1, 2, 4, 8, \dots$;

(d) $2, 6, 18, 54, \dots$;

(e) $1, 3, 7, 15, 31, \dots$;

(f) $-3, 3, -3, 3, \dots$.

3. On a motorway a driver keeps his speedometer showing a steady 70 m.p.h. and checks the milometer reading every 3 minutes. If at his first check the reading is 7115·4, what should the checks show as the readings over the next quarter of an hour?

4. Upon losing a bet, a gambling man doubles his stake for the next bet, and goes on in this way until he wins. His initial stake is 30p and his first win is after a losing run of 9 bets. How much is his final stake?

5. If the 'add 4' instruction in the flow chart of Question 1 is replaced by 'multiply the last number written down by 3', find the first four terms of the sequence. Can you work out u_{12} easily? Give an expression for u_{12}.

6. The following are the first few terms of sequences which display simple patterns. Write down the next 3 terms of each. Which sequences can be generated by simple flow charts? For which can u_{20} be found without working out the preceding terms? In these cases, give the values of u_{20}.

(a) $0, 0.25, 0.5, 0.75, \dots$;

(b) $1, \frac{1}{2}, \frac{1}{3}, \frac{1}{4}, \dots$;

(c) $1, 4, 9, 16, \dots$;

(d) $3, -6, 12, -24, \dots$;

(e) $0.02, 0.1, 0.5, 2.5, \dots$;

(f) $2, 4, 6, 8, \dots$;

(g) $0, 1, 0, 2, 0, 3, 0, 4, \dots$;

(h) $1, 1, 2, 3, 5, 8, 13, \dots$.

2. FLOW CHARTS AND COMPUTERS

2.1　Notation. Generating a particular sequence on a computer is one of the easiest tasks for a programmer. His first job would be to draw up a suitable flow chart. In order to write the flow charts more concisely, we shall use a notation which is closely linked with computer programming. Figure 3 produces the sequence 2, 5, 8, …. of Section 1.

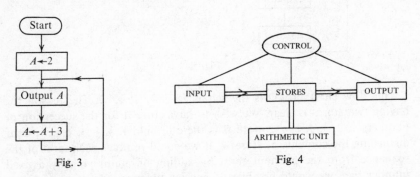

Fig. 3　　　　　　　　　　　　Fig. 4

Let us take these instructions and describe what happens in terms of a computer, shown schematically in Figure 4. A is the 'address' of one store; a computer will have several thousand stores, but as in this chapter we shall only require a few, we shall use capital letters $A, B, C \ldots$ for their addresses.

Within the computer, calculations are carried out in the arithmetic unit. When the instruction $A \leftarrow A+3$ is reached, the control unit will see that the number in store A and the number 3 are transferred to the part of the arithmetic unit which performs addition. The result is then sent back to store A to replace the number there previously.

The arithmetic unit can only carry out the basic operations of $+$, $-$, $\times$, $\div$. It is the function of the control unit to see that the correct arithmetic operation is carried out at each stage, that the numbers are fed in from the correct sources, and that the answer goes to the correct destination.

The results of a program are almost always wanted in printed form, and the output device is usually a typewriter connected to the computer or a line printer, which prints the results a complete line at a time.

How could the flow chart of Figure 3 be modified to produce sequences starting (i) 2, 6, 18, 54, (ii) 2, 6, 10, 14, (iii) 1, 6, 11, 16?

Figure 3 used one store only. Sometimes it is necessary to use two or more stores. Work through the chart in Figure 5 which produces one of the sequences of Exercise A, Question 6. Can you produce this sequence conveniently with one store only?

3

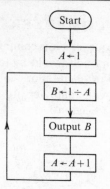

This means 'replace the contents of store B by the amount $1/A$'. A remains the same, whatever was in B is *overwritten*.

Fig. 5

This flow chart produces the sequence $1, \frac{1}{2}, \frac{1}{3}, \frac{1}{4}, \dots$. The reason for having two stores is clear. We wish to have store A for the succession of numbers $1, 2, 3, 4, 5, \dots$; store B is there to hold $1, \frac{1}{2}, \frac{1}{3}, \frac{1}{4}$, etc. without disturbing the contents of store A. If we could produce each term of the sequence from the previous term by adding or multiplying by a fixed number then we would be able to generate the sequence using one store only; there is no such simple relationship between the terms of the sequence here.

2.2   Dry runs and loops. We can find out what is happening in a flow chart by carrying out a *dry run*. To do this we set out in a table the contents of each store at each stage of the computation. For example, a dry run for Figure 5 would be:

A	B
1	1
2	$\frac{1}{2}$
3	$\frac{1}{3}$ etc.

Note that we set out as many stores as the chart uses, even though only the contents of store B are printed out in this case. Whenever we construct a flow chart, a dry run will enable us to see that the chart works correctly.

The flow charts in Figures 3 and 5 are incomplete in as much as they have no (Stop) instruction. If applied to a computer program, they would cause the sequence to go on being printed out indefinitely. They are very simple examples of an infinite loop. In long programs with complicated flow charts, an infinite loop might occur without the programmer realizing it; it is a pitfall he will do his best to avoid.

We need an instruction that tells the computer to leave the loop and go on with the rest of the program at the appropriate moment. We cannot insert verbal questions of the sort used so far in this chapter, but it is

4

possible for the computer to compare two numbers and, depending on the
result, either continue with the loop or not. *A decision box* (diamond-
shaped) is used in a flow chart for this type of instruction.

In order to come out of a loop after a certain number of cycles, we may
incorporate into the flow chart a *counter*, which increases by 1 each time
a loop is traversed, and a decision box. Write out dry runs for the flow
charts of Figure 6, where this method is illustrated.

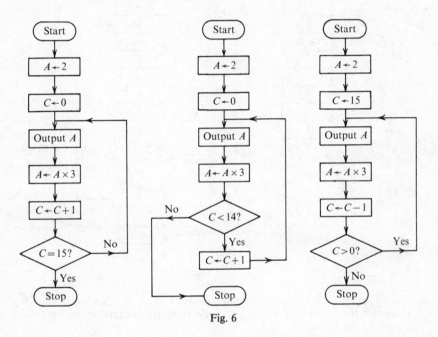

Fig. 6

You can see that each one does exactly the same thing, which is to print
out the first 15 terms of the sequence 2, 6, 18, 54, ... In each case the
program stops after 2×3^{14} has been printed, and leaves store A containing
the number 2×3^{15}. Care has to be taken to ensure that the loop is used
exactly the right number of times, and that the decision box contains the
right conditional instruction.

Decision boxes are used either to compare the contents of one store with
a given number, or to compare the contents of two stores. Any of the
symbols $=, >, \geqslant, <, \leqslant, \neq$ may be used, so, for example, a decision box
may contain questions such as '$C \leqslant 0$?' or '$A = B$?'.

5

Exercise B

1. What is printed out by the following flow charts?

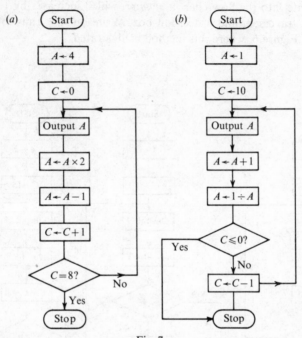

Fig. 7

2. The addresses of five stores in a computer are A, B, C, D, E and the stores A, B, C contain the numbers x, y, z respectively. Write flow charts for working out and printing the values of:

(a) $x(y+z)$; (b) $xy+z$;

(c) $x-(y-z)$; (d) $\dfrac{x}{y+z}$.

Each arithmetic instruction should be limited to a single operation.

3. Construct flow charts for printing out the first 24 terms of simple sequences beginning:

(a) 1, 3, 5, 7; (b) 1, 1·1, 1·21, 1·331;

(c) 5, −10, 20, −40; (d) 1, −3, 5, −7.

4. For the sequence 1, 3, 6, 10, 15, ..., find a simple method of getting from one number to the next. Hence, write a flow chart for printing out successive numbers of the sequence. First 10·

6

5. $k!$, where k is a positive integer, is called *factorial k*, and denotes the product $k \times (k-1) \times (k-2) \times \ldots \times 2 \times 1$. Write a flow chart to print out the value of $k!$, where k is entered into store A of a computer. Check by carrying out a dry run for values of k such as 3 or 4.

6. Find the output of the following flow charts:

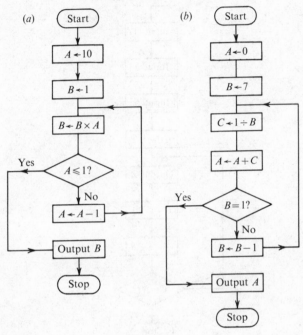

Fig. 8

7. Construct a flow chart for printing a table of values of $n!$ for values of n from 1 to 25.

8. Write flow charts for printing out the first 20 terms of the sequences of Exercise A, Question 6 (*c*), (*g*), (*h*).

2.3 Data lists. Two special types of sequence occurred many times in Exercise A. We give them names.

A sequence in which each term is produced from the preceding term by adding a fixed number (positive or negative) is called an *arithmetic progression* (A.P. for short). One produced in a similar way by multiplication by a fixed number is called a *geometric progression* (G.P.).

Construct flow charts for generating 20 terms of the arithmetic progression 1, 4, 7, 10, ..., and 30 terms of the arithmetic progression 7, 9, 11, 13,.... Write out the two flow charts side by side and compare them. What is it that all flow charts for arithmetic progressions have in common?

Figure 9 generates any A.P., the first term, common difference and the number of terms being supplied independently and fed into the stores A, B, N at the beginning of the program.

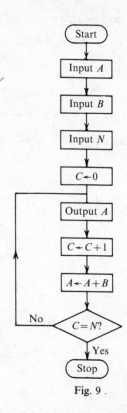

Fig. 9

The whole of the main program is fed into the computer first, and stored. The input data is then placed in the input device. When the program is run, the first input instruction causes the first number in the data to be read into store A. If this was on a punched card, the card is then placed automatically in the 'out-tray', the next number comes to the top of the pile and is read when the next input instruction is reached. If the data is on paper tape, one can watch it passing jerkily through the tape reader, each input instruction in the program causing the data tape to advance a centimetre or two.

A data tape with the numbers 1, 3, 20 used in conjunction with the program of Figure 9 would produce the first 20 terms of the sequence 1, 4, 7, ... What would the data tape 3, 7, 6 give?

8

As another example, write out a dry run for the flow chart in Figure 10, given the data list $\boxed{24,\ 31,\ 26,\ 29,\ -999}$.

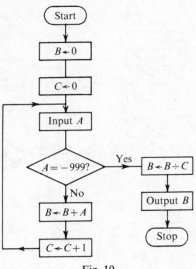

Fig. 10

The numbers 24, 31, 26, 29 form the data and -999 is an arbitrary number, known not to belong to the data, which signals that all the data have been read in.

Notice that in this example, which works out the mean of any list of numbers, the input instruction occurs within the loop. Each number is fed into A, added to the 'running total' in B, and then is overwritten by the next number.

Another way by which the computer can be made to recognize that the input of data is completed is to start the data list with the number n of items to be read in (see Exercise C, Question 2).

Exercise C

1. (a) Construct a flow chart to generate 12 terms of the geometric progression 2, 3, 4·5, 6·75, ...

(b) Now construct a flow chart to generate any G.P. What data list would result in the sequence of (a) being printed? What would happen if the numbers were placed on the data list in the reverse order?

2. Work through the flow charts of Figure 11 with the given data lists. Notice that the structure of the second one is made clearer by the simplified way the instructions are boxed.

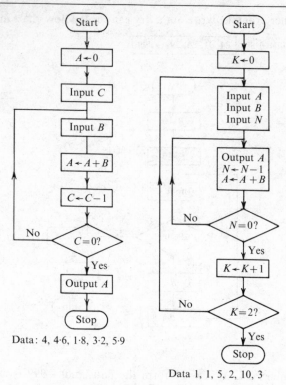

Data: 4, 4·6, 1·8, 3·2, 5·9

Data 1, 1, 5, 2, 10, 3

Fig. 11

3. Construct a flow chart to find and print the largest number of a list given on a data list. Let the first number on the list give the number of numbers to be read in after it.

[*Hint*. Read in two numbers, compare them, reject the smaller, compare the larger with the next one read in, and so on.]

4. Write a program to find the sum of the squares of a given set of numbers.

3. SEQUENCES

3.1 Defining a sequence. What do we mean by 'the sequence 2, 4, 6, 8, ...'? There are many different sequences which begin in this way. If we are interested, for example, only in the last digits of the multiples of 2, we have a sequence starting 2, 4, 6, 8, 0, 2, 4.

Perhaps you are expected to notice that the difference between each pair of consecutive terms is 2, and assume that this pattern persists, i.e. that $u_9 = u_8 + 2$, $u_{14} = u_{13} + 2$, etc. One way of defining this sequence precisely is to generalize these statements and say

$$u_{k+1} = u_k + 2 \quad \text{for all positive whole numbers } k.$$

10

This, together with the starting value $u_1 = 2$, determines the sequence precisely. We call this an *inductive definition*; 'inductive' means 'leading on'. Such definitions for sequences require starting values and rules for leading on.

Here we have

$$\begin{cases} u_1 = 2, \\ u_{k+1} = u_k + 2 \quad \text{for all positive whole numbers } k. \end{cases}$$

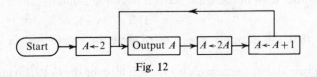

Fig. 12

Many of the flow diagrams we have used for sequences embody inductive definitions. The first 4 terms of the sequence given by Figure 12 are 2, 5, 11, 23, and the inductive definition is

$$\begin{cases} u_1 = 2, \\ u_{k+1} = 2u_k + 1 \quad \text{for all positive whole numbers } k. \end{cases}$$

Write down inductive definitions for sequences starting (*a*) 2, 10, 50, 250, (*b*) 1, -2, -5, -8.

An alternative way of defining a sequence is to give an *algebraic formula* for the general term. If we write $u_n = 2n$,

$$n = 1 \quad \text{gives} \quad u_1 = 2,$$
$$n = 2 \quad \text{gives} \quad u_2 = 4,$$
$$n = 3 \quad \text{gives} \quad u_3 = 6 \quad \text{etc,}$$

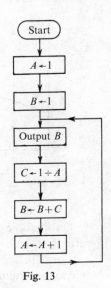

and we have the first sequence discussed in this section.

Write down the first 4 terms of the sequences defined by the formulae (*a*) $u_n = 5n - 3$, (*b*) $u_n = \frac{3}{2} \times 2^n - 1$.

Many sequences can be simply defined both inductively and by algebraic formulae, but there are others for which one method or the other is preferable. For example, the sequence produced by the flow chart of Figure 13 is given inductively by the statements

$$\begin{cases} u_1 = 1, \\ u_{k+1} = u_k + \frac{1}{k} \quad \text{for all positive whole numbers } k. \end{cases}$$

What are the first few terms of this sequence?

In this example, we cannot find a formula for u_n.

Fig. 13

11

3.2 Arithmetic and geometric progressions. A.P.s and G.P.s have featured prominently in this chapter because of their simplicity. They are important sequences, and we note here that for both it is easy to proceed from inductive definitions to algebraic formulae.

Earlier in the chapter we discovered that we could write down the 100th term of the A.P. starting 2, 5, 8, 11.

In fact
$$u_{100} = 2 + 99 \times 3 = 299.$$

Any other term of the sequence can be found similarly. In general,
$$u_n = 2 + (n-1)\,3 = 3n - 1.$$

Check that this formula does indeed give the correct values for $n = 4$ and $n = 7$.

Can you find an expression for the nth term of the G.P. starting 2, 6, 18, 54?

The second term, 6, is produced when we have multiplied by 3 once. The third term, 18, is produced when we have multiplied by 3 twice. The nth term comes from multiplying $n-1$ times by 3, so
$$u_n = 2 \times 3^{n-1}.$$

We see that this formula is correct for $n = 2, 3, 4$, etc. Is it correct also for $n = 1$? In Chapter 8, we shall show that it is convenient to define 3^0 to be 1.

The difference between arithmetic and geometric progressions may be illustrated by the idea of simple and compound interest. If you invest £100 at 5 % per annum simple interest, the capital value after 1, 2, 3 ... years will be £105, 110, 115, ... which is represented graphically by a straight line (see Figure 14(a)).

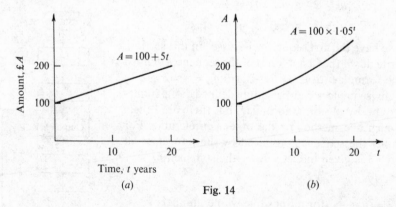

(a)   Fig. 14   (b)

On the other hand, investing £100 at 5 % compound interest will give after 1, 2, 3, ... years a capital value of £100 × 1·05, 100 × 1·05², 100 × 1·05³, ... or £105, 110·25, 115·76, ..., represented graphically by a growth curve (see Figure 14(b)).

12

3.3 Natural numbers The connection is evident between sequences and the set of positive whole numbers, or *natural numbers*,

$$\mathbb{N} = \{1, 2, 3, \dots\}.$$

When we use the symbol u_n for the typical term of a sequence we understand that n is to be a natural number, i.e. $n \in \mathbb{N}$. To each element n belonging to $\mathbb{N}$ there corresponds a unique number u_n, so we can think of a sequence as arising from a *function* with domain the set of natural numbers.

Exercise D

1. Write down the first five terms of the sequences given by the formulae below. Identify those sequences that are arithmetic or geometric progressions:

(a) $u_n = 2n - 5$; (b) $u_n = 6n + \frac{1}{2}$; (c) $u_n = 3 \times 4^n$;

(d) $u_n = n^2 + 1$; (e) $u_n = (n-1) 2^n$; (f) $u_n = 3^n$;

(g) $u_n = (-1)^{n+1} \times n$; (h) $u_n = (-1)^n \times (\frac{1}{2})^{n+1}$.

2. Find an expression for u_n for sequences starting as follows:

(a) $1, 5, 9, 13$; (b) $0, \frac{2}{3}, \frac{4}{5}, \frac{6}{7}$;

(c) $3, -6, 12, -24$; (d) $10, -16, 22, -28$.

3. Write down the first five terms of the sequences defined inductively below.

(a) $u_1 = 1$, $u_{k+1} = u_k + 2^k$; (b) $u_1 = 2$, $u_{k+1} = u_k + k$;

(c) $u_1 = 1$, $u_{k+1} = 2u_k + 1$; (d) $u_1 = 1$, $u_{k+1} = u_k + (k+1)$;

(e) $u_1 = 1$, $u_{k+1} = u_k \times \dfrac{k+2}{k}$.

4. Each of the flow charts shown in Figure 15 produces a sequence. Write down the first few terms, and give an inductive definition of each sequence.

Write a flow chart, with one instruction fewer than (b), that produces the same sequence.

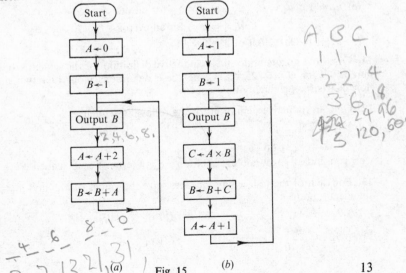

Fig. 15

13

5. Give the next three terms of simple sequences starting as follows, and state which of them are arithmetic or geometric progressions:

(a) $10, 1, -8, -17$;

(b) $\frac{1}{2}, \frac{1}{5}, \frac{1}{8}, \frac{1}{11}$;

(c) $\frac{1}{6}, \frac{1}{2}, 1\frac{1}{2}, 4\frac{1}{2}$;

(d) $3, 6, 11, 18$;

(e) $2a, 2a+1, 2a+2, 2a+3$;

(f) $6, 3, 1\frac{1}{2}, \frac{3}{4}$;

(g) $\frac{1}{2}, \frac{1}{6}, \frac{1}{12}, \frac{1}{20}$;

(h) $2a, 3a+1, 4a+2, 5a+3$.

6. The following terms belong respectively to the sequences given in Question 5. For each one, state which term of the sequence it is.

(a) -107;

(b) $\frac{1}{47}$;

(c) $364\frac{1}{2}$;

(d) 171;

(e) $2a+n$;

(f) $\frac{3}{256}$;

(g) $\frac{1}{156}$;

(h) $na+n-2$.

7. A large piece of paper has thickness $\frac{1}{8}$ mm. If you were to tear it in half several times, each time putting the two halves together, how many times would you have to do this to obtain a thickness of more than 3 cm? What is the thickness after carrying out the operation n times?

8. If you invest £625 at 8 % p.a. compound interest, how much more is this worth to you after 4 years than if you had invested the sum at 8 % p.a. simple interest for 4 years? How much more is it worth after n years?

9. (a) Find the first five terms of the sequence defined by the formula

$$u_n = 2n+(n-1)(n-2)(n-3)(n-4).$$

(b) Find a formula giving a sequence with first five terms 1, 2, 4, 8, 20.

10. For the sequences defined as follows, write down the first 5 terms and the 100th term.

(a) $u_1 = 3$, $u_{k+1} = u_k+2$ for all $k \in \mathbb{N}$.

(b) $u_1 = 1$, $u_{k+1} = 2/u_k$ for all $k \in \mathbb{N}$.

(c) $u_1 = 2$, $u_{k+1} = u_k+(-1)^k$ for all $k \in \mathbb{N}$.

(d) $u_1 = 3$, $u_{k+1} = 1/(1-u_k)$ for all $k \in \mathbb{N}$.

(e) $u_1 = 1$, $u_2 = 0$, $u_{k+2} = u_k+1$ for all odd $k \in \mathbb{N}$,

$u_{k+2} = u_k$ for all even $k \in \mathbb{N}$.

(f) $u_n =$ the last digit of 2^n for all $n \in \mathbb{N}$.

11. Give both an algebraic and an inductive definition for the sequence of square numbers 1, 4, 9, 16, 25, ... Using these definitions, construct two different flow charts for producing this sequence.

12. Give an inductive definition for the following sequences:

(a) $1, \frac{1}{2}, \frac{1}{3}, \frac{1}{4}, ...$;

(b) $1!, 3!, 5!, 7!, ...$;

(c) $1, \frac{1}{2}, \frac{2}{3}, \frac{3}{5}, \frac{5}{8}, \frac{8}{13}, ...$.

Can you find an algebraic formula for the nth term of each sequence?

13. For each of the following sequences, give the values of u_{100} and u_{1000} to 1 significant figure.

(a) $2, 5, 8, 11, ...$;

(b) $\frac{1}{2}, \frac{1}{5}, \frac{1}{8}, \frac{1}{11}, ...$;

(c) $u_n = \dfrac{n}{n+10}$;

(d) $u_n = 6+\dfrac{1}{n}$;

14

(e) $u_n = \dfrac{n-10}{n^2+1}$;   (f) $u_n = \dfrac{n^2+4}{n+12}$;

(g) $u_n = 2+(-1)^n$;   (h) $u_n = \dfrac{2+(-1)^n}{n}$;

(i) $u_n = 2+n(-1)^n$.

4. BEHAVIOUR OF A SEQUENCE FOR LARGE VALUES OF *n*

4.1 Limits. In later chapters we shall often wish to know, for particular sequences, about values of u_n when n is large. In some sequences in Exercise D, Question 13, u_n approaches some fixed number. In (*b*) the limit is 0, and in (*d*) the limit is 6. In how many of the other sequences does u_n tend to a limit? The idea of a limit occurs frequently in mathematics and is fundamental to the study of calculus.

A graph provides a good illustration. For a sequence, this will consist of a set of isolated points.

Example 1

$$u_n = \frac{n}{2n+3}.$$

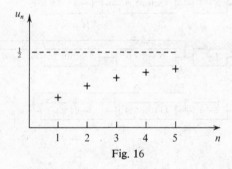

Fig. 16

As *n* increases, the $+3$ in the denominator affects the value of u_n less and less, and we see that u_n approaches $n/2n = \tfrac{1}{2}$.

4.2 Sequences which do not tend to a limit. For some sequences, u_n tends to a limit as *n* increases without limit, but there are several alternatives. Look back at the sequences of Exercise D, Questions 10 and 13, and categorize them according to their behaviour for large *n*. Which oscillate finitely? Which oscillate infinitely? Which increase without limit?

15

Exercise E

1. Write down the first few terms of the sequences defined as follows, and display them on graphs. Describe the behaviour of u_n for large n in each case.

(a) $u_n = 2 + \dfrac{1}{n}$;　　(b) $u_n = (-\tfrac{1}{2})^n$;　　(c) $u_n = \dfrac{2n}{1+2n}$;

(d) $u_n = n(2 + (-1)^n)$;　　(e) $u_n = \dfrac{n^2 - n}{n+1}$;　　(f) $u_n = \dfrac{n^2 + n}{n^2 + 1}$.

2. For the following sequences, find an expression for u_n and describe the behaviour of u_n for large n.

(a) $120, 60, 40, 30, 24, \ldots$;　　(b) $-1, 0, 3, 8, 15, \ldots$;

(c) $0, \tfrac{1}{3}, \tfrac{2}{5}, \tfrac{3}{7}, \tfrac{4}{9}, \ldots$;　　(d) $\dfrac{2 \times 3}{1!}, \dfrac{3 \times 4}{2!}, \dfrac{4 \times 5}{3!}, \ldots$.

3. Decide whether the sequences generated by the following flow charts tend to a limit or not. If a limit exists, state what you think it is.

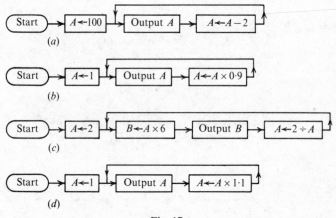

Fig. 17

4. Write down the first few terms of the sequence produced by Figure 18, and interpret them with regard to the angles of regular polygons. What is the geometrical interpretation of u_n, the nth term of the sequence? Give an expression for u_n. State the limit to which u_n tends and justify your answer (a) geometrically, (b) algebraically.

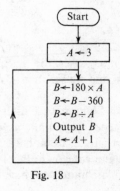

Fig. 18

16

5.

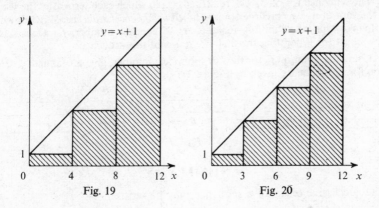

Fig. 19   Fig. 20

Show that the total area of the shaded rectangles in Figure 19 is 60, and find the corresponding area in Figure 20.

u_n is defined as the sum of the areas of n rectangles of equal width drawn under the graph of $y = x+1$ between $x = 0$ and $x = 12$. Thus Figures 19 and 20 give u_3 and u_4. Evaluate u_2 and u_6. Would you expect u_n to tend to a limit as n increases infinitely?

6. For a sequence defined as in Question 5 but with rectangles under the graph of $y = x^2+4$ between $x = 1$ and $x = 5$, find u_1, u_2 and u_4. Would you expect u_n to increase without limit as n increases? If the sequence tends to a limit, what would this represent?

7. A sequence is defined by $u_1 = 5$, $u_{k+1} = \frac{1}{2}(u_k + 10/u_k)$. Obtain u_2, u_3, u_4 and u_5 (slide-rule accuracy will suffice), and square each term. Comment.

If you have computing facilities available, write a program to generate more terms of the sequence.

Miscellaneous Exercise

1. Write down the first six terms of the sequence defined inductively as follows:

$$\begin{cases} u_1 = 2, \\ u_{k+1} = 3u_k - 2 \quad \text{for all } k \in \mathbb{N}. \end{cases}$$

Devise a flow chart for calculating the hundredth term. Find a formula for u_n.

2. Give the next two terms of the sequence 5, 9, 17, 33, 65, 129, ..., and write down an inductive definition for it.

Write a flow chart for generating the first n terms of this sequence, and find a formula for u_n.

3. A sequence is defined inductively as follows:

$$\begin{cases} u_1 = 1, \\ u_{k+1} = \frac{1}{2}\left(u_k + \frac{3}{u_k}\right) \quad \text{for all } k \in \mathbb{N}. \end{cases}$$

What are the values of the first five terms? Construct a flow chart which will print the first 50 terms of the sequence.

17

4. The sequence 1, 1, 2, 3, 5, 8, 13, 21, 34, ..., in which each term after the second is the sum of its two predecessors, is called a *Fibonacci sequence*. Write down an inductive type of definition for the nth Fibonacci number, f_n. Construct a flow chart for generating the first 100 terms of this sequence.

5. Using the notation f_k for the kth Fibonacci number, give an inductive definition for the sequence given by Figure 21.

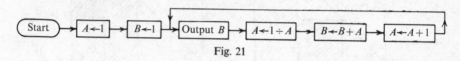

Fig. 21

SUMMARY

The successive terms of a sequence may be written

$$u_1, u_2, u_3, u_4, ..., u_n, ...$$

A sequence may be defined
(i) by a formula for u_n that holds for all natural numbers,
(ii) by an inductive definition where u_1 is given together with an equation connecting u_{k+1} and u_k that holds for all $k \in \mathbb{N}$.
($\mathbb{N}$ is the set of natural numbers $\{1, 2, 3, ...\}$.)

An *arithmetic progression* is a sequence such that

$$\begin{cases} u_1 = a, \\ u_{k+1} = u_k + d \quad \text{for all } k \in \mathbb{N}, \end{cases}$$

where a and d are any two numbers.

A *geometric progression* is a sequence such that

$$\begin{cases} u_1 = a, \\ u_{k+1} = u_k \times r \quad \text{for all } k \in \mathbb{N}, \end{cases}$$

where a and r are any two numbers.

Flow chart notation

$A \leftarrow 5$	means: put the number 5 into store A.
$A \leftarrow A + 1$	means: increase the number in A by 1.
$A \leftarrow B$	means: replace the contents of A by the number in B. Whatever was in A is over-written, while the contents of B are not affected.
$A \leftarrow B \times C$	means: multiply the number in B by the number in C, and store the result in A.
Input A	means: read the next number on the data tape into the store with address A.
Output A	means: print out the contents of store A.

18

2

MATHEMATICAL MODELS AND FUNCTIONS

1. INTRODUCTION

A large number of problems can be resolved by obtaining and analysing relations between quantities that can take a variety of values.

Examples of these problems are given in the first section of this chapter. We shall then discuss functions in greater detail and so lay the foundations for more advanced methods of analysis—an examination that will continue throughout the A-level course.

Example 1

What has been the effect of television on other communication media? To help answer this question, information was collected and some of it is shown in graphical form in Figure 1.

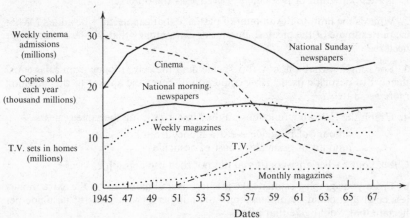

Fig. 1. From *The Effects of Television* edited by James D. Halloran (Panther) p. 141.

Do the graphs help you to reach any conclusions? Comment upon the trends you can observe. Do you think that any of these trends conflict with such theories as the following?

Television has caused the decline in cinema attendances.

Television now makes the morning papers unnecessary.

Television has increased the demand for monthly magazines.

Example 2

This next problem is much more detailed and specific. The information is given, not as a graph, but as a set of pairs of observations.

A certain sort of grass-worm reduces the beef-mass of cattle that eat it. To get rid of the worm, a pesticide can be sprayed over the grass containing it. What is the best amount of pesticide to use? What data should be collected?

The relation between the extra money obtained from improved beef sales and the amount of pesticide used is given in the following table (each measure is calculated per hectare):

Amount of pesticide (kg/ha)	0	1	2	3	4	5	6	7	8
Extra money gained (p/ha)	0	100	150	175	187	193	196	198	199

The pesticide itself costs 35p per kilogram. What advice would you give the farmer as to the most profitable and so the most economical amount to use?

Confirm that your suggestions are sound, by answering the following questions.

Exercise A

1. Is each kilogram of pesticide as effective as the others?

2. What is the limit to the amount of pesticide that can usefully be added? What is your estimate of the greatest amount of extra money that can be obtained per hectare?

3. For roughly what amount of pesticide does the extra money from sales equal the cost of pesticide used? How could you discover the answer to this question more accurately?

4. Graph the following functions on the same axes using the same scales:

amount of pesticide → extra money from beef sales,
amount of pesticide → cost of pesticide.

Check your earlier answers (if you did not then use a graph).

5. From your graphs, estimate the greatest overall gain (that is the extra money less cost) that could be obtained and the number of kilograms of pesticide per hectare that would give that gain.

2. MATHEMATICAL MODELS

2.1 Numerical and graphical models. In Example 2, the real situation involved people, cattle, fields, money etc. But to deal with the specific problem of the efficient use of pesticide, measurements were taken of only two quantities—mass and money. This information acts, in a limited way, as a *numerical model* of the real situation.

20

But the observed readings were only a small sub-set of all the possible ordered pairs (mass, money) that could have been recorded. Plotting the points corresponding to the data gave us a *graphical model* of the situation and enabled us to estimate the intermediate ordered pairs, and, eventually, a maximum value for the profit. But what assumptions were we making in doing this? Were we right to assume the existence of intermediate points and that they lay along a smooth curve? Should there have been kinks or discontinuities in the graph?

Contrast Example 2 with the following:

Example 3

In 1967, a local council required an estimate of the number of unemployed to be expected that year and the next so that they could try to provide new jobs. The January and June figures for the previous six years were:

	1961	1962	1963	1964	1965	1966
Jan	150	175	330	190	140	135
June	95	150	180	120	105	100

Would you be prepared to estimate the unemployment figures for intermediate months or to predict the values for 1967 and 1968? How would you display the data graphically? What might account for the June figures being generally lower than the January figures?

Example 4

An investigation is being made into the morning rush-hour conditions in a city. At a certain set of traffic lights, observations were made of the number of cars that were being delayed. The total of stopped cars was noted at the end of the first 'red' period that followed the given times.

Times	6.45	7.00	7.15	7.30	7.45	8.00	8.15	8.30	8.45
Number of cars	0	6	15	19	18	18	21	20	20

Is there any sign of a trend in this case? Draw a graph.

In general, the construction of graphs is a matter of common sense. Figure 2 shows a graph for Example 3. Obviously any estimation of intermediate values is nearly valueless (though no doubt they could have been obtained from the records). There appears to be a trend (omitting the January 1963 figure which was caused by exceptional weather), but for 1967 and 1968 the figures were:

Jan 1967	June 1967	Jan 1968	June 1968
300	256	315	262

You will understand the danger of prediction unless a great deal of extra information is available.

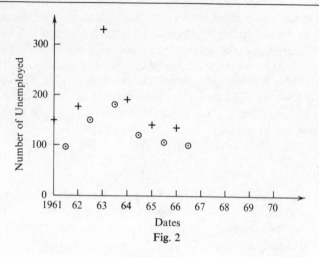

Dates

Fig. 2

Figure 3 shows the graph for Example 4. A continuous curve would not be appropriate here as the 'red' periods are separated from each other. On the other hand, there is evidently a trend of some sort for the readings do appear to lie close to a curve: it is possible, or it would be possible if the observations were repeated several times, to estimate the likely values of intermediate numbers for the separate red periods.

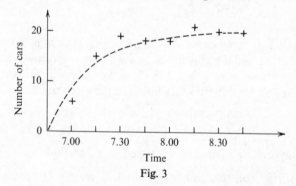

Time

Fig. 3

Exercise B

1. The population of an island at various times, expressed as a percentage of the number of inhabitants in 1905 is recorded as:

Date	D	1905	1909	1914	1918	1922	1926	1930	1939	1944
Population	P	100	104	101	90	92	104	125	80	22

When do you think the population was greatest? For what proportion of the time was the population greater than the 1905 figure? Discuss the assumptions you are making. In drawing a graph would you join the plotted points with curved or straight lines?

22

2. Graph the following information which describes the cooling of a cup of tea:

Time (min)	t	0	4	8	12	16	20
Temperature (in °C above room temp.)	T	80	65	52	41	32	26

At the end of the first four minutes the temperature was 0·81 of what it was at the start. What is the ratio of the temperatures when $t = 8$ and $t = 4$? What would you expect to be the reduction in the next four minutes? What do you expect the temperature to be after 40 minutes, and when should it be down to 10 °C above room temperature?

3. Manufactured articles sometimes become less costly (per article) the more that are manufactured at a time. Such an advantage is occasionally offset by the cost of storing articles.

The following data was once collected on the costs connected with manufacturing magnum champagne bottles:

Number in order	N	1000	2000	3000	4000	5000	6000
Cost per bottle (p)	C	70	35	23	18	14	12

The cost of storing the empty but beautiful bottles is given by:

Number in order	N	1000	3000	5000
Storage cost per bottle (p)	S	10	20	30

Carry out an investigation similar to Exercise A to find the best number to order at a time.

4. A parachutist jumped from an aircraft, fell freely for a while and then opened his parachute. A film provided the following table of distances fallen:

Time of fall (s)	t	0	$\frac{1}{2}$	1	$1\frac{1}{2}$	2	$2\frac{1}{2}$	3	$3\frac{1}{2}$	4	$4\frac{1}{2}$	5	$5\frac{1}{2}$
Distance (m)	d	0	1	4	9	16	25	36	42	46	49	52	55

At approximately what time did he open his parachute?

What estimate would you give for the fastest he was falling (in m/s) before and after opening his parachute?

5. In designing cars, tests are made to discover the effects of collision impact at various speeds. The number of tests is necessarily limited by expense to one at each speed. Measurements were taken of the gap between the head of the steering column and the back of the driver's seat after impact. The function 'speed → gap' is given by the following table:

Speed (km/h)	10	20	30	40	50	60	70	80	90	100	110	120
Gap (cm)	105	102	96	89	65	79	56	92	32	32	32	32

Plot the points given by the ordered pairs of the table and consider how they should be joined up. What is your impression of the collapse of the steering column at the different impact-speeds?

6. Figure 4 shows the length of the queue for lunch in a military dining hall at various times. Service started at 1.00 p.m. and finished at 1.40 p.m. The counters serve 20 people a minute.

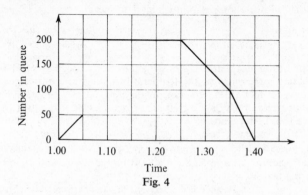

Fig. 4

(a) How many joined the queue between 1.10 and 1.20?
(b) At what rate were people joining the queue between 1.00 and 1.05?
(c) What happened at five past one?
(d) Atkins joined the queue at 1.20. When was he served?
(e) What was happening between 1.25 and 1.35?
(f) What was happening between 1.35 and 1.40?

2.2 Algebraic models. For each of the models so far mentioned, the information given has consisted of a set of pairs of numbers. When these exhibit a definite pattern, it may be possible to define the model alternatively by an algebraic equation.

For the first 3 seconds of the parachutist's fall (see Exercise B, Question 4), we had:

Time	t	0	$\frac{1}{2}$	1	$1\frac{1}{2}$	2	$2\frac{1}{2}$	3
Distance fallen	d	0	1	4	9	16	25	36

Clearly, $d = (2t)^2 = 4t^2$. We describe $d = 4t^2$ as an *algebraic model* of the situation. We expect this relation to hold at intermediate times during the first 3 seconds but not, of course, after the parachute is opened.

Exercise C

1. The height, h metres, of a stone thrown upward with an initial speed of 15 m/s is taken to be, at time t seconds,

$$h = 15t - 5t^2.$$

Either by trying different values for t or by graphical methods, estimate the highest point reached and the stone's speed when $t = 2$.

2. In Exercise B, Question 3, the total cost per bottle could be related to the number of bottles made by the formula

$$C = \frac{70000}{N} + \frac{1}{200}N + 5.$$

Using graphical methods confirm your answer to that question.

24

3. Plot the graph of

$$E = \frac{300\,A}{A+2}.$$

Compare it with the graph of the grass-worm example, Example 2. Would you consider this an adequate algebraic model?

Consider $E = 200 - 200/2^A$ as an alternative model.

4. The volume of a cylindrical oil drum is to be 1 cubic metre. We wish to find the smallest area of sheet metal needed to contain this volume. Write down the formulae for the volume of a cylinder and the surface area (including both ends) and hence show that an expression for the area in terms of the radius is

$$A = \frac{2}{r} + 2\pi r^2.$$

Draw the graph of this relation and so find approximately the smallest area that can be used. What is the radius to give that area and what is the height?

5. Fibre glass swimming pools come in various sizes. Their prices are given in the following table:

Diameter (m)	d	4	5	6	8	10
Cost (£)	c	60	90	126	216	330

Suggest the cost of a pool of diameter 7 m. What does this assume about the intermediate values? Does the cost increase evenly with the increase of diameter? What seems to be happening? Do you think that this rate of increase is justified in terms of the materials needed for construction of the pools?
Find an algebraic relation between c and d.

6. The following readings were obtained in an experiment:

x	1	2	4	7	10
y	5·5	4·5	4	3·8	3·7

Draw the graph of $1/x \rightarrow y$. Hence suggest a suitable algebraic relation and the expected value of y when $x = 12$.

7. In an experiment to investigate how the volume of a certain quantity of air varies under different pressures, the following results were obtained:

Pressure (N/cm²)	P	20	25	30	35	40	50
Volume (cm³)	V	158	115	105	90	79	63

Suggest a suitable algebraic model and hence which reading is probably incorrect.

8. 'Noon' can be defined as the moment when the sun is due south. According to our watches, this event occurs at a different time each day. The total variation is given by $T_1 + T_2$; the individual variations T_1 and T_2 arise from different causes and, when measured in minutes, are given by

$$T_1 = 7 \sin 30t°,$$

$$T_2 = 10 \sin (60t + 30)°,$$

where t is the time in months from 1 January.

Approximately when do the two time systems (sun time and clock time) agree and what is the greatest difference between them?

25

3. FUNCTIONS

The text examples and those of Exercises B and C have something in common. Each one involves the consideration of two sets of numbers and the relation between them—year and number going to the cinema, amount of pesticide and extra money received, number of bottles and cost, time and distance of fall. You will have noticed moreover that all the relations are *functions*. At any moment we could know exactly how far the parachutist has fallen. He cannot be in two places at once. To each element of the first set there corresponds just one element of the second set. Is this true for the population of Exercise B, Question 1? At any particular date there is a unique size of population, though there are many pairs of dates on which the population is the same, for instance 1909 and 1926. This relation is another example of a function.

The first set is called the *domain* and the second set the *codomain*. So far the elements of the domain and codomain have been numbers. In fact, the elements of any two sets may be related; for example, girls in a form and colours of the spectrum related by 'colour of eye'.

The number pairs of time and distance only give us partial information about the fall of the parachutist. He has a position at all intermediate times and we take the domain for the algebraic model $d = 4t^2$ to be the set of all real numbers between 0 and 3. How far do you think he fell in the first 1·7 seconds? By contrast, the domain of the cinema attendance function is a set of integers {1945, 1946, ..., 1968}. We do not talk about attendance in year 1951·8! In the same way, codomains may be sets of integers or rational numbers or real numbers. Discuss the nature of the domains and codomains of other functions in Examples 1 and 2.

3.1 Notation. We shall often use the familiar arrow notation when expressing functions in algebraic form, e.g. $t \to 4t^2$. Before reaching this stage, we might refer in a vague way to the function $t \to d$.

When both the domain and codomain of a function consists of real numbers, we indicate this by the symbols $\mathbb{R} \to \mathbb{R}$, where $\mathbb{R}$ is the set of real numbers. We also have $\mathbb{Z} \to \mathbb{Z}$ functions, $\mathbb{R} \to \mathbb{Z}$ functions, $\mathbb{Q} \to \mathbb{Q}$ functions etc ($\mathbb{Z}$ is the set of integers, $\mathbb{Q}$ the set of rational numbers).

When a function is defined, its domain must be specified. Then the elements of the codomain actually 'used' form the *range* of the function. For $t \to 4t^2$ with domain $\{t: 0 \leqslant t \leqslant 3\}$, the range is $\{d: 0 \leqslant d \leqslant 36\}$.

3.2 Mapping diagrams. In some work, functions are named. For a function f, the general usage is, as you will remember, that the image of x under f (i.e. the element of the codomain corresponding to the element x in the domain) is written $f(x)$. Thus for $f: x \to 4x^2$, we may write

26

$f(x) = 4x^2$ and, for instance, $f(5) = 4 \times 5^2$. When the images are associated with the possible values of another quantity as in the statement $d = 4t^2$, then $f(t) = 4t^2$ and also $d = f(t)$.

A graph provides a useful illustration of a function, as we have seen. An alternative pictorial representation is a mapping diagram (see Figure 5 (*b*)); in this, representative elements from the domain are joined to their images in the codomain. We shall use both types of display, choosing on each occasion the one which suits our purposes better.

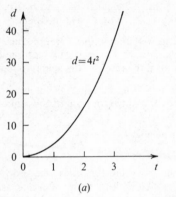

(*a*)   (*b*)

Fig. 5

3.3 Functions with other domains.

Even in simple situations concerned with numbers, the elements of the domain need not be single numbers. If a car is driven fast and the tyres get hot, the tyre pressures change. Will they increase or decrease? The pressure depends on the temperature T as well as the mass of air m. For a particular tyre, if values of m and T are known, we should expect to get a unique value for the pressure p. How might you draw a graph of the function $(m, T) \to p$? The domain is a set of ordered pairs of real numbers and the codomain is a set of single real numbers. Such a function is often referred to as a function $\mathbb{R} \times \mathbb{R} \to \mathbb{R}$ or, briefly, $\mathbb{R}^2 \to \mathbb{R}$.

Transformations of the plane give further examples of more general functions. We can write the translation $\binom{2}{3}$ in the form

$$(x, y) \to (x+2, y+3).$$

This is a function $\mathbb{R}^2 \to \mathbb{R}^2$.

Exercise D

1. For the function $f: t \to 15t - 5t^2$ with domain $\{t: 0 \leqslant t \leqslant 3\}$ (see Exercise C, Question 1), state the values of $f(\frac{1}{2}), f(1), f(1\frac{1}{2})$ and $f(3)$. Draw a mapping diagram and state the range of the function.

27

2. A supermarket normally sells tins of peas at 9p a tin, and has a turnover of 400 tins weekly. The manager estimates that for every $\frac{1}{2}$p reduction in price he will sell an extra 100 tins weekly. He buys the tins for 5p each. Make a table to show his weekly profit for selling prices from 5p to 10p. Find an appropriate algebraic model for this, stating the domain. What is the most profitable price? What if every $\frac{1}{2}$p reduction only increases sales by 40 tins weekly?

3. For the function $g: A \to 300A/(A+2)$ of Exercise C, Question 3, find $g(18)$ and $g(28)$. What is the range if the domain is the set of all positive real numbers?

4. For the function $f: t \to \sin t°$, write down from your tables the values of $f(20)$ and $f(85)$. What are $f(90)$ and $f(95)$? State the values of $f(180)$ and $f(270)$, and give the range of the function if the domain is the set of all real numbers.

5. The height in metres of the tide at Neapswell at any time T hours after midnight is predicted to be $H = 2 \sin 30T°$. Explain why it is perfectly reasonable to have -15 as an element of the domain. What is the range of the height function?

6. Chapter 1 was concerned with functions $n \to u_n$ in which the domain was always the set of natural numbers. Describe the range for each of the sequences defined as follows:

(a) $u_n = 4n$;   (b) $u_1 = 3$, $u_{k+1} = u_k + 6$;
(c) $u_1 = 8$, $u_{k+1} = 12/u_k$.

7. Draw mapping diagrams illustrating the following functions whose domain and codomain are both the set $\mathbb{R}$, and describe each in terms of simple transformations of the number line:

(a) $x \to -x$;   (b) $x \to x-4$;
(c) $x \to \frac{1}{2}x$;   (d) $x \to 3x-2$.

8. Draw a mapping diagram for $x \to \sqrt{x}$. Suggest suitable sets for the domain and the codomain.

9. Draw a mapping diagram for the function $x \to x^2$ with domain

$$\{x: -3 \leqslant x \leqslant 3\}.$$

What is the range?

10. How many functions are there

(i) with domain $\{a, b, c\}$ and codomain $\{p, q\}$,
(ii) with domain $\{a, b, c\}$ and range $\{p, q\}$?

4. COMPOSITE FUNCTIONS

We saw in the O-level course how two functions f and g can be combined to give functions fg and gf.

For example, with $f: x \to 4x^2$ and $g: x \to x-3$, the function fg is

$$fg: x \to 4(x-3)^2.$$

Remember that the order, as with matrices, matters; fg means first g then f. What would be the function gf in our example?

28

Mapping diagrams are particularly useful in illustrating composite functions (see Figure 6). Could the combination of functions be shown by means of graphs?

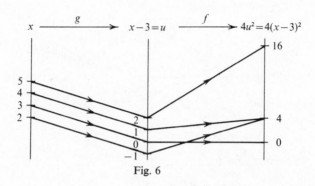

Fig. 6

Example 5

A cinema proprietor noticed that by raising the temperature on the central heating thermostat he could increase the sales of ice cream in the interval. From his observations he decided that the proportion A of his audience who bought ices was approximately $A = 1 - 8/T$, where T is the temperature in degrees Celsius. He makes 3p profit on each ice sold, but the cost of central heating for each session is a basic £1 plus an extra 5p for each degree above zero. What temperature would bring him the greatest profit? Would you recommend such a temperature?

Let us for the moment assume there is an audience of 200. The functions involved are most easily expressed as formulae rather than mappings. They are:

$$\text{numbers:} \qquad\qquad N = 200(1 - 8/T)$$

$$\text{gain from sales of ices:} \quad G = 3N$$

$$\text{cost of heating:} \qquad\quad C = 100 + 5T.$$

Substitution gives $\qquad\qquad G = 3(200 - 1600/T).$

Here $f: T \to 200 - 1600/T$ is combined with the trebling function

$$g: N \to 3N \quad \text{to get} \quad gf: T \to 3(200 - 1600/T).$$

It is equally useful to be able to break down a function into simpler parts. You will probably have noticed that f itself is a composite function. Its constituent parts are easily obtained from considering the flow chart for evaluating a particular value of $f(T)$.

$$T \xrightarrow{} \boxed{\text{Divide into 1600}} \xrightarrow{\;1600/T\;} \boxed{\text{Subtract from 200}} \xrightarrow{\;200 - 1600/T\;}$$

Fig. 7

Figure 8 shows the mapping diagram for this composite function.

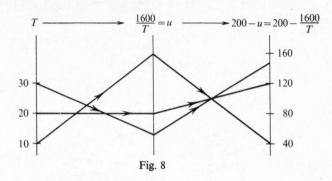

Fig. 8

The proprietor's profit is given by

$$P = 3(200 - 1600/T) - (100 + 5T).$$

How can you find the temperature for which P is a maximum? It is about 31 °C, which is impractically hot.

Exercise E

1. Find the cinema proprietor's profit (with an audience of 200) when $T = 10$, 20, 30. What temperature will lead to the sale of 80 ices?

2. Find the formula for the cinema proprietor's profit when there is an audience of 300. What temperature would give him the greatest profit?

3. Functions f and g which map $\mathbb{R} \to \mathbb{R}$ are defined:

$$f : x \to \frac{1}{x}, \quad g : x \to 1 + x.$$

Find the images of the number 2 under the functions f, g, fg, ff and gg. Repeat the question for the number a. Express gf, fg, ff and gg each by a single formula.

What numbers must be excluded from the domains of f and g if fg and gf are to be defined?

4. Give geometrical interpretations of the functions

$$f : x \to -x, \quad g : x \to 2 - x$$

which map $\mathbb{R} \to \mathbb{R}$, in terms of points on the number line. Express the function gf by a single formula, and interpret this geometrically.

5. Let f and g denote the mappings:

$$f : \begin{pmatrix} x \\ y \end{pmatrix} \to \begin{pmatrix} a & b \\ c & d \end{pmatrix} \begin{pmatrix} x \\ y \end{pmatrix}, \quad g : \begin{pmatrix} x \\ y \end{pmatrix} \to \begin{pmatrix} p & q \\ r & s \end{pmatrix} \begin{pmatrix} x \\ y \end{pmatrix}.$$

Suggest domains and codomains for which f and g would be functions. What is fg?

6. Let s denote the function $x \to x^2$ and q the function $x \to x+1$. Express the following functions in terms of s and q:

(a) $x \to x^2+1$;   (b) $x \to (x+1)^2$;

(c) $x \to (x^2+1)^2$;   (d) $x \to x+2$;

(e) $x \to (x+2)^2$;   (f) $x \to x^4$.

7. e, f, g, h are defined as follows:

$$e: x \to x; \qquad f: x \to \frac{1}{x};$$

$$g: x \to -x; \qquad h: x \to -\frac{1}{x}.$$

Verify that f^2, g^2, h^2 are all equal to e, and simplify fg, gf, fh, hf, gh and hg. Copy and complete the following table:

		Function written second			
		e	f	g	h
Function	e				
written	f				
first	g				
	h				

8. Let f and g be defined by

$$f: x \to 1-x, \quad g: x \to \frac{1}{x}.$$

Find and simplify formulae for various composite functions such as fg, gf, gfg, $fggf$.... How many different functions can you obtain? Allocate a single letter to stand for each function and express the complete set in a table as in Question 7.

4.1 Inverse functions.

Let us continue the example of the previous section, where
$$f: T \to 200 - 1600/T$$
gave the numbers of ice creams sold for any given temperature T, that is, $f(T) = N$.

What temperature leads to sales of 75 ices? In other words, for what value of T does $f(T) = 75$? This question requires the function to be used in reverse. The new function which carries out this process is called the *inverse* function, and is denoted by f^{-1}.

For the function $h: x \to 4x+7$, $h(5) = 27$ and $h^{-1}(27) = 5$. Give the values of $h(-4)$ and $h^{-1}(-9)$. What is $h^{-1}(15)$? Explain why the inverse function is $h^{-1}: x \to \frac{1}{4}(x-7)$.

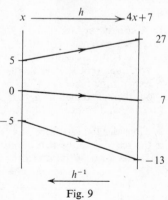

Fig. 9

31

The basic condition for a relation to be a function is that, for every element of the domain, there is *just one* associated element of the co-domain. In a mapping diagram, one and only one arrow points to the right from each mark on the left.

If we consider the mapping in reverse, however, from the codomain to the domain, the situation may be quite different. There is no restriction on the number of arrows which may lead to a particular element of the codomain; for some elements there may be several, whilst for others there may be none at all. If, however, each element of the codomain is associated with a unique element of the domain, the function is described as 'one to one', and an inverse function exists. The squaring function $s: x \to x^2$ has no inverse function unless its domain is restricted; if the domain of s is the set of positive real numbers, s^{-1} exists and is $x \to \sqrt{x}$.

The temperature leading to sales of 75 ice creams can be found by using the composite mapping diagram of Figure 8 backwards. The corresponding number on the u-axis is 125 and on the T-axis 12·8. We notice that the inverse of a composite function is found by taking the inverses of the simple functions in reverse order. Note that both the functions here are self-inverse.

The general result for the inverse of a composite function may be expressed as follows:

If
$$h = fg, \quad \text{then} \quad h^{-1} = g^{-1}f^{-1}.$$

As an example, take $f: x \to x+8$ and $g: x \to 3x$; then $h = fg$ maps x onto $3x+8$.

Now the inverse functions are $f^{-1}: x \to x-8$, $g^{-1}: x \to \frac{1}{3}x$, and

$$h^{-1} = g^{-1}f^{-1} \quad \text{maps } x \text{ onto} \quad \tfrac{1}{3}(x-8).$$

Illustrate this example (as in the O-level course) with flow charts like Figure 7.

Exercise F

1. A circuit consists of a 12 volt battery with internal resistance 2 ohms and a variable resistance of R ohms. The electrical current is $I = 12/(R+2)$ amps.

What is the current when the resistance is 18 ohms?

What value of R gives $I = 0.5$?

Express the function $R \to I$ as the combination of two simpler functions, and show them together in a mapping diagram. Write down the inverse of each function and so express the function $I \to R$ algebraically.

2. Consider the functions $f: x \to 2\pi x$ and $g: x \to \pi x^2$, where the domain of each is the set of positive real numbers. Express the inverse functions f^{-1} and g^{-1} in the same form. Write down the composite functions fg^{-1} and gf^{-1}.

The above functions may be written using formulae as

$$c = 2\pi x \quad \text{and} \quad a = \pi x^2.$$

Express x in terms of c and of a. Have these results anything to do with the inverse functions f^{-1} and g^{-1}? Express c in terms of a and a in terms of c, and relate your results to the above composite functions.

3. Find the inverses of the following functions, expressing your answers in the same form.

(a) $f: x \to 2x-3$;

(b) $f: x \to 3-5x$;

(c) $f: x \to \dfrac{1}{x}+3$;

(d) $f: x \to \dfrac{1}{x+3}$;

(e) $f: x \to \dfrac{3}{2-7x}$;

(f) $f: x \to 8-\dfrac{10}{1-x}$.

4. If f and g are functions for which inverse functions are defined, and if $fg = h$, show that $f = hg^{-1}$ and that $g = f^{-1}h$. Illustrate these results with a mapping diagram.

5. If f is any function and e is the identity function, what are ef and fe?

If f is a function for which an inverse is defined, explain why ff^{-1} and $f^{-1}f$ are both equal to e.

6. Assume that $u = a+y$ and $y = bt^2$, where a and b are constants. Express u in terms of t (i.e. eliminate y from the formulae, leaving an expression containing only t's and constants). What is the inverse of this function, i.e. what is the expression giving t in terms of u and constants?

From the original formulae, express y in terms of u and t in terms of y. Combine these expressions eliminating y. Does this answer agree with the other expression for t in terms of u?

5. AN EXTENDED EXAMPLE

Imagine a small factory making record players, with a steady output of 100 a month. Components are obtained from other firms, and, in particular, an order for 300 loudspeakers is placed every three months with one supplier.

Every loudspeaker costs £3, and there is an extra cost of £15 for each order placed. The latter may be thought of as the cost of transport and is independent of the size of the order. There is one other cost we should consider: there is a time lag between paying for components and receiving payment for finished products and this may be financed by borrowing from a bank. We calculate the cost per annum as 10 % of the value of the average size of the stock of loudspeakers.

Here is a numerical situation in which we can pose various questions. It is expressed in words at present, and our first aim is to translate it into mathematical terms.

Exercise G

1. If the stock of loudspeakers is down to 0 just as a consignment arrives, write down the size of the stock after (a) $\frac{1}{2}$ month, (b) 1 month, (c) $2\frac{1}{2}$ months, (d) 4 months, (e) 6 months.

33

2. Draw a graph showing the size of the stock over a period of 8 months beginning as a consignment arrives. When does the stock consist of 120 loudspeakers?

3. What is a 'month' in this context? What account should we take of weekends and holidays?

4. Is the graph 'continuous'? Is the portion of the graph between the arrival of one order and the next continuous?

5. Would you describe the stock size as a function of time? If so, can you express it algebraically? What is the domain? What is the average size of the stock of loudspeakers?

6. Show that the total annual cost of purchasing and stocking the loudspeakers is £3705.

7. List some of the other factors contributing (*a*) to the £15 cost of an order, (*b*) to the 10 % cost of holding stock.

8. If orders for 200 were placed every two months instead, calculate the new total annual cost.

9. Make some more calculations similar to those in Questions 6, 8, and suggest the best policy.

10. Would your advice in Question 9 be affected if the price of loudspeakers changed?

5.1   Some possible models. You probably had no difficulty with Question 1, except in (*e*) where there is ambiguity. But if the question had asked for the stock level after $\frac{1}{3}$ month, the answer $266\frac{2}{3}$ is suggested, and this is not meaningful. Furthermore, we should consider what we mean by $\frac{1}{3}$ month. Perhaps we should eliminate weekends and holidays, find that there are 240 working days in the year and divide this into 12 periods of 20 days. Then the production rate of 100 a month is exactly equivalent to 5 a day, and it is easy to state the stock level after any integral number of days. We should prefer not to consider fractions of a day.

With these suggestions adopted, we have a clearly defined relation between the time t months and the stock size s. When $t = 1$, $s = 200$; when $t = 1\frac{3}{20}$, $s = 185$; when $s = 50$, $t = 2\frac{1}{2}$ or $5\frac{1}{2}$ or $8\frac{1}{2}$ etc. The graph of this relation consists of a set of distinct points at intervals of $\frac{1}{20}$ in the t-direction (see Figure 10).

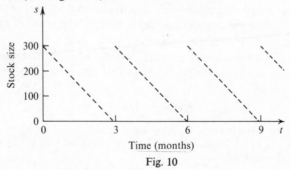

Time (months)

Fig. 10

The final stage in constructing a mathematical model is dictated more by whim and convenience than by necessity.

Take

$$y = 300 - 100x \quad \text{for} \quad 0 \leqslant x < 3,$$
$$y = 300 - 100(x-3) \quad \text{for} \quad 3 \leqslant x < 6,$$
$$y = 300 - 100(x-6) \quad \text{for} \quad 6 \leqslant x < 9, \quad \text{etc.}$$

This is an abstract function for which we choose as domain the set of all real numbers. The essential feature of a function is that there should be a single element of the codomain or image-set for each element of the domain. s is not a function of t unless we resolve the ambiguity about its value when t is a multiple of 3. This difficulty can be avoided in the model in a variety of ways, one of which has been adopted above. The graph of the model (Figure 11) now consists of straight line segments.

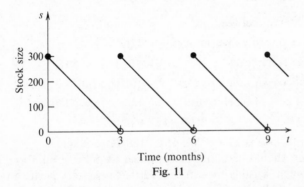

Time (months)

Fig. 11

Let us now return to the stock control problem of Question 9. The time interval (T months) between orders can be varied, and for each value of T there is a unique value of C (the total annual cost, in £, of buying and holding stock), as calculated in Exercise G, Questions 6, 8. Thus C is a function of T. For this function we produce in turn (i) a table of values, (ii) a graph (Figure 12), (iii) an algebraic description.

T	1	2	3	4	6	12
No. of orders per annum	12	6	4	3	2	1
Average stock level	50	100	150	200	300	600
Annual cost of holding stock	15	30	45	60	90	180
Annual cost of placing orders	180	90	60	45	30	15
Annual cost of components	3600	3600	3600	3600	3600	3600
C	3795	3720	3705	3705	3720	3795

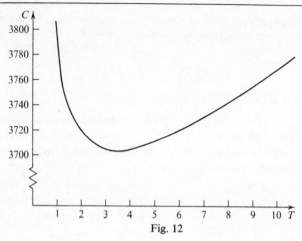

Fig. 12

If the

time interval between orders	$= T$ months,
number of orders per annum	$= 12/T$,
average stock level	$= \frac{1}{2} \times 100T = 50T$,
annual cost of holding stock	$= 10/100 \times 50T \times 3 = 15T$,
annual cost of placing orders	$= 12/T \times 15 = 180/T$.

$$C = 3600 + 15T + 180/T,$$

i.e. the cost function is $T \to 3600 + 15T + 180/T$.

The domain should certainly be restricted to positive numbers, and it might be thought sensible to restrict it further to certain positive rational numbers (e.g. multiples of $\frac{1}{20}$). However, when we wish to calculate the value of T giving minimum C—the ultimate objective—it will pay to work with the model in which T can take all real positive values. This must be left until Chapter 5.

Miscellaneous Exercise

1. Which of the following define functions from x to y, with domain the real numbers?

(a) $y = x^2$;   (b) $x = y^2$;

(c) $y = \sqrt{x}$;   (d) $y > x^2$;

(e) $y = \sin x°$;   (f) $x^2 + y^2 = 4$.

2. Relations are sometimes divided into the following categories: one–one, many–one, one–many, many–many.

A one–many relation, for example, is a relation in which an element of the domain may be associated with several elements in the range but an element in the range may be associated with only one element in the domain.

Categorize the relations of Question 1 in this way, choosing suitable domains and codomains.

36

3. When two dice are thrown, the possible totals form a set of values from 2 to 12. What are the probabilities usually assigned to the elements of this set? Is the relation you have obtained a function? Can you think of any situation in which the relation between events and their probabilities is not a function?

4. A function $\mathbb{R}^2 \to \mathbb{R}^2$ is defined by $f: \begin{pmatrix} x \\ y \end{pmatrix} \to \begin{pmatrix} 2 & 4 \\ 3 & 6 \end{pmatrix} \begin{pmatrix} x \\ y \end{pmatrix}$. Find $f\begin{pmatrix} 1 \\ 0 \end{pmatrix}$, $f\begin{pmatrix} 0 \\ \frac{1}{2} \end{pmatrix}$, $f\begin{pmatrix} 1 \\ 1 \end{pmatrix}$ and $f\begin{pmatrix} 3 \\ -1 \end{pmatrix}$. Show these on a diagram and describe the range of the function.

5. Find examples of functions f and g for which $fg = gf$ where the domains of the functions are (a) $\mathbb{R}$, (b) $\mathbb{R}^2$.

6. The spot on a T.V. screen traces out 625 lines in $0 \cdot 1$ seconds moving from left to right at a steady rate and shooting back to the start of the next line in negligible time. Is the position of the beam a function of the time t? Would you describe it as $\mathbb{R} \to \mathbb{R}$, $\mathbb{R}^2 \to \mathbb{R}$, $\mathbb{R} \to \mathbb{R}^2$, or what?

7. All the apples in a box are of mass 180 grams. They are sold at 8p for half a kilogram. A customer asking for K kg gets the least number of apples N that will tilt the scales. How many apples does he get if he asks for $1\frac{1}{2}$ kg? Suggest a suitable domain and codomain for the function $K \to N$, and state the corresponding range.

8. A stone is thrown upwards so that its height (in metres) above the ground after t seconds is given by
$$t \to 5t(1-t)+10.$$

What restrictions are there on the domain of this function? Draw a mapping diagram and state the range.

What is the maximum height the stone reaches?

9. The number of admissions to the school sanatorium on the nth day of an epidemic is given approximately by
$$A = 10+30n-3n^2.$$

Describe the domain of the function $n \to A$. Find the greatest number of admissions on any one day and the total number of admissions.

10. A boy gets £1 pocket money per month and spends, on average, 25p a week. Formulate carefully an algebraic model to give the amount of money he has at any given time.

SUMMARY

A *function* is a relation between two sets, the *domain* and the *codomain*, in which each element of the domain is related to one and only one element of the codomain.

The element of the codomain to which an element x of the domain is connected by the function f is called the *image* of x and is denoted by $f(x)$.

The set of images of all members of the domain is called the *range*.

We illustrate functions either by *mapping diagrams* or by *graphs*.

37

We can combine two functions f and g to produce a composite function fg, mapping x onto $f[g(x)]$. The notation thus implies that the function g is to be applied first, followed by f.

If a function is *one–one*, meaning that every element of the range is the image of one and only one member of the domain, there is an *inverse function* f^{-1}, which reverses the action of f; $a = f^{-1}(b)$ implies $b = f(a)$.

3

GRAPHS

1. GRAPHICAL REPRESENTATION
OF FUNCTIONS

1.1 Introduction. In Chapter 2 we found graphs useful for representing functions whose domain and codomain were both sets of real numbers. For example, in the mathematical model of the cost situation in Section 5, we had the function $T \to 3600 + 15T + 180/T$. When we sketched its graph, we saw that there is a value of T for which the cost is a minimum.

A similar function is $x \to x + 3/x$. Draw its graph and estimate where its minimum value occurs.

1.2 Graph sketching. In drawing the graph of $x \to x + 3/x$ in Section 1.1, did you produce a table of values, plot the corresponding points and join them up? While this is a perfectly suitable method, it is laborious; in this chapter we will develop methods of sketching a graph quickly, incorporating in the sketch all the important features. We shall find many situations in which a rough sketch tells us what we want to know about a function, and a graph accurately calculated and plotted would be no more useful.

Example 1

We illustrate the main ideas by considering the function $x \to x + 3/x$.

First write $y = x + 3/x$, and look at the table of values below:

x	1	2	3	4	5	10
y	4	3·5	4	4·75	5·6	10·3

It is clear that x and y are approximately equal when they are large. This can be seen from the form of the function without having to substitute values for x, for when x is large and positive, $3/x$ is small and $x + 3/x$ is approximately equal to x. Thus the graph approaches the line $y = x$ as x becomes larger and larger. (The line $y = x$ is called an *asymptote*.)

In the table of values, only positive values of x were taken. This is reasonable if the function is a model of a real-life situation, but in this chapter we shall always take the domain to be the set of all real numbers for which the function under discussion is defined. We should therefore consider negative values and zero. Negative values give:

x	−10	−4	−3	−2	−1
y	−10·3	−4·75	−4	−3·5	−4

Now $x = 0$ presents a problem since we cannot divide by 0, and we say 3/0 is undefined. We must exclude 0 from the domain, but we can have numbers as near 0 as we like, both positive and negative.

x	-0.1	-0.01	$+0.01$	$+0.1$
y	-30.1	-300.01	300.01	30.1

It emerges that when x is small and positive, the term $3/x$ in $x + 3/x$ is very large and positive, and the term x is negligible. If x is small and negative, then $3/x$ is large and negative, and so is y. We can now sketch the graph as in Figure 1. The graph is said to have a *discontinuity* at $x = 0$, and the y-axis is another asymptote.

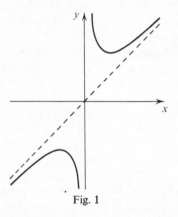

Fig. 1

If y is the image of x under the function $x \rightarrow x + 3/x$ we see that the curve in Figure 1 contains the points (x, y) and only such points. The relation $y = x + 3/x$ is called the *equation* of the graph, and it is important to realize that the coordinates of any point on the graph do in fact satisfy this equation.

This chapter deals in a more leisurely way with each of the ideas required for this example. At the end, each sketch graph should take only a minute or two. While experience is being gained, you may have to plot a few specific points; when you do, always look for patterns of behaviour which you might be able to predict on later occasions.

Example 2

Sketch the graph of the function $x \rightarrow 2x + 1$.

We know from the O-level course that the graph is a straight line. All straight lines can be sketched easily by noting the gradient and the point where the line cuts the y-axis (i.e. where $x = 0$).

For $x \rightarrow 2x + 1$, the image of 0 is 1, and the gradient is 2. Hence the graph can be sketched as in Figure 2.

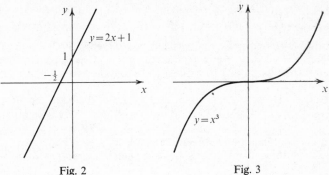

Fig. 2   Fig. 3

Example 3

Sketch the graph of $y = x^3$.

When $x = 0$, $y = 0$ and this is the only point at which the graph crosses the x-axis or the y-axis. What happens when x is large and positive (say 10^2)? The value of y is much larger ($x = 10^2 \Rightarrow y = 10^6$) and the graph of $y = x^3$ gets steeper and steeper as x gets larger. Similarly, when x takes larger and larger negative values (e.g. -10^2, -10^3, -10^4), y takes even larger negative values and the graph again gets steeper.

When x lies between 0 and 1, y is smaller than x (e.g. $y = \frac{1}{8}$ when $x = \frac{1}{2}$). The graph 'flattens out' as we approach the origin from the right. This is also true when we approach the origin from the left. The graph of $y = x^3$ is sketched in Figure 3.

Exercise A

1. Sketch the graphs of the functions:

   (*a*) $x \to 2x$;   (*b*) $x \to 2x+2$;   (*c*) $x \to 2x-1$;

   (*d*) $x \to -3x+2$;   (*e*) $x \to \frac{1}{2}x-1$;   (*f*) $x \to -\frac{1}{3}x+2$.

2. Sketch the graphs of

   (*a*) $y = 3x$;   (*b*) $y = 3x+1$;   (*c*) $y = 3x-2$;

   (*d*) $3y = 2x$;   (*e*) $3y = -x-4$;   (*f*) $5y = 4x+3$;

   (*g*) $y+x+1 = 0$;   (*h*) $2x-3y+4 = 0$.

3. What is the connection between the graphs of Questions 1 (*a*), (*b*) and (*c*)?

4. What is the connection between the graphs of Questions 2 (*a*), (*b*) and (*c*)?

5. Sketch the graphs of (*a*) $x \to x^2$, (*b*) $x \to x^4$, (*c*) $x \to x^5$.

6. Sketch the graphs of (*a*) $x \to \dfrac{1}{x}$, (*b*) $x \to \dfrac{1}{x^2}$.

7. Sketch the graphs of (*a*) $x \to \sqrt{x}$, where $\sqrt{x}$ means the positive square root of x, (*b*) $x \to \sqrt[3]{x}$.

41

8. Sketch the graphs of

(a) $y = x^2 + 1$;　　　(b) $y = -\frac{1}{2}x^2$;　　　　　　(c) $y = 2x - x^2$.

9. Describe any symmetries you can find in the graphs of Questions 5–8. (For example, $x \to x^2 + 1$ is symmetrical about the y-axis.) Can you tell by looking at a function whether its graph is (i) symmetrical about the y-axis, (ii) unchanged by a half turn about O?

10. Write in order of ascending value $1/x^2$, $1/x$, x, $\sqrt{x}$, $\sqrt[3]{x}$, (i) if $0 < x < 1$, (ii) if $x > 1$.

11. What is the connection between the graphs of $x \to x^2$ and $x \to x^2 + 1$?
　　Without plotting many points, quickly sketch the graphs of $x \to (x+1)^2$, $x \to x^2 + 2$, $x \to (x-2)^2 - 3$.

12. Sketch the graphs of

(a) $y = 1/(x+1)$;　　　　　　(b) $y = x/(x-1)$;

(c) $y = 1/(x^2+1)$;　　　　　　(d) $x^2y = 1$.

2. GRAPHS OF STANDARD FUNCTIONS

2.1　Powers of x. What are the graphs of $x \to x^2$, $x \to x^3$, $x \to 1/x$, $x \to 1/x^2$? Simple functions of this kind occur so frequently that we should be able to sketch their graphs without any hesitation. Consider the graphs in Figure 4; notice that $y = 1/x$ and $y = 1/x^2$ are not defined when $x = 0$, and that $y = \sqrt{x}$ is not defined when $x < 0$. Sketch the graphs of $y = x^5$, $y = 1/x^4$ and $y = \sqrt[5]{x}$ and compare them with those in Figure 4.

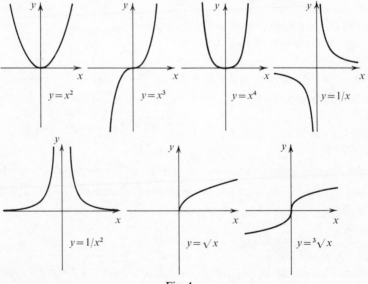

Fig 4

2.2　Location of graphs in quadrants. In Example 1 we saw that for $y = x+3/x$, when x is positive so is y, and when x is negative y is also negative. It follows that the curve lies completely in the first and third quadrants, where the plane is divided into four quadrants by the coordinate axes as in Figure 5.

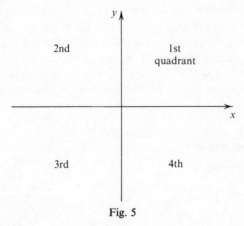

Fig. 5

Similarly we can see that the graph of $y = 1/x$ must lie in the first and third quadrants, while that of $y = 1/x^2$, for which y is always positive, lies in the first and second quadrants. For $y = \sqrt{x}$ we must have *both* x and y positive, and this graph lies in the first quadrant.

In which quadrants do the graphs of $y = -x^2$ and $y = 1/x^3$ lie?

2.3　Transformations of graphs of powers of x. How are the graphs of $y = x^2+1$, $y = -x^2$ and $y = 3x^2$ related to the graph of $y = x^2$?

x	-2	-1	0	1	2
x^2	4	1	0	1	4
x^2+1	5	2	1	2	5
$-x^2$	-4	-1	0	-1	-4
$3x^2$	12	3	0	3	12

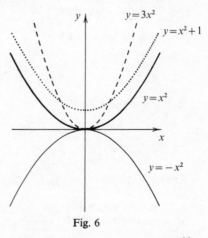

Fig. 6

43

The graph of $y = x^2 + 1$ is one unit higher at every point than the graph of $y = x^2$, so it is produced from the latter by a translation of 1 unit in the direction of the y-axis. The graph of $y = -x^2$ is a reflection in the x-axis of the graph of $y = x^2$. Finally the graph of $y = 3x^2$ is obtained from that of $y = x^2$ by stretching it upwards by a factor of 3.

These transformations are confirmed by the table of values with Figure 6. For example, corresponding to the point $(2, 4)$ on $y = x^2$, we have the point $(2, 12)$ on $y = 3x^2$, and this is the image under the stretch of factor 3.

It follows from this example that we can quickly sketch the graphs for equations such as $y = 2x^3$, $y = x^4 + 3$, $y = -1/x$. Each is obtained from the graph of a simple power of x by a stretch, translation or reflection.

Exercise B

1. Sketch the graphs of

(a) $y = x^6$;   (b) $y = x^7$;   (c) $y = \dfrac{1}{x^3}$;   (d) $y = \dfrac{1}{x^4}$;

(e) $y = \sqrt[4]{x}$;   (f) $y = \sqrt[5]{x}$;   (g) $y = \dfrac{1}{\sqrt{x}}$;   (h) $y = \dfrac{1}{\sqrt[3]{x}}$.

2. Sketch the graph of $y = \sqrt{x^3}$.

3. Superimpose on the same diagram the graphs of $y = x^2$ and $y = x^3$. Where do they cut? How do they compare for $0 < x < 1$ and for $x > 1$?

4. Superimpose on the same diagram the graphs of $y = 1/x$ and $y = 1/x^2$. Where do they cut? How do they compare for $0 < x < 1$ and for $x > 1$?

5. Where do the graphs of $y = x^2$ and $y = 1/x$ cut? Where do those of $y = x^2$ and $y = 1/x^2$ cut?

6. How is the graph of $y = \sqrt{x}$ related to that of $y = x^2$? How are those of $y = \sqrt[3]{x}$ and $y = x^3$ related?

7. Sketch the graphs of

(a) $y = x^2 - 5$;   (b) $y = 1/x + 3$;   (c) $y = \sqrt{x} + 9$;

(d) $y = 2x^2$;   (e) $y = 3x^3$;   (f) $y = \frac{1}{4}x$.

8. Sketch the graphs of

(a) $y = -x^3$;   (b) $y = -\dfrac{1}{x^2}$;   (c) $y = -\sqrt{x}$;

(d) $y = -\dfrac{2}{x}$;   (e) $y = -3x^4$;   (f) $y = -\frac{1}{2}\sqrt[3]{x}$;

(g) $y = 3x^2 - 1$;   (h) $y = -\sqrt{x} + 4$;   (i) $y = -5x^2 + 2$.

9. What can you say about the natural number n if the graph of $y = x^n$ is (a) symmetrical about the y-axis; (b) symmetrical under a half turn about O?

10. By comparing the shapes of $y = x^n$ for small integers n, make a rough sketch of the graphs of (a) $y = x^{99}$, (b) $y = x^{100}$.

11. Where do the graphs of the following meet the x-axis

(a) $y = (x-1)^2$;

(b) $y = (x+1)(x+2)$;

(c) $y = x(x+1)$;

(d) $y = \sqrt{[x(x+1)]}$?

12. For what values of x is y very large and (i) positive, (ii) negative if

(a) $y = \dfrac{1}{x(x+1)}$,

(b) $y = \dfrac{1}{(x-1)^2(x+1)}$?

13. As x becomes larger and larger, what value does y approach in each of the following? Is y greater than or less than this value when (i) x is large and positive, (ii) x is large and negative?

(a) $y = 2 - \dfrac{1}{x}$;

(b) $y = 1 + \dfrac{1}{x+2}$;

(c) $y = \dfrac{x+1}{x+2}$;

(d) $y = \dfrac{x+1}{x^2+1}$.

3. SKETCHING GRAPHS

This section summarizes and carries further the ideas suggested by the earlier exploratory questions. It is important to develop a facility for sketching such graphs quickly. The general shape is usually all that is required, and we will not be concerned with plotting more than a few points.

We first deal with simple properties that are apparent from the form of the function, and then consider the vital question 'What happens when x is large?'. We next examine for what values of x the function is undefined, and the behaviour for nearby values of x, and finish by giving one or two examples sketched completely.

3.1 Simple properties.

(i) *Quadrants*. In Section 2.2 we discovered that it is sometimes possible to find that the quadrants in which the graph lies are limited.

(ii) *Range and domain*. The domain can usually be stated at once. For example, for $x \to (2-x)\sqrt{x}$ the domain is $\{x : x \geqslant 0\}$ since $\sqrt{x}$ is undefined for negative x. The range is sometimes (not always) obvious; for example if $y = 1/(x^2+1)$ the range is $\{y : 0 \leqslant y \leqslant 1\}$, since x^2 is positive or zero and hence the denominator is always greater than or equal to 1.

(iii) *Intercepts on the x-axis*. It is usually easy to see where the graph cuts the x-axis by putting $y = 0$ in its equation. If $y = (x+1)/(2x+1)$ then $y = 0$ for $x = -1$ and for no other value. If all such points are marked in, then the x-axis forms a 'barrier'—it cannot be crossed at any other point.

3.2 Behaviour when x is large: asymptotes. When x is large (either large and positive or large and negative) x^2 is much larger than x, x^3 is larger than x^2 and when terms are added it is the *highest* power of x that matters: the others can be neglected when we are considering the approximate shape of the graph for large x. Thus we can often compare the shape with that of the standard functions described in Section 2.1.

Example 4

Consider the graph of $y = (2-x)\sqrt{x}$ for large values of x.

When $x = 10^2$, 10^4 the values of this function are -980 and $-999\,800$. The corresponding values of $-x\sqrt{x}$ are -1000 and -10^6, and are close to those of the function (in the sense that the percentage difference is small). We see that the dominant term of $2\sqrt{x} - x\sqrt{x}$ is $-x\sqrt{x}$ and the function behaves, for large positive x, like $y = -x\sqrt{x}$ and its graph has the shape shown in Figure 7. (y is undefined when x is negative.)

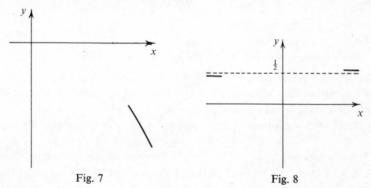

Fig. 7   Fig. 8

Example 5

Consider the graph of $y = (x+1)/(2x+1)$ for large values of x.

Here let us put $x = 10, 100, 1000$. Then $y = \frac{11}{21}, \frac{101}{201}, \frac{1001}{2001}$ respectively, which when expressed in decimal form give $0\cdot52$, $0\cdot502$, $0\cdot5002$. We see that these values are close to $0\cdot5$. This is because when x is large $x+1$ behaves like x (the 1 is negligible compared with x) and $2x+1$ behaves like $2x$. So $y \approx x/(2x) = \frac{1}{2}$. The same applies when x is large and negative. Thus the line $y = \frac{1}{2}$ gives a good approximation to the curve far from the origin; we approach as close as we please to this line provided we take x large enough. We say that y tends to $\frac{1}{2}$ as x gets larger and larger either through positive or negative values (written : $y \to \frac{1}{2}$ as $x \to \pm\infty$). The line $y = \frac{1}{2}$ is an asymptote.

We see moreover that $y > \frac{1}{2}$ when x is large and positive (e.g. when $x = 100$, $y = \frac{101}{201}$, which is greater than $\frac{1}{2}$). We say that $y \to \frac{1}{2}$ *from above*. Similarly when x is large and negative, $y < \frac{1}{2}$ (e.g. when $x = -100$,

46

$y = -99/-199$). As $x \to -\infty$, $y \to \frac{1}{2}$ *from below*. Thus the shape of the graph for large x, positive and negative, is as in Figure 8.

Example 6

Consider the graph of $y = 2x/(x^2-1)$ for large values of x.

Here the dominant terms for large x are $2x$ and x^2, and so the function behaves like $2x/x^2 = 2/x$, This tells us not only that $y = 0$ is an asymptote but also that as $x \to \infty$, $y \to 0$ from above and as $x \to -\infty$, $y \to 0$ from below. This is shown in Figure 9.

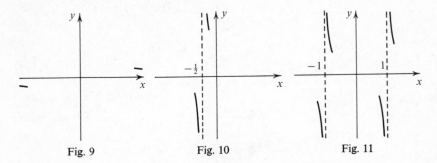

Fig. 9   Fig. 10   Fig. 11

3.3 Asymptotes parallel to the *y*-axis. Discontinuities.

Example 5 (cont.)

$y = (x+1)/(2x+1)$ is undefined when $x = -\frac{1}{2}$, since $2x+1 = 0$ and we cannot divide by 0. What happens for values of x close to $-\frac{1}{2}$? y is clearly very large and it only remains to discover whether y is positive or negative. Now when x is just greater than $-\frac{1}{2}$ (e.g. $-0\cdot499$) both $x+1$ and $2x+1$ are positive and hence y is positive. We say $y \to +\infty$ when $x \to -\frac{1}{2}$ from above.

Similarly $y \to -\infty$ as $x \to -\frac{1}{2}$ from below; since when x is just less than $-\frac{1}{2}$ (e.g. $-0\cdot501$), $x+1$ is still positive, but $2x+1$ is now negative. The shape of the curve near the asymptote $x = -\frac{1}{2}$ is given in Figure 10. The graph has a discontinuity at $x = -\frac{1}{2}$. Such a discontinuity will always occur when there is a value of x which makes the denominator of an expression zero.

Example 6 (cont.)

$y = 2x/(x^2-1)$ is undefined when $x = -1$ or 1.

By considering values of x just less than and just greater than -1, check that $y \to -\infty$ as $x \to -1$ from below, and $y \to +\infty$ as $x \to -1$ from above. Near $x = 1$ we proceed in a similar manner, obtaining finally the form shown in Figure 11.

47

Discontinuities can arise when the value of the function is subject to 'jumps'. Figure 12 shows the graph of the function $x \to [x]$, where $[x]$ means the greatest integer not exceeding x. Thus $[1\cdot3] = 1$, $[\pi] = 3$, $[5] = 5$, $[-1\cdot7] = -2$, and $[-1] = -1$. We use a circle to show that the end-point is not included, and a disc to show that it is.

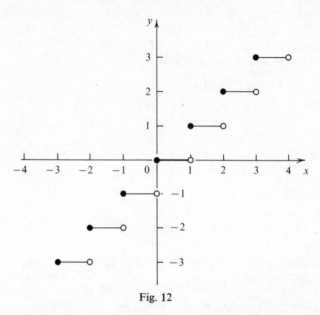

Fig. 12

3.4 Examples of curve sketching. We now show the whole process of sketching curves for some examples, three of which we have already dealt with in part.

Example 4 (cont.)

Sketch $y = (2-x)\sqrt{x}$.

In Figure 7 we showed the form for large positive x, and mentioned that the domain was $\{x : x \geqslant 0\}$. We note that $y = 0$ when $x = 0$ and $x = 2$. What happens near the origin? When x is small and positive the x in the term $(2-x)$ may be neglected in comparison with the 2, and $y \approx 2\sqrt{x}$. This shows us the form at O, and the whole graph must be as in Figure 13.

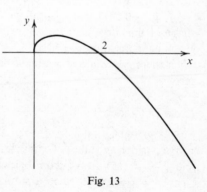

Fig. 13

Example 5 (cont.)

Sketch $y = (x+1)/(2x+1)$.

We have shown the form near the asymptotes $y = \frac{1}{2}$ and $x = -\frac{1}{2}$ in Figures 8 and 10.

$y = 0$ when $x = -1$, and when $x = 0$, $y = 1$. Except at these two points the axes form barriers. The complete graph is then as in Figure 14.

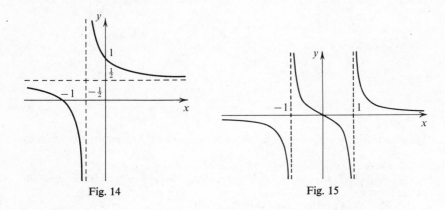

Fig. 14   Fig. 15

Example 6 (cont.)

Sketch $y = 2x/(x^2-1)$.

Figures 9 and 11 show us the form near the asymptotes. When $x = 0$, $y = 0$ and the axes form barriers, except at the origin. The graph is as shown in Figure 15.

We conclude with a complete example.

Example 7

Sketch the graph of $y = x^3/(x-1)$.

   (i)   The only 'gate' in either axis is at the origin.

   (ii) When x is large $y \approx x^3/x = x^2$; this gives the part of Figure 16 marked A and B.

   (iii) When $x = 1$, y is undefined and $x = 1$ is an asymptote. When x is greater than 1, y is positive and when x is just less than 1, y is negative. We now have the parts of Figure 16 marked C and D.

We can now complete the sketch (Figure 17). Some extra information is given by noting that when x is small we may neglect the x in the denominator in comparison with the -1, and hence $y \approx -x^3$.

49

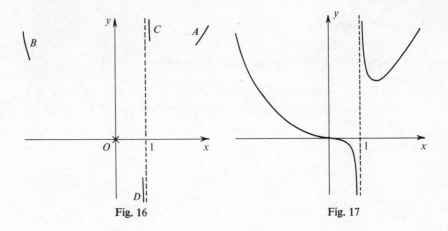

Fig. 16   Fig. 17

Exercise C

When sketching graphs it is useful to follow a more or less standard procedure as follows.

(i) Look for any restrictions on possible values of x and y.

(ii) Find where the graph cuts the axes: apart from these points the axes will act as barriers.

(iii) Find the behaviour for large x.

(iv) Find the values of x which give discontinuities, and the behaviour near these values.

By now it should be possible to sketch the graph.

Each member of the class should sketch the graphs of a few of the functions in Questions 1–5, chosen in such a way that all are considered.

1. (a) $y = (x-1)(x-2)$;   (b) $y = (x+1)(x-1)$;

(c) $y = x(x-1)$;   (d) $y = x^2(2x-1)$;

(e) $y = x(x-1)(x+1)$;   (f) $y = (x-1)(x+2)(x-3)$;

(g) $y = x^2(x-1)$;   (h) $y = x(x-1)^2$.

2. (a) $y = \dfrac{1}{x-1}$;   (b) $y = \dfrac{x}{x+2}$;

(c) $y = \dfrac{x}{1-x}$;   (d) $y = \dfrac{x+1}{x-3}$;

(e) $y = \dfrac{2x}{(x+1)(x+2)}$;   (f) $y = \dfrac{1}{x(x+1)}$;

(g) $y = \dfrac{x^3}{2x-1}$;   (h) $y = \dfrac{x(x-1)(x-2)}{x+1}$.

3. (a) $y = 1 + \dfrac{1}{x}$;   (b) $y = 1 + \dfrac{1}{x^2}$;

(c) $y = 2 - \dfrac{1}{x-1}$;

(d) $y = \dfrac{1}{1+x^2}$;

(e) $y = x - 1 + \dfrac{1}{x+1}$;

(f) $y = \dfrac{x}{1+x^2}$.

4. (a) $y = \sqrt{(x+1)}$;

(b) $y = \sqrt{(x^2-1)}$;

(c) $y = 1 + \sqrt{(x^2-1)}$;

(d) $y = (x+1)\sqrt{x}$;

(e) $y = \dfrac{\sqrt{(x+1)}}{x}$;

(f) $y = \dfrac{x^2}{\sqrt{(x-1)}}$.

5. (a) $y = \dfrac{1}{(x-2)^2}$;

(b) $y = \dfrac{x}{(x-1)^2}$;

(c) $y = \dfrac{x+1}{(x-1)^2}$;

(d) $y = \dfrac{1}{x^2(x-1)}$.

6. On the same diagram sketch the graphs of $y = x^3$, $y = 1 + x^3$, $y = 2 + x^3$. What is the relationship between these?

7. Sketch the graphs of $y = 1/x$, $y = 1/(x+1)$, $y = 1/(x+2)$. What is the relationship between these?

8. Sketch the graphs of $y = (x-5)\sqrt{x}$, $y = (2x-5)\sqrt{(2x)}$, $y = (\tfrac{1}{4}x-5)\sqrt{(\tfrac{1}{4}x)}$. What is the relationship between these?

9. Sketch the graphs of

(a) $y = [x]$;   (b) $y = [x]+2$;   (c) $y = [x-\tfrac{1}{2}]$;

(d) $y = 3[x]$;   (e) $y = [3x]$;

where $[x]$ means the greatest integer not exceeding x.

10. A stone is thrown into the air with a velocity of u m/s upwards. After t seconds, the height s metres is given approximately by the function $s = ut - 5t^2$. Sketch the graph of this in the cases when

(a) the initial velocity is 10 m/s;

(b) the stone is dropped from rest;

(c) the stone is thrown downwards initially with a speed of 10 m/s.

11. For a cylinder of radius r, total surface area A (including the circular ends), and volume V, it can be shown that $V = \tfrac{1}{2}rA - \pi r^3$. Sketch the graph of V as a function of r when A is fixed and equals (a) 2; (b) 10. If r is fixed, what is the graph of V as a function of A? Suggest suitable domains for these functions.

12. If for a lens of focal length f the distance of an object from it is u and the distance of its image from the lens is v, we know that $\dfrac{1}{u} + \dfrac{1}{v} = \dfrac{1}{f}$. Find v in terms of u and draw the graph of this function for lenses of focal length 1, 5, 10.

13. For a cone of radius r and height h, the curved surface area is $\pi r \sqrt{(r^2+h^2)}$ and the total surface area is $\pi r \sqrt{(r^2+h^2)} + \pi r^2$. Sketch the graphs of both these functions of r, treating h as fixed, on the same diagram.

51

14. Sketch the graphs of all the following, which will be used in the next few questions.

(a) $y = 1 + x^4$;   (b) $y = x - x^3$;   (c) $y = \dfrac{1}{2 + x^2}$;

(d) $y = \sqrt{(1 + x^2)}$;   (e) $y = \dfrac{1}{x(x^2 - 1)}$;   (f) $y = \dfrac{1}{1 + x}$;

(g) $y = (1 - x^2)(4 - x^2)$;   (h) $y = \dfrac{1 + x^2}{x}$.

Which of the curves have (a) reflective symmetry in the y-axis, (b) rotational half turn symmetry about the origin?

15. For those curves of Question 14 which have reflective symmetry in the y-axis what happens (a) if we put $x = 3$ and then -3 in the equations, (b) if we put $x = c$ and then $-c$ in the equations?

16. Repeat Question 15 for those curves of Question 14 which have half turn symmetry.

17. What is special about the equations of the curves of Question 14 which have reflective symmetry about the y-axis? Can you tell straight away from an equation that its graph will have such symmetry?

18. Repeat Question 17 for those curves which have half turn symmetry about the origin O.

4. TRANSFORMATIONS APPLIED TO GRAPHS

4.1   Reflection and even functions. The graph of $y = -x^2$ (Figure 6) is the reflection of the graph of $y = x^2$ in Ox (the x-axis). In general, the reflection in Ox of the graph of any function $y = f(x)$ has equation $y = -f(x)$. But is there any similar result for reflection in Oy (the y-axis)?

Sketch the graph of $y = 1/(4 + x)$ and its image after reflection in Oy. What do you think is the equation of the reflected graph? Make tables of values, taking integral values of x from -3 to 3, for the function $y = 1/(4 + x)$ and also for the function $y = 1/(4 - x)$. Note that the second equation gives the points on the image curve.

The equation of the image graph under reflection in Oy is given by replacing x by $-x$. Thus the reflection of $y = (2 - x)\sqrt{x}$, whose domain is $\{x : x \geqslant 0\}$ is $y = (2 + x)\sqrt{(-x)}$, with domain $\{x : x \leqslant 0\}$ (see Figure 18).

What is the reflection in Oy of $y = x^2$? Sketch the graph of $y = (-x)^2$.

A function for which $f(-x) = f(x)$ is called an *even* function. Its graph has reflective symmetry about the y-axis, because if (a, b) is a point of the graph, $f(a) = b$ and so $f(-a) = b$ and $(-a, b)$ is also a point of the graph. Thus if P is on the graph, so is its image P' under reflection in Oy. (See Figure 19.)

52

Such functions are called 'even' because all even powers of x have this property. For example $(-x)^2 = x^2$. Any algebraic function containing only even powers of x and constant terms is an even function: check that

$$x \to x^4 + 3x^2 + 2, \quad x \to 1/(1-x^2) \quad \text{and} \quad x \to x^2/(1+x^2)$$

are all even functions.

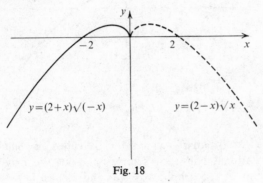

Fig. 18

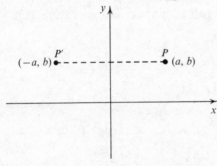

Fig. 19

4.2 Rotation and odd functions.

What is the effect of reflection in Ox followed by reflection in Oy? Carry out these two reflections on the graph of $y = \sqrt{x}$. What single transformation have you effected? The result of these two reflections is equivalent to a rotation through 180° about the origin. If $y = \sqrt{x}$ is transformed by reflection in Ox, giving $y = -\sqrt{x}$, followed by reflection in Oy, giving $y = -\sqrt{(-x)}$, this is equivalent to a half turn about O.

In general, $y = f(x)$ becomes $y = -f(-x)$ after a half turn about O. Thus $y = (2-x)\sqrt{x}$ becomes $y = -(2-(-x))\sqrt{(-x)} = -(2+x)\sqrt{(-x)}$. (See Figure 20.)

What does the graph of $y = x^3$ become after a half turn about O? Sketch the graph of $y = -(-x)^3$. What is the equation of the image of the graph of $y = x+3/x$ (Figure 1) under a half turn about O?

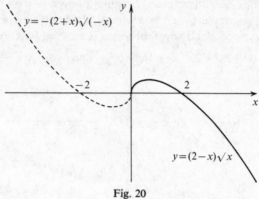

Fig. 20

A function for which $f(-x) = -f(x)$ is called an *odd* function. Its graph has rotational half turn symmetry about the origin, because if (a, b) is a point of the graph, $b = f(a)$ and so $-b = f(-a)$ and hence $(-a, -b)$ is also a point of the graph. Thus if P is on the graph, so is its image P' under a half turn about O. (See Figure 21.)

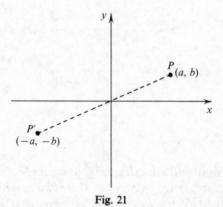

Fig. 21

Such functions are called 'odd' because all odd powers of x have this property: for example $(-x)^3 = -x^3$.

It is not however true that if a function contains only odd powers of x it must be odd. Thus, for example, $x \to (x^5 - x^3)/x$ is an *even* function, because

$$\frac{(-x)^5 - (-x)^3}{(-x)} = \frac{x^5 - x^3}{x}.$$

The function in Example 6 is an odd function, and its graph of course has half turn symmetry about O.

Care must be taken about pronouncing functions odd. Thus, although $1/(x^2-1)$ is clearly even, $1/(x-1)$ is neither odd nor even; for

$$\frac{1}{(-x)-1} = \frac{-1}{x+1},$$

which bears no relation to the original $1/(x-1)$. Most of the functions we deal with are neither odd nor even.

4.3 Translation and periodic functions. In Exercise C we sketched the graphs of $y = 1/x$, $y = 1/(x+1)$ and $y = 1/(x+2)$, and discovered that the second of these is obtained from the first by a translation of 1 unit parallel to Ox but to the left and the third is obtained from the first by a translation of 2 units to the left.

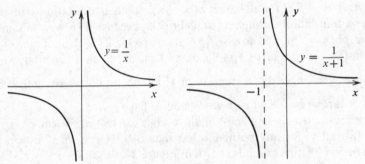

Fig. 22

Thus replacing x by $x+1$ in an equation produces a translation of 1 to the left; similarly replacing x by $x-1$ would cause a translation of 1 to the right. What translation would map the graph of $y = 1/x^2$ to that of $y = 1/(x+4)^2$? Sketch the graphs.

In general, when the graph of any function $y = f(x)$ is translated a units along Ox to the right, it becomes that of $y = f(x-a)$.

The direction of the translation can be confirmed by substituting one value for x. For example, the graph of $y = (x-8)^2$ is obtained from that of $y = x^2$ by a translation of 8 units parallel to Ox (Figure 23). Note that $y = 0$ when $x = 8$, so the graph lies *to the right* of that of $y = x^2$.

Translations parallel to Oy are straightforward. For example if the graph of $y = x^2$ is translated through 3 units upwards, the equation of the new graph is $y = x^2+3$. Also, under the translation $\binom{4}{1}$, the graph of $y = x^2$ maps onto the graph of $y = (x-4)^2+1$.

3-2   55

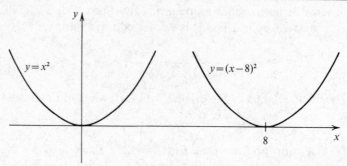

Fig. 23

Sketch the graph of $y = x - [x]$, where $[x]$ is defined as in Section 3.3. What is its image under the translation $\begin{pmatrix} -3 \\ 0 \end{pmatrix}$? Sketch the graph of $y = (x+3) - [x+3]$.

If $f(x+a) = f(x)$ for all values of x, the graph has translation symmetry under a translation through a parallel to Ox, because if (p, q) is a point of the graph, $q = f(p)$ and so $q = f(p+a)$ and $(p+a, q)$ is also a point of the graph. (So are $(p+2a, q)$, $(p+3a, q)$, and so on.) Such a function, whose graph is unchanged by a translation $\begin{pmatrix} a \\ 0 \end{pmatrix}$ (and by no translation with a smaller throw) is said to be *periodic* and to have *period a*.

For example, $\sin(x+360)^\circ = \sin x^\circ$ but $\sin(x+a)^\circ = \sin x^\circ$ is not true (for all x) for any positive a less than 360. Hence $\sin x^\circ$ is periodic with period 360; its graph is shown in Figure 24.

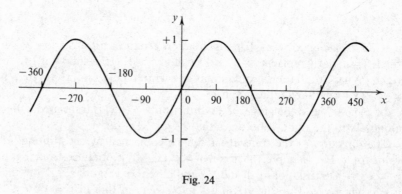

Fig. 24

Check, from their graphs, that $\cos x^\circ$ is periodic with period 360 whereas $\tan x^\circ$ is periodic with period 180. These three functions are by far the most important periodic functions.

Figure 25 is the graph of the periodic function $x \to x - [x]$. What is its period?

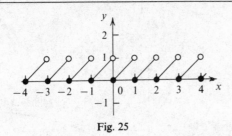

Fig. 25

4.4　Graphs of inverse functions. Figure 26 shows the graphs of $x \to x^3$ and its inverse $x \to \sqrt[3]{x}$. What is the connection between these two curves? Sketch pairs of functions which are inverse to each other and see if this same connection holds (e.g. try $x \to 2x+1$ and $x \to \frac{1}{2}(x-1)$ or $x \to 1/(x-1)$ and $x \to 1/x+1$).

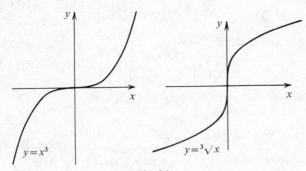

Fig. 26

You should have found that the graph of the inverse of a function is obtained by reflection in the line $y = x$. For suppose the point (a, b) lies on the graph of $y = f(x)$ then $b = f(a)$. If the inverse function f^{-1} exists, then $a = f^{-1}(b)$, i.e. the point (b, a) lies on the graph of $y = f^{-1}(x)$. But (a, b) and (b, a) are reflections of each other in the line $y = x$, so the graph of the inverse function f^{-1} is the reflection of that for f in the line $y = x$. (We are assuming that the scales on the two axes are the same.)

*4.5　Formal method for transformations. A general method of dealing with transformations of graphs is demonstrated in the following example.

Example 8

What is the equation of the image of the graph of $y = \sqrt{(x-2)}$ under a quarter turn about the origin?

57

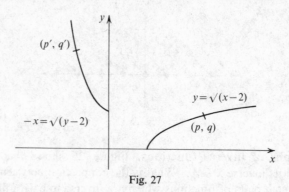

Fig. 27

Let a typical point of the first graph be (p, q) and let (p', q') be its image. Then

$$\begin{pmatrix} p' \\ q' \end{pmatrix} = \begin{pmatrix} 0 & -1 \\ 1 & 0 \end{pmatrix}\begin{pmatrix} p \\ q \end{pmatrix}$$

describes the rotation, and

$$\begin{pmatrix} p \\ q \end{pmatrix} = \begin{pmatrix} 0 & 1 \\ -1 & 0 \end{pmatrix}\begin{pmatrix} p' \\ q' \end{pmatrix}$$

the inverse rotation, so that $p = q'$ and $q = -p'$.

Now

$$(p, q) \text{ lies on } y = \sqrt{(x-2)} \Leftrightarrow q = \sqrt{(p-2)}$$

$$\Leftrightarrow -p' = \sqrt{(q'-2)}$$

$$\Leftrightarrow (p', q') \quad \text{lies on} \quad -x = \sqrt{(y-2)}.$$

Hence $-x = \sqrt{(y-2)}$ is the equation of the image curve.

With a general transformation $\mathbf{T}$ applied to $y = f(x)$,

$$\begin{pmatrix} p' \\ q' \end{pmatrix} = \mathbf{T}\begin{pmatrix} p \\ q \end{pmatrix} \quad \text{and} \quad \begin{pmatrix} p \\ q \end{pmatrix} = \mathbf{T}^{-1}\begin{pmatrix} p' \\ q' \end{pmatrix}.$$

Now p and q are connected by the relation $q = f(p)$. We substitute in this, obtain an equivalent relation connecting p' and q', and hence find the equation of the image curve.

The appearance of $\mathbf{T}^{-1}$ in the working explains, for example, why a translation of $\begin{pmatrix} +4 \\ 0 \end{pmatrix}$ corresponds to replacing x by $x-4$ in the equation.

Similarly, with $y = \sqrt{(x-2)}$, if we replace x by $3x$ and y by $3y$ giving $3y = \sqrt{(3x-2)}$, we get an enlargement with scale factor $\frac{1}{3}$.

58

Exercise D

1. For the functions given, find $f(-x)$ and hence determine whether the function is (i) odd, (ii) even, or (iii) neither. Sketch rough graphs of the functions.

(a) $x \to 2x^5$;

(b) $x \to \dfrac{2}{x}$;

(c) $x \to x^3 - x + 2$;

(d) $x \to x^4 + x^2 + 1$;

(e) $x \to \dfrac{1}{2 + x^2}$;

(f) $x \to \dfrac{x}{2 + x}$;

(g) $x \to x + \dfrac{1}{x}$;

(h) $x \to \sqrt{(1 + x^3)}$.

2. Are there functions which are (a) both odd and even, (b) neither odd nor even? If so, give examples.

3. Describe any reflections, rotations or translations that map the graph of $y = \sin x°$ onto itself.

4. Use simple translations of standard graphs to sketch graphs of the following, in each case giving the standard equations and the translation used:

(a) $y = x^2 + 7$;

(b) $y = (x-1)^2$;

(c) $y = \dfrac{1}{x + \frac{1}{2}}$;

(d) $y = x^3 - 2$;

(e) $y = \sqrt{(x - \frac{1}{2})}$;

(f) $y = x^2 + 2x$.

(Note that $x^2 + 2x$ may be written as $(x+1)^2 - 1$.)

5. Find the equation of the graphs obtained when the curve $y = x^3$ is translated (a) through $\begin{pmatrix} 1 \\ 0 \end{pmatrix}$; (b) through $\begin{pmatrix} 0 \\ 2 \end{pmatrix}$; (c) through $\begin{pmatrix} 2 \\ 4 \end{pmatrix}$.

6. Sketch the graphs of (a) $y = 1/x$, (b) $y = 1/2x$, (c) $y = 1/(2x-1)$, and state how the second and third are obtained from the first by simple transformations.

7. What is the equation obtained from $y = x^2 - 6x$ by applying the following transformations to its graph?

(a) a reflection in Ox;

(b) a reflection in Oy;

(c) a translation $\begin{pmatrix} -3 \\ 2 \end{pmatrix}$;

(d) a half turn about O.

8. What is the equation obtained from $y = 9 - x^2$ by applying the following transformations to its graph?

(a) a reflection in $\bullet x$;

(b) a stretch parallel to Ox, scale factor 2, with Oy invariant;

(c) a stretch parallel to Oy, scale factor $\frac{1}{2}$, with Ox invariant;

(d) an enlargement with centre O and scale factor 3.

9. What can you say about (i) $f(x) + g(x)$, (ii) $f(x) g(x)$, (iii) $fg(x)$ if f and g are both odd functions? Repeat with both functions even, and with one odd and the other even.

10. Give the inverse function f^{-1} for each of the following, restricting the domain of f where necessary. In each case sketch the graphs of f and f^{-1}.

(a) $f: x \to \frac{1}{2}x+3$;   (b) $f: x \to x^2+2$;   (c) $f: x \to 1/x$;

(d) $f: x \to 1/x^2$;   (e) $f: x \to \dfrac{x}{x-1}$.

*11. Use the method of Section 4.5 to show that the graph of $y = 1/(2-x)$ may be obtained from that of $y = 1/x$ by a reflection in the line $x = 1$.

*12. Use the method of Section 4.5 to find the image of $y = x^3$ under the shear $\begin{pmatrix} 1 & 0 \\ 1 & 1 \end{pmatrix}$.

5. GRAPHS OF RELATIONS

So far we have confined ourselves to the graphs of relations which are functions. We now extend the ideas to more general relations, including those expressed by inequalities.

Example 9

Sketch the graph of $x^2+4y^2 = 36$ and shade in the region for which $x^2+4y^2 \leqslant 36$.

When $x = 0$, $y = \pm3$ and when $y = 0$, $x = \pm6$. Note also that since $x^2 \geqslant 0$, $y^2 \leqslant 9$ and so $-3 \leqslant y \leqslant 3$. Similarly $-6 \leqslant x \leqslant 6$.

Since only even powers of x occur there is symmetry about Oy. Similarly, since only even powers of y occur there is symmetry about Ox.

Note that a one way stretch would convert the circle $x^2+y^2 = 36$ into the graph of $x^2+4y^2 = 36$. So the graph is as in Figure 28.

Check the value of x^2+4y^2 for several points inside and outside the curve. We should find that $x^2+4y^2 < 36$ for all points (x, y) inside the curve.

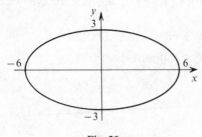

Fig. 28   Fig. 29

Example 10

Sketch the graph of $x^2-y^2 = 1$.

Here $y^2 = x^2-1$, so that since $y^2 \geqslant 0$, $x^2 \geqslant 1$ and x cannot lie between -1 and 1. But $x^2 = y^2+1$ and so y can take any value.

The graph has symmetry about both axes (only even powers of both x and y occur.)

$x = 0$ is not possible but $y = 0$ when $x = \pm 1$.

When x is large, $y = \pm \sqrt{(x^2-1)} \approx \pm x$ and so the graph is close to the lines $y = \pm x$ at large distances from O. Also the curve lies below the asymptote $y = x$ in the first quadrant since then $y = \sqrt{(x^2-1)} < \sqrt{x^2} = x$. The behaviour elsewhere is obtained by symmetry.

Exercise E

1. Sketch the graphs of the relations (a) $y^2 = x^2$; (b) $y^2 = x^3$; (c) $y^2 = x^4$. For what natural numbers n does $y^2 = x^n$ touch the x-axis at the origin?

2. Find the points of intersection of $(x-y)^2 = (x+y)$ with $y = tx$. What happens when $t = 1$? Explain the significance of this. Use the results to sketch the graph of $(x-y)^2 = (x+y)$.

3. Sketch the graph of $x^2+2y^2 = 4$ and the region for which $x^2+2y^2 \geqslant 4$.

4. Sketch the graphs of
   (a) $y^2 = x^2(1-x)$;   (b) $y^2 = (x-1)(x+2)$;
   (c) $y^2 = x^2+2x+1$;   (d) $y^2 = x(x-1)^2(x-2)^3$.

5. By comparing the shapes of $x^n+y^n = 1$ for small natural numbers n, sketch the graphs of (a) $x^{100}+y^{100} = 1$; (b) $x^{100}-y^{100} = 1$.

Miscellaneous Exercise

1. Sketch the graphs of:
   (a) $y(x^2-1) = x$;   (b) $x^2 = y(x+1)^2$;   (c) $x^2y = x^3-4$;
   (d) $x = y(x^3-1)$;   (e) $y = \sqrt{x}+\sqrt{(-x)}$.

2. Sketch the graphs of:
   (a) $y = \dfrac{1}{x+3}$;   (b) $y = \dfrac{1}{(x+3)^2}$;   (c) $y = 2+\dfrac{1}{(x+3)^2}$;
   (d) $y = \sqrt[3]{x}-1$;   (e) $y = \sqrt[3]{(x-1)}$.

3. Sketch the graphs of:
$$y = \frac{1}{x+1}, \quad y = \frac{1}{2x+1}, \quad y = \frac{1}{2(x+1)}.$$

How are these graphs related to one another?

4. For each of the graphs sketched roughly in Figure 30, produce a suitable equation whose graph it might be.

61

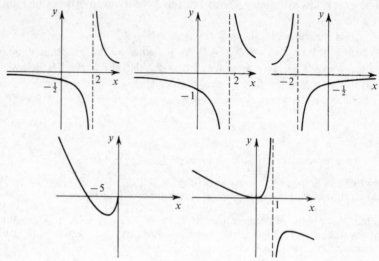

Fig. 30

5. Sketch the graphs of:

(a) $y = \left[\dfrac{x}{2}\right]$; (b) $y = [x^2]$; (c) $y = \left[\dfrac{1}{x}\right]$;

(d) $y = \dfrac{[x]}{x}$; (e) $y = \dfrac{x}{[x]}$; (f) $[y] = [x]$.

6. Under what transformations are the graphs of the following functions obtained from that of $y = f(x)$:

(a) $y = f(x) + a$; (b) $y = f(x+a)$; (c) $y = f(x-a) + b$;
(d) $y = af(x)$; (e) $y = f(ax)$; (f) $y = f(a-x)$?

7. Sketch the graphs of:

(a) $y = \sin 2x°$; (b) $y = 2 \sin x°$; (c) $y = \sin x° - 1$;
(d) $y = \sin (x-90)°$; (e) $y = 3 \sin (4x+90)°$.
State the period of each function.

8. Draw the graph of $y = f(x) = \sqrt{(2-x)}$ and sketch on the same diagram the graphs of:

(a) $y = f(-x)$; (b) $y = \frac{1}{2}(f(x)+f(-x))$; (c) $y = \frac{1}{2}(f(x)-f(-x))$.

9. A function f is defined for all real values of x. Find an odd function g and an even function h such that $g(x)+h(x) = f(x)$ for all x.

10. Show that, if the graph of $f(x)$ is mapped onto itself by a half turn about $(a, 0)$, then $f(x) = -f(2a-x)$. Hence show that if the graph is mapped onto itself by half turns about two points on the x-axis it is periodic, and is mapped onto itself by an infinite number of half turns. Do you know any functions that behave like this?

11. Sketch the graph of $y = \dfrac{4}{(x+1)\,(x-5)}$ and show that it has reflectional symmetry.

12. What is the result of applying a stretch of $\frac{1}{2}$ parallel to Ox and of 2 parallel to Oy to the graph of $y = 1/x$?

13. Show that when x is small $1/(x+1) \approx 1-x+x^2$. Deduce that when $x = 0$ the tangent to the graph of $y = 1/(x+1)$ is the line $y = 1-x$ and that the curve lies above this line near $x = 0$. In a similar way find how the graphs of (a) $y = x/(x+1)$ and (b) $y = 1/(x^2+1)$ behave near $x = 0$.

14. Show that
$$\frac{x^2}{x-1} = x+1+\frac{1}{x-1}$$

and deduce that $y = x+1$ is an asymptote to the graph of $y = x^2/(x-1)$. Deduce also that the graph lies above the asymptote when $x \to +\infty$ and below when $x \to -\infty$. Sketch the curve.

15. Sketch the graph of $y = x^3/(x-1)$.

16. What can you say about a, b, c, d if $f: x \to \dfrac{ax+b}{cx+d}$ is self-inverse? Choose simple values for a, b, c, d and (a) sketch the graph of f, (b) confirm algebraically that $ff(x) = x$.

17. Sketch the graph of $(x-1)^2+(y-1)^2 = 2^2$. Suggest part of the graph which, taken by itself, would be the graph of a function of x.

18. Find the image of $x^2-y^2 = 2$ under rotation through $+45°$ about O.

SUMMARY

Procedure for sketching graphs

(i) Look for any restrictions on possible values of x and y, and any quadrants in which the curve must lie.

(ii) Find the behaviour for large x.

(iii) Find the values of x which give discontinuities, and the behaviour near these values.

(iv) Find where the graph cuts the axes; apart from these points the axes will act as barriers.

Graphs of powers of x are shown in Figure 4.

Symmetry

An *even* function is one for which $f(-x) = f(x)$; its graph has reflective symmetry about Oy.

63

An *odd* function is one for which $f(-x) = -f(x)$; its graph has half turn rotational symmetry about O.

A function containing only even powers of x is even, and a relation which contains only even powers of y has symmetry about Ox.

A *periodic* function of period a is one for which $f(x+a) = f(x)$ for all x, with no smaller positive a satisfying this condition.

The graph of the *inverse* function is obtained by reflecting in the line $y = x$.

4

POLYNOMIALS AND ALGEBRAIC FRACTIONS

Exercise A

1. Look at the expressions in each part of this question, and decide which you think are equivalent and which are different from the other expressions. Then check by working out the value of each expression when $a = 12$, $b = 2$, $c = 4$, and $d = 3$.

(i) $\dfrac{a}{b} + \dfrac{c}{b}$, $\dfrac{(a+c)}{b}$, $\dfrac{ad+cd}{bd}$;

(ii) $a \times c/b$, $(a/b) \times c$, $a/(b \times c)$, $a/b/c$;

(iii) $c^2 + d^2$, $(c+d)^2$, $c^2 + 2cd + d^2$;

(iv) $2c^2 + 2d^2$, $2(c^2 + d^2)$, $(2c + 2d)^2$, $4(c+d)^2$;

(v) $a(b+c)$, $ab+c$, $ab+ac$;

(vi) $c^3 - d^3$, $(c-d)^3$, $(c-d)(c^2-d^2)$, $(c-d)(c-d)(c-d)$;

(vii) $(c-b)^2$, $c^2 - b^2$, $(c-b)(c-b)$, $(c-b)(c+b)$;

(viii) $2c^2 - 2b^2$, $(2c-2b)(c+b)$, $(c-b)(2c+2b)$, $(2c-2b)(2c+2b)$.

2. State whether the two expressions given in each part are equivalent:

(i) $\dfrac{x^2+y^2}{x+y}$, $x+y$;

(ii) $\sqrt{(a+b)}$, $\sqrt{a} + \sqrt{b}$;

(iii) $\dfrac{a-b}{\sqrt{a}-\sqrt{b}}$, $\sqrt{a} + \sqrt{b}$;

(iv) $(x-y)(x+y)$, $x^2 - y^2$;

(v) $\sqrt{(x^2-y^2)}$, $x-y$;

(vi) $\dfrac{x^2-y^2}{x+y}$, $x-y$;

(vii) $(\sqrt{a}+\sqrt{b})^2$, $a+b$;

(viii) $(\sqrt{a} \times \sqrt{b})^2$, ab.

When you have decided which of these are the same, check your answers by giving x, y, a, b some simple values such as 7, 5, 64 and 36.

If you have had trouble with this question it is because you are not yet really familiar with the two basic relations

$$(p+q)(p+q) = p^2 + 2pq + q^2 \quad \text{and} \quad (p+q)(p-q) = p^2 - q^2.$$

1. CONVENTIONS AND LAWS

Some of the answers to the above questions depend entirely on conventions. In an expression like $a \times b + c$, it is understood that the multiplication is to be carried out before the addition. If we wish to give the addition precedence, this can be provided by the use of brackets: $a \times (b+c)$. On the other hand $a \times c/b$ is unambiguous since the same result is obtained whether we multiply first or divide first. How about $a/b \times c$?

Some of these conventions are changing. What is the value of $24 \div 6 \div 2$ for example? You may well say that it has no meaning until brackets are inserted to show which division is to be done first; but ask a computer to work out $24 \div 6 \div 2$ and it will give the answer 2 (not 8) because, in computer conventions, expressions of this sort are always worked out starting at the left-hand end. It is possible that in the future as people become more used to reading what is written for computers this convention will come to be adopted in normal arithmetic. Some of the new shorthand symbols used in computer languages may also come to be more widely recognized: for example $*$ used for the multiplication sign and $\uparrow$ used to denote an index so that 3^2 is written $3\uparrow2$. The latter is sometimes called the exponentiator. The conventions as regards priority are the same as in normal use, i.e. brackets bind numbers together more tightly than any other operator, then the exponentiator, then with equal priority multiplication and division and finally addition and subtraction. So $3*x\uparrow2$, like $3x^2$, means that the x has to be squared before being multiplied by the three.

What is the value of $4*3\uparrow(5-3) \div 6+2$?

(i) Combining the numbers in the brackets gives $4*3\uparrow2 \div 6+2$;

(ii) combining the numbers connected by the exponentiator gives $4*9 \div 6+2$;

(iii) taking multiplication and division from the left gives $36 \div 6+2$ then $6+2$;

(iv) finally combining the numbers connected by addition gives 8.

So much for conventions. Justification for the answers to other questions in Exercise A involves correct use of the commutative, associative and distributive laws.

In this chapter we will take a closer look at the processes of algebraic manipulation.

Exercise B

1. Using the computer conventions mentioned in Section 1, work out the values of

(i) $3/6*2$;

(ii) $3/6/2$;

(iii) $5+3\uparrow4/2$;

(iv) $((5-2)/(3-1))\uparrow2*4$.

If the answers to (i), (ii), (iii) and (iv) are respectively a, b, c and d then
$$(c-a/2)/d \times b = a+b.$$
Use this to check whether your answers are correct.

2. $(x\uparrow2-2)/(3*x+5)/(2*x\uparrow2+1)$ would normally be written $\dfrac{(x^2-2)}{(3x+5)(2x^2+1)}$. What are the particular advantages of each notation?

3. Use the distributive law to expand the following:

  (i) $3x(5x-2)$;   (ii) $(x+1)(2x+3)$;

  (iii) $2x^2(x-3)-x(x^2+2)$;   (iv) $(x-1)(3x+2)$;

  (v) $(2x-3)(2x+3)$;   (vi) $(3x-2)(3x-2)$.

4. Simplify as much as you can:

  (i) $3x^2-6+5x-5x^2+x^3-2(3x^2+4)$;

  (ii) $x^2+2xy-y(2x+y)+3x(y-x)$;

  (iii) $4x^5-3x^3+2x(5-x^2)+x^2(x^2+1)-3x^4+8x$.

In Questions 5–8, $\mathbf{I}$ is the unit matrix $\begin{pmatrix} 1 & 0 \\ 0 & 1 \end{pmatrix}$.

5. If $\mathbf{A} = \begin{pmatrix} 1 & 2 \\ -1 & 4 \end{pmatrix}$, show that $\mathbf{A}^2-5\mathbf{A}+6\mathbf{I}$ is the zero matrix. Are $\mathbf{A}-3\mathbf{I}$ and $\mathbf{A}-2\mathbf{I}$ zero matrices? What is their product?

6. Show that in matrix algebra, $(\mathbf{B}-\mathbf{I})(\mathbf{B}-3\mathbf{I}) = \mathbf{B}^2-4\mathbf{B}+3\mathbf{I}$. Verify for a particular 2×2 matrix $\mathbf{B}$ of your own choice.

7. Use the distributive laws to expand

  (a) $(x-1)(x^2+x+1)$,   (b) $(\mathbf{M}-\mathbf{I})(\mathbf{M}^2+\mathbf{M}+\mathbf{I})$.

Verify the result of (a) by replacing x by 3 and the result of (b) by replacing $\mathbf{M}$ by $\begin{pmatrix} 1 & -1 \\ 2 & 0 \end{pmatrix}$.

8. Let $\mathbf{X}$ and $\mathbf{Y}$ be 2×2 matrices.

  (a) Is $\mathbf{X}^2-\mathbf{I}$ always equal to $(\mathbf{X}-\mathbf{I})(\mathbf{X}+\mathbf{I})$?

  (b) Is $\mathbf{X}^2-\mathbf{Y}^2$ always equal to $(\mathbf{X}-\mathbf{Y})(\mathbf{X}+\mathbf{Y})$?

2. MANIPULATION OF POLYNOMIAL EXPRESSIONS

2.1 Polynomials. An expression like $2x^3-3\cdot4x^2+\sqrt{7}x+5$ which contains only positive, whole number powers of x is called a *polynomial* in x. Thus $3x+4/x^2$ is not a polynomial, while $x^7-5/9$ is. If the highest power of x is x^3, the polynomial is said to be of third degree and can contain four terms, one in x^3, one in x^2, one in x, and a constant term. Polynomials are generally written with the highest power of x first and other powers following in descending order; occasionally they are written with the constant first and the powers of x in ascending order. So the example above might be written $5 + \sqrt{7}x - 3 \cdot 4x^2 + 2x^3$.

Here, $-3 \cdot 4$ is the *coefficient* of x^2. Although the coefficients can be fractions, irrational numbers and so on, we will mostly be concerned with polynomials with integral coefficients in this chapter.

For the present we shall say nothing about the symbol x, except that it obeys the usual rules for combining numbers. In fact, although we shall often wish to replace x by a number, there are occasions when polynomial expressions are used in which x has some other significance; it might, for example, be a matrix.

2.2   Multiplication and addition. Can you multiply two polynomials together? What, for example, is the product of $4x^2 - x + 3$ and $-x^3 + 3x + 2$? The multiplication of polynomials is essentially the same as multiplication of integers in arithmetic as it is based on the distributive property of multiplication over addition.

$$(4x^2 - x + 3)\,(-x^3 + 3x + 2)$$

$$= 4x^2(-x^3 + 3x + 2) - x(-x^3 + 3x + 2) + 3(-x^3 + 3x + 2)$$

$$= (-4x^5 + 12x^3 + 8x^2) + (x^4 - 3x^2 - 2x) + (-3x^3 + 9x + 6).$$

Using the associative and commutative properties of addition, we can add these polynomials with no more difficulty than adding and subtracting directed integers. It is best to be systematic and start with the highest power of x, adding up the coefficients mentally as the terms containing each power are picked out of the line:

$$-4x^5 + x^4 + (12 - 3)\,x^3 + (8 - 3)\,x^2 + (-2 + 9)\,x + 6$$

$$= -4x^5 + x^4 + 9x^3 + 5x^2 + 7x + 6.$$

The similarity with long multiplication in arithmetic is clearly seen when the work is set out in the following way:

$-x^3 \qquad +3x+2$		1032
$+4x^2 \ -x+3$		413
$-4x^5 \qquad +12x^3+8x^2$		4128
$x^4 \qquad -3x^2-2x$		1032
$-3x^3 \qquad +9x+6$		3096
$-4x^5+x^4 \ +9x^3+5x^2+7x+6$		426216

In the algebra, there are minus signs and there is no 'carrying'.

68

An alternative format, called the method of detached coefficients, is useful when programming a computer to handle polynomials:

x^5	x^4	x^3	x^2	x^1	1
		-1	0	3	2
			4	-1	3
-4	0	12	8		
	1	0	-3	-2	
		-3	0	9	6
-4	1	9	5	7	6

With practice, it will be found that multiplication of polynomials can be done mentally. For example, it can be seen that the term involving x^3 in the product above will come from $(4x^2)\,(3x)$ and $(+3)\,(-x^3)$; this term is therefore $(12-3)\,x^3$, or $9x^3$.

Exercise C

In the first three questions, let

$$A = 3x^2 - 5x + 2, \quad B = 4x^3 - 3x + 4, \quad C = 2x^4 - 3x^3 + 4x^2 - x.$$

1. Write the following expressions as polynomials in descending powers of x:

(i) $A - B$;   (ii) $B + C$;   (iii) $A - B + C$;   (iv) $B + C - A$.

Add together your answers to parts (iii) and (iv). Can you say before you start what the answer should be?

2. If $B + B$ is written $2B$, express as polynomials

(i) $2A - 2B$,   (ii) $2(A - B)$ (use your answer to 1(i)).

3. Find (i) $A \times B$ and (ii) $A \times C$, writing the working out in full using (a) the 'along the line' method, (b) the 'long multiplication' format.

4. If $P = 2x + 1$ and $Q = 3x - 2$, work out the following as polynomials in descending powers of x:

(i) P^2 (i.e. $P \times P$);   (ii) Q^2;

(iii) $P + Q$;   (iv) $P - Q$;

(v) $(P + Q)^2$;   (vi) $(P - Q)^2$;

(vii) $2 \times P \times Q$;   (viii) $(P + Q)(P - Q)$.

5. Check your answers to Question 4 by verifying that

$$(P + Q)^2 = P^2 + 2PQ + Q^2,$$

$$(P - Q)^2 = P^2 - 2PQ + Q^2,$$

$$(P + Q)(P - Q) = P^2 - Q^2.$$

6. If $A = (2x-5)$, $B = (3x+2)$, $C = (5-2x)$, $D = (-2-3x)$, $E = (4x-10)$, express as polynomials in descending powers of x:

(i) AB; (ii) CD.

E is related to A since $E = 2A$. Can you state similar relations between A and C, and between B and D?

7. Write each polynomial in (a) ascending order, (b) descending order, and give the degree of the polynomial.

(i) $2x^3 - 4x^2 + 5x - 1$; (ii) $x^2 - 7x^4 + 3x - 5x^3$;

(iii) $4 - x^3 + x^5 - 2x^2$.

For the polynomials A and B in Questions 8–10, give

(a) the sum $A+B$, (b) the difference $A-B$, (c) the product AB.

8. $A = 2 - 4x + 3x^2$, $B = 1 + 5x - 2x^2$.

9. $A = x^3 - 2x^2 + 4$, $B = 2x^3 + x - 3$.

10. $A = x^2 - 4x^3 + 5x$, $B = 4x^3 - 3x + 2$.

11. With as little working as possible, write down as polynomials:

(i) $(x-1)(2x+1)$; (ii) $(x-3)(x+2)$;

(iii) $(2x+3)^2$; (iv) $(2x+3)(2x-3)$;

(v) $(3-x)(2+4x)$; (vi) $(4x-3)^2$;

(vii) $(6x-5)(x+3)$; (viii) $(20x-1)(20x+1)$;

(ix) $(20x-1)(20x-1)$; (x) $(9x+5)^2$.

12. Write as a polynomial $(3+x-2x^3)^2$.

Write down (without any intermediate working) the coefficients named in the products of Questions 13 and 14.

13. Coefficients of x^2 and of x^3 in $(2+3x)(1+5x-2x^2)$.

14. Coefficients of x and of x^2 in $(x^2-3x+2)(5x^2+6x+4)$.

Write down (without intermediate working) the products in Questions 15–19.

15. $(3+2x)(4-x)$. **16.** $(x^2-5)(x+2)$.

17. $(x-2)(x^3+2x^2+4x+8)$. **18.** $(x^2+2x-3)(x^2-2x+3)$.

19. $(1+x)^2$, $(1+x)^3$, $(1+x)^4$, $(1+x)^5$ and $(1+x)^6$.

20. Fill in, where possible, the missing signs in the brackets:

(i) $(x\ \ 1)(x\ \ 2) = x^2 + 3x + 2$;

(ii) $(x\ \ 1)(x\ \ 2) = x^2 - 3x + 2$;

(iii) $(x\ \ 1)(x\ \ 2) = x^2 + x - 2$;

(iv) $(x\ \ 1)(x\ \ 2) = x^2 - x + 2$.

3. FACTORS

We know that $(x-1)(2x+1) = 2x^2-x-1$. The *factors* of $2x^2-x-1$ are $x-1$ and $2x+1$. It is useful to be able to split up a polynomial into the product of simple factors. Can you find the factors of x^2-x-6? Look again at Exercise C, Question 11 (ii).

Exercise D

Fill in the brackets in the following questions. Check by multiplying out the brackets.

1. $x^2+3x+2 = (x \quad 1)(x \quad 2)$.

2. $x^2+3x-4 = (x \quad 1)(x \quad 4)$.

3. $x^2-5x+6 = (x \quad 2)(x-3)$.

4. $x^2-2x-8 = (x \quad 2)(x \quad 4)$.

5. $2x^2+5x-12 = (x \quad 4)(2x \quad 3)$.

6. $2x^2+x-21 = (2x+7)(\quad)$.

7. $3x^2+2x-8 = (3x-4)(\quad)$.

8. $x^2-9x+20 = (\quad)(\quad)$.

9. $x^2+2x-24 = (\quad)(\quad)$.

10. $x^3+x^2+x-3 = (x^2+2x+3)(\quad)$.

In arithmetic we say that when 35 is divided by 4 the quotient is 8 and the remainder 3; but when 35 is divided by 5 there is no remainder and therefore 5 is a 'factor' of 35. Moreover 37 is a 'prime number' because it has no factors other than itself and one. When we talk about prime numbers we are thinking only of integers; otherwise we could say that 37 has factors 2 and $18\frac{1}{2}$. Similarly, we shall for the moment limit ourselves to seeking factors with integral coefficients for polynomials with integral coefficients.

'Find the quotient and remainder when 373 is divided by 17' is a very different problem from 'Show that 373 is a prime number'. We can only say a number is prime when we have considered all the prime numbers up to a certain limit and shown that none is a factor. When we try to factorize a polynomial, we have no convenient list of 'primes', but in the process of guessing and trial there are some other things that can help us. First let us consider how to factorize quadratic polynomials.

3.1 Factors of quadratic polynomials. What patterns emerged from Exercise D? The factors of a quadratic polynomial are of the form $(px+q)(rx+s)$ where p, q, r, s are integers. Multiplying gives

$$(px+q)(rx+s) = prx^2+(qr+ps)x+qs.$$

71

So if we are trying to factorize $2x^2-7x-15$, for example, we require pr to be 2 and qs to be -15. This means $p=2, r=1$ or $p=1, r=2$ or $p=-2$, $r=-1$ or $p=-1, r=-2$. We choose the first of these, and note later that the others would not lead to essentially different results. The choice for q and s is fairly restricted if $qs=-15$; possible pairs are $+15, -1$ and $-15, +1$ and $-1, +15$ and $+1, -15$ and $+5, -3$, and $-5, +3$ and $-3, +5$ and $+3, -5$. Mental multiplication of $(2x\ 15)(x\ 1)$ and $(2x\ 1)(x\ 15)$ with either plus or minus signs fails to produce the required $-7x$; but $(2x+3)(x-5)$ gives the right combination. Even with this fairly simple example there are 8 possibilities, but with practice most combinations can be eliminated quickly.

Here we have $\qquad 2x^2-7x-15 = (2x+3)(x-5).$

With $p=-1$ and $r=-2$, we would obtain the correct alternative

$$2x^2-7x-15 = (-x+5)(-2x-3).$$

Explain how the two answers are related, and write down the other two possible forms for the factors.

Exercise E

Fill in the signs in the brackets in the following questions:

1. $x^2+5x+6 = (x\ 3)(x\ 2)$.
2. $x^2+5x-6 = (x\ 6)(x\ 1)$.
3. $x^2-8x+15 = (x\ 5)(x\ 3)$.
4. $x^2+11x+18 = (x\ 9)(x\ 2)$.
5. $x^2-11x+18 = (x\ 9)(x\ 2)$.
6. $3x^2-7x-6 = (3x\ 2)(x\ 3)$.
7. $6-x-x^2 = (3\ x)(2\ x)$.
8. $2x^2-x-15 = (2x\ 5)(x\ 3)$.

Complete the factors:

9. $2x^2-x-3 = (2x\ 3)(\quad)$.
10. $6x^2-19x+10 = (3x\ 2)(\quad)$.
11. $2x^2+11x+15 = (2x\ 5)(\quad)$.
12. $12+x-6x^2 = (4\ 3x)(\quad)$.
13. $x^4+10x^2+24 = (x^2\ 6)(\quad)$.

Factorize:

14. x^2+6x+8.
15. $x^2-7x-18$.
16. $3+x-2x^2$.
17. $2x^2+7x$.
18. $25x^2-9$.
19. $4x^2-12x+9$.
20. $4x^2+33x-27$.
21. $8x^2+6x-9$.
22. $4x^2-10x-14$.
23. x^4-5x^2+4.

3.2 Constant factors. When factorizing a polynomial, first examine the terms to see whether they have any numerical factor in common. In $7x^2+14x-56$, for example, the coefficients have a common factor of 7, and the polynomial can be re-written as $7(x^2+2x-8)$. It is easier to look for factors of x^2+2x-8 than of $7x^2+14x-56$.

We obtain
$$7x^2+14x-56 = 7(x+4)(x-2).$$
Show that

$$7x^2+14x-56 = (7x+28)(x-2) = (x+4)(7x-14),$$

and that both forms are equivalent to the previous answer.

In just the same way, a composite number in arithmetic may perhaps be expressible as a product of two factors in a variety of ways, but its expression in prime factors is unique.

For example,
$$30 = 2 \times 15 = 3 \times 10 = 5 \times 6.$$

In prime factors, $\qquad 30 = 2 \times 3 \times 5.$

The corresponding algebraic result is this. The expression of a given polynomial as a product of polynomials which cannot be factorized further using only integers is essentially unique. That is, any two such expressions differ only in a redistribution of numerical factors.

3.3 Factors of polynomials with rational coefficients.

How would you factorize a polynomial with fractions as coefficients, such as $\frac{3}{4}x^2+1\frac{1}{2}x-6$? The best technique for this is to proceed as follows:

$$\begin{aligned}
\tfrac{3}{4}x^2+1\tfrac{1}{2}x-6 &= \tfrac{3}{4}x^2+\tfrac{6}{4}x-\tfrac{24}{4} && \text{(common denominator 4)} \\
&= \tfrac{1}{4}(3x^2+6x-24) && \text{(common factor } \tfrac{1}{4}) \\
&= \tfrac{3}{4}(x^2+2x-8) && \text{(common factor 3)} \\
&= \tfrac{3}{4}(x+4)(x-2).
\end{aligned}$$

In this way, the task of factorizing a polynomial with rational coefficients can be reduced to that of factorizing one with integral coefficients. Moreover, we now state (without proof) an important theorem:

Any polynomial with integral coefficients which can be separated into factors with rational coefficients can be separated into factors which are essentially the same but with integral coefficients.

In consequence, even if we allow rational coefficients in the factors, there is nothing to be gained by using them.

Exercise F

Factorize, where possible:

1. $6x^2+19x+10$.   2. $6x^2-17x+12$.

3. $36x^2+33x+6$.   4. $60+4x-8x^2$.

5. $3x^2+48$.   6. $8x^2-14$.

73

7. $7x^2 - 19x - 6$.   **8.** $12x^2 + 7x - 10$.

9. $12x^2 - 7x - 10$.   **10.** $12x^2 - 7x + 10$.

11. $14x^2 - 26x - 4$.   **12.** $\frac{1}{4}x^2 + \frac{1}{2}x - 2$.

13. $10\frac{1}{2}x^2 - 14x + 3\frac{1}{2}$.   **14.** $\frac{1}{5}x^2 + \frac{3}{10}x - \frac{1}{2}$.

In the following questions, fill in the blank bracket.

15. $\frac{1}{6}x^3 - 5x^2 + 3x = \frac{1}{6}x($ $)$.

16. $10ax^2 + 5a^2x - 15a^3 = 5a($ $)$.

17. $-6x^2 + 3x = -3x($ $)$.

18. $-x + 1 = -($ $)$.

19. $x(x+1) - 3(x+1) = (x+1)($ $)$.

20. $x(x-1) + 2(1-x) = (x-1)($ $)$.

21. $x^3 - 5x^2 + 2x + 8 = (x-2)($ $)$.

22. $2x^3 + x^2 - 10x + 15 = (x+3)($ $)$.

3.4 Factors of higher degree polynomials.

(i) The observation of Section 3.2 applies to general polynomials. When factorizing a polynomial with integer coefficients which have a common factor, simplify that algebraic problem by taking out the common factor: e.g. $3x^3 - 12x^2 + 15x + 30 = 3(x^3 - 4x^2 + 5x - 10)$. Note also that $5x^4 - 3x^3 - 2x^2 = x^2(5x^2 - 3x - 2)$, so that the problem of factorizing a fourth degree polynomial in which the constant term and the first degree term are missing is reduced to the problem of factorizing the quadratic polynomial $5x^2 - 3x - 2$. Also we may use the method of Section 3.3 to remove fractions from coefficients.

(ii) If a polynomial with integer coefficients has a linear factor of the form $ax + b$ with integer coefficients, the choice for a and b is restricted. Suppose that $3x^3 - 5x^2 - 4x + 4$ has a linear factor, then the other factor must be quadratic and we can write the polynomial in the form

$$(ax+b)(cx^2+dx+e).$$

Multiplication then shows that ac must be 3 and be must be 4, so that a can only be ± 1 or ± 3, while b can be ± 1, ± 2 or ± 4. We normally choose the $+$ sign for a (Why are we justified in doing this?), so possible linear factors are limited to $x \pm 1$, $x \pm 2$, $x \pm 4$, $3x \pm 1$, $3x \pm 2$, $3x \pm 4$, a total of twelve possibilities which can be tested. Analogous work occurs in arithmetic; we can only say that 1427 is prime when we have tried dividing it by all prime numbers up to $\sqrt{1427}$.

74

One method of testing for a possible algebraic factor is by reversing the multiplication process. If we write

$$3x^3 - 5x^2 - 6x + 4 = (x-2)(\qquad), \qquad (1)$$

we soon see that the first term of the missing factor must be $3x^2$ and the last term -2.

$$(x-2)(3x^2 \qquad -2). \qquad (2)$$

We now choose the middle term so that the required coefficient of x^2 is obtained when the multiplication is carried out. Formally, we require $bc + ad = -5$, with a, b, c now chosen as $1, -2, 3$; this gives $d = 1$. Mentally, we should reason in this way. Multiplying out the incomplete form (2) gives $-6x^2$, whereas we require $-5x^2$ altogether; the missing term must give rise to $+x^2$ when multiplied by the first term in the other bracket. Hence the missing term must be $+x$.

We now have $(x-2)(3x^2 + x - 2)$, with the second bracket chosen to give the required coefficients of x^3 and x^2 and the required constant term. But what is the coefficient of x in the expanded form? When we see that this is -4 instead of the desired -6 we conclude that $x-2$ is *not* a factor of $3x^3 - 5x^2 - 6x + 4$.

Exercise G

In Questions 1–6 determine whether the polynomial B is a factor of A.

1. $A = 3x^2 - 5x - 2$, $B = x - 2$.

2. $A = x^3 + 4x^2 + 2x - 3$, $B = x + 3$.

3. $A = 6x^3 - x^2 + 1$, $B = 2x + 1$.

4. $A = 3x^3 + 4x^2 - x + 2$, $B = 3x + 2$.

5. $A = 2x^4 + x^2 + x + 1$, $B = x^2 - x + 1$.

6. $A = 2x^4 - 3x^3 - 3x - 4$, $B = x^2 + 1$.

7. What number must be added to $x^3 + 5x^2 + 10x + 1$ to make $x + 1$ a factor?

8. What number must be added to $x^3 + x^2 - 2x + 15$ to make $x + 3$ a factor?

In the following questions list the possible linear factors and test them. If you find a factor, go on to see whether the polynomial can be factorized further.

9. $3x^3 + 5x^2 + x - 1$.

10. $x^3 - 2x^2 - x + 2$.

11. $2x^3 + 3x^2 - 5x - 6$.

12. $4x^3 - 20x^2 - 3x + 6$.

3.5 Division. If a pile of 2837 beads is to be shared among 13 tribesmen, one might start by making 13 piles of 200 beads, leaving 237:

$$2837 = 13 \times 200 + 237.$$

75

Now suppose 13 piles of 10 are taken. This leaves 107 and we note that

$$2837 = 13 \times 210 + 107.$$

Finally, each tribesman can have another 8, and we have

$$2837 = 13 \times 218 + 3.$$

We say that when 2837 is divided by 13, the *quotient* is 218 and the *remainder* is 3.

Polynomial division follows similar lines. Let us divide

$$A = x^3 + 5x^2 + 10x + 15 \quad \text{by} \quad B = x + 2.$$

We start by subtracting x^2 lots of B (i.e. $x^3 + 2x^2$) from A. Then

$$A - x^2 B = 3x^2 + 10x + 15;$$

this removes the x^3 term in much the same way as the thousands were removed in the arithmetical example. Next we remove the x^2 term by subtracting $3xB$ (i.e. $3x^2 + 6x$), leaving $4x + 15$, and finally we subtract $4B$, leaving 7. The process can be written out as follows, and each step checked by multiplication.

$$\begin{aligned} x^3 + 5x^2 + 10x + 15 &= (x+2)\,(x^2) + 3x^2 + 10x + 15 \\ &= (x+2)\,(x^2 + 3x) + 4x + 15 \\ &= (x+2)\,(x^2 + 3x + 4) + 7. \end{aligned}$$

We say that when $x^3 + 5x^2 + 10x + 15$ is divided by $x + 2$, the quotient is $x^2 + 3x + 4$ and the remainder is 7.

The process is equivalent to the un-multiplication of the last section, and with a little practice can be carried out mentally. We start by writing

$$x^3 + 5x^2 + 10x + 15 = (x+2)\,(\qquad) + \qquad,$$

and fill in the quotient bracket from the left, in such a way that on multiplication first the x^3 terms, then the x^2 and x terms in turn tally. The remainder is then determined by the constant term.

In arithmetic, the quotient q and remainder r when the integer a is divided by the integer b are defined formally as the integers for which

$$a = bq + r, \quad 0 \leqslant r < b.$$

Are q and r unique? How can this definition be adapted for polynomials? What is the equivalent of the condition that the remainder must be less than the divisor?

As a second example, divide

$$A = 6x^3 - 5x^2 + 4x - 1 \quad \text{by} \quad B = 2x^2 + x - 3.$$

76

If we multiply B by $3x$ and subtract from A, we remove the term in x^3.

$$A - 3xB = (6x^3 - 5x^2 + 4x - 1) - (6x^3 + 3x^2 - 9x)$$
$$= -8x^2 + 13x - 1.$$

We now subtract $-4B$ and remove the term in x^2.

$$A - 3xB - (-4)B = 17x - 13.$$

Here we stop. The quotient is $3x - 4$, the remainder $17x - 13$, and

$$6x^3 - 5x^2 + 4x - 1 = (2x^2 + x - 3)(3x - 4) + (17x - 13),$$

which is of the form $\qquad A = BQ + R.$

Q is the polynomial which makes $A - BQ$ as 'small' as possible. This does not refer to the size of the coefficients of R but to its *degree*. We continue until the degree of the remainder is less than the degree of the divisor. With a linear divisor, as in our first example, the remainder is a number (or polynomial of degree zero); with a quadratic divisor, the remainder will in general be a linear polynomial.

3.6 Long division format. The examples of the last section can be set out as 'long divisions':

$$
\begin{array}{r}
218 \\
13\overline{)2837} \\
26 \\
\hline
23 \\
13 \\
\hline
107 \\
104 \\
\hline
3
\end{array}
\qquad
\begin{array}{r}
x^2 + 3x + 4 \\
x+2\overline{)x^3 + 5x^2 + 10x + 15} \\
x^3 + 2x^2 \\
\hline
3x^2 + 10x \\
3x^2 + 6x \\
\hline
4x + 15 \\
4x + 8 \\
\hline
7
\end{array}
$$

Divide (*a*) 4397 by 31, (*b*) $6x^3 - 5x^2 + 4x - 1$ by $2x^2 + x - 3$, using long division.

This is the most succinct format which shows all the intermediate steps, but you may still prefer to un-multiply.

As a further illustration, we find the quotient and remainder when $2x^3 - 5x + 1$ is divided by $2x + 3$.

$$
\begin{array}{r}
x^2 - 1\frac{1}{2}x - \frac{1}{4} \\
2x+3\overline{)2x^3 + 0x^2 - 5x + 1} \\
2x^3 + 3x^2 \\
\hline
-3x^2 - 5x \\
-3x^2 - 4\frac{1}{2}x \\
\hline
-\frac{1}{2}x + 1 \\
-\frac{1}{2}x - \frac{3}{4} \\
\hline
1\frac{3}{4}
\end{array}
$$

77

The quotient is therefore $x^2 - 1\frac{1}{2}x - \frac{1}{4}$ and the remainder is $1\frac{3}{4}$. The answers can be checked by finding $BQ + R$ and showing that it is equal to A; thus

$$(2x+3)(x^2 - 1\frac{1}{2}x - \frac{1}{4}) + 1\frac{3}{4} = 2x^3 + (3-3)x^2 + (-4\frac{1}{2} - \frac{1}{2})x - \frac{3}{4} + 1\frac{3}{4}$$
$$= 2x^3 - 5x + 1.$$

Two points should be noted:

(i) When carrying out this process for polynomials, the coefficients must be thought of as rational numbers rather than integers. For instance, in the above example $2x^3 - 5x + 1$ and $2x + 3$ are polynomials with integral coefficients but the quotient and remainder both contain coefficients which are not integers.

(ii) If a coefficient in one of the polynomials is zero, it is important to allow for this in setting out the calculation.

Exercise H

1. Find the quotient and remainder when 253 is divided by 14.

In Questions 2–9 give the quotient and remainder when A is divided by B.

2. $A = x^3 - 2x^2 + 3x - 5$, $B = x$.

3. $A = x^3 - 2x^2 + 3x - 5$, $B = x + 2$.

4. $A = 2x^3 - 5x + 3$, $B = x - 1$.

5. $A = 3x + 4$, $B = 2x - 1$.

6. $A = 4x^3 + x^2 - 1$, $B = 2x + 1$.

7. $A = x^3 + 3x^2 + 2x$, $B = x^2 - x + 2$.

8. $A = x^4 + 2x^3 - 4x^2 - 2x + 1$, $B = x^2 - 1$.

9. $A = 2x^3 - 3x^2 + x - 1$, $B = 2x^2 + x - 2$.

10. Consider the set of integers $450 - 13n$, where n is any integer.
(a) What is the difference between 'consecutive' members of the set?
(b) Can two members of the set lie in the interval $0 \leqslant x \leqslant 12$?
(c) What is the significance of the member of the set which lies in this interval? Must there be one that does?

11. Find a polynomial P such that $x^3 + 3x^2 - 2 - P(x^2 + x + 1)$ has degree less than 2. Are there other polynomials with this property?

In Questions 12 and 13, B is a factor of A. Find the other factor. These results are useful and should be noted for future reference.

12. (i) $A = x^3 + 1$, $B = x + 1$.
(ii) $A = x^3 + 8$, $B = x + 2$.
(iii) $A = x^3 + c^3$, $B = x + c$.

13. (i) $A = x^3 - 1$, $B = x - 1$.
(ii) $A = x^3 - 27$, $B = x - 3$.
(iii) $A = x^3 - c^3$, $B = x - c$.

14. Find the remainder when $A = 2x^3 + 3x^2 - 5x - 6$ is divided by (a) $x - 1$, (b) $x - 2$, (c) $x + 2$. Express A as the product of three linear factors.

15. List the possible linear factors of the following polynomials, and test them by division or otherwise. If you find a factor, go on to see whether the polynomial can be factorized further.

(a) $2x^3 + 7x^2 + 4x - 4$, (b) $4x^3 + 12x^2 - x - 3$,
(c) $2x^3 + 5x^2 - 3x - 3$, (d) $2 + 4x - 5x^2 + 3x^3$.

4. EXPRESSIONS CONTAINING TWO OR MORE LETTERS

Sometimes polynomials contain two or more letters, for example

$$x^3 + y^3 - 3x^2 y + 2x - 6.$$

For the moment we shall assume that the letters all stand for numbers and that therefore the commutative law for multiplication holds, as well as the usual other laws; in other words $3xy$ is the same as $3yx$. As we have already seen, the letters may sometimes stand for matrices in which case this will not be true.

Exercise I

In the following questions, multiply out the brackets using the fact that multiplication is distributive over addition.

1. $3x^2(x + 2y^2)$. **2.** $(x + y + 1)(x^2 + 2)$.

3. $(x + 2y - 3z)(xy - 5)$. **4.** $(x + 3y)(2x - y)$.

5. $(2x + 3y)^2$. **6.** $(x + y + 1)(x - y + 1)$.

7. Say which of the following statements are true for all x and y and which are false. If you are in doubt, check whether your answer makes sense when x and y are given simple values such as 2 and 3.

(i) $4xy + 3xy = 7x^2 y^2$; (ii) $4xy + 3xy = 12xy$;
(iii) $5yx - 2xy = xy(5 - 2) = 3xy$; (iv) $x^2 y + xy^2 = x^2 y^2$;
(v) $2x^2 y + 3xy^2 = xy(2x + 3y)$.

8. Remove the brackets and simplify the resulting expressions as far as possible.

(i) $(5x - 2y)(3x + y) + 3(5x^2 - 2y^2) - (2x - y)^2$;
(ii) $(x + y)(x - y) + (y - x)(y + x)$;
(iii) $(x + 2y)^3$;
(iv) $3x^2(2x + y) + 2xy(x - y) - 3y^2(4x - 3y)$;
(v) $(x + y)(x^2 - xy + y^2) + (x - y)(x^2 + xy + y^2)$.

9. In each part, show that B is a factor of A, and find the other factor.

(a) $A = x^3 - 2x^2 y - 7xy^2 + 2y^3$, $B = x + 2y$;
(b) $A = 8x^3 - y^3$, $B = 2x - y$;
(c) $A = 9x^3 + 5xy^2 + 6y^3$, $B = 3x + 2y$.

10. (*a*) Show that $x-y$ is a factor of (i) x^2-y^2, (ii) x^3-y^3, (iii) x^4-y^4. Find the other factor in each case, and describe the pattern in the answers.

(*b*) Investigate whether $x+y$ is a factor of x^n+y^n with $n = 2, 3, 4, 5$. Generalize.

11. Factorize the following expressions, where possible.

(*a*) $x^2-5xy+6y^2$,   ◂(*b*) $2x^2+4xy-30y^2$,

(*c*) $3x^2-13xy-4y^2$,   (*d*) x^2-4y^2,

(*e*) x^3-8y^3,   ◂(*f*) x^4-y^4.

12. (i) If $\mathbf{A} = \begin{pmatrix} 2 & 1 \\ 0 & 3 \end{pmatrix}$ and $\mathbf{B} = \begin{pmatrix} 1 & -1 \\ -1 & 2 \end{pmatrix}$, work out

$$(\mathbf{A}+\mathbf{B})\,(2\mathbf{A}-3\mathbf{B}) \quad \text{and} \quad \mathbf{A}^2-\mathbf{A}\mathbf{B}-3\mathbf{B}^2.$$

(ii) Given that $\mathbf{C}$ and $\mathbf{D}$ are 2×2 matrices, write in expanded form

$$(\mathbf{C}+\mathbf{D})\,(2\mathbf{C}-3\mathbf{D}) \quad \text{and} \quad (4\mathbf{C}-\mathbf{D})\,(\mathbf{C}-5\mathbf{D}).$$

5. SOME APPLICATIONS OF FACTORS

(i) Work out $\dfrac{3^2 \times 7 \times 13}{5 \times 17} \times \dfrac{2^3 \times 5^2 \times 17}{7 \times 13}$.

(ii) Find all the factors of $(1-x)^4+3(1-x)^5$.

Anyone who multiplies out the fractions in (i), getting $\dfrac{819}{85} \times \dfrac{3400}{91}$,

and then does some long multiplication, $\dfrac{2\,784\,600}{7735}$,

and then some long division, 360,

would rightly be accused of making unnecessary work for himself.

Similarly, in (ii), we can multiply out and collect terms, giving

$$4-19x+36x^2-34x^3+16x^4-3x^5,$$

and then set about the laborious task of factorization. But this is absurd.

In essence, 'a number to the fourth power is to be added to three times the same number to the fifth power'. It is much the same as $7^4+3 \times 7^5$ or $y^4+3 \times y^5$, and these can be factorized to give

$$7^4(1+3 \times 7) \quad \text{and} \quad y^4(1+3y).$$

Then $(1-x)^4+3(1-x)^5 = (1-x)^4\,[1+3(1-x)]$

$$= (1-x)^4\,[1+3-3x]$$

$$= (1-x)^4\,(4-3x).$$

The important thing is to get used to thinking of an expression like $x-1$ or $2x+3$ simply as one number. Now can you simplify

$$\tfrac{1}{6}(x+1)\,(x+2)\,(2x+3)-(x+1)^2,$$

giving the answer in factors? It is best to multiply the second term by $\frac{6}{6}$ so that the common fractional factor $\frac{1}{6}$ can be got out of the way; then $x+1$ is a common factor. Try it yourself before looking at the working below.

$$\frac{1}{6}(x+1)(x+2)(2x+3)-(x+1)^2$$

$$= \frac{1}{6}(x+1)(x+2)(2x+3)-\frac{6}{6}(x+1)(x+1)$$

$$= \frac{1}{6}(x+1)[(x+2)(2x+3)-6(x+1)] \tag{1}$$

$$= \frac{1}{6}(x+1)[2x^2+7x+6-6x-6] \tag{2}$$

$$= \frac{1}{6}(x+1)[2x^2+x]$$

$$= \frac{1}{6}(x+1)x(2x+1) \tag{3}$$

$$= \frac{1}{6}x(x+1)(2x+1). \tag{4}$$

Notes (1) This stage is really no different from saying $abc-6a^2 = a(bc-6a)$.

(2) The brackets within the square bracket must be multiplied out to enable the subtraction to be done.

(3), (4) The factorization is completed and the x moved to the beginning where it is less likely to be overlooked.

Exercise J

1. Factorize $2(x+1)^2+7(x+1)-4$. (Start by treating it the same way as you would $2a^2+7a-4$.)

2. Factorize $(x^2+6)^2-2x(x^2+6)-35x^2$.

3. Simplify $(3x+5)^3-(3x+4)^3$. Refer to Exercise H, Question 13.

Simplify the expressions in Questions 4–7, leaving the answers in factors.

4. $(x+1)(2x+1)(2x+3)-3(2x+1)^2$.

5. $x(x+1)(x+4)(x+5)+4(x+1)(x+3)(x+5)$.

6. $\frac{1}{12}(x+1)(x+2)(x+3)(3x+4)-(x+1)^2(x+2)$.

7. $\frac{1}{4}(x+1)^2(x+2)^2-(x+1)^3$.

8. Simplify

(i) $\dfrac{b-a}{\sqrt{b}-\sqrt{a}}$, (ii) $(\sqrt{b}-\sqrt{a})(b+\sqrt{(ba)}+a)$, (iii) $(\sqrt{b}-\sqrt{a})^2(\sqrt{b}+\sqrt{a})^2$.

(It may help to substitute x for $\sqrt{b}$ and y for $\sqrt{a}$.)

6. FRACTIONS IN ALGEBRA

The rules for manipulating algebraic fractions are identical to those for arithmetical fractions.

6.1 Multiplication and division. As in arithmetic, multiplication and division of fractions are easier than addition and subtraction.

Example 1

$$\frac{3}{4} \times \frac{2}{5} = \frac{3 \times 2}{4 \times 5} = \frac{3}{2 \times 5}.$$

The numerators and denominators are multiplied and the result reduced to the simplest equivalent fraction by dividing 'top' and 'bottom' by any common factors.

Example 2

$$\frac{5}{6} \div \frac{3}{4} = \frac{5}{6} \times \frac{4}{3} = \frac{5 \times 4}{6 \times 3} = \frac{5 \times 2}{3 \times 3}.$$

Can you justify the rule 'turn the divisor upside down and multiply'?

Example 3

$$\frac{x-2}{x^2+2x+1} \times \frac{x+1}{x^2-4} = \frac{(x-2)\,(x+1)}{(x^2+2x+1)\,(x^2-4)}$$

$$= \frac{(x-2)\,(x+1)}{(x+1)^2\,(x+2)\,(x-2)}$$

$$= \frac{1}{(x+1)\,(x+2)}.$$

It is important to express each polynomial in factors so that factors common to numerator and denominator can be spotted. The answer is best left in factors.

Exercise K

Express the following fractions in their simplest form.

1. $\dfrac{1617}{3927}$.

2. $\dfrac{x^2-3x+2}{x^2-4}$.

3. $\dfrac{x^2+6x+5}{x^2+4x-5}$.

4. $\dfrac{2x^2+2}{x^2+3x+2}$.

5. $\dfrac{x^3-1}{x^2-1}$.

Simplify:

6. $\dfrac{x-y}{x+y} \times \dfrac{xy+y^2}{x^2-xy}$.

7. $\dfrac{x^2-49}{x^2-9} \div \dfrac{x+7}{x-3}$.

8. $\dfrac{x^2+5x+6}{x^2-25} \div \dfrac{x+3}{5-x}$.

9. $\dfrac{4x^2-1}{8y^3-1} \div \dfrac{1+2x}{1-2y}$.

10. $\dfrac{6-5x+x^2}{x^2-16} \times \dfrac{x^2+5x+4}{x^2-4} \div \dfrac{x-3}{x-4}$.

6.2   Addition and subtraction

Example 4 $\frac{9}{10} - \frac{1}{6} = \frac{27}{30} - \frac{5}{30} = \frac{22}{30} = \frac{11}{15}.$

We find the L.C.M. of the denominators, and express each fraction in an equivalent form with this as denominator. After subtraction we reduce the answer to its simplest form.

In such a simple example, it would not matter if we used a larger common multiple, e.g. 60.

$$\frac{9}{10} - \frac{1}{6} = \frac{54}{60} - \frac{10}{60} = \frac{44}{60} = \frac{11}{15}.$$

In algebra, the denominators should be factorized and the *lowest* common multiple found. Otherwise the working is likely to be excessively complicated.

Example 5

$$\frac{x-6}{x^2-4} - \frac{x}{x^2+3x+2} = \frac{x-6}{(x-2)(x+2)} - \frac{x}{(x+2)(x+1)}$$

$$= \frac{(x-6)(x+1)}{(x-2)(x+2)(x+1)} - \frac{x(x-2)}{(x-2)(x+2)(x+1)}$$

$$= \frac{(x^2-5x-6)-(x^2-2x)}{(x-2)(x+2)(x+1)} \qquad (1)$$

$$= \frac{-3x-6}{(x-2)(x+2)(x+1)}$$

$$= \frac{-3(x+2)}{(x-2)(x+2)(x+1)}$$

$$= \frac{-3}{(x-2)(x+1)}.$$

Note that the denominator has been left in factors throughout. At stage (1), the numerators had to be multiplied out so that they could be combined. The numerator was then factorized and the common factor $x+2$ revealed.

6.3   Applications to functions

Example 6

If f and g are the functions $f\colon x \to \dfrac{3+x}{2-x}$, $g\colon x \to \dfrac{2x+1}{x-1}$, find $gf(5)$ and $gf(x)$.

$f(5) = -\frac{8}{3}$ and hence $gf(5) = g(-\frac{8}{3}) = \dfrac{-\frac{16}{3}+1}{-\frac{8}{3}-1}$. This may be simplified by multiplying above and below the bar by 3. Then

$$gf(5) = \frac{-16+3}{-8-3} = \frac{-13}{-11} = \frac{13}{11}.$$

Similarly,

$$gf(x) = \frac{2\left(\dfrac{3+x}{2-x}\right)+1}{\left(\dfrac{3+x}{2-x}\right)-1}$$

$$= \frac{2(3+x)+(2-x)}{(3+x)-(2-x)}, \quad \text{multiplying top and bottom by } 2-x,$$

$$= \frac{6+2x+2-x}{3+x-2+x}$$

$$= \frac{8+x}{1+2x}.$$

Now work out $fg(x)$ and compare with $gf(x)$.

Example 7

If f is the function $f: x \to (3+x)/(2-x)$, what is its inverse f^{-1}?

Let us write $y = f(x)$; then $x = f^{-1}(y)$. We wish to change the subject of the formula $y = (3+x)/(2-x)$ so as to express x in terms of y.

$$y = \frac{3+x}{2-x}.$$

Multiply both sides of the equation by $(2-x)$.

$$y(2-x) = 3+x,$$

and so $\qquad 2y-xy = 3+x.$

Collect all the terms containing x on one side of the equation; in this case the right is chosen to avoid minus signs.

$$2y-3 = x+xy.$$

Factorize the right-hand side.

$$2y-3 = x(1+y).$$

Divide both sides by $(1+y)$.

$$\frac{2y-3}{1+y} = x = f^{-1}(y).$$

Hence the inverse function is

$$f^{-1}: x \to \frac{2x-3}{1+x}.$$

Exercise L

Simplify:

1. $\dfrac{1}{x}+\dfrac{1}{3x}+\dfrac{1}{2x}.$

2. $\dfrac{x-3}{3}-\dfrac{x-4}{4}.$

3. $\dfrac{1}{x+1}+\dfrac{1}{x-1}.$

4. $\dfrac{6}{2x-3}-\dfrac{3}{3-2x}.$

5. $\dfrac{3}{1-x}+\dfrac{4}{(1-x)^2}.$

6. $\dfrac{x-2}{x^2-x-2}+\dfrac{x-4}{x^2-5x+4}.$

In Questions 7–14 express the sums and products as single fractions in their simplest forms.

7. $\dfrac{2x}{3}+\dfrac{3x}{2}.$

8. $\dfrac{2x-1}{3}+\dfrac{1+x}{6}.$

9. $\dfrac{x}{3}\times\dfrac{5}{x}.$

10. $\dfrac{x}{3}-\dfrac{5}{x}.$

11. $\dfrac{x}{3}+\dfrac{5}{x}.$

12. $\dfrac{3}{4x}-\dfrac{5}{8x}.$

13. $\dfrac{4}{x}\times\dfrac{5}{x}-\dfrac{1}{4}\times\left(\dfrac{6}{x}\right)^2.$

14. $\dfrac{3x}{x-2}-\dfrac{6}{x-2}.$

For the fractions given in Questions 15–20 calculate $A+B$, $A-B$, AB and $A\div B$.

15. $A=\dfrac{1}{x+2},\quad B=\dfrac{2}{x+1}.$

16. $A=\dfrac{x-2}{x+2},\quad B=\dfrac{x+2}{x-2}.$

17. $A=\dfrac{x}{1-x^2},\quad B=\dfrac{1}{(1-x)^2}.$

18. $A=\dfrac{x+5}{5},\quad B=\dfrac{5}{x-5}.$

19. $A=\dfrac{x+1}{x^2-3x+2},\quad B=\dfrac{x-2}{x^2-1}.$

20. $A=\dfrac{2}{2x+x^2},\quad B=\dfrac{3}{3x+x^2}.$

Simplify:

21. $\dfrac{1}{x^2-4x+3}+\dfrac{1}{x^2-5x+6}+\dfrac{1}{x^2-3x+2}.$

22. $\dfrac{3x}{x^2-3x+2}+\dfrac{4}{1-x}+\dfrac{1}{x-2}.$

23. $\dfrac{4}{x^2+2x}-\dfrac{3x}{x+2}+\dfrac{3x-2}{x}.$

24. $\dfrac{1}{2(x-2)}+\dfrac{1}{(x-2)(x-3)}+\dfrac{1}{(x-2)(x-3)(x-4)}.$

25. Find the inverses of the following functions:

(a) $f: x \to \dfrac{x+4}{x-3}$;   (b) $g: x \to \dfrac{2x+3}{x-1}$;   (c) $h: x \to \dfrac{3x-5}{x-3}$.

26. For the functions given in Question 25, find, in the simplest form:

(a) fg;   (b) $(fg)^{-1}$;   (c) $g^{-1}f^{-1}$.

27. For each of the following functions, write $f(b)-f(a)$ as a single fraction, and simplify $\dfrac{f(b)-f(a)}{b-a}$:

(i) $f: x \to \dfrac{1}{x}$;   (ii) $f: x \to \dfrac{1}{3x-2}$;   (iii) $f: x \to \dfrac{1}{x^2}$.

In the following questions you are given $f(n)$ and another expression E. In each case show that $f(n)+E = f(n+1)$.

28. $f(n) = \dfrac{n}{n+1}$ and $E = \dfrac{1}{(n+1)(n+2)}$.

29. $f(n) = \frac{1}{3}n(4n^2-1)$ and $E = (2n+1)^2$.

30. $f(n) = \dfrac{n}{3n+1}$ and $E = \dfrac{1}{(3n+1)(3n+4)}$.

31. $f(n) = 1 - \dfrac{2}{(n+1)(n+2)}$ and $E = \dfrac{4}{(n+1)(n+2)(n+3)}$.

Miscellaneous Exercise

1. A polynomial may be specified by its coefficients alone, e.g. $2+7x-9x^2$ by $(2, 7, -9)$.

Find the sum and product of the polynomials the coefficients of which are, in ascending order:

(i) $(3, -4, 1, 2)$ and $(2, -5)$;

(ii) $(1, 0, 3, -4)$ and $(3, 6, -1)$;

(iii) (a_0, a_1, a_2) and (b_0, b_1, b_2, b_3).

2. Two polynomials A and B have degrees m and n respectively. What can you say about the degrees of $A+B$, $A-B$, AB? Can you give any meaning to the statement $A > B$?

3. If A and B are polynomials, and r and s are numbers, prove that $rA+sB$ is a polynomial. (Are there any exceptions to this?)

Find the numbers r and s if A is $2+3x$, B is $4-x$ and $rA+sB$ is $7x-5$.

4. If P, Q, R, S are polynomials, which of the following are true?

(a) $PQ = PR \Rightarrow Q = R$.

(b) $P(Q+R) = PQ+PR$.

(c) $\dfrac{P}{Q}+\dfrac{R}{S} = \dfrac{P+R}{Q+S}$.

(d) $\dfrac{P}{Q}-\dfrac{R}{S} = \dfrac{PS-QR}{QS}$.

5. If the polynomial A, of degree 6, described by the coefficients in descending order $(a_6, a_5, \ldots, a_0)$, is divided by the linear polynomial $x - k$, and if the quotient is $(c_5, c_4, \ldots, c_0)$ and the remainder r, show that

$$c_5 = a_6, \quad c_4 = a_5 + kc_5,$$

and write similar equations for c_3, c_2, c_1, c_0, and r. Write this in the form of a flow chart for a program to compute the quotient and remainder when the co-efficients of A and the number k are given. Generalize this for the case when the polynomial A has degree n.

Use this procedure to obtain the quotient and remainder when

$$2x^6 - 3x^5 + x^3 - 4x^2 + 5$$

is divided by $x - 2$.

6. In Question 5, show that the remainder is given explicitly by the formula

$$a_0 + k(a_1 + k(a_2 + k(a_3 + k(a_4 + k(a_5 + ka_6))))),$$

and that this can be written as

$$a_6 k^6 + a_5 k^5 + a_4 k^4 + a_3 k^3 + a_2 k^2 + a_1 k + a_0.$$

Express this rule in words.

7. A polynomial A of degree 5 is divided by $x - k$ to give a quotient B and remainder r_0. B is then divided by $x - k$ to give a quotient C and remainder r_1; and so on. Prove that the last quotient F, which is a simple number, is equal to the coefficient of x^5 in A. Denoting this by a_5, prove that the original polynomial A can be written in the form

$$a_5(x - k)^5 + r_4(x - k)^4 + r_3(x - k)^3 + r_2(x - k)^2 + r_1(x - k) + r_0.$$

Carry out this calculation where A is $3x^5 + 2x^4 + 4x^3 - x + 5$ and $k = 2$, using the result of Question 5 to set out your work in as orderly a manner as possible.

SUMMARY

The processes for addition, subtraction, multiplication and division of polynomials are similar to those for combining integers in arithmetic.

Algebraic fractions are manipulated also in much the same way as arithmetical fractions.

Some factors

$$x^2 + 2ax + a^2 = (x + a)^2,$$

$$x^2 - 2ax + a^2 = (x - a)^2,$$

$$x^2 - a^2 = (x + a)(x - a),$$

$$x^3 - a^3 = (x - a)(x^2 + ax + a^2),$$

$$x^3 + a^3 = (x + a)(x^2 - ax + a^2).$$

5

DERIVATIVES AND DERIVED FUNCTIONS

Continuing the study of functions begun in Chapter 2, we now concentrate on rates of change. The techniques developed in Chapters 3 and 4 will be required.

Exercise A

1. A film of a model boat in motion provided the following information:

Time (in seconds) from the first frame	0	1	2	3	4	5	6
Distance travelled (in metres)	0	3	6	9	12	15	18

What can you say about the boat's motion during this period?

2. The position of a car was observed at 5 second intervals to see if it was obeying the speed limit.

Time (s)	0	5	10	15	20	25	30	35	40
Distance travelled (m)	0	100	200	290	370	430	510	610	720

Calculate the average speed for the whole period, and for each 5 second interval. Give an estimate of the car's speed after 20 seconds. Estimate also for how long the speed was less than 18 m/s.

3. The population of a city has grown as follows:

Year	1935	1940	1945	1950	1955	1960	1965	1970
Population (in thousands)	135	149	165	182	201	223	246	272

Find the average rates of growth (in thousands per year) for each ten year period. Express each rate of growth as a percentage of the current size of population. Comment on your answers.

4. In a film of the last 10 seconds of a horse race, the distance of the leader from the finish can be estimated using the railings in the background, which are 2 m apart.

Time (s)	0	1	2	3	4	5	6	7	8	9	10
Number of rails from end	100	89	78	68	57	46	38	30	20	10	0

Was the horse travelling at a constant speed? Calculate its average speed over each one second interval.

5. A parachutist jumps from an aircraft at a great height and delays the opening of his parachute. The distance he has fallen at various times after leaving the aircraft are:

Time of fall (s)	t	0	2	4	6	8
Distance fallen (m)	d	0	20	80	180	320

Find the average speed for each time interval of length 2 seconds.

Draw a mapping diagram to display this information.

Show that there is a simple relation between the time of fall and the distance fallen. From this relation calculate the average speed for the third second (from $t = 2$ to $t = 3$) and for the ninth second.

6. Fibre glass paddling pools come in various diameters. Their prices are given in the following table:

Diameter (m)	x	2	$2\frac{1}{2}$	3	4	5
Cost (£)	y	16	$20\frac{1}{2}$	26	40	58

Draw a mapping diagram for the function $x \to y$.

Is there a pattern in the cost increases per extra metre in diameter? Give one reason why you would expect the price to increase with size in this sort of way.

Show that there is a relation between diameter and cost of the form $y = a + bx^2$.

1. AVERAGE SCALE FACTORS

In this chapter we are concerned with how things change. In Exercise A, some of the tables showed regular patterns which could be described by algebraic formulae. In others (e.g. Question 4), no pattern existed and these are of little further interest from a mathematical viewpoint.

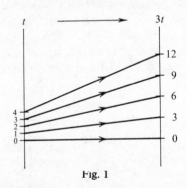

Fig. 1

The distances in Question 1 are clearly given by the trebling function $t \to 3t$. Figure 1 displays this function, and if we think of the domain as a length of elastic, the mapping has the effect of stretching the elastic uniformly. It is evident that each portion of the domain becomes stretched by a factor of 3, and this corresponds to the speed of the boat (in m/s).

Both Questions 5 and 6 involved the squaring function, so we look at this next.

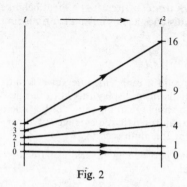

Fig. 2

Here, there is no single scale factor for the mapping, and it appears from Figure 2 that there is a sort of 'variable stretch' needed to map the domain onto the range, with the scale factor increasing as t increases. The portion of the domain between 3 and 4, of length 1, is stretched to an interval of length 7, so we can describe the function as having average scale factor 7 here. For a function mapping time to displacement, the average scale factor is an alternative name for average velocity.

1.1 Average scale factor for a general function. For the squaring function, $5 \to 25$ and $7 \to 49$, so the interval $\{x: 5 \leqslant x \leqslant 7\}$ of the domain is stretched by a factor $(49-25)/(7-5) = 12$ on average, though we appreciate that the part nearer 5 is stretched less while the part nearer 7 is stretched more. What are the average scale factors for the intervals $\{x: 7 \leqslant x \leqslant 10\}$ and $\{x: 10 \leqslant x \leqslant 12\}$?

In what follows it is convenient to refer to the set of real numbers between a and b as 'the interval $[a, b]$'. Thus, for example, the interval $[2, 5]$ is $\{x: 2 \leqslant x \leqslant 5\}$.

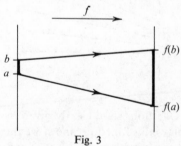

Fig. 3

Then, for a general function f, the *average scale factor over the interval* $[a, b]$ is defined as

$$\frac{f(b)-f(a)}{b-a}.$$

90

Example 1

Draw the mapping diagram for $x \to -2x+8$, and find the average scale factor over $[-1, 2]$. Interpret the answer.

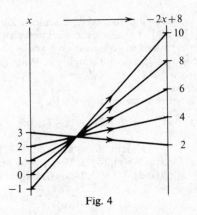

Fig. 4

Since $-1 \to 10$ and $2 \to 4$, the definition gives the average scale factor as

$$\frac{4-10}{2-(-1)} = -2.$$

The fact that the scale factor is negative implies that an increase in the value of x within the domain has given rise to a decrease in the value of $f(x)$ in the range.

It also appears from the diagram that this linear function has a constant scale factor. This can be confirmed by taking a general interval $[a, b]$. For this interval, the average scale factor is

$$\frac{(-2b+8)-(-2a+8)}{b-a} = \frac{-2b+2a}{b-a} = \frac{-2(b-a)}{b-a} = -2.$$

Exercise B

1. Sketch the mapping diagram for $x \to 4+3x$. Onto what intervals do $[0, 1]$ and $[-1, 3]$ map? What is the scale factor for this mapping?

2. What are the scale factors for

  (a) $x \to 2x+1$;   (b) $x \to (3+x)/2$;   (c) $x \to px+q$?

3. In what way are the scale factors of $x \to 2+4x$ and $x \to 2-4x$ different? How does this difference show up on a mapping diagram?

4. Find the average scale factor over the interval $[4, 7]$ for each of the following functions.

  (a) $x \to x^2$;   (b) $x \to x^2+10$;   (c) $x \to 10x^2$.

5. The displacement of a body (in metres) is given as a function of time (t seconds) by $t \to t^2 + 6t + 10$. Find the average velocity between $t = 4$ and $t = 7$.

6. A body is oscillating on the end of a vertical spring. Its height above the floor at time t seconds is $0.8 + 0.2 \sin (100t)°$ metres. Find its average velocity over the time interval $[0.1, 0.3]$.

7. For the function $x \to x^2$, find the average scale factors over the intervals $[5, 7]$, $[5, 6]$, $[5, 5.5]$, $[5, 5.1]$ and also over the intervals $[3, 5]$, $[4, 5]$, $[4.5, 5]$, $[4.9, 5]$. Can you spot a pattern in your answers? Write down an expression for the average scale factor over $[5, b]$, and simplify it. What can you say about the average scale factor when b is close to 5?

8. Repeat Question 7, with the same intervals, for

   (a) $x \to 3x^2$,   (b) $x \to 6x$,   (c) $x \to 3x^2 + 6x + 7$,   (d) $x \to x^3$.

9. For the function $x \to x^2 - 3x$, write down an expression for the average scale factor over the interval $[4, b]$ and simplify it. Hence write down the average scale factors over $[4, 6]$, $[4, 5]$, $[4, 4.5]$, $[4, 4.1]$, $[4, 4.001]$. Is it possible to speak of a scale factor *at* $x = 4$?

2. DERIVATIVES

For any function expressed algebraically, we can calculate the average scale factor for any given interval of the domain. This is equivalent to calculating the average velocity of (say) a car between two points in time.

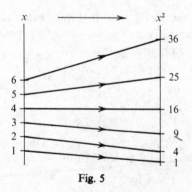

Fig. 5

But is it possible to deduce the actual velocity at a given instant (without looking at the speedometer) just from knowledge of the car's position? We may know the average stretch experienced by an interval of the domain for a given function, but can we associate a stretch with a single point of the domain?

Consider the squaring function again, and the point 3 in particular. As we approach the point 3 from above we get:

Interval	Average scale factor
[3, 6]	9
[3, 5]	8
[3, 4]	7
[3, 3·5]	6·5
[3, 3·1]	6·1
[3, 3·01]	6·01

What value of the scale factor does this suggest at the point 3?
 Also, as we approach the point 3 from below we get:

Interval	Average scale factor
[3, 0]	3
[3, 1]	4
[3, 2]	5
[3, 2·5]	5·5
[3, 2·9]	5·9
[3, 2·99]	5·99

The shorter we make the interval of the domain, the nearer the average scale factor gets to 6. This number, the limit of the average scale factor, is called the *local scale factor* or *derivative* at 3.

Rather than calculating all these average scale factors separately, we prefer to establish the pattern algebraically, as suggested in Exercise B, Questions 7, 8 and 9.

Over the interval [3, b], the average scale factor is

$$\frac{b^2-9}{b-3} = \frac{(b-3)(b+3)}{b-3} = b+3 \quad \text{if} \quad b \neq 3.$$

From this, all the above numbers can be written down and we see that as b tends to 3, the average scale factor tends to 6.

Example 2

Find the derivative of $x \to x^2 - 5x$ at $x = 4$.
 The average scale factor over [4, b] is

$$\frac{(b^2-5b)-(16-20)}{b-4} = \frac{b^2-5b+4}{b-4} = \frac{(b-1)(b-4)}{b-4} = b-1.$$

As a check, we might note that $4 \to -4$, $7 \to 14$, giving $\dfrac{14-(-4)}{7-4} = 6$ as the average scale factor over $[4, 7]$, which is in agreement with the formula $b-1$ when $b = 7$.

Interval	Average scale factor
[4, 2]	1
[4, 3]	2
[4, 3·9]	2·9
[4, 4·1]	3·1
[4, 5]	4
[4, 6]	5

The above table, though not strictly necessary, shows how the average scale factor approaches 3 as the interval is shortened, i.e. as b tends to 4. We say that the derivative at 4 is 3.

Exercise C

1. For each of the following functions, find the images of the intervals $[3, 5]$, $[3, 4]$, $[3, 3·1]$, and of the intervals $[1, 3]$, $[2, 3]$, $[2·9, 3]$ and illustrate with a mapping diagram. Find the average scale factors over these intervals and state the derivative at $x = 3$.

(a) $x \to 2x^2$;   (b) $x \to 7x$;   (c) $x \to 2x^2 + 7x$.

2. For each of the functions in Question 1, write down and simplify the average scale factor over the interval $[3, b]$.

3. Write down and simplify the average scale factor for each of the following functions over the interval $[5, b]$. Then write down the average scale factors for several short intervals with 5 as one endpoint and state the derivative at 5.

(a) $x \to x^3$; (b) $x \to \frac{1}{2}x^2 - 3$;

(c) $x \to x - x^2$; (d) $x \to 1/x$.

4. A stone is thrown vertically upwards and its height in metres after t seconds is given by the function $t \to 12t - 5t^2$. Find its velocity when $t = 1$ and when $t = 2$.

5. Show that the average scale factor for $x \to \sqrt{x}$ over the interval $[9, b]$ is equal to $\dfrac{1}{\sqrt{b}+3}$. Deduce the derivative at 9.

6. Find the derivative at 1 of the following functions.

(a) $x \to x^4$; (b) $x \to 1/x$; (c) $x \to 1/x^2$;

(d) $x \to \sqrt{x}$; (e) $x \to \sqrt[3]{x}$.

7. Making use of any results so far obtained, find the derivatives of each of the following functions at $x = 2, 3, 4$ and 5.

Comment on your answers.

(a) $x \to x^2$,   (b) $x \to 8x^2$,   (c) $x \to x^2+8$,

(d) $x \to x^2+3x+8$,   (e) $x \to x^3$.

Suggest in each case a formula for the derivative at $x = a$.

8. For each of the functions in Question 7, write down and simplify the average scale factor over the interval $[a, b]$. What can you deduce?

9. Repeat Question 8, using the interval $[a, a+h]$.

3. DERIVED FUNCTIONS

For the squaring function $f: x \to x^2$, every element of the domain has its derivative, expressing the local scale factor (stretch) at that point.

Element	2	3	4	5
Derivative	4	6	8	10

This itself defines a function, element $\to$ derivative, which is called the *derived function* and denoted by f'.

In this example, the derived function is actually the doubling function:

$$f: x \to x^2 \;\Rightarrow\; f': x \to 2x.$$

Thus the derivative at -6 is -12. We write this $f'(-6) = -12$.

Our task is to find derived functions corresponding to all the functions which might be useful in mathematical models in which rates of change are relevant. These include trigonometric, exponential and logarithmic functions. The quest has been started in Exercise C, and will be continued in Section 4 and later chapters.

Example 3

Find the average scale factor over $[a, b]$ for $f: x \to 1/x$, and deduce the derived function f'.

The average scale factor is

$$\frac{1/b - 1/a}{b - a}.$$

This is an awkward expression to handle, so we first simplify the numerator:

$$\frac{1}{b} - \frac{1}{a} = \frac{a-b}{ab} = \frac{-(b-a)}{ab}.$$

The average scale factor over $[a, b]$ is

$$\frac{-(b-a)}{ab} \div (b-a) = -\frac{1}{ab}.$$

95

For the moment we regard a as fixed. Then the limit of the average scale factor $-1/ab$ as b tends to a is $-1/a^2$, and this is a formula for the derivative at $x = a$. Thus, for example, at $x = 2$ the derivative is $-\frac{1}{4}$ and at $x = 5$ the derivative is $-\frac{1}{25}$.

As the result is true for all a in the domain of f, we can write

$$f(x) = \frac{1}{x} \;\Rightarrow\; f'(x) = -\frac{1}{x^2}.$$

3.1 Summary of derived functions. The method of Example 3 may be used to establish the following results, many of which have been proved or suggested in earlier exercises.

$f(x)$	$f'(x)$	
x^4	$4x^3$	
x^3	$3x^2$	
x^2	$2x$	
x	1	
1	0	Basic results
$1/x$	$-1/x^2$	
$1/x^2,$	$-2/x^3$	
$\sqrt{x}$	$1/(2\sqrt{x})$	
$5x^3$	$15x^2$	We can multiply or divide
$x^2/7$	$2x/7$	by a constant
x^3+4x-6	$3x^2+4$	We can add or subtract

Example 4

A drop of oil is spreading over a smooth surface. The circular region covered has radius (in cm) given approximately by the function $f: t \to 3\sqrt{t+1}$, where t is the time in seconds. Find the rate at which the radius is increasing when $t = 4$ and when $t = 9$.

The rate of increase is the derivative.

$$f(t) = 3\sqrt{t+1} \;\Rightarrow\; f'(t) = 3 \times 1/(2\sqrt{t}).$$

Then $f'(4) = \frac{3}{4}$ and $f'(9) = \frac{1}{2}$, and so the rates of change are $\frac{3}{4}$ cm per second and $\frac{1}{2}$ cm per second.

Exercise D

1. Use the results in Section 3.1 to write down the derived functions for:

(a) $f: x \to 5x^2+3x,$ (b) $f: x \to 2x+3,$

(c) $f: x \to x^3+2/x,$ (d) $f: x \to 4\sqrt{x}-x^2,$

(e) $f: x \to 2x^3+8x-5,$ (f) $f: x \to 3/x+4x.$

2. Find $f(4)$ and $f'(4)$ for each of the following functions.

(a) $f: x \to x^2 - 2x + 3$,   (b) $f: x \to 5\sqrt{x}$,

(c) $f: x \to 2x - 1/x$,   (d) $f: x \to 12/x^2$,

(e) $f: x \to (x-3)^2$,   (f) $f: x \to (x+1)(x+2)$.

3. If $f: t \to 30t - 4t^2$ gives the displacement of a body as a function of the time t, write down the function f' mapping time to velocity.

Find the position and velocity of the body when $t = 1, 2, 3$ and 4.

Where is the body when its velocity is zero?

4. DIFFERENTIATING FROM FIRST PRINCIPLES

The process of finding a derived function is called *differentiation*. In Example 3, we showed how to differentiate $f: x \to 1/x$ to give $f': x \to -1/x^2$. To prove this result, it was necessary to work algebraically, starting from the definition of a derivative.

Example 5

Find the derived function of $f: x \to \dfrac{1}{3x+2}$.

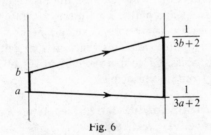

Fig. 6

First we find the average scale factor (A.S.F.) for the interval $[a, b]$.

$$
\begin{aligned}
(b-a) \times \text{A.S.F.} &= \frac{1}{3b+2} - \frac{1}{3a+2} \\
&= \frac{(3a+2) - (3b+2)}{(3b+2)(3a+2)} \\
&= \frac{3(a-b)}{(3b+2)(3a+2)} \\
&= \frac{-3(b-a)}{(3b+2)(3a+2)}.
\end{aligned}
$$

So the average scale factor is $-3/[(3b+2)(3a+2)]$. As b approaches a, from above or below, this gives $-3/(3a+2)^2$ as the derivative at a.

Hence $f'(a) = -3/(3a+2)^2$ and the derived function is $f': x \to -3/(3x+2)^2$.

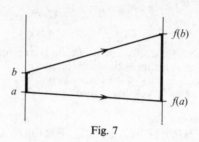

Fig. 7

In general the average scale factor is

$$\frac{f(b)-f(a)}{b-a}.$$

The derivative at a is the limiting value of this as b approaches a from above or below. This is written

$$f'(a) = \lim_{b \to a} \frac{f(b)-f(a)}{b-a}.$$

Finding a derived function by evaluating a limit is known as differentiating *from first principles*. Such a phrase is necessary because (as we have seen in Section 3.1 and Exercise D) we soon develop a number of rules and some expertise for differentiating functions which save us from always having to use the limiting process. Of course the derivatives of any new functions have to be found from first principles.

4.1 Alternative form for the derivative. Replacing b by $a+h$ in the definition of a derivative gives

$$f'(a) = \lim_{h \to 0} \frac{f(a+h)-f(a)}{h}.$$

This is sometimes more convenient than the form used in Example 5.

Example 6

Differentiate $f: x \to x^3$ from first principles.

$$f'(a) = \lim_{h \to 0} \frac{(a+h)^3-a^3}{h} = \lim_{h \to 0} \frac{a^3+3a^2h+3ah^2+h^3-a^3}{h}$$

$$= \lim_{h \to 0} (3a^2+3ah+h^2)$$

$$= 3a^2.$$

Hence $f'(x) = 3x^2$, proving the result given in Section 3.1.

98

Note that whichever form is used, it is necessary to simplify the average scale factor before attempting to proceed to the limit. Otherwise both numerator and denominator tend to zero, which is unhelpful since 0/0 is meaningless.

Exercise E

1. Differentiate the following from first principles.

(a) x^2,   (b) x^4,   (c) x,

(d) $1/x^2$,   (e) $1/(x+2)$,   (f) $\dfrac{x+3}{x+2}$.

2. By considering $f'(a)$ for $f: x \to x^n$ and $n = 1, 2, 3, 4$, suggest a possible formula for $f'(a)$ in terms of a and n. Does your formula work for $n = 5$?

3. Find from first principles the derived function of $f: x \to \sqrt{x}$.
(Note that $b-a$ may be replaced by $(\sqrt{b}-\sqrt{a})(\sqrt{b}+\sqrt{a})$.)
Find also the derived function of $g: x \to \sqrt[3]{x}$.

4. The functions f and g have derived functions f' and g'. If $p(x) = f(x)+g(x)$ and $q(x) = mf(x)$ where m is any real number, write down expressions for $p'(x)$ and $q'(x)$. Justify your answers.

5. GRADIENTS OF GRAPHS

So far in this chapter, we have used mapping diagrams to illustrate functions, and the derivative $f'(a)$ has been interpreted as the local scale factor at a for the mapping. But we might also use a graphical representation. What is then the interpretation of $f'(a)$?

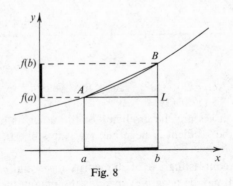

Fig. 8

Figure 8 shows that the average scale factor

$$\frac{f(b)-f(a)}{b-a} = \frac{LB}{AL},$$

and this is the gradient of the chord AB.

The limiting process for turning the average scale factor into a local scale factor, or derivative, at $x = a$ is equivalent simply to sliding B down the graph towards A so that the gradient of the chord AB approaches that of the tangent at A. So we conclude that $f'(a)$ is the gradient of the tangent at A.

In the O-level course, we associated rates of change with gradients of tangents of graphs. In the early part of this chapter we developed the link between rates of change and local scale factors of mapping diagrams. We could have inferred that derivatives are gradients of graphs, as demonstrated above.

In particular, velocities are gradients of displacement–time graphs and derivatives of functions mapping time to displacement. Similarly, accelerations are gradients of velocity–time graphs and derivatives of functions mapping time to velocity.

Example 7

The height of a stone thrown straight up is $20t - 5t^2$ metres after t seconds. Find its velocity (a) when $t = \frac{1}{2}$, (b) when $t = 3$, and interpret on a graph.

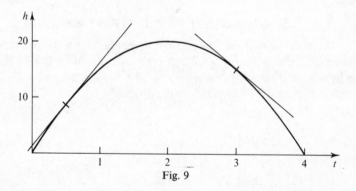

Fig. 9

Write $h = f(t) = 20t - 5t^2$. Then the velocity $v = f'(t) = 20 - 10t$. Hence $f'(\frac{1}{2}) = 15$ and $f'(3) = -10$.

These derivatives are the gradients of the tangents drawn in Figure 9. When $t = 3$ the gradient is negative, and the stone is falling with speed 10 m/s.

Notice our contrasting use of the words *speed* and *velocity*. Velocity is 'directed' and may be negative; speed is the magnitude of the velocity.

There is also possible confusion between *distance* and *displacement*. In the first 3 seconds, the stone moves a distance of 25 metres (20 metres upwards and 5 metres downwards); its displacement during this time interval is 15 metres, meaning that it is 15 metres above its starting point at the end of the interval.

100

*5.1   Intervals and endpoints. A small difficulty has been ignored so far. The average scale factor was introduced as the ratio of lengths of intervals, and this led to the formula

$$\frac{f(b)-f(a)}{b-a},$$

with the tacit assumption that both $f(b)-f(a)$ and $b-a$ were positive. We then took this formula as our definition of average scale factor, and allowed $f(b) < f(a)$ or $b < a$ or both. This gives us negative scale factors whenever the displacement from a to b along the number line is in the opposite direction to the displacement from $f(a)$ to $f(b)$. We are pleased to see that these negative scale factors match negative gradients on the corresponding graphs. But in such cases it is wrong to describe the average scale factor as the ratio of the *lengths* of intervals; lengths cannot be negative.

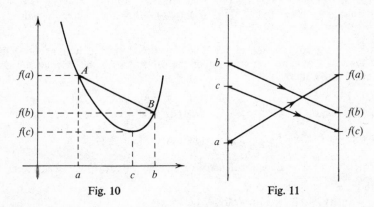

Fig. 10   Fig. 11

Moreover, Figures 10 and 11 show another situation in which our original interpretation of $(f(b)-f(a))/(b-a)$ does not apply. The set $\{x: a \leqslant x \leqslant b\}$ here maps onto the set $\{y: f(c) \leqslant y \leqslant f(a)\}$ so that the length of the image interval is quite different from $f(b)-f(a)$.

This situation arises in Example 7, where over the first 3 seconds the average velocity is $\frac{15}{3} = 5$ m/s, found by dividing the net displacement (*not* the total distance travelled) by the length of the time interval.

We stick to our formal definition of average scale factor. Its interpretation as the gradient of the chord of the graph is always correct, but with mapping diagrams we must bear in mind the special cases which may arise.

5.2   Alternative notation. We refer so frequently to $b-a$ and $f(b)-f(a)$ that it is convenient to write them simply as δx and δy; this is a shorthand for 'the increase in x' and 'the increase in y'. The average scale factor is then written $\dfrac{\delta y}{\delta x}$, and its limit is written $\dfrac{dy}{dx}$.

Similar symbols can be used whatever letters are chosen to denote the two variables. If $h = 20t - 5t^2$, as in Example 7, we may write

$$v = \frac{dh}{dt} = 20 - 10t.$$

This notation for the derivative is particularly useful in applications where several variables are involved. $\frac{dv}{dt}$ will represent the gradient of the $t \to v$ graph. The height h may be considered as a function of v; $\frac{dh}{dv}$ denotes the derivative of this function.

Exercise F

1. Draw the graph of the function $f: x \to x^2 - 4x$, and, by drawing tangents, find the gradient at (a) (0, 0), (b) (2, −4), (c) (4, 0). Also calculate the values of $f'(0), f'(2)$ and $f'(4)$.

2. Sketch the graph of each of the following functions and its tangent at the point named. Compare the gradient of the tangent with the calculated value of the derivative there.

(a) $f: x \to 3x^3$, $(\frac{1}{2}, \frac{3}{8})$; (b) $f: x \to \frac{1}{2}(x^3 + 1)$, (1, 1);

(c) $f: x \to 4/x$, (1, 4); (d) $f: x \to x^3 - 3x$, $(\pm 1, \mp 2)$;

(e) $f: x \to x^2 + 2x$, $(-1, -1)$; (f) $f: x \to x^2 + \dfrac{1}{x}$, (1, 2).

3. Write down expressions for dy/dx if (a) $y = x^3 - 10x^2$, (b) $y = 2x - \sqrt{x}$.

4. Find the value of dy/dx

(a) at (2, 18) on the graph of $y = 6x^2 - 7x + 8$,

(b) at (4, 28) on the graph of $y = x(x + 3)$.

5. At what points on the graphs of the following is the value of dy/dx equal to zero, and what is the significance of such points?

(a) $y = 3x^2 - 12x + 4$, (b) $y = 2x^3 - 6x^2$.

6. The distance, x metres, of a car from a camera which is filming it is given by $x = 100 - 15t$, where t is measured in seconds, and $0 \leqslant t \leqslant 6$. Write down the velocity of the car, and interpret your answer.

7. A stone is dropped over a cliff 80 metres high and the distance, s metres, fallen in the first t seconds is given by $s = 5t^2$. When does the stone land and at what speed is it then travelling? When is it travelling at 30 m/s?

8. For $10 \leqslant t \leqslant 500$, the velocity of a car t seconds after leaving a motorway service station is $(30 - 100/t)$ m/s. Find the velocity and acceleration when $t = 20$, and the acceleration when the velocity is 28 m/s.

9. The height in metres of a ball above the ground is given by $x = 15t - 5t^2$, where t is the time in seconds. What are its velocity and acceleration when $t = 0, 1, 1\frac{1}{2}, 2, 3$?

10. The volume V of a sphere is given by $V = \frac{4}{3}\pi r^3$, where r is the radius in cm. What is dV/dr when $r = 2$, and what does it represent, in words?

11. The total cost, in pounds, of producing n articles a week in a small factory is given by
$$f(n) = 50 + 5n - \tfrac{1}{100} n^2.$$
Calculate $f(26) - f(25)$ and compare with $f'(25)$.

$f'(n)$ is approximately the amount by which the total cost is increased if production is increased by one unit. It is called the *marginal cost*. Find the marginal cost when $n = 10$ and when $n = 30$.

12. The position of a ball t seconds after leaving the thrower's hand is given by $x = 3t$ and $y = 20t - 5t^2$, where x and y are the displacements (in metres) horizontally and vertically from the point of projection. Draw the graph of its path. Calculate dx/dt and dy/dt when $t = 0, 1, 2$. What do they tell you about the ball's velocity? When does it stop rising, and what is its greatest height?

6. MAXIMUM AND MINIMUM POINTS

Sketch the graph of $f: x \to 3x^2 - 10x + 14$. Start by finding the intercept on the y-axis, and considering the behaviour for large x (positive and negative).

The derived function $f': x \to 6x - 10$ gives us valuable extra information. What is $f'(0)$? What does this tell you about the graph? Find the gradient of the graph at $(2, 6)$. For what value of x is the gradient zero? Draw a new sketch graph incorporating all the information you now have. Then sketch the graph of $g: x \to 1 + 5x - 2x^2$, using the derived function to help find the highest point.

In graph sketching, we often wish to find the coordinates of points where the gradient is zero. These are called *stationary points*.

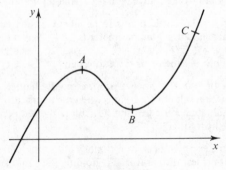

Fig. 12

For the graph of $y = x^3 - 6x^2 + 9x + 2$, drawn in Figure 12, A is called a *maximum point* and B a *minimum point*. Notice that a maximum point is only a local maximum; for example, the value of y is greater at C than at A.

103

Now gradients are here given by

$$\frac{dy}{dx} = 3x^2 - 12x + 9$$

$$= 3(x^2 - 4x + 3)$$

$$= 3(x-1)(x-3).$$

Show that A is the point $(1, 6)$ and find the coordinates of B.

Exercise G

1. For the function $f: x \to 4 + 6x - x^2$, find the value of a for which $f'(a) = 0$, and sketch the graph of $y = f(x)$.

2. Taking each of the following expressions in turn as $f(x)$, find the set of values for which $f'(x) = 0$; then sketch the graph of the function, showing the co-ordinates of all the stationary points.

(a) $x^2 + 10x$,   (b) $x^2 - 4x + 4$,

(c) $x^3 - 9x$,   (d) $2x^3 - 9x^2 + 12$,

(e) $x + 1/x$,   (f) $x - 6\sqrt{x}$,

(g) $x^4 - 8x^2 + 12$,   (h) $x^2 + 16/x$.

3. In the final example in Chapter 2 (about the record player factory), we had the function
$$T \to 3600 + 15T + 180/T = C.$$

What must T (the interval between orders) be in order to minimize the cost C of buying and storing the loudspeakers?

4. The cost $£C$ of producing n armchairs is about $£(100 + 5n + n^2)$. Write down the average cost, and the marginal cost, dC/dn. Minimize the average cost, and show that it is then equal to the marginal cost. Explain why this is so.

5. The area of a rectangular cattle pen is to be 64 square metres. If x metres is the length of one side, show that the perimeter is $2x + 128/x$ metres.
    Sketch the graph of $x \to 2x + 128/x$. —
    What is the minimum perimeter of the cattle pen? $-x = 8$.

6. With an audience of 100, the cinema proprietor of Chapter 2 made a profit of $(300 - 2400/T)$ pence on sales of ice creams when the temperature was T degrees, but paid out $(100 + 5T)$ pence for heating. Calculate the temperature that leads to the greatest overall profit.

7. A manufacturer of canned beef traditionally uses tins with approximately rectangular bases with sides in the ratio 2:1, holding 243 cm³ each. What height should the tins be to use as little metal as possible?

8. A manufacturer wishes to sell soup in cylindrical tins, each holding 128π cm³ of soup and using the minimum area of sheet metal. Show that if the radius is r cm, the total surface area of a tin is $2\pi(r^2 + 128/r)$ cm². Hence find the best dimensions for the tins.

9. Write down the derived function of $f: x \to x^3 - 6x^2 + 5$. f' is also a function and it too has a derived function. Write this down and denote it by f''.

Sketch the graphs of all three of these functions. For each graph say what is special about the point where $x = 2$.

10. For the following functions, sketch the graphs of f, f' and f''. Explain the significance with regard to the graph of f of the values of x for which $f''(x) = 0$, and of the sign of $f''(x)$ when $f'(x) = 0$.

(a) $f: x \to x^4 - 6x^2 + 9$;

(b) $f: x \to x^3 - 3/x$;

(c) $f: x \to x^3 - 3x^3 + 3x$.

6.1 Second derivatives. For the first few seconds, the displacement, in metres, of a school-built rocket is given by

$$s = t^3 - 3t^2,$$

where t is the time in seconds after ignition. Where is the rocket after 4 seconds, and how fast is it then travelling?

Fig. 13

Differentiation gives the velocity:

$$v = 3t^2 - 6t.$$

When $t = 4$, $s = 16$ and $v = 24$, representing a displacement of 16 m and a velocity of 24 m/s. Repeat the calculations for $t = 1$.

It seems that after release, the rocket starts by moving backwards down its ramp. The velocity is negative for the first 2 seconds.

Differentiating again, we get the rate of change of velocity, i.e. the acceleration:

$$a = 6t - 6.$$

It is interesting to compare the graphs of displacement, velocity and acceleration with time.

For the first second, the rocket has negative acceleration and moves backwards with increasing speed. The displacement–time graph has negative gradient and is getting steeper.

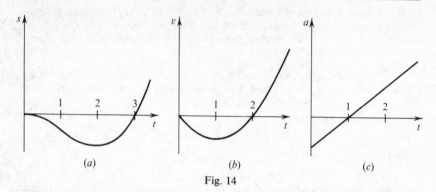

Fig. 14

For the next second, it continues to move backwards but the acceleration is positive so that the velocity is becoming less negative. Thereafter it has a positive velocity, passes its initial position after 3 seconds, and shoots off with rapidly increasing speed.

The acceleration gives the gradient of the velocity graph, and the velocity gives the gradient of the displacement graph. But can you say what the acceleration tells us about the displacement graph?

The acceleration was obtained by differentiating twice; it is a *second derivative*. The two alternative notations are as follows:

$$\text{Displacement} \qquad s = f(t).$$

$$\text{Velocity} \qquad v = \frac{ds}{dt} = f'(t).$$

$$\text{Acceleration} \quad a = \frac{dv}{dt} = \frac{d^2s}{dt^2} = f''(t).$$

In general, a second derivative $g''(a)$ measures the rate of change of the derived function g' at $x = a$. Thus, if $g''(a) > 0$, $g'(x)$ will be increasing around $x = a$, and the graph of g is *concave upwards*. Figure 15 shows the three possible shapes, depending upon whether $g'(a)$ is itself positive, negative or zero. If $g'(a) = 0$, the graph has a minimum point at $x = a$.

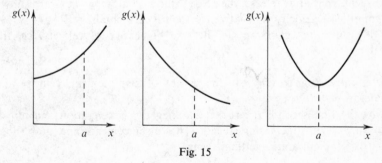

Fig. 15

In the same way, if $g''(a) < 0$, the gradient is decreasing and the graph of g is *concave downwards*. (See Figure 16.)

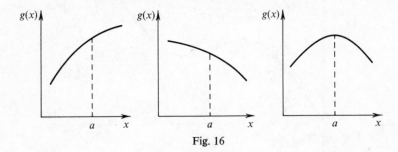

Fig. 16

Where a graph is neither concave upwards nor concave downwards (see Figure 17), the second derivative is zero, and we have a *point of inflexion*.

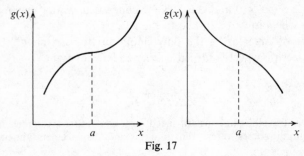

Fig. 17

Look back at Figure 14, and notice that for $t < 1$, the acceleration is negative and the displacement graph is concave downwards. For $t > 1$, the acceleration is positive and the displacement graph is concave upwards. There is a point of inflexion where $t = 1$.

Example 8

A Z-bend on a road is represented by the graph of $f: x \to x^3 - 6x^2 + 11x$, for $0 \leqslant x \leqslant 5$. Find the point of inflexion and explain its significance.

$$f(x) = x^3 - 6x^2 + 11x$$

$$\Rightarrow f'(x) = 3x^2 - 12x + 11$$

$$\Rightarrow f''(x) = 6x - 12.$$

For a point of inflexion, $f''(x) = 0$. The only point of inflexion occurs where $x = 2$; $f(2) = 6$ and $f'(2) = -1$ give the y-value and the gradient at this point.

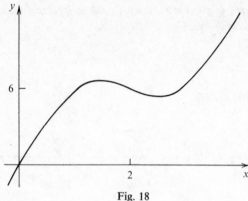

Fig. 18

When $x < 2$, $f''(x) < 0$ and the curve is concave downwards. Driving from $(0, 0)$ towards $(2, 6)$, the steering wheel is always turned to the right. When $x > 2$, $f''(x) > 0$ and the curve is concave upwards. Beyond $(2, 6)$ the steering wheel must be turned to the left.

The point of inflexion is the only point on this stretch of the road where the steering wheel is turned neither to left nor right.

Exercise H

1. A car, after travelling at constant speed for a while, first accelerates and then decelerates until it comes to rest. Illustrate this on a displacement–time graph.

2. Sketch graphs of the following, indicating clearly where d^2y/dx^2 is positive, zero, negative:

(a) $y = 9x^2 - x^3$,   (b) $y = x^4 - 6x^2$.

3. For each of the following, find $f(2), f'(2)$ and $f''(2)$; also sketch the portion of the graph near the point where $x = 2$.

(a) $f: x \to 5x - x^2$;   (b) $f: x \to x^3 - 10x^2$;

(c) $f: x \to x + 9/x$;   (d) $f: x \to 5x^4 - 2x^5 - 8x$.

4. Find the points of inflexion (if any) on the graphs of the following, and sketch the curves.

(a) $y = x^3$;   (b) $y = x^2 + 10x$;

(c) $y = x^3 - 3x + 1$;   (d) $y = x^2 - 1/x$;

(e) $y = x^3 + 3x - 4$;   (f) $y = x^4 - 6x^2 + 5$.

5. Describe the points on the graph of $y = f(x)$ where $x = b$ and $x = c$ given that $f'(b) = 0, f''(b) < 0, f'(c) = 0$ and $f''(c) > 0$.

6. Find the point of inflexion on the graph of $y = x^3 - 3x^2 + 3x$ and the gradient at this point. Sketch the curve.

7. Find the stationary points on the graphs of the following and state whether each is a maximum, minimum or point of inflexion.

(a) $y = x^3 + 2x^4$;   (b) $y = 3x^5 - 5x^3$;

(c) $y = x^2(x-6)^2$;   (d) $y = 4 - x - 9/x$.

Miscellaneous Exercise

1. For the function $f: x \to \log_{10} x$, find average scale factors approximately equal to $f'(3), f'(6)$ and $f'(9)$. Comment on your answers.

2. (i) Show that

$$\frac{b\sqrt{b} - a\sqrt{a}}{b-a} = \frac{b + \sqrt{ba} + a}{\sqrt{b} + \sqrt{a}},$$

and deduce the derivative at a of $f: x \to x\sqrt{x}$.

(ii) Sketch the graph of $y = x\sqrt{x} - 2\sqrt{x}$ and find the coordinates of the minimum point.

3. If $\dfrac{f(b) - f(a)}{b-a}$ does not tend to a limit as b tends to a, we say that f is not differentiable at a. Investigate which of the following are differentiable at 0, illustrating with sketch graphs.

(a) $f: x \to \sqrt[3]{x}$;   (b) $f: x \to x\sqrt{x}$;

(c) $f: x \to |x|$, where $|x|$, the modulus of x, is defined as x for $x \geqslant 0$, $-x$ for $x < 0$;

(d) $f: x \to |x + \frac{1}{2}|$.

4. Find the minimum values of

(a) $|x|$,   (b) $|x-3|$,

(c) $|x| + |x-3|$,   (d) $|x| + |x-3| + |2x-11|$.

Illustrate with sketch graphs.

5. For $f: x \to [x]$, where $[x]$ is the greatest integer less than or equal to x, state for what values of x there is no derivative. What is $f'(a)$ for other values of a?

6. Investigate, using average scale factors of small intervals, the nature of the derived function of $f: x \to \sin x°$.

7. Show, by considering the intersection of the two graphs, that $y - 9 = m(x-3)$ is tangent to $y = x^2$ if m is replaced by $f'(3)$, where f is the function $x \to x^2$.

Show further that for any other value of m, the line intersects the curve in two distinct points, and that these points become closer as m tends to 6.

8. An electrical circuit consists of a 12 volt battery with internal resistance 5 ohms and a variable resistance of R ohms. The power developed in the circuit is given by $I^2 R$ watts, where the current $I = 12/(R+5)$ amps. Find the value of R giving maximum power. (Take $x = R+5$ as variable.)

9. A beam 3 m long is supported at one end A, and at a point B 1 m from the other end. The *bending moment* M at a point x m from A is given by

$$M = 2x^2 - 3x \quad \text{when} \quad x \leqslant 2$$

and by

$$M = 2(3 - x)^2 \quad \text{when} \quad x \geqslant 2.$$

Find the point where the bending moment is numerically greatest (the point where the beam is most likely to break). (Sketch a graph.)

10. The height, in metres, of a rocket t minutes after blast-off is given by

$$h = \tfrac{1}{4}t(36 - 24t + 10t^2 - t^3).$$

Calculate the maximum velocity and maximum acceleration attained.

11. If $y = \sqrt{x}$, then $x = y^2$. Find, when $x = 16$ and $y = 4$, the values of

(a) $\dfrac{dy}{dx}$, (b) $\dfrac{dx}{dy}$, (c) $\dfrac{d^2y}{dx^2}$, (d) $\left(\dfrac{dy}{dx}\right)^2$, (e) $\dfrac{d^2x}{dy^2}$.

In this case, is it true that

(i) $\dfrac{dy}{dx} \times \dfrac{dx}{dy} = 1$; (ii) $\left(\dfrac{dy}{dx}\right)^2 = \dfrac{d^2y}{dx^2}$; (iii) $\dfrac{d^2y}{dx^2} \times \dfrac{d^2x}{dy^2} = 1$?

12. If $y = t^3$ and $x = t^2$, find an expression for y in terms of x only, and write down the values when $t = 5$ of

(a) $\dfrac{dx}{dt}$, (b) $\dfrac{dy}{dt}$, (c) $\dfrac{dy}{dx}$, (d) $\dfrac{d^2x}{dt^2}$, (e) $\dfrac{d^2y}{dt^2}$, (f) $\dfrac{d^2y}{dx^2}$.

In this case is it true that

(i) $\dfrac{dy}{dx} = \dfrac{dy}{dt} \div \dfrac{dx}{dt}$; (ii) $\dfrac{d^2y}{dx^2} = \dfrac{d^2y}{dt^2} \div \dfrac{d^2x}{dt^2}$?

SUMMARY

The average scale factor for the function f over the interval $[a, b]$ is

$$\frac{f(b) - f(a)}{b - a}.$$

On the graph of f, this is the gradient of the chord joining the points where $x = a$ and $x = b$.

If the average scale factor tends to a limit as b tends to a, this limit is called the local scale factor or derivative of f at a, and is written $f'(a)$. The derivative is the gradient of the tangent to the graph of f at the point where $x = a$.

An equivalent definition is

$$f'(a) = \lim_{h \to 0} \frac{f(a+h) - f(a)}{h}.$$

110

Notation

If $y = f(x)$, an alternative way of writing the derivative is $\dfrac{dy}{dx}$.

Derived functions

The set of derivatives of a function f defines a function f', the derived function. The derived functions of various simple functions are given on Page 96.

Second derivative

The derivative of the derived function is written $f''(x)$ or $\dfrac{d^2y}{dx^2}$. Where the second derivative is positive, the graph of the function is concave upwards; where it is negative, the graph is concave downwards. At a point of inflexion, $f''(x) = 0$ and the curve is neither concave upwards nor downwards.

Maxima, minima and points of inflexion

At a stationary point of a graph, the gradient is zero. This may be a maximum point, minimum point or a point of inflexion.

REVISION EXERCISES

1. FLOW CHARTS AND SEQUENCES

1. Draw a diagram of the path you would follow if you obeyed the instructions in Figure 1.

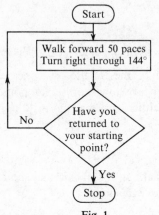

Fig. 1

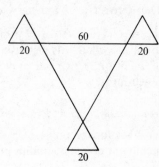

Fig. 2

Produce a similar flow chart to draw Figure 2, in which all the triangles are equilateral.

2. Write flow charts to produce the first 20 terms of sequences starting as follows:

(a) 8, 12, 18, 27;   (b) 2, 6, 12, 20;

(c) 20, 26, 32, 38;   (d) $\frac{2}{7}, \frac{2}{9}, \frac{-2}{11}, \frac{-2}{13}$;

(e) 3, 11, 35, 107.

3. For each of your sequences in Question 2, give (a) an inductive definition, (b) a formula for u_n.

4. Write down the first five terms of the sequences defined as follows; in (b) and (c) give your answers as fractions. Write flow charts to produce the first 12 terms of the sequences.

(a) $u_1 = 10$, $u_{k+1} = 2u_k - 9$ for all $k \in \mathbb{N}$;

(b) $u_1 = 3$, $u_{k+1} = \dfrac{u_k}{u_k + 1}$ for all $k \in \mathbb{N}$;

(c) $u_1 = 1$, $u_{k+1} = \dfrac{u_k + 2}{u_k + 1}$ for all $k \in \mathbb{N}$.

In (c) find the squares of the first 5 terms, and comment.

5. The flow charts of Figure 3 generate sequences. For each sequence give (a) the first 4 terms, (b) an inductive definition, (c) a formula for the nth term.

112

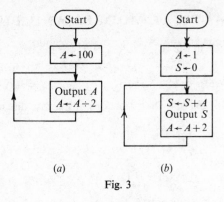

(a)   (b)

Fig. 3

6. Construct a flow chart for the calculation of

$$f(r) = 1^3 + 2^3 + 3^3 + \ldots + r^3,$$

for all values of r up to and including 15.

Tabulate the values contained in all the stores on the completion of each instruction, as far as $r = 3$.

7. Give an inductive definition of the following sequence and construct a flow chart that would generate it. (Notice the relation between the sum of two consecutive terms and the next.)

$$0, 1, 2, 6, 16, 44, 120, \ldots.$$

8. In Figure 4, $r(A, B)$ means 'the remainder when A is divided by B'. Do a complete dry run with $p = 144$ and $q = 60$.

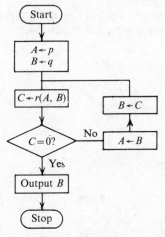

Fig. 4

If p and q are positive integers and $p > q$, suggest what is being calculated.

113

2. MATHEMATICAL MODELS AND FUNCTIONS

1. Given the functions $f: x \to 2x-3$, $g: x \to 4-3x$, find

$$f(5), \qquad gf(5), \qquad fg(5), \qquad fg(x), \qquad gf(x),$$
$$f^{-1}(5), \qquad g^{-1}(5), \qquad g^{-1}f^{-1}(x), \qquad f^{-1}g(x), \qquad g^{-1}f(x).$$

2. Find the ranges of the following functions, given that the domain of each is $\{x: 0 \leqslant x \leqslant 6\}$.

(a) $x \to \dfrac{12}{x+2}$; 　　　　(b) $x \to \tfrac{1}{3}x^3$; 　　　　(c) $x \to (x-2)^2$;

(d) $x \to |x-5|$; 　　　　(e) $x \to [2x]$.

3. Express in terms of the functions $f: x \to \sqrt{x}$, $g: x \to x+3$,

(a) $x \to \sqrt{(x+3)}$; 　　　　(b) $x \to \sqrt{x}+3$; 　　　　(c) $x \to \sqrt{(x-3)}$;

(d) $x \to \sqrt{x}+6$; 　　　　(e) $x \to x^4+3$.

Draw mapping diagrams for f and g separately, and composite mapping diagrams for the functions in (a), (b) and (c).

4. Find inverse functions of

(a) $x \to 7x+10$; 　　　　(b) $x \to \dfrac{6-8x}{3}$;

(c) $x \to \dfrac{1}{4x-5}$; 　　　　(d) $x \to 4-x^2$.

State any restrictions on the domains that you require.

5. A tropical rain gauge (see Figure 5) consists of four cylindrical sections of radius 2, 4, 6, 4 cm and each of height 4 cm. When the rainfall has been x cm, the depth of water in the gauge is y cm. The function $x \to y$ is denoted by f.

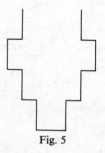

Fig. 5

(a) Express in words what $f(3)$ and $f^{-1}(6)$ represent, and find their values.
(b) What is the domain of f if the range is $\{y: 0 \leqslant y \leqslant 12\}$?
(c) Draw the graph of f and give an algebraic description of the function.
(d) Find the value of p for which $f(p) = p$.

114

6. Mrs Quintle's five children were born at exactly 2 year intervals. The average age of her children x years after the birth of the eldest was $f(x)$ years.

(a) Find $f(4\frac{1}{2})$, $f(5\frac{1}{2})$ and $f(6\frac{1}{2})$. How should $f(6)$ be defined?

(b) Find p and q if $f(p) = 0 \cdot 8$ and $f(q) = 6$.

(c) When was the average age $3 \cdot 2$ years, and when was it $4 \cdot 2$ years?

(d) Sketch the graph of the function f. Does f have an inverse function?

(e) Which of the following is an algebraic description of f if the domain is $\{x: 0 \leqslant x < 10\}$:

(i) $x \to x - \frac{1}{2}[x]$, (ii) $x \to x - [\frac{1}{2}x]$, (iii) $x \to x - 2[\frac{1}{4}x]$?

7. It is an 1100 km drive across France to my villa on the Riviera. In my old age I am not prepared to drive for more than 4 hours a day. It has been estimated that my car covers 10 km per litre of petrol at average speeds up to 60 km/h, and $(16 - \frac{1}{10}v)$ km per litre at v km/h where $60 \leqslant v \leqslant 100$. Form a mathematical model giving the total cost of my journey at various average speeds, stating the amounts you allocate for hotel accommodation, cost of meals and the price of petrol, and any other assumptions you make. What would you advise?

3. GRAPHS

1. Sketch the graphs of the following and explain how they are related.

(a) $y = x^3$; (b) $y = (x+1)^3$; (c) $y = (x-2)^3$;

(d) $y - 2 = x^3$; (e) $y + 1 = (x-5)^3$.

2. For the graphs of each of the following,

(i) discuss the behaviour for large x,

(ii) discuss the behaviour near asymptotes parallel to the y-axis,

(iii) give the coordinates of points where the graph cuts the axes,

(iv) give a complete sketch of the graph.

(a) $y = \dfrac{2x+1}{x-4}$; (b) $y = \dfrac{1}{x^2} - x$; (c) $y = \dfrac{x^2}{(x-1)(x+6)}$;

(d) $y = \dfrac{\sqrt{(x-2)}}{x-5}$; (e) $y = \dfrac{x^3}{2x-1}$.

3. (a) With the same axes, sketch the graphs of $y = \dfrac{1}{x-1}$ and $y = \dfrac{1}{x+1}$.

(b) Show that $\dfrac{x}{x^2-1} = \dfrac{1}{2}\left(\dfrac{1}{x-1} + \dfrac{1}{x+1}\right)$.

(c) Sketch the graph of $y = \dfrac{x}{x^2-1}$ and explain how to obtain it from the other two graphs.

4. State what is meant when a function is described as (i) even, (ii) odd. What is the relation between these algebraic properties and the symmetries of the corresponding graphs?

Determine whether the following functions are odd, even or neither.

(a) $x \to \dfrac{x}{1+x^2}$; (b) $x \to \dfrac{x^2}{1+x^2}$; (c) $x \to \dfrac{x^3}{1+x^2}$;

(d) $x \to \sqrt{(9-x^2)}$; (e) $x \to \sqrt{(8-x^3)}$; (f) $x \to [1+x^2]$;

(g) $x \to |2x+3|$; (h) $x \to |2x| + 3$.

115

5. Sketch the graphs of the functions in Question 4.

6. Give the equation of the image of the graph of $y = \sqrt{x}$ under each of the following transformations.

(a) The translation $\begin{pmatrix} 2 \\ 0 \end{pmatrix}$;   (b) the translation $\begin{pmatrix} -1 \\ 5 \end{pmatrix}$;

(c) reflection in Oy;   (d) reflection in Ox;

(e) reflection in $y = x$;

(f) enlargement with centre O and scale factor 4;

(g) an anticlockwise quarter turn about O.

Write down the image of (25, 5) under each of these transformations, and hence check your equations.

7. (a) Sketch the graph of $f: x \rightarrow \dfrac{10+3x}{3+x}$. Find a formula for the inverse function f^{-1} and sketch its graph.

(b) Repeat (a) for the function $g: x \rightarrow -\left(\dfrac{10+3x}{3+x}\right)$.

4. POLYNOMIALS AND ALGEBRAIC FRACTIONS

1. Express $P+Q$ and PQ as polynomials in descending order, given

(a) $P = x^3+6x^2-10$ and $Q = x+5$;

(b) $P = x^3+7x+2$ and $Q = x^2+4x-3$;

(c) $P = 2x^3-x^2+8x+2$ and $Q = 2x+1$.

In each part, find also the quotient and remainder when P is divided by Q.

2. Factorize

(a) $x^2-13x-48$,   (b) $6x^2+13x-33$,

(c) $16x^4-81$,   (d) x^3-125,

(e) $6x^2-29x+30$,   (f) $4x^3+12x^2-x-3$.

3. Find the quotient and remainder when x^4+3x^2-1 is divided by x^2+x+2.

4. (a) If $x-2$ is a factor of $x^3-6x^2+11x+k$, find the value of k. When k has this value, find the remaining factors.

(b) Divide $2x^4-9x^3+11x^2-4x-6$ by x^2-2x+2. Hence factorize completely this fourth degree polynomial.

5. Express $\dfrac{f(x+h)-f(x-h)}{2h}$ in its simplest form if

(a) $f(x) = x^3$;   (b) $f(x) = \dfrac{1}{x}$;   (c) $f(x) = x^2+4x-5$.

6. Express each of the following as a single fraction, with numerator and denominator fully factorized. Simplify as much as possible.

(a) $\dfrac{1}{(x+1)^2} - \dfrac{1}{x^2-1}$,   (b) $\dfrac{2x-3}{3x+2} - \dfrac{x-3}{x+2}$,

(c) $\dfrac{7}{3x-4}+\dfrac{5}{4-3x}$,

(d) $\dfrac{x^2-5x-6}{x^2-36}\div\dfrac{x+1}{x-3}$,

(e) $\dfrac{4x+8}{x^2+3x+4}\times\dfrac{x^2-16}{x^2+6x+8}$,

(f) $\dfrac{x^3+8}{x^3-8}\times\dfrac{x^2+4}{x^2-4}$.

7. Simplify the following, giving your answers in factors.

(a) $\tfrac{1}{4}(x+1)(x-2)(3x-4)-(x-1)(x-2)$,

(b) $\dfrac{n(n-1)(n-2)}{6}+\dfrac{n(n-1)}{2}$.

8. Work out $f(n+1)-f(n)$ where $f(x)=\dfrac{2x}{2x+1}$.

9. Show that $(x+2)$ is a factor of x^3-3x+2 and hence find the other factors. Sketch the graph of $x\to x^3-3x+2$. Write down the solution set of the inequality $x^3-3x+2\leqslant 0$.

5. DERIVATIVES AND DERIVED FUNCTIONS

1. Write down the derived functions for

(a) $f: x\to 3x^7-4x^4+6x^2-12x+7$;

(b) $f: x\to \sqrt{x}-1/\sqrt{x}$;

(c) $f: x\to (2x+3)^2$;

(d) $f: x\to (2x+3)/x$.

2. For each of the following functions, find $f(3)$, $f'(3)$ and $f''(3)$ and interpret your answers in terms of the graph of the function.

(a) $f: x\to 2-x^2+4x$;

(b) $f: x\to x^3-3x^2-9x$;

(c) $f: x\to \dfrac{27}{x}-x^2$;

(d) $f: x\to x^{\frac{1}{2}}+x^{-\frac{1}{2}}$.

3. State the two formulae for differentiation from first principles. Using either of these, find

(a) $f'(3)$ when $f(x)=4-x^2$;

(b) $f'(a)$ when $f(x)=\dfrac{1+x^2}{x}$;

(c) the derived function of $g: x\to\dfrac{1}{1+x^2}$.

4. A metal ball is being heated; at time t (in seconds) its radius is r cm and its temperature is θ °C.

If $r=3+0\cdot0002\theta$, show that the radius increases uniformly with the temperature.

If also $\theta=16+0\cdot4t$ for $0\leqslant t\leqslant 60$ and $\theta=200-9600/t$ for $t>60$, show that the radius is expanding at a rate of 8×10^{-5} cm/s when $t=30$ and find the rate of expansion when $t=100$ and when $t=200$.

5. (a) Find the coordinates of the point on the graph of $y=x^2-x+3$ where the tangent to the curve is parallel to the line $y=7x-2$.

(b) Show that the graph of $y=-x^2+x+3$ intersects the curve in (a) at right angles.

117

6. Find all the stationary points on the graphs of the following, and classify them as maxima, minima or points of inflexion.

(a) $y = x^4 - 18x^2$;   (b) $y = x + 5/x$;   (c) $y = x^4 + 8x^3 + 18x^2$.

7. A square sheet of metal of side 30 cm has four equal squares removed from the corners and the sides are then turned up to form an open box. Find the depth of the box if the volume is a maximum.

8. A piece of wire, 1 metre long, is to be bent to form the boundary of a shape consisting of a semicircle at one end of a rectangle. Find the necessary measurements in order to enclose the greatest possible area.

$$\text{Sin } 30 = \tfrac{1}{2} \quad \Big| \quad 60 = \tfrac{\sqrt{3}}{2} \quad \Big| \quad 45 = \tfrac{1}{\sqrt{2}}$$

$$\text{Cos } 30 = \tfrac{\sqrt{3}}{2} \quad \Big| \quad 60 = \tfrac{1}{2} \quad \Big| \quad 45 = \tfrac{1}{\sqrt{2}}$$

$$\text{Tan } 30 = \tfrac{1}{\sqrt{3}} \quad \Big| \quad 60 = \sqrt{3} \quad \Big| \quad 45 = 1$$

6

CIRCULAR FUNCTIONS

1. INTRODUCTION

In the last chapter, we developed a method of calculating some 'rate of change' functions. This involved the limiting process called differentiation and we shall now attempt to extend the process from algebraic to trigonometric functions.

Exercise A

1. The pedals of a child's bicycle are such that AO is 10 cm, and O is 20 cm above the ground. y cm is the height of pedal A above the road, t seconds after an instant when A is at its highest point. The pedal is rotating at a steady rate of one complete revolution every 2 seconds.

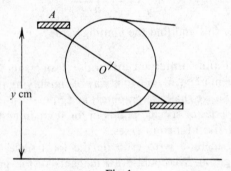

Fig. 1

(a) Find y when $t = 0, 0.5, 1, 1.5, 2$.
(b) Find y when $t = 0.1, 0.2, 0.3, 0.4$.
(c) Draw the graph of the function $t \rightarrow y$, taking values of t from 0 to 4.
(d) Estimate the rate of change of y when $t = 0.3, 0.6, 1.5, 3.2$.
(e) Can you suggest a formula which will connect t and y? Can you differentiate the formula to find the rate of change?

2. The depth, y metres, of water about the mean during spring tides at Liverpool is given approximately by $y = 5 \sin 30t°$, where t is the number of hours after midnight on a certain day. Draw a graph to represent this relation over a period of 36 hours. At what times do the high and low tides occur during this period? When is the depth increasing, decreasing at the fastest rate? Estimate the fastest rate of increase of depth. Can you answer any of these questions by differentiation?

1.1 The nature of the mathematical model. Both the questions in Exercise A deal with trigonometric functions. In the O-level course, the sine and cosine functions were used in the calculation of displacements associated with given angles. But now we find that we are concerned with situations of which angles are not always an essential part. Whenever we find a graph looking like a sine or cosine graph, we can employ these functions in our model, and use all our knowledge of them (including the appropriate pages of our tables).

In order to *calculate* rates of change in examples like these, we need to know the derived functions for $x \to \sin x°$ and $x \to \cos x°$.

1.2 To find the derived function. From the last chapter, we know that the derivative at any element a in the domain is defined as

$$\lim_{b \to a} \frac{f(b) - f(a)}{b - a} = f'(a).$$

Applying this definition to the sine function, the derivative at a is given as

$$\lim_{b \to a} \frac{\sin b° - \sin a°}{b - a}.$$

Can you simplify this and find the limiting value?

1.3 Graphical and numerical methods. Using algebraic methods, there does not seem to be any obvious way of simplifying the expression of the last section. So we shall use graphical and numerical ideas to estimate derivatives at a series of specific points in the domain and then try to see what form the derived function takes.

The graphical method is to estimate the local scale factor from the gradient of the graph. We could draw tangents to the graph at various points, measure their gradients and plot the new function

$$x \to \text{gradient at } x.$$

The shape of this second graph may suggest the form of the derived function. For instance, suppose that we did not know the derived function of $f: x \to x^3$. By measurement from Figure 2 we obtain the third row of the table of values below, and then Figure 3 suggests that $f'(x) = 3x^2$.

x	-3	-2	-1	0	1	2	3
$f(x)$	-27	-8	-1	0	1	8	27
Gradient at x	28	11·6	3·2	0	3·2	11·6	28

The numerical method is similar but more accurate. Instead of drawing tangents we estimate the local scale factors from the average scale factors over short intervals.

120

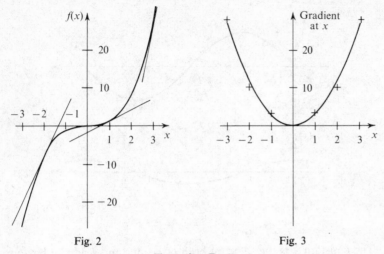

Fig. 2   Fig. 3

Exercise B

1. Draw carefully the graph of $f: x \to 4 - 2x^2$ over the domain $\{x: -2 \leqslant x \leqslant 2\}$. Measure the gradients at integral values of x and draw the 'gradient' graph as in Figure 3. Of what function is this the graph? Does this agree with the derived function obtained by differentiation?

2. Draw carefully the graph of $f: x \to \sin x°$ over the domain $\{x: 0 \leqslant x \leqslant 180\}$, taking values of x that are multiples of 30. Measure the gradients when $x = 0$, 30, 60, and draw the graph of the gradient function.

Use your knowledge of the sine function to extend the gradient graph. What do you think is the formula for the function f'?

3. (*a*) Find the average scale factors for $f: x \to \sin x°$ for the intervals $[-1, 1]$, $[9, 11]$, $[19, 21]$, ..., $[89, 91]$. Taking these average scale factors as estimates of $f'(0)$, $f'(10)$, ..., $f'(90)$, draw the graph of f' for the interval $[0, 90]$. Use the symmetries of the graph of f to extend the graph of f'.

(*b*) What is the greatest value of $f'(x)$? How accurately can this be obtained, using only four figure tables?

(*c*) Comment on the shape of the graph in (*a*), and suggest a formula for the function f'.

4. Investigate (along the lines of Question 3) the derived function of $x \to \cos x°$.

2. THE DERIVED FUNCTIONS

From your answers to the last exercise, the following perhaps unexpected result may have emerged.

If
$$f(x) = \sin x°, \quad \text{then} \quad f'(x) = k \cos x°.$$

The graphs are as shown in Fig. 4.

Also (see Exercise B, Question 4),

$$\text{if} \quad g(x) = \cos x°, \quad \text{then} \quad g'(x) = -k \sin x°.$$

121

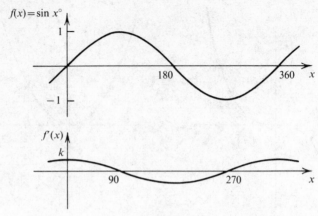

Fig. 4

The constant k is the same on both occasions and seems to be approximately equal to 0·017. It is possible to find the value of k accurately, by the following argument.

Assuming that $f(x) = \sin x°$ implies $f'(x) = k \cos x°$, then

$$f'(0) = k \cos 0° = k.$$

But we know that $f'(0)$, the gradient at the origin, is given by

$$\lim_{h \to 0} \frac{\sin h°}{h}.$$

So if we can find the value of this limit, we have the value of k.

One way of doing this is to consider the arc of the circle in Figure 5. Let $OP = 1$ and angle $PON = h°$. Then

(i) $\sin h° = PN$,

(ii) $\text{arc } PA = \dfrac{h}{360} \times 2\pi = \dfrac{\pi h}{180}$,

i.e. $h = \dfrac{180}{\pi} \times \text{arc } PA$.

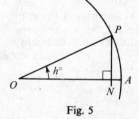

Fig. 5

From these results, $\dfrac{\sin h°}{h} = \dfrac{\pi}{180} \times \dfrac{PN}{\text{arc } PA}$.

From the diagram, it seems that as P approaches A and $h \to 0$, the lengths of PN and the arc PA become more and more nearly equal to each other so that

$$\lim_{h \to 0} \frac{PN}{\text{arc } PA} = 1.$$

If that is true, then

$$\lim_{h \to 0} \frac{\sin h°}{h} = 1 \times \frac{\pi}{180} = \frac{\pi}{180} = k.$$

Now $\pi/180 \approx 0·017453$, which confirms our previous value for k.

122

The results at the beginning of this section can now be written

$$f(x) = \sin x° \Rightarrow f'(x) = \frac{\pi}{180} \cos x°,$$

and

$$g(x) = \cos x° \Rightarrow g'(x) = -\frac{\pi}{180} \sin x°.$$

But notice that we are relying upon our assumptions (i) that the gradient functions really are sines and cosines, (ii) that the limiting value of $(\sin h°)/h$ is $\pi/180$ as $h \to 0$. A more formal proof of (i) will be given in Section 5.

2.1 Extension to more general functions. From the last section, we know, for example, that the derivative of $x \to \sin x°$ at $x = 60$ is

$$0·017453 \cos 60° = 0·017453 \times 0·5 = 0·008727.$$

Two remarks might be made. In the first place, we still cannot differentiate the function representing the movement of the tide at Liverpool which started the chapter, because it was of the form $x \to \sin 30x°$ and we do not yet know what to do with the 30. The second point is that every time we differentiate we have to introduce the factor $\pi/180$. It turns out that if we learn how to deal with the first problem, we can see how to reduce the inconvenience caused by the second. Work through Exercise C to find out the results we need.

Exercise C

1. Sketch the graph of $g: x \to \sin 2x°$, considering points at intervals of 15 over the domain $\{x: 0 \leqslant x \leqslant 180\}$. How does the greatest value of the gradient compare with the greatest value of the gradient of the graph of $f: x \to \sin x°$? What would be your estimate of K assuming that the gradient function is of the form

$$g': x \to K \cos 2x°?$$

Check by finding the average scale factor over the interval [29, 31] and comparing with $g'(30)$.

2. Repeat Question 1 for

(a) $y = 5 \sin x°$,   (b) $y = 5 \sin x° + 12$,

(c) $y = 5 \sin 2x° + 12$.

Sketch the graphs, deduce the derived functions and check for one particular element of the domain.

3. The formulae used in Questions 1 and 2 of Exercise A were

(1) $y = 20 + 10 \cos 180t°$;

(2) $y = 5 \sin 30t°$.

Using the results suggested by the first two questions of this exercise, write down the derived functions in both these cases. Check some of the answers obtained in Exercise A.

123

2.2 Scale factors. It is likely that the results you obtained from Exercise C were as follows:

if $p(x) = \sin 2x°$, then $p'(x) = 2 \times \dfrac{\pi}{180} \times \cos 2x°$;

if $q(x) = 5 \sin x°$, then $q'(x) = 5 \times \dfrac{\pi}{180} \times \cos x°$;

if $r(x) = 20 + 10 \cos 180x°$, then $r'(x) = -10 \times 180 \times \dfrac{\pi}{180} \times \sin 180x°$.

We should endeavour to see why the extra scale factors have to be included in differentiating these more complicated functions. The transformations which map the graph of $x \to \sin x°$ onto the graphs of p, q, r provide an explanation.

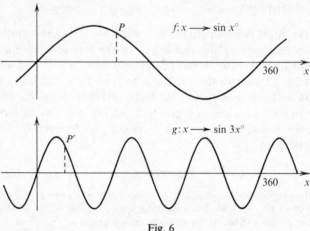

Fig. 6

The graph of $g: x \to \sin 3x°$ can be obtained from that of $f: x \to \sin x°$ by applying a stretch of $\frac{1}{3}$ parallel to Ox. The two graphs are shown in Figure 6. The point P (120, 0·87) on the graph of f corresponds to P' (40, 0·87) on the graph of g. It is clear that the gradient at P' is 3 times the gradient at P, and that the period of g is 120.

The derived function of g also has period 120, and is given by

$$g': x \to 3 \times \frac{\pi}{180} \cos 3x°.$$

Consider next the function $x \to 7 \sin 3x°$. Its graph is found by a further stretch, this time parallel to Oy. The gradient is now increased by a factor of 7. Sketch the graph to confirm this.

In general, $\quad f(x) = c \sin ax° \Rightarrow f'(x) = ca \times \dfrac{\pi}{180} \cos ax°,$

and a similar result holds for cosine functions.

124

3. RADIAN MEASURE

We now show how to eliminate the factor $\pi/180$ which has had to be introduced whenever we differentiate.

This factor is a consequence of the units in which we measure angles. Had we chosen 'mils', where 1000 mils $= 360°$, as has been suggested for a metric measure of angle, we should have a new sine function $x \to \sin x^m$.

Show (using tables) that $5 \to 0\cdot0314$ under this function. Sketch the graph of this function and describe the transformation mapping the graph of $\sin x°$ onto the graph of $\sin x^m$. If A and B are the points $(30, 0\cdot5)$ and $(36, 0\cdot588)$ on the graph of $\sin x°$, find the gradient of AB. Find also the coordinates of the corresponding points and the gradient of the corresponding chord on the graph of $\sin x^m$. Explain why

$$f(x) = \sin x^m \Rightarrow f'(x) = \frac{\pi}{500} \cos x^m.$$

Now that our attention is directed towards rates of change, a third unit and consequently another sine function proves more convenient. When mils were introduced, this corresponded to stretching the sine graph by a factor of $1000/360$ and reducing derivatives by a factor of $360/1000$.

We choose our new unit, the radian (written 1^c), in such a way that the graph of $x \to \sin x^c$ has gradient 1 where $x = 0$, and hence the derived function is $x \to \cos x^c$.

This requires a scale factor of $\pi/180$, in other words

$$1 \text{ degree} = \frac{\pi}{180} \text{ radians,}$$

or $$180 \text{ degrees} \approx 3\cdot142 \text{ radians.}$$

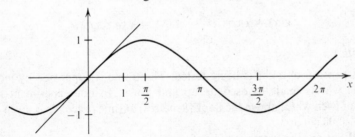

Fig. 7

Figure 7 shows part of the graphs of $x \to \sin x$ and $x \to x$. From now on, we shall use this sine function almost to the exclusion of all other sine functions, and for this reason we allow ourselves to drop the ^{c}. Notice that the degree symbol has been printed meticulously on every occasion earlier in the chapter when the other sine function was involved.

125

New cosine and tangent functions are introduced in the same way and tables of all three functions are printed in the S.M.P. *Advanced Tables* under the title 'Circular Functions'.

We must realize that these functions and also the previous trigonometric functions map real numbers onto real numbers. This is important when we use them for mathematical models in which angles may play no part. In Exercise A, where $y = 5 \sin 30t°$ described the height of tide, we chose to have t and y as numbers, the measures of the time and displacement in our chosen units. We can calculate that when $t = 2$, $y = 4.33$ and the derivative is 1·31. The units reappear when we wish to interpret these numbers as meaning that the height of tide at 02.00 was 4·33 metres above the mean level and rising at a rate of 1·31 metres per hour.

In future we shall prefer to express our models in terms of the new sine and cosine functions, largely because their derived functions are simple.

3.1 Summary. The introduction of radian measure, where $\pi^c = 180°$, leads to the definition of the circular functions $x \rightarrow \sin x$ and $x \rightarrow \cos x$. These are functions with domain and codomain the real numbers, and both functions have period 2π.

The limit as $x \rightarrow 0$ of $\dfrac{\sin x}{x}$ is 1.

It follows that $$f(x) = \sin x \Rightarrow f'(x) = \cos x,$$

and $$g(x) = \cos x \Rightarrow g'(x) = -\sin x.$$

The same reasoning as used in Section 2.2 shows that

$$f(x) = c \sin ax \Rightarrow f'(x) = ca \cos ax,$$

and $$g(x) = c \cos ax \Rightarrow g'(x) = -ca \sin ax.$$

Example 1

The suspension of a car is being tested. The frame is supported by jacks and the wheels made to oscillate up and down. In one experiment the height of each wheel above the floor (h metres) at time t seconds is given by $h = 1 + 0.08 \sin 5t$.

(a) What are the greatest and least heights?

(b) What is the period of the oscillation?

(c) Find the height, velocity and acceleration when $t = 0.1$.

(a) The greatest and least values for $\sin 5t$ are $+1$ and -1, so the greatest and least heights are 1·08 and 0·92 metres.

(b) The function $x \rightarrow \sin x$ has period 2π. The function $t \rightarrow \sin 5t$ has period $2\pi/5$, and this is therefore the period of the height function also.

126

(c) $h = 1 + 0.08 \sin 5t \Rightarrow \dfrac{dh}{dt} = 0.4 \cos 5t$

and $\qquad\qquad\qquad\qquad \dfrac{d^2h}{dt^2} = -2 \sin 5t.$

When $t = 0.1$,

$\qquad h = 1 + 0.08 \times 0.4794 \quad$ (from the circular function tables)

$\qquad\quad = 1.038.$

The velocity is given by dh/dt and the acceleration by d^2h/dt^2 and we find their values when $t = 0.1$ by substitution.

Exercise D

1. (a) Draw the graph of $f: x \to \sin x$ from $x = 0$ to $x = 1.5$ using the circular function tables. Extend the graph by using the given table of values.

x	2	2.5	3	3.5	4	4.5	5	5.5	6	6.5
$\sin x$	0.91	0.60	0.14	-0.35	-0.76	-0.98	-0.96	-0.71	-0.28	0.21

    (b) Mark the numbers $\frac{1}{2}\pi$, π, $\frac{3}{2}\pi$, 2π on the x-axis.
    (c) Write down the values of $\sin \frac{1}{2}\pi$, $\sin \frac{5}{6}\pi$, $\sin (-\frac{3}{2}\pi)$.
    (d) Find from your tables $f(0.3)$, $f'(0.3)$, $f(1.1)$, $f'(1.1)$.
Does your graph support these answers?
    (e) Write down the values of $f'(0)$ and $f'(\pi)$.

2. (a) Sketch the graph of $g: x \to \cos x$ for $-2\pi \leqslant x \leqslant 2\pi$.
    (b) Write down the values of $\cos \pi$, $\cos \frac{1}{3}\pi$, $\cos (-\frac{1}{2}\pi)$.
    (c) Simplify $\cos (\pi + x)$ and $\cos (\frac{1}{2}\pi - x)$.
    (d) Find $g'(0.3)$, $g'(0.6)$ and $g'(1.2)$.

3. Draw separate sketch graphs of $\cos x$, $\cos 2x$, $\cos (x - \frac{1}{3}\pi)$, and $\cos 2(x - \frac{1}{3}\pi)$. Mark clearly where they meet the x-axis.

4. Differentiate

    (a) $3 \cos x$,   (b) $\sin x + \cos x$,   (c) $2 \sin x + 5 \cos x$,

    (d) $\cos 3x$,   (e) $\sin 2x + \cos 5x$,   (f) $4 \sin 3x + 6 \cos x$.

5. The height of the water above a sand-bar t hours after noon on a certain day was x metres, where $x = 7 + 5 \sin \frac{1}{2}(t - 2)$.
    (a) What was the greatest depth of water, and what was the least depth at the bar?
    (b) When was high tide that afternoon?
    (c) How many hours elapsed between successive tides?
    (d) How fast was the water rising at 2 p.m., and at 4 p.m.?

6. A cube is oscillating in a vertical line at the end of a spring. Its height, y metres, above the floor at time t seconds is given by $y = 0.5 + 0.2 \sin 10t$.

(a) What are its greatest and least heights?

(b) What is the period of the oscillation?

(c) Find the height, velocity and acceleration when

$$t = 0.1, 0.3, 0.5.$$

7. (a) A body is oscillating so that its displacement x from its central position is given by $x = 2 \sin kt$, where t is the time from the beginning of the oscillation. What is the period of the oscillation when k has the following values: (i) 1, (ii) 2, (iii) $\frac{1}{2}$, (iv) 10?

(b) The frequency of an oscillation is defined as the number of complete oscillations per unit of time. The period T is therefore the reciprocal of the frequency f:

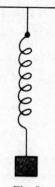

Fig. 8

$$T = \frac{1}{f}.$$

Write down the formulae for the position of the body in (a) for the following frequencies: (i) 1, (ii) 10, (iii) 200.

8. A tuning fork is oscillating with a frequency of 256 oscillations per second. What is the period? The formula for the displacement in millimetres of a tip of the tuning fork from its central position is given by

$$s = 0.4 \sin kt.$$

Find k. What are the displacements when t is 10 and 0.2? What is the maximum speed of the tip of the tuning fork? At what times is the acceleration zero?

9. A pendulum is pulled to one side and then released from rest. It completes one oscillation in 2 seconds. Its displacement (d cm) from the central position measured along the arc of motion is given by

$$d = 1.5 \cos kt.$$

(a) What is the value of k?

(b) What is the greatest displacement from the central position?

(c) What are the formulae for the velocity and acceleration at time t?

(d) At what times are the velocity and acceleration zero and at their maximum values?

10. Modify the equation of Question 6 so that the oscillations have period $\frac{1}{4}\pi$ seconds and y varies from 1.4 to 1.6. Find the speed when $y = 1.55$.

11. Justify the statement in the Summary of Section 3.1 that

$$\lim_{h \to 0} \left(\frac{\sin h}{h} \right) = 1,$$

(a) from the graph of $\sin x$;

(b) by repeating the working of Section 2 using radian measure.

Use your tables to find the values of h for which $\dfrac{\sin h}{h}$ is greater than 0.95.

128

4. ARC LENGTH AND THE AREA OF A SECTOR

The measure of one whole turn is 2π radians, and so if the angle POA in Figure 9 is θ radians,

$$\text{arc } AP = \frac{\theta}{2\pi} \times 2\pi r = r\theta,$$

and

$$\text{area of sector } POA = \frac{\theta}{2\pi} \times \pi r^2 = \tfrac{1}{2}r^2\theta.$$

An added advantage of radian measure is that these formulae are so simple.

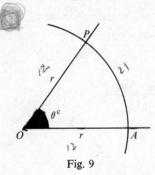

Fig. 9

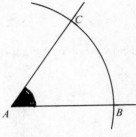

Fig. 10

Exercise E

1. Write down the measures in radians (using π) of : $135°, 270°, 300°, 390°, 720°, 765°, 67\tfrac{1}{2}°, 36°, 108°, 110°$.

2. Write down the measures in degrees of the angles whose radian measures are :

$$\tfrac{1}{8}\pi, \tfrac{-3}{10}\pi, \tfrac{7}{2}\pi, \tfrac{5}{6}\pi, \tfrac{11}{12}\pi, \tfrac{2}{3}\pi, 3\pi, \tfrac{9}{4}\pi, \tfrac{13}{18}\pi, \tfrac{27}{20}\pi.$$

3. What are $\cos 3\pi$, $\tan \tfrac{1}{4}\pi$, $\sin \tfrac{1}{3}\pi$, $\cos \tfrac{5}{6}\pi$?

4. Find a formula for the area of the segment cut off by a chord subtending an angle θ radians at the centre of a circle of radius r.

5. A sector is bounded by two radii of length 12 cm and an arc of length 21 cm. Find the angle and area of the sector.

6. The radian measure of an angle is, arc BC/AB (see Figure 10). This ratio is independent of the length of AB. In a similar way we can define a 'solid angle'; for example, the 'angle' subtended at my eye by the moon's disc, or by the image on a T.V. screen. What do you think this means, and can you suggest a way of measuring it?

7. What would be the formula for (*a*) the area of a 'cap', (*b*) the volume of a sector, of a sphere of radius r if a solid angle ω is subtended at the centre?

129

5. DIFFERENTIATION FROM FIRST PRINCIPLES

We have yet to establish by theoretical means the main result of this chapter, namely

$$\text{if } f(x) = \sin x, \text{ then } f'(x) = \cos x.$$

This was deferred because of the difficulty of simplifying

$$\frac{\sin b - \sin a}{b - a}.$$

In the last chapter, an alternative form for the derivative was given,

$$f'(a) = \lim_{h \to 0} \frac{f(a+h) - f(a)}{h},$$

and now we shall use another,

$$f'(a) = \lim_{h \to 0} \frac{f(a+h) - f(a-h)}{2h}.$$

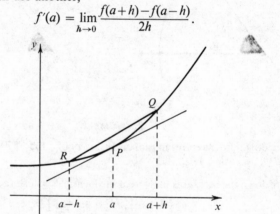

Fig. 11

This formula can be used when it is known that $f'(a)$ exists, and is equivalent to saying that as $h \to 0$ the gradient of the chord QR in Figure 11 tends to the gradient of the tangent at P.

The scheme we shall develop starts by reorganizing the numerator; this requires alternative formulae for $\sin(a+h)$ and $\sin(a-h)$. If you work through the next exercise you will develop these relations.

Exercise F

1. Figure 12 shows the unit square $OAUB$ and its image under a rotation about O. In each of the following examples the image of A is given. Find the image of B and hence write down the rotation matrix.

(a) A' is $(\frac{4}{5}, \frac{3}{5})$,　(b) A' is $(\frac{12}{13}, \frac{5}{13})$,　(c) A' is $(-\frac{3}{5}, \frac{4}{5})$,

(d) A' is $(\frac{15}{17}, -\frac{8}{17})$,　(e) A' is $(-\frac{7}{25}, -\frac{24}{25})$.

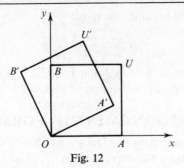

Fig. 12

2. Find the matrix representing the general rotation about O through an angle θ radians.

3. If $\mathbf{R}_a$ and $\mathbf{R}_b$ are the matrices of Question 1 parts (a) and (b), calculate $\mathbf{R}_a\mathbf{R}_b$ and $\mathbf{R}_b\mathbf{R}_a$. What do you find, and what transformation is represented by $\mathbf{R}_a\mathbf{R}_b$? Repeat for $\mathbf{R}_a\,\mathbf{R}_c$ and $\mathbf{R}_b\,\mathbf{R}_c$.

4. Write down the matrices representing rotation about the origin of θ, ϕ, and $\theta+\phi$ radians.

Form the product of the first two matrices and show that equating this with the third matrix leads to the formulae

$$\cos(\theta+\phi) = \cos\theta\cos\phi - \sin\theta\sin\phi,$$
$$\sin(\theta+\phi) = \sin\theta\cos\phi + \cos\theta\sin\phi.$$

5. Obtain expressions similar to those in Question 4 for $\cos(\theta-\phi)$ and $\sin(\theta-\phi)$ either by replacing ϕ by $-\phi$ or by combining the matrices for rotation through θ and $-\phi$.

6. Verify that $\qquad \sin(a+h) - \sin(a-h) = 2\sin h\cos a$

and develop the argument to show that

$$\lim_{h\to 0}\left(\frac{\sin(a+h) - \sin(a-h)}{2h}\right) = \cos a.$$

5.1   The derived functions obtained. In case the last question of Exercise F was not entirely clear, the working is set out below.

We have the results

$$\sin(a+h) = \sin a\cos h + \cos a\sin h, \quad \text{from Question 4,}$$

and $\qquad \sin(a-h) = \sin a\cos h - \cos a\sin h, \quad$ from Question 5.

So if $f(x) = \sin x$, then

$$f'(a) = \lim_{h\to 0}\frac{\sin(a+h) - \sin(a-h)}{2h}$$

$$= \lim_{h\to 0}\frac{2\cos a\sin h}{2h}$$

$$= \cos a\times\lim_{h\to 0}\frac{\sin h}{h}, \quad \text{since } \cos a \text{ does not vary with } h,$$

$$= \cos a.$$

131

The final step still requires the result

$$\lim_{h \to 0} \frac{\sin h}{h} = 1,$$

which was discussed in Section 3 and Exercise D, Question 11.

Use a similar argument to show that if $g(x) = \cos x$, then $g'(x) = -\sin x$.

6. TRIGONOMETRIC FORMULAE

The four formulae introduced in Questions 4 and 5 of Exercise F are called the *addition formulae*, and have great importance in work on periodic functions. They are set out in the Summary at the end of this chapter, and in the S.M.P. *Advanced Tables*. It is worth digressing for a while to learn how to use them and how to develop other related formulae.

Example 2

Show that $\sin^2 a = \frac{1}{2}(1 - \cos 2a)$.

Put $b = a$ in the addition formula

$$\cos (a+b) = \cos a \cos b - \sin a \sin b;$$

then $\cos 2a = \cos^2 a - \sin^2 a,$

where $\cos^2 a$ is written for $(\cos a)^2$ and $\sin^2 a$ for $(\sin a)^2$.

But we know that $\cos^2 a + \sin^2 a = 1,$

so $\cos 2a = 1 - 2\sin^2 a,$

$$\sin^2 a = \frac{1}{2}(1 - \cos 2a).$$

Example 3

Find a formula for $\tan (a+h)$ in terms of $\tan a$ and $\tan h$.

$$\tan (a+h) = \frac{\sin (a+h)}{\cos (a+h)} = \frac{\sin a \cos h + \cos a \sin h}{\cos a \cos h - \sin a \sin h}.$$

The required form is reached by dividing the top and bottom of the fraction by $\cos a \cos h$. This gives

$$\tan (a+h) = \frac{\tan a + \tan h}{1 - \tan a \tan h}.$$

Exercise G

1. Put $\phi = \theta$ in the formula for $\cos (\theta - \phi)$.

State the result and explain how it is related to Pythagoras's Theorem.

2. If $\theta = 0.4$, $\phi = 0.7$, evaluate *directly*

(a) $\sin \theta \cos \phi + \cos \theta \sin \phi$;   (b) $\cos \theta \cos \phi + \sin \theta \sin \phi$;

(c) $\cos^2 \theta + \sin^2 \theta$;   (d) $\cos^2 \theta - \sin^2 \theta$.

Verify your answers to (a), (b), (c) using the relevant formulae, and comment on your answer to (d).

132

3. If $\theta = 40$, $\phi = 70$, evaluate directly $\sin\theta° \cos\phi° + \cos\theta° \sin\phi°$ and check that your answer is the same as $\sin 110°$. Similarly, set and answer questions like $2(b)$, (c), (d) with these values for θ and ϕ.

4. ABC is an equilateral triangle of side 2 units, and AN is drawn perpendicular to BC. What are the lengths of BN and AN? Write down values for $\sin 30°$, $\cos 30°$, $\sin 60°$, $\cos 60°$ (using $\sqrt{3}$ if needed, without substituting a numerical value for it). Check the results of using these values in the addition formulae.

5. If $\theta + \phi = \frac{1}{2}\pi$, then $\cos\theta = \sin\phi$. What does $\sin\theta$ equal? What result does the formula for $\sin(\theta + \phi)$ give?

6. Use the addition formulae to simplify
$$\sin(\pi + \theta), \quad \sin(2\pi - \theta), \quad \cos(\tfrac{1}{2}\pi + \theta), \quad \cos(\pi - \theta).$$

7. If $0 < \theta < \frac{1}{2}\pi$, $0 < \phi < \frac{1}{2}\pi$, and $\sin\theta = \frac{3}{5}$, $\cos\phi = \frac{-8}{17}$, calculate $\cos\theta$ and $\sin\phi$. Calculate also $\sin(\theta + \phi)$, $\cos(\theta + \phi)$ and $\sin(\phi - \theta)$.

8. Find the possible values of $\sin\theta$ if $\cos\theta = -\frac{21}{29}$.

9. Put $\phi = \theta$ in the formulae for $\sin(\theta + \phi)$ and obtain an expression for $\sin 2\theta$ in terms of $\sin\theta$ and $\cos\theta$. Sketch the graphs of $\sin\theta$, $\cos\theta$ and $\sin 2\theta$ on the same axes.

10 Put $\phi = \theta$ in the formula for $\cos(\theta + \phi)$ and obtain an expression for $\cos 2\theta$ in terms of $\sin\theta$ and $\cos\theta$. Use the identity $\sin^2\theta + \cos^2\theta = 1$ to obtain $\cos 2\theta$ (a) in terms of $\sin\theta$ alone, and (b) in terms of $\cos\theta$ alone.

11. On the same axes, sketch the graphs of

   (a) $\cos 2\theta$, (b) $\cos 2\theta + 1$, (c) $\frac{1}{2}(\cos 2\theta + 1)$.

12. On the same axes, sketch the graphs of (a) $\cos\theta$, (b) $\cos^2\theta$. Compare with Question $11(c)$, and explain your answer.

13. Sketch the graph of $\sin^2\theta$, and show how it can be obtained from that of $\cos 2\theta$ by a combination of simple transformations.

14. What are the periods of $\sin^2\theta$, $\cos^2\theta$ and $\cos 2\theta$?

15. Show that $\sin 3\theta = 3\sin\theta - 4\sin^3\theta$; use the addition formula for $\sin(2\theta + \theta)$, and then the double angle formulae of Questions 9 and 10.
   Find a similar formula for $\cos 3\theta$ in terms of $\cos\theta$.

16. From the result of Example 3, deduce a formula for $\tan 2\theta$ in terms of $\tan\theta$. If $\tan\theta = \frac{1}{5}$, find $\tan 2\theta$ and $\tan 4\theta$.

17. Simplify:

   (a) $\sin 2A \cos A - \cos 2A \sin A$;

   (b) $\sin(P + Q) + \sin(P - Q)$;

   (c) $\cos(P - Q) + \cos(P + Q)$;

   (d) $\cos X \cos(X + Y) + \sin X \sin(X + Y)$;

   (e) $\sqrt{(1 - \sin^2 x)}$, $0 < x < \frac{1}{2}\pi$;

   (f) $\sqrt{(1 - \sin^2 x)}$, $\frac{1}{2}\pi < x < \pi$;

   (g) $\dfrac{\sin x}{\sqrt{(1 - \sin^2 x)}}$.

18. Given that
$$\sin 1 = 0{\cdot}8415, \ \cos 1 = 0{\cdot}5403, \ \sin 0{\cdot}01 = 0{\cdot}0100, \ \cos 0{\cdot}01 = 1{\cdot}0000$$
to four decimal places, calculate $\sin 1{\cdot}01$, $\cos 1{\cdot}01$, $\sin 1{\cdot}02$, $\cos 1{\cdot}02$. Check from the tables.

19. Given that $\sqrt{3} = 1{\cdot}7321$, $\sin 1° = 0{\cdot}0175$, $\cos 1° = 1{\cdot}0000$ to four decimal places, calculate $\sin 61°$ and $\cos 59°$ and check from the tables.

Miscellaneous Exercise

1. Explain why the graph of $y = \cos\left(\frac{1}{2}\pi - x\right)$ is the image of the graph of $y = \cos x$ under reflection in $x = \frac{1}{4}\pi$. Hence write $\cos\left(\frac{1}{2}\pi - x\right)$ in a simpler form.

2. What transformations map the graph of $y = \sin x$ onto the graphs of

   (a) $y = \sin(\pi + x)$,   (b) $y = \sin(2\pi - x)$,   (c) $y = \sin\left(\frac{1}{2}\pi + x\right)$?

Deduce simpler forms for these equations and check your answers by using the addition formulae.

3. When a violin string tuned to A is bowed, the displacement y mm of a particular point P on the string is given by $y = 0{\cdot}5 \sin 144000t°$.

   (a) Show that the period of the oscillations is $0{\cdot}0025$ seconds, and hence that the frequency of the musical note is 400 cycles/second.

   (b) Re-write the equation using the 'radian' sine function.

   (c) Find the greatest velocity of P during each oscillation.

4. In Figure 13, the circle has unit radius, and RP is parallel to Ox.

   (i) Using the fact that triangle OPQ is isosceles, show that

$$\text{angle } RQP = \left(a + \tfrac{1}{2}h\right) \text{ radians.}$$

   (ii) Show that

$$\frac{\sin(a+h) - \sin a}{h} = \frac{QR}{\text{arc } QP}$$
$$= \cos\left(a + \tfrac{1}{2}h\right) \times \frac{QP}{\text{arc } QP}.$$

   (iii) What result is obtained by letting h tend to 0?

   (iv) Draw Figure 13 again with $\frac{1}{2}\pi < a < \pi$. Re-consider (i), (ii) and (iii) for this diagram.

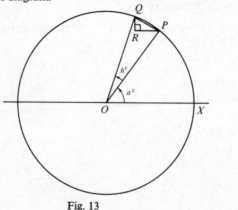

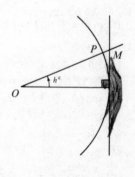

Fig. 13   Fig. 14

134

5. (i) Use Figure 14 and a method similar to that of Section 2 to show that

$$\lim_{h \to 0} \frac{\tan h}{h} = 1.$$

(ii) Use the result of Example 3 to write $\dfrac{\tan (a+h) - \tan a}{h}$ in an alternative form.

(iii) From (i) and (ii), deduce that if $f(x) = \tan x$, then $f'(a) = 1 + \tan^2 a$.

SUMMARY

The two circular functions we have studied are:
(i) $\theta \to \sin \theta$, an odd function with period 2π;
(ii) $\theta \to \cos \theta$, an even function with period 2π.
The domain and codomain are, in both cases, the real numbers.

The addition formulae

$$\sin (\theta + \phi) = \sin \theta \cos \phi + \cos \theta \sin \phi,$$

$$\cos (\theta + \phi) = \cos \theta \cos \phi - \sin \theta \sin \phi,$$

$$\sin (\theta - \phi) = \sin \theta \cos \phi - \cos \theta \sin \phi,$$

$$\cos (\theta - \phi) = \cos \theta \cos \phi + \sin \theta \sin \phi.$$

Similar formulae hold for $\sin (\theta \pm \phi)°$ and $\cos (\theta \pm \phi)°$.

Connection between the circular functions

$$\cos^2 \theta + \sin^2 \theta = 1; \quad \tan \theta = \frac{\sin \theta}{\cos \theta}.$$

Deductions from the addition formulae

$$\sin 2\theta = 2 \sin \theta \cos \theta,$$

$$\cos 2\theta = \cos^2 \theta - \sin^2 \theta = 2 \cos^2 \theta - 1 = 1 - 2 \sin^2 \theta,$$

$$\tan(\theta + \phi) = \frac{\tan \theta + \tan \phi}{1 - \tan \theta \tan \phi}, \quad \tan 2\theta = \frac{2 \tan \theta}{1 - \tan^2 \theta}.$$

Limits and derivatives

$$\lim_{x \to 0} \frac{\sin x}{x} = 1.$$

$$\frac{d}{dx}(\sin x) = \cos x, \quad \frac{d}{dx}(\cos x) = -\sin x.$$

$f: x \to \sin (ax+b)$ has derived function $f': x \to a \cos (ax+b)$ and period $2\pi/a$.

$g: x \to \cos (ax+b)$ has derived function $f': x \to -a \sin (ax+b)$ and period $2\pi/a$.

135

MATHEMATICS FOR THE MILLIONS!

$\dfrac{dy}{dx}$ of $\sin x = \cos x$

Circular measure

$$1 \text{ radian } = 180/\pi° = 57\cdot3° \text{ approximately.}$$

The arc of a circle of radius r which subtends an angle θ radians at the centre has length $r\theta$, and the area of the corresponding sector is $\frac{1}{2}r^2\theta$.

7

KINEMATICS

1. VECTORS

1.1 Introduction. Kinematics is the analysis of motion. It is not concerned with the causes or effects of motion. This chapter deals with displacement, velocity and acceleration and their expression in mathematical terms. For motion in a straight line, we know that velocity is defined as the rate of change of displacement and acceleration as the rate of change of velocity. But we live in a three dimensional world. How do we describe the motion of an aircraft circling an airfield while losing height? Are the definitions of velocity and acceleration still applicable?

Example 1

We shall begin by considering the position of a ship as shown on the radar screen at a coastguard station.

Let us suppose that the radar antenna rotates once every 30 seconds. The ship appears as a bright blip on the screen and the series of blips, a new one appearing approximately every 30 s, suggests the path taken by the ship.

In Figure 1, the points P_1 and P_2 represent successive blips on the screen.

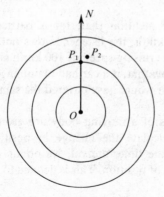

Fig. 1

The centre, O, of the screen represents the coastguard station and the concentric circles represent distances of 1, 2, 3 kilometres from the station.

137

We see that, initially, the ship is 2 km due north of the coastguard station. The second blip appears on the screen 30 seconds later and shows the ship's new position as 2·2 km on a bearing 006°. If the ship is moving at a constant speed in a straight line throughout the interval, in what direction is it travelling and at what speed?

From a scale diagram, the change in position from P_1 to P_2 can be found by measurement. This change in position can be represented by the *displacement vector* $\mathbf{P_1 P_2}$.

$\mathbf{P_1 P_2}$ represents a change in position of 0·3 km in a direction 051°. Since this change occurs in a little over 30 seconds, we conclude that the ship's velocity over the interval is about 36 km/h in the direction 051°.

1.2 Average velocity. Without the assumptions of constant speed and direction, would the two blips of Figure 1 have given us any information about the movement of the ship? Its speed could be increasing or decreasing and it may also be changing course.

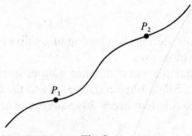

Fig. 2

Similarly, when we mention that, for a particular car journey, the *average speed* was 60 km/h, the listener knows nothing about the delays at traffic lights nor the cruising speed of 100 km/h along the dual carriageways. He can only know that, if a car had maintained a steady speed equal to our average speed, it would have covered the same distance in the same total time.

When two positions of a moving body are given, in two or three dimensions, we can calculate the change in position (the displacement vector). Dividing by the time interval, we obtain an expression for the average rate of change of position. This is defined to be the *average velocity* over the interval.

In Figure 2, if P_1 is the position at time t_1 and P_2 is the position at time t_2, the average velocity is

$$\frac{\mathbf{P_1 P_2}}{t_2 - t_1}.$$

1.3   Position vectors and vector subtraction. In Example 1, to describe a velocity in two dimensions, we gave its magnitude and direction. The magnitude, 36 km/h, would not be sufficient by itself. Velocities are vector quantities, and it will be no surprise that our description of motion in two and three dimensions will be couched in vector language.

We shall describe the position of an object by its *position vector*, the vector **r** from a fixed origin O to its present position P. For a moving body, **r** is a function of t, the time.

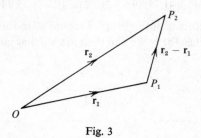

Fig. 3

Now vectors are added by the triangle law, and for Figure 3 this gives
$$\mathbf{r}_2 = \mathbf{r}_1 + \mathbf{P}_1\mathbf{P}_2.$$
It is natural to write $\mathbf{P}_1\mathbf{P}_2 = \mathbf{r}_2 - \mathbf{r}_1$, and then the average velocity for $t_1 \leqslant t \leqslant t_2$ may be written
$$\frac{\mathbf{r}_2 - \mathbf{r}_1}{t_2 - t_1}.$$

The equation $\mathbf{P}_1\mathbf{P}_2 = \mathbf{r}_2 - \mathbf{r}_1$ is, in effect, a definition of vector subtraction. We define the vector $\mathbf{c} - \mathbf{b}$ as the vector **a** for which $\mathbf{a} + \mathbf{b} = \mathbf{c}$ (see Figure 4). Notice that $\mathbf{c} - \mathbf{b} = \mathbf{c} + (-\mathbf{b})$; **a** can be found by drawing a vector **c**, and following it by a vector $(-\mathbf{b})$, the inverse of **b** (Figure 5). The arrows of Figure 4 are appropriately placed to show $(\mathbf{c} - \mathbf{b}) + \mathbf{b} = \mathbf{c}$.

Fig. 4   Fig. 5

In practice, we usually give vectors in component form, employing unit vectors in the directions of the coordinate axes as in the following example.

Example 2

The position of a certain aircraft is given in terms of t, the time in seconds after take-off. At time t, its height is $\frac{1}{20}t^3$ metres and it is vertically above a point on the ground which is $40t$ metres from the point of take-off.

We write this in vector form as

$$\mathbf{r} = 40t\mathbf{i} + \tfrac{1}{20}t^3\mathbf{j},$$

where $\mathbf{i}$ and $\mathbf{j}$ are horizontal and vertical unit vectors and the point of take-off is chosen as the origin.

Sketch the path for $0 \leqslant t \leqslant 10$, and find the average velocity for the time interval from $t = 4$ to $t = 6$.

t	0	2	4	6	8	10
$\mathbf{r}$	$0\mathbf{i}+0\mathbf{j}$	$80\mathbf{i}+0{\cdot}4\mathbf{j}$	$160\mathbf{i}+3{\cdot}2\mathbf{j}$	$240\mathbf{i}+10{\cdot}8\mathbf{j}$	$320\mathbf{i}+25{\cdot}6\mathbf{j}$	$400\mathbf{i}+50\mathbf{j}$

The position vectors at intervals of 2 seconds are found by substituting the appropriate values for t. We can then draw a diagram of the flight path (Figure 6).

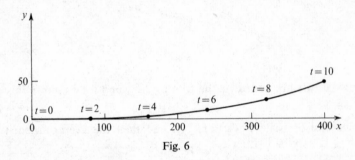

Fig. 6

The displacement vector from the position when $t = 4$ to that when $t = 6$ is given by

$$(240\mathbf{i} + 10{\cdot}8\mathbf{j}) - (160\mathbf{i} + 3{\cdot}2\mathbf{j}) = 80\mathbf{i} + 7{\cdot}6\mathbf{j},$$

and hence the average velocity (in m/s) for this 2 second interval is

$$\frac{80\mathbf{i} + 7{\cdot}6\mathbf{j}}{2} = 40\mathbf{i} + 3{\cdot}8\mathbf{j}.$$

Fig. 7

From Figure 7, we can calculate that this average velocity has magnitude 40·2 m/s and is at an angle of 5·4° to the horizontal.

Exercise A

1. (a) If $\mathbf{i}$ and $\mathbf{j}$ are unit vectors in the x and y directions, and $\mathbf{p} = 3\mathbf{i}+2\mathbf{j}$, $\mathbf{q} = 2\mathbf{i}-5\mathbf{j}$, show on a single diagram the vectors $\mathbf{p}, \mathbf{q}, -\mathbf{q}, \mathbf{p}+\mathbf{q}, \mathbf{p}-\mathbf{q}$.

(b) Repeat (a) taking $\mathbf{p}$ as a vector of 4 units due north and $\mathbf{q}$ as a vector of 3 units in the direction 060°.

2. A fielder throws a cricket ball to the wicketkeeper and its position relative to the point of projection, O, is given by

$$\mathbf{r} = 20t\mathbf{i} + (15t - 5t^2)\,\mathbf{j},$$

where $\mathbf{i}$, $\mathbf{j}$ are unit vectors along the horizontal and the upward vertical. Distances are in metres, times in seconds.

Find the position of the ball when $t = \frac{1}{2}$, 1, $1\frac{1}{2}$, 2, $2\frac{1}{2}$, 3. Draw a graph of its path and find the average velocity between $t = \frac{1}{2}$ and $t = 1$.

In each of Questions 3–8, in which $\mathbf{i}$ and $\mathbf{j}$ are unit vectors in the x and y directions,

(a) mark on a sketch graph the positions P_1 and P_2 at the given times,
(b) sketch the path followed between P_1 and P_2,
(c) show the displacement $\mathbf{P_1P_2}$ with a heavy line,
(d) state the average velocity (i) in vector form, (ii) by giving its magnitude and direction relative to the x-axis.

3. $\mathbf{r} = t^2\mathbf{i} + t\mathbf{j}$ between $t = 1$ and $t = 4$.

4. $\mathbf{r} = t^3\mathbf{i} + (t^2 - 3)\mathbf{j}$ between $t = 0$ and $t = 2$.

5. $\mathbf{r} = (2+t)\mathbf{i} + (1-t)\mathbf{j}$ between $t = 0$ and $t = 3$.   *velocity $= \dfrac{s}{t}$*

6. $\mathbf{r} = t^3(\mathbf{i} + \mathbf{j})$ between $t = 1$ and $t = 2$.

7. $\mathbf{r} = \mathbf{i} + t\mathbf{j}$ between $t = 0$ and $t = 5$.

8. $\mathbf{r} = t\mathbf{i} + \cos t\mathbf{j}$ between $t = 0$ and $t = \frac{1}{2}\pi$.

9. The useful, everyday idea of average speed can be defined as the total distance travelled divided by the time taken.

(a) If A and B are two towns 16 km apart as the crow flies but 24 km apart by road, and if the road journey takes 20 minutes, calculate the average speed and the magnitude of the average velocity.

(b) A man ran one complete circuit of a 400 m track in 50 s. Calculate his average speed and his average velocity.

(c) Describe circumstances under which the average speed and the magnitude of the average velocity are equal.

10. A fast motor launch passes 1 km due north of the coastguard station of Example 1 at time $t = 0$. The radar antenna rotates once every half minute and Figure 8 shows two successive blips on the screen. P_2 is $\frac{2}{5}$ km east and $\frac{1}{5}$ km north of P_1.

Show on a single diagram the position of the launch when $t = 0, \frac{1}{4}, \frac{1}{2}$ (t being measured in minutes) in each of the following cases:

(i) the launch is moving with constant velocity in the direction $\mathbf{P_1P_2}$;

(ii) the launch is moving on a parabolic path through P_1 and P_2 such that

$$x = \tfrac{4}{5}t, \quad y = 1 + \tfrac{4}{5}t^2,$$

where the x and y axes are in an easterly and northerly direction respectively;

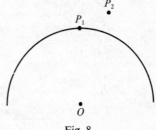

Fig. 8

141

(iii) the launch is moving on a path through P_1 and P_2 such that

$$x = \tfrac{2}{5}(1 - \cos \pi t), \quad y = 1 + \tfrac{1}{5} \sin \pi t.$$

In which of these three cases is the launch moving fastest at P_2?

11. (*a*) For the cricket ball of Question 2, in which $\mathbf{r} = 20t\mathbf{i} + (15t - 5t^2)\,\mathbf{j}$, find the position of the ball when $t = 0, \tfrac{1}{20}, \tfrac{1}{10}$. Estimate the direction of the ball when it leaves the point of projection. What is its speed at this instant?

(*b*) Find the displacement of the ball between $t = 1$ and $t = 1 + h$, and the average velocity in this interval. Can you say what the velocity of the ball is when $t = 1$?

12. An airliner, waiting to land at London Airport, moves anticlockwise on a horizontal circle of radius 5 km with centre above Epsom. If at zero time it is over Ashtead flying south-east and it moves through a quadrant in 1 minute, find by drawing and measurement the average velocity in the first (*a*) minute, (*b*) $\tfrac{1}{2}$ minute, (*c*) $\tfrac{1}{4}$ minute, (*d*) $\tfrac{1}{8}$ minute.

Estimate the velocity over Ashtead.

2. INSTANTANEOUS VELOCITY

If the radar antenna in Example 1 were able to rotate twice as fast, what extra information would this give us about the ship? We could now calculate its average velocity over 15 second intervals, and this would give us a clearer picture of its actual motion. The faster the antenna rotates, the shorter the time interval between blips and the greater our knowledge about the ship's movements. In fact, average velocities do not tell us very much about the motion of bodies unless the time intervals are relatively short.

Example 2 (cont.)

For the aircraft taking off, where $\mathbf{r} = 40t\mathbf{i} + \tfrac{1}{20}t^3\mathbf{j}$, we showed that the average velocity for $4 \leqslant t \leqslant 6$ is $40\mathbf{i} + 3\cdot 8\mathbf{j}$. This is a vector in the direction of **AD** in Figure 9 (which is greatly distorted).

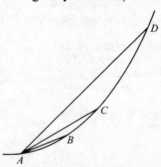

Fig. 9

Show that the average velocity for $4 \leqslant t \leqslant 4+h$ is $40\mathbf{i}+\frac{1}{20}(48+12h+h^2)\mathbf{j}$. Proceeding exactly as in Chapter 5 when differentiating from first principles, we see that as h tends to 0, the average velocity approaches $40\mathbf{i}+2\cdot4\mathbf{j}$.

Figure 9 shows the displacements $\mathbf{AD}$, $\mathbf{AC}$, $\mathbf{AB}$ over the intervals $[4, 6]$, $[4, 5]$, $[4, 4\frac{1}{2}]$ It is clear that the direction of the average velocity gets closer and closer to the direction of the tangent at A. The limit of the average velocity is the instantaneous velocity at $t = 4$, and this is a vector in the direction of the tangent to the path at this point.

2.1   The general result. Can you suggest a formula for the velocity $\mathbf{v}$ at time t if $\mathbf{r} = f(t)\mathbf{i}+g(t)\mathbf{j}$? This is easily obtained. For if $\mathbf{r} = \mathbf{r}_1$ when $t = a$ and $\mathbf{r} = \mathbf{r}_2$ when $t = b$, the average velocity for $a \leqslant t \leqslant b$ is

$$\frac{\mathbf{r}_2-\mathbf{r}_1}{b-a} = \frac{f(b)\mathbf{i}+g(b)\mathbf{j}-f(a)\mathbf{i}-g(a)\mathbf{j}}{b-a}$$

$$= \frac{f(b)-f(a)}{b-a}\mathbf{i}+\frac{g(b)-g(a)}{b-a}\mathbf{j}.$$

The limit as b tends to a is
$$f'(a)\mathbf{i}+g'(a)\mathbf{j}.$$

Hence $$\mathbf{v} = f'(t)\mathbf{i}+g'(t)\mathbf{j}.$$

The components of velocity are found by differentiating separately the components of the position vector.

Example 3

A man at a circus is fired from a cannon and lands in a tank of water. The muzzle of the gun and the surface of the water are both 2 metres above ground level. The equation of the trajectory is given by

$$\mathbf{r} = 20t\mathbf{i}+(10t-5t^2)\mathbf{j},$$

where $\mathbf{i}$ and $\mathbf{j}$ are horizontal and vertical unit vectors respectively, t is the number of seconds after projection and distances are measured in metres.

Give an expression for the velocity $\mathbf{v}$ at time t, and find the velocity at which the man hits the water.

The expression for the velocity is obtained immediately by differentiation

$$\mathbf{v} = 20\mathbf{i}+(10-10t)\mathbf{j}.$$

He lands in the tank when his vertical displacement since projection is zero, i.e. when $10t-5t^2 = 0$. This occurs when $t = 2$, and at this instant $\mathbf{v} = 20\mathbf{i}-10\mathbf{j}$ (see Figure 10).

At the highest point of the trajectory, the man passes through a paper hoop. How high is this, and what is the man's velocity at this point?

143

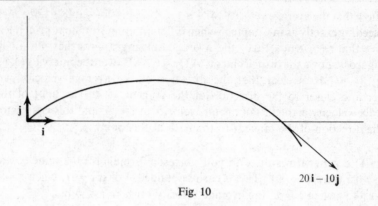

$$20\,\mathbf{i} - 10\,\mathbf{j}$$

Fig. 10

2.2 Velocity and speed. In one dimension we distinguish between velocity and speed. The sign of the velocity indicates the direction of motion; the speed cannot be negative. Likewise we appreciate that the total *displacement* during an interval may be different from the total *distance* travelled in that interval.

In two and three dimensions the distinctions are even clearer. Displacements and velocities are vectors; distances and speeds are scalars (i.e. just numbers). A velocity can be described by its components in specified directions or by its magnitude and direction. The magnitude of the velocity of a body is what we term its speed. In Example 3, the final velocity as the man lands is $20\mathbf{i} - 10\mathbf{j}$; his speed is $\sqrt{500}$. The units of both are metres per second. Notice that we have chosen to use the notation m/s (km/h, cm/s) rather than m s^{-1} (km h^{-1}, cm s^{-1}): both should be understood.

Exercise B

In Questions 1–5, **i** and **j** are fixed unit vectors at right angles. For each question,
  (*a*) find the position vectors when $t = 0, 1, 2, 3$ and sketch the path,
  (*b*) differentiate to find **v**,
  (*c*) find the velocities when $t = 0, 1, 2, 3$ and calculate their magnitudes and directions,
  (*d*) mark each velocity on the curve, using a straight line roughly proportional to the speed.

1. $\mathbf{r} = t^2\mathbf{i} + 3t\mathbf{j}.$ **2.** $\mathbf{r} = (t^2 - 2t)\mathbf{i} + (t^2 + 1)\,\mathbf{j}.$

3. $\mathbf{r} = (2 + t)\mathbf{i} + (3 - 2t)\,\mathbf{j}.$ **4.** $\mathbf{r} = \cos\left(\tfrac{1}{6}\pi t\right)\mathbf{i} + \sin\left(\tfrac{1}{6}\pi t\right)\mathbf{j}.$

5. $\mathbf{r} = t\mathbf{i} + \sin \pi t\,\mathbf{j}.$

In Questions 6–10 we shall use the convention that **e**, **n**, **u** are unit vectors in the directions east, north and vertically upward from a point H on level ground.

144

6. The position of an aircraft relative to the point H is given by

$$\mathbf{r} = 3\mathbf{u} + 1000t(\mathbf{n}+\mathbf{e});$$

t being measured in hours and the magnitudes of the vectors in kilometres. Describe its altitude, speed and course and calculate its distance from H five minutes after passing over H.

7. A dog and its master are exercising in a field. The position of the dog is given by

$$\mathbf{r} = (2t + 5 \sin \tfrac{1}{2}\pi t)\,\mathbf{n} + (t + 6 \sin \pi t)\,\mathbf{e},$$

and the position of the master by $\mathbf{r} = t(2\mathbf{n}+\mathbf{e})$.

How far apart are they and what are their velocities (in vector form) when $t = 1$ and $t = 10$?

8. A bullet has a velocity $\mathbf{v} = 700\mathbf{e} - 10t\mathbf{u}$.

Is the speed increasing or decreasing?

What is the new velocity if the bullet is deflected through $60°$ clockwise in the horizontal plane without loss of speed? (The vertical component remains unchanged.)

9. The position of a tracer shell fired from a ship is given by

$$\mathbf{r} = t(16\mathbf{n}+12\mathbf{e}) + (48t - 5t^2)\,\mathbf{u},$$

distances being measured in metres and time in seconds.

(i) Find the velocity of projection of the shell.

(ii) The shell has a time fuse which causes it to burst after 4 s. Find the height, velocity and distance from the ship of the tracer shell at this instant.

(iii) If the time fuse failed to ignite and the shell continued to move on the given path, find (a) the height of the highest point of the trajectory and (b) the distance that the shell lands from the ship.

10. (a) Given that $\mathbf{v} = \mathbf{e} + 3\mathbf{n}$ and $\mathbf{w} = 2\mathbf{e} - \mathbf{n}$, express the sum of these velocities in vector form and find the resulting speed and direction.

(b) Given that $\mathbf{v}$ is a velocity of 30 km/h in the direction due north, and $\mathbf{w}$ is a velocity of 20 km/h in the direction due east, express the sum $\mathbf{v} + 2\mathbf{w}$ in vector form and find the resulting speed and direction.

(c) Given that $\mathbf{v}$ is a velocity of 40 km/h in the direction north $30°$ west, and $\mathbf{w}$ is a velocity of 60 km/h in the direction north $60°$ east, express the sum of $\mathbf{v}$ and $\mathbf{w}$ in vector form and find the resulting speed and direction.

11. A ball is thrown and, at time t its position relative to the point of projection is given by

$$\mathbf{r} = 12t\mathbf{i} + (24t - 5t^2)\,\mathbf{j}.$$

Let $\mathbf{v}_1$ and $\mathbf{v}_2$ be the velocities at times t_1 and t_2. Find

$$\frac{\mathbf{v}_2 - \mathbf{v}_1}{t_2 - t_1}$$

(which we shall call the average acceleration) for

(a) $t_1 = 0$, $t_2 = 1$;   (b) $t_1 = 1$, $t_2 = 4$;   (c) $t_1 = \tfrac{1}{2}$, $t_2 = 3$.

What do you notice about the answers? What is the physical significance of this?

12. If $\mathbf{r} = (t^2+2t)\mathbf{i}+(t^3-1)\mathbf{j}$, find the average acceleration (as defined in Question 11) for the intervals

  (a) $1 \leqslant t \leqslant 3$;   (b) $1 \leqslant t \leqslant 1\frac{1}{2}$;   (c) $1 \leqslant t \leqslant 1+h$.
What do you conclude?

3. ACCELERATION

We have investigated the way in which average velocity tends to a limit and gives rise to instantaneous velocity as the time interval is reduced, and we discovered that the components of instantaneous velocity are obtained simply by differentiating the corresponding components of the position vector. Since velocity is itself a vector we can now pose some new questions:

  Is the change of *velocity* over a time interval worth investigating?

  If so, what happens as the time interval tends to zero?

  If a limit is reached, can this easily be obtained from the component forms of $\mathbf{r}$ and $\mathbf{v}$?

  In one dimension, you will have encountered the concept of rate of change of speed and given it a name, acceleration. In more general motion, we start by defining *average acceleration* over a time interval to be

$$\frac{\text{change in velocity}}{\text{length of time interval}}.$$

  The units are those of velocity divided by the units of time and typical ones are: km/h per second (km h^{-1} s^{-1}) and m/s per second (m/s^2 or ms^{-2}).

  What do you expect the formula for the acceleration at time t to be, given $\mathbf{r} = f(t)\mathbf{i}+g(t)\mathbf{j}$ and hence $\mathbf{v} = f'(t)\mathbf{i}+g'(t)\mathbf{j}$?

Example 4

Find the average acceleration of the aircraft of Example 2 over the time intervals (i) 4 to 6 seconds, (ii) 4 to $4+h$ seconds.

  What happens to this average acceleration as the length of the interval near 4 is made very small?

  The position of the aircraft on the flight path is given by

$$\mathbf{r} = 40t\mathbf{i}+\tfrac{1}{20}t^3\mathbf{j}.$$

Differentiating, we get $\mathbf{v} = 40\mathbf{i}+\tfrac{3}{20}t^2\mathbf{j}.$

  (i) When $t = 6$, $\mathbf{v} = 40\mathbf{i}+5\cdot4\mathbf{j}.$
    When $t = 4$, $\mathbf{v} = 40\mathbf{i}+2\cdot4\mathbf{j}.$
Change in velocity $= 3\mathbf{j}$. Average acceleration $= \tfrac{3}{2}\mathbf{j}$.

  (ii) Show that for the interval from 4 to $4+h$ seconds, the average acceleration is

$$\frac{24+3h}{20}\mathbf{j}.$$

146

As h tends to zero, the average acceleration tends to 1·2**j**.

This example leads us to the conclusion that the average acceleration tends to a limit. This limit is the instantaneous rate of change of velocity (*instantaneous acceleration*) at $t = 4$. Furthermore, we see that its components are obtainable from **v** by differentiation:

$$\mathbf{v} = 40\mathbf{i} + \tfrac{3}{20}t^2\mathbf{j} \;\Rightarrow\; \mathbf{a} = 0\mathbf{i} + \tfrac{3}{10}t\mathbf{j},$$

giving $\mathbf{a} = 1\cdot2\mathbf{j}$ when $t = 4$.

We have, in general, that the acceleration **a** of an object with velocity **v** is defined to be the rate of change of **v**, and the components of acceleration are obtained from the corresponding components of **v** by differentiation.

$$\mathbf{r} = f(t)\mathbf{i} + g(t)\mathbf{j} \;\Rightarrow\; \mathbf{v} = f'(t)\mathbf{i} + g'(t)\mathbf{j} \;\Rightarrow\; \mathbf{a} = f''(t)\mathbf{i} + g''(t)\mathbf{j}.$$

This result can be reached formally exactly as in Section 2·1.

Fig. 11

In calculating an average acceleration, the change in velocity can be found from a vector triangle. Figure 11 displays the vectors of (i) in this way.

Example 5

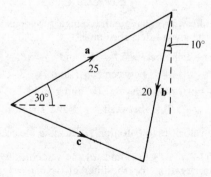

Fig. 12

A stone thrown at 25 m/s at an angle of 30° above the horizontal experiences an average acceleration of 10 m/s² in a direction 10° (backwards) from the downward vertical during the first 2 seconds. What is its velocity after 2 seconds?

The vector **a** in Figure 12 represents the original velocity and **b** the change in velocity in 2 s, of magnitude 2×10 m/s. The final velocity is therefore represented by $\mathbf{c} (= \mathbf{a} + \mathbf{b})$ and is 19·6 m/s at 21·6° below the horizontal.

3.1 Alternative notation. If $\mathbf{r} = f(t)\mathbf{i} + g(t)\mathbf{j}$, we may write $x = f(t)$ and $y = g(t)$. Then

$$\mathbf{v} = \frac{dx}{dt}\mathbf{i} + \frac{dy}{dt}\mathbf{j}.$$

Newton invented a convenient notation, called the 'dot' notation, for derivatives of functions of time and we will use it here, writing $\dot{x}$ for dx/dt, $\ddot{x}$ for d^2x/dt^2, etc.

Now
$$\mathbf{v} = \dot{x}\mathbf{i} + \dot{y}\mathbf{j} \quad \text{and} \quad \mathbf{a} = \ddot{x}\mathbf{i} + \ddot{y}\mathbf{j}.$$

Moreover, we shall write

$$\mathbf{v} = \dot{\mathbf{r}} \quad \text{and} \quad \mathbf{a} = \dot{\mathbf{v}} = \ddot{\mathbf{r}}.$$

So far in this chapter we have used unit vectors whenever describing vectors in component form. You will be familiar also, from the O-level course, with the column vector notation. In this,

$$\mathbf{r} = \begin{pmatrix} x \\ y \end{pmatrix}, \quad \mathbf{v} = \begin{pmatrix} \dot{x} \\ \dot{y} \end{pmatrix}, \quad \mathbf{a} = \begin{pmatrix} \ddot{x} \\ \ddot{y} \end{pmatrix}.$$

The two notations for vectors in component form are interchangeable, and we shall use whichever is the more convenient.

Exercise C

1. In each of the following, calculate the change in velocity and hence the average acceleration over the given interval of time.

(a) $\mathbf{v} = (1 + t^2)\mathbf{i} + 2t^2\mathbf{j}$ between $t = 2$ and $t = 3$.

(b) $\mathbf{v} = t^3\mathbf{i} + (t^2 - 3t + 2)\mathbf{j}$ between $t = 1$ and $t = 3$.

(c) $\mathbf{v} = \cos t\mathbf{i} + \sin t\mathbf{j}$ between $t = 0$ and $t = \frac{1}{2}$.

(d) $\mathbf{v} = 10t\mathbf{i} + (15t - 5t^2)\mathbf{j}$ between $t = 1$ and $t = 4$.

2. For each of the velocities in Question 1, calculate the acceleration when $t = 0$.

3. If $\mathbf{r} = (t^3 - 4t^2)\mathbf{i} + (t^2 + t + 5)\mathbf{j}$, find (a) the velocities when $t = 1$ and $t = 3$, (b) the average acceleration for the interval from $t = 1$ to $t = 3$, and (c) the instantaneous accelerations when $t = 1$, $t = 2$ and $t = 3$.

4. A model aircraft is flying at 10 m/s in a horizontal circle of radius 15 m. Draw a vector triangle to find the change in velocity in the interval in which its velocity changes direction from 000° to 030°, and hence find the average acceleration. In what direction would you expect its acceleration to be at the instant when it is flying in the direction 000°?

5. A stone thrown horizontally with a speed of 25 m/s over a cliff edge experiences a constant downwards acceleration of 10 m/s². What is its velocity after $\frac{1}{2}$ s, 1 s, 2 s, 10 s?

6. A jet of water issues at 20 m/s at an upward angle of 70° to the horizontal. If each particle of water has a downward acceleration of 10 m/s², find by drawing its velocity after $1\frac{1}{2}$ seconds. In what direction is such a particle moving at the highest point of its path? How long does it take to reach this point, and what is its speed then?

7. An electron in a television tube leaves the cathode with a speed of 8×10^6 m/s and passes through an electric field which gives it an acceleration of 2×10^{15} m/s² at right angles to its original direction for a period of 3×10^{-9} s. What is its final speed and through what angle has it been deflected?

8. What is the average acceleration of a cricket ball, moving in a horizontal plane, if its direction of motion is changed through an angle of 120° in $\frac{1}{20}$ s and its speed is increased from 17 m/s to 20 m/s? In approximately what direction do you think the batsman played the ball?

9. The position of an electron is given by $\mathbf{r} = (t^2 - 7)\,\mathbf{i} + t^3\mathbf{j}$. Find the acceleration when it is moving parallel to the vector $\mathbf{i} + \mathbf{j}$.

10. Find, in terms of the time t, the magnitude and direction of the velocity and acceleration of the particle whose path is given by $x = \cos t$, $y = 1 + \sin t$ and state any obvious relation between the velocity and acceleration. What sort of path do you think it is?

11. The position of a particle is given by

$$\mathbf{r} = \begin{pmatrix} t^3 - 12t - 11 \\ 2t^3 + 9t^2 - 60t \end{pmatrix}.$$

Find at what time its velocity is zero and its position and acceleration at this instant.

4. POSITIONS, PATHS AND PARTICLES

Vector equations have been used to describe the paths of particles in the earlier sections of this chapter. In this section we work through two examples in which the paths of particles are sketched and their velocities at selected points represented on the diagram. A velocity will be shown in a diagram by a line segment proportional to its magnitude and marked with a single arrow. An acceleration is similarly represented but the marking will consist of double arrowheads.

It is hoped that practice of this sort will give the reader a 'feel' for the motion of particles and an appreciation of the relationships between position, velocity and acceleration for a variety of different paths.

Example 6

Sketch the path given by $\mathbf{r} = 4t^2\mathbf{i} + t^3\mathbf{j}$ and show the velocities and accelerations at $t = 0, 1, 2$, on your diagram.

Differentiation of $\mathbf{r}$ gives $\mathbf{v} = 8t\mathbf{i} + 3t^2\mathbf{j}$ and $\mathbf{a} = 8\mathbf{i} + 6t\mathbf{j}$. The vectors are most easily written in column form.

Time	Position	Velocity	Acceleration.
0	$\begin{pmatrix} 4t^2 \\ t^3 \end{pmatrix} = \begin{pmatrix} 0 \\ 0 \end{pmatrix}$	$\begin{pmatrix} 8t \\ 3t^2 \end{pmatrix} = \begin{pmatrix} 0 \\ 0 \end{pmatrix}$	$\begin{pmatrix} 8 \\ 6t \end{pmatrix} = \begin{pmatrix} 8 \\ 0 \end{pmatrix}$
1	$\begin{pmatrix} 4 \\ 1 \end{pmatrix}$	$\begin{pmatrix} 8 \\ 3 \end{pmatrix}$	$\begin{pmatrix} 8 \\ 6 \end{pmatrix}$
2	$\begin{pmatrix} 16 \\ 8 \end{pmatrix}$	$\begin{pmatrix} 16 \\ 12 \end{pmatrix}$	$\begin{pmatrix} 8 \\ 12 \end{pmatrix}$

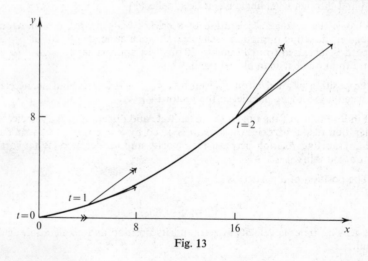

Fig. 13

The path is sketched from $t = 0$ to 2 in Figure 13 and velocities and accelerations have been marked on a scale of $\frac{1}{2}$ with respect to distance. The directions of the acceleration vectors indicate that the particle's speed is increasing and that the path is curving to the left.

Example 7

A particle moves in a plane so that its Cartesian coordinates at time t are $x = \sin 2t$, $y = \cos t$. Discuss the motion.

The velocity and acceleration components are:

$$\dot{x} = 2\cos 2t, \quad \dot{y} = -\sin t,$$
$$\ddot{x} = -4\sin 2t, \quad \ddot{y} = -\cos t.$$

The following table gives the components of the position, velocity and acceleration vectors at a succession of times.

t		$\mathbf{r}$	$\mathbf{v}$	$\mathbf{a}$
0	A	$\begin{pmatrix}0\\1\end{pmatrix}$	$\begin{pmatrix}2\\0\end{pmatrix}$	$\begin{pmatrix}0\\-1\end{pmatrix}$
$\frac{1}{6}\pi$	B	$\begin{pmatrix}\frac{1}{2}\sqrt{3}\\\frac{1}{2}\sqrt{3}\end{pmatrix}$	$\begin{pmatrix}1\\-\frac{1}{2}\end{pmatrix}$	$\begin{pmatrix}-2\sqrt{3}\\-\frac{1}{2}\sqrt{3}\end{pmatrix}$
$\frac{1}{4}\pi$	C	$\begin{pmatrix}1\\1/\sqrt{2}\end{pmatrix}$	$\begin{pmatrix}0\\-1/\sqrt{2}\end{pmatrix}$	$\begin{pmatrix}-4\\-1/\sqrt{2}\end{pmatrix}$
$\frac{1}{3}\pi$	D	$\begin{pmatrix}\frac{1}{2}\sqrt{3}\\\frac{1}{2}\end{pmatrix}$	$\begin{pmatrix}-1\\-\frac{1}{2}\sqrt{3}\end{pmatrix}$	$\begin{pmatrix}-2\sqrt{3}\\-\frac{1}{2}\end{pmatrix}$
$\frac{1}{2}\pi$	E	$\begin{pmatrix}0\\0\end{pmatrix}$	$\begin{pmatrix}-2\\-1\end{pmatrix}$	$\begin{pmatrix}0\\0\end{pmatrix}$

When these positions, together with other positions for times between $\frac{1}{2}\pi$ and 2π are plotted, the path of the particle is as shown in Figure 14. The velocities and accelerations at these points are represented by line segments proportional to their magnitude.

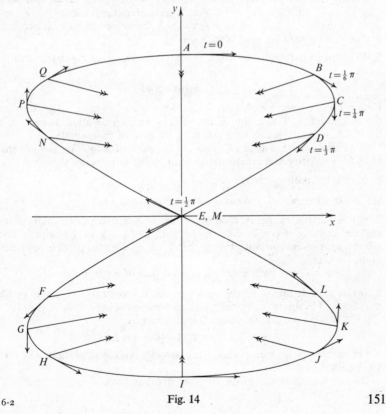

Fig. 14

From Q (at top left) the speed increases to A, where the acceleration is at right angles to the velocity; then decreases to a minimum somewhere between B and C, where again the acceleration and velocity are perpendicular and where the inward acceleration is large so that the turn is sharp; then increases to a maximum at E, where there is no acceleration; and similarly over the other sections of the path. A complete cycle takes 2π units of time.

Exercise D

1. A particle moves so that its position at time t is given by $x = 8t$, $y = 8t - t^2$. Find the velocity and acceleration components when $t = 1$, 4 and 7, and hence by drawing or calculation the magnitude and direction of the velocity and acceleration at each of these times. Show these velocities and accelerations on a sketch of the path of the particle.

2. Repeat Question 1 but with $x = t^2$, $y = t^3$, for $t = -2$, -1, 0, 1 and 2.

3. The path of an electron is given by $\mathbf{r} = (t^2 - 7)\,\mathbf{i} + t^3\mathbf{j}$ (see Exercise C, Question 9). Sketch the path for $t = 0$ to $t = 3$ marking in the velocity and acceleration at 1 second intervals.

4. An upright wheel, of radius 1 metre, rolls without slipping along the ground at 1 metre per second. The Cartesian coordinates of a point on the rim are (x, y) where $x = t - \sin t$, $y = 1 - \cos t$. Sketch the locus of the point during two revolutions of the wheel and show on the sketch the velocities and accelerations at five or more points for each revolution.

5. Relative to perpendicular axes, the position vector of a particle at time t is given by
$$\mathbf{r} = \begin{pmatrix} t^3 \\ 10t^2 - 20t \end{pmatrix}.$$

Find $\mathbf{r}$, $\dot{\mathbf{r}}$ and $\ddot{\mathbf{r}}$ when $t = 0$, 1, 2, 3, and hence by drawing or calculation obtain the magnitude and direction of the velocity and acceleration at each of these times. Show these vectors on a sketch of the path of the particle.

In general, at what type of point on the path of a moving particle do you expect the velocity and acceleration vectors to be in the same direction?

6. Sketch the path given by $\mathbf{r} = t^2\mathbf{i} + (t^4 - 1)\,\mathbf{j}$.

What sort of curve is it? What is its Cartesian equation?

7. (a) A particle moves in a plane so that its Cartesian coordinates at time t are $x = \cos t$, $y = \cos 2t$. Sketch the path and mark in the velocity and acceleration at several instants. From what direction does the particle approach the point $(-1, 1)$?

(b) Show that the path obtained in (a) is part of a parabola.

8. (a) A particle moves on the path given by $\mathbf{r} = \cos \pi t\,\mathbf{i} + (1 - \cos \pi t)\,\mathbf{j}$. Sketch the path and evaluate the velocity and acceleration when $t = 0, \frac{1}{4}, \frac{1}{2}, \frac{3}{4}, 1$.

(b) A second particle moves on a path given by
$$\mathbf{r} = \tfrac{1}{2}(1 + \cos 2t)\,\mathbf{i} + \tfrac{1}{2}(1 - \cos 2t)\,\mathbf{j}.$$

Sketch this path and evaluate the velocity and acceleration when $t = 0, \frac{1}{4}\pi, \frac{1}{2}\pi, \frac{3}{4}\pi, \pi$.

Discuss the behaviour of the particles in (a) and (b).

152

9. For each of the following, give a sketch of the path and show on it the velocities and accelerations at several points.

(*a*) $\mathbf{r} = 2 \cos 3t\mathbf{i} + 2 \sin 3t\mathbf{j}$,

(*b*) $\mathbf{r} = 10 \cos 4t\mathbf{i} + 10 \sin 4t\mathbf{j}$,

(*c*) $\mathbf{r} = 5 \sin 2t\mathbf{i} + 5 \cos 2t\mathbf{j}$.

What can you say about the direction of the acceleration? What is the relation connecting the magnitude of the acceleration and the speed in these examples?

10. An aircraft is turning on an arc of radius 15 km with constant speed 1600 km/h. What is its acceleration?

11. Show that a particle with position vector

$$\mathbf{r} = (1 + 3 \cos 5t)\,\mathbf{i} + (4 + 3 \sin 5t)\,\mathbf{j}$$

at time t follows a circular path with constant speed. Give the radius and centre of this circle and the speed of the particle. Show that the acceleration is always directed towards the centre of the circle. $\quad speed = \sqrt{\dot{x}^2 + \dot{y}^2}$

5. MOTION IN A CIRCLE

One particular motion—motion in a circle with constant speed—is worth a special mention. This has arisen in Exercise C, Questions 4 and 10, and in Exercise D, Questions 9, 10 and 11.

If $x = r \cos \omega t$, $y = r \sin \omega t$, where r and ω are constants, the path is a circle of radius r with the origin as centre. The circle is traced anticlockwise (see Figure 15), starting at A. Angle $AOP = \omega t$ radians, and so ω represents the rate (in radians per second) at which the angle is increasing. This is called the *angular velocity*.

Now $\qquad \dot{x} = -r\omega \sin \omega t, \qquad \dot{y} = r\omega \cos \omega t,$

$$\ddot{x} = -r\omega^2 \cos \omega t, \qquad \ddot{y} = -r\omega^2 \sin \omega t.$$

The velocity is clearly always perpendicular to the position vector. It has magnitude $r\omega$, as illustrated in Figure 16. We may write $v = r\omega$, the speed v being the magnitude of the velocity $\mathbf{v}$.

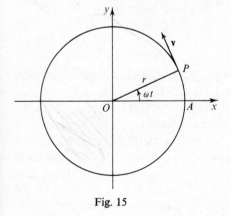

Fig. 15   Fig. 16

We notice that

$$\ddot{x} = -\omega^2(r \cos \omega t) = -\omega^2 x \quad \text{and} \quad \ddot{y} = -\omega^2 y,$$

and hence
$$\mathbf{a} = \begin{pmatrix} \ddot{x} \\ \ddot{y} \end{pmatrix} = -\omega^2 \begin{pmatrix} x \\ y \end{pmatrix} = -\omega^2 \mathbf{r}.$$

The acceleration is always directed towards the centre and has magnitude $\omega^2 r$. This is equal to $\omega^2 r^2 / r = v^2 / r$. At first sight it may seem strange that a body moving with constant speed should have an acceleration. However, its direction, and so its velocity, is changing. The inwards acceleration causes the curvature of the path, and the fact that the acceleration is always perpendicular to the velocity shows that the speed is constant.

Summary. For a body moving round a circle with constant speed,

  (i) $v = r\omega$,
  (ii) $a = r\omega^2 = v^2 / r$,

where ω is the angular velocity of the radius vector.

5.1 Angular velocity. A common example of circular motion is the rotation of a long-playing record. In this case, not only is the velocity of any point on the record variable (because its direction is changing), but also the speeds of points nearer the centre are different from the speed of the rim. There is, however, one thing constant and that is the angular velocity. The whole record is rotating at a constant $33\frac{1}{3}$ revolutions per minute.

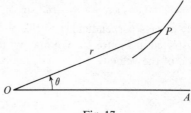

Fig. 17

When the position of a particle P in a plane is given in polar coordinates (r, θ) relative to a fixed point O and some fixed direction OA, its movement will usually involve changes in both r and θ. The rate at which the direction of the line OP changes with time is called the angular velocity of the line OP. Sometimes it is loosely referred to as the 'angular velocity of the point P about O', but more correctly it is a property of the line OP rather than the point P.

The angular velocity is denoted by $\dot{\theta}$ or, as in the last section, by the Greek letter ω (omega). If, as is usual, θ is measured in radians and time in

154

seconds, then ω is in rad/s. Other units which are sometimes employed are degrees per second, revolutions per minute, and so on.

The *angular acceleration* of a line is defined in the obvious way, and is denoted by $\ddot{\theta}$ or $\dot{\omega}$. In Section 5, we had $\ddot{\theta} = 0$, $\dot{\theta} = \omega =$ constant, and $\theta = \omega t$.

Example 8

Convert the angular velocity of the turntable of a record player from $33\frac{1}{3}$ revolutions per minute to radians per second and find the speed and acceleration of a point on the turntable 16 cm from the centre.

Since 1 rev $= 2\pi$ radians,

$$\omega = 33\frac{1}{3} \text{ rev/min}$$

$$= \frac{100}{3} \times \frac{2\pi}{60} \text{ rad/s} \approx 3 \cdot 5 \text{ rad/s}.$$

Using the formulae $v = r\omega$ and $a = \omega^2 r$, the speed and acceleration of a point 16 cm from the centre are approximately, 56 cm/s and 196 cm/s².

Exercise E

1. An outboard motor is started by pulling a cord wound round a grooved wheel of radius 10 cm. If the cord is pulled at 1 m/s what is the angular velocity of the wheel in rad/s and revolutions per minute?

2. A helicopter's rotor blade is 4 m long and is rotating at 50 revolutions per minute. Express this rate in rad/s and find the speed of the tip of the blade.

3. A dentist's drill turns at the rate of 4000 revolutions per second. Find the speed of the cutting edge of a drill 1·5 mm in diameter, and the total distance travelled by a point on the cutting edge during 2 s of drilling.

4. A star is situated 4000 light years from the centre of a rotating nebula and is moving at 100 km/s. Find how long the star takes to make a circuit of the centre of the nebula. (The speed of light is 300000 km/s.)

5. Discuss the angular velocity of a camera on a fixed tripod filming an athlete who is running at a steady speed around a circular track, if the camera is close to, but just inside, the track.

6. In a device for simulating the accelerations produced in rocket flights, a horizontal arm of length 7 m is rotated about a vertical axis. If it is desired to produce an acceleration of 100 m/s² (about 10 times the acceleration due to gravity), at what rate must the arm rotate?

7. What is the acceleration of an aircraft flying at a constant speed of 2000 km/h in a circular arc of radius 16 km?

8. A car is travelling at a constant speed of 120 km/h round a bend consisting of part of a circle. The radial acceleration is 30 m/s². What is the radius of the bend?

155

9. Calculate the speed (in m/s) and the acceleration towards the polar axis (in m/s²) due to the earth's rotation, of a person (*a*) on the equator and (*b*) in latitude 60°. (The circumference of the earth is 40000 km.)

10. A space station in orbit rotates steadily so that a man at 20 m from the axis of rotation experiences an acceleration of 9·8 m/s²—about equivalent to that in the earth's gravitational field. What is the rate of rotation and how does the acceleration vary with the rate of rotation?

11. A man 2 m tall in a space station which is rotating at 1 rad/s has the top of his head 8 m from the centre of rotation. How far from the centre are his feet? When he is standing with his head and feet along a radius from the centre of rotation he holds a small body in front of him at head height, immediately above his feet. Show that, if released, the body will land about 1 m from his feet.

Miscellaneous Exercise

1. (i) Find two functions $f(t)$, $g(t)$ of the form t^n (where n is a natural number) such that $\mathbf{r} = f(t)\mathbf{i}+g(t)\mathbf{j}$ gives the path with Cartesian equation $y^3 = x^2$. Sketch the path given by your vector equation for values of t between -1 and 1.

(ii) Will the vector equation in (i) serve to describe the graph with Cartesian equation $\sqrt{y} = \sqrt[3]{x}$?

2. The following 3 vector equations give a part of a circle of radius 2, centre the origin.

(*a*) $\mathbf{r} = \sqrt{(4-t)}\mathbf{i}+\sqrt{t}\mathbf{j}$ $0 \leqslant t \leqslant 4$.

(*b*) $\mathbf{r} = 2\cos t\mathbf{i}+2\sin t\mathbf{j}$ $0 \leqslant t \leqslant \frac{1}{2}\pi$.

(*c*) $\mathbf{r} = 2\cos t^2\mathbf{i}+2\sin t^2\mathbf{j}$ $0 \leqslant t \leqslant \sqrt{(\frac{1}{2}\pi)}$.

Comment on the behaviour of particles starting at (2, 0) if the above 3 vector equations are the equations of the paths, t being regarded as measuring time.

What happens to particles moving on paths (*a*), (*b*), (*c*) if t is allowed to increase beyond the limits given alongside each vector equation?

3. Sketch the path of the particle whose Cartesian coordinates are given parametrically in terms of the time t by $x = t^2$, $y = \sin t$. Calculate and show on the sketch the values of the velocity and acceleration at $t = 0$, $\frac{1}{2}\pi$, π, $\frac{3}{2}\pi$ and 2π. What is the gradient of the graph at $t = 2\pi$? Show that the acceleration and the velocity have the same direction when $\tan t = -1/t$ and give the approximate solutions of this equation when t is large.

4. A particle is projected with speed V and its position at time t is given by $\mathbf{r} = Vt\cos\theta\mathbf{i}+(Vt\sin\theta-\frac{1}{2}gt^2)\mathbf{j}$.

(i) Write down an expression for the velocity vector **v**.

(ii) By putting $t = 0$ in the expression for **v** find the significance of the angle θ.

(iii) At what time will the particle reach a point with position vector $R\mathbf{i}$ (where $R \neq 0$)? Express R in terms of V, g and θ.

(iv) By writing $\sin\theta\cos\theta = \frac{1}{2}\sin 2\theta$, or otherwise, show that for given V, R is greatest where $\theta = \frac{1}{4}\pi$.

156

5. The sixteenth century astronomer Tycho Brahe, on whose results much of Kepler's work on orbits depended, produced the following argument against the theory that the Earth rotates from west to east: 'Set up two identical cannons with identical elevation, shot and charge, facing east and west respectively. Fire them, and observe that the shots have equal range. But if the Earth were rotating from west to east, the shot directed to the east would appear to have a shorter range than the other since the cannon on the ground would tend to catch up with its shot which was travelling through the air.'

Produce a counter-argument.

6. Assuming the planets move in circular orbits, one of Kepler's laws states that T^2/D^3 is constant, where T is the time for a complete revolution of a planet about the sun and D is its distance from the sun. If the angular velocity of the line from the sun to the planet is ω and the speed of the planet is v (assumed constant), find similar laws relating ω with D, v with D and ω with v.

7. A tennis ball of radius 3·8 cm is moving at 25 m/s carrying top spin of 10 rev/s. What are the speeds of the top and bottom points of the ball?

8. A wheel of radius $\frac{1}{2}$ m is rolling along the ground and its centre has a speed of 10 m/s. What is the angular velocity of the wheel in (rad/s)? What are the linear velocities of (*a*) the top point and (*b*) the foremost point (level with the centre) of the wheel?

SUMMARY

Velocity

The average velocity from position $\mathbf{r}_1$ at time t_1 to $\mathbf{r}_2$ at t_2 is

$$\frac{\mathbf{r}_2 - \mathbf{r}_1}{t_2 - t_1}.$$

The instantaneous velocity $\mathbf{v}$ at time t_1 is the limit of the average velocity as t_2 tends to t_1.

Acceleration

The average acceleration from velocity $\mathbf{v}_1$ at time t_1 to $\mathbf{v}_2$ at t_2 is

$$\frac{\mathbf{v}_2 - \mathbf{v}_1}{t_2 - t_1}.$$

The instantaneous acceleration is the limit of the average acceleration.

Components

If
$$\mathbf{r} = f(t)\,\mathbf{i} + g(t)\,\mathbf{j},$$
then
$$\mathbf{v} = f'(t)\,\mathbf{i} + g'(t)\,\mathbf{j},$$
and
$$\mathbf{a} = f''(t)\,\mathbf{i} + g''(t)\,\mathbf{j}.$$

157

Alternative notation

If
$$\mathbf{r} = \begin{pmatrix} x \\ y \end{pmatrix},$$

then
$$\mathbf{v} = \lim_{\delta t \to 0} \frac{\delta \mathbf{r}}{\delta t} = \frac{d\mathbf{r}}{dt} = \dot{\mathbf{r}} = \begin{pmatrix} \dot{x} \\ \dot{y} \end{pmatrix}$$

and
$$\mathbf{a} = \lim_{\delta t \to 0} \frac{\delta \mathbf{v}}{\delta t} = \frac{d\mathbf{v}}{dt} = \dot{\mathbf{v}} = \begin{pmatrix} \ddot{x} \\ \ddot{y} \end{pmatrix}.$$

Motion in a circle with constant speed

If r is the radius and ω the angular velocity, the angle rotated through in time t is $\theta = \omega t$, the speed $v = r\omega$ in the direction of the tangent, the acceleration is $\omega^2 r = v^2/r$ towards the centre.

8

INDICES AND LOGARITHMS

When using a slide-rule to *multiply* two numbers, we find that we have to *add* lengths of ruler. Previously, this surprising action was justified by pointing out that since $8 = 2^3$, $4 = 2^2$ and $32 = 2^5$, we could obtain $8 \times 4 = 32$ from the working $3 + 2 = 5$, i.e. the product of some numbers can be obtained by the addition of other numbers (in this case indices). In the O-level course, the introduction of logarithms was based on this idea but some difficulties had to be glossed over. For example, we use logarithms and slide-rules to multiply, not just whole number powers of 2 or 10, say, but *any* real numbers, e.g. 3.75×0.81. Now, are there values m and n such that $3.75 = 10^m$ and $0.81 = 10^n$? And, if so, can we find them?

We start this chapter by seeing how expressions like $2^{\frac{3}{4}}$ and $3^{-0.6}$ are defined.

1. INDICES

Exercise A

1. Find the exact value of each of the following and, where possible, express the answer in index form with a prime number base.

(a) $2^3 \times 2^4$; (b) $3^2 \times 3^5$; (c) $2^4 + 2^5$;

(d) $3^2 + 2^2$; (e) $4^3 \div 4^2$; (f) $3^6 \div 3^4$;

(g) $2^5 - 2^3$; (h) $(2^3)^2$; (i) $(3^2)^4$.

2. Use the ideas of Question 1 to simplify:

(a) $5^a \times 5^b$; (b) $4^a \div 4^b$; (c) $(3^a)^b$.

3. By combining the indices, simplify the following:

(a) $5^4 \times 5^2$; (b) $10^2 \times 10^3 \times 10^6$; (c) $\dfrac{2^3 \times 2^4 \times 2^5}{2^2 \times 2^6}$;

(d) $(3^2)^7$.

4. Solve:

(a) $3^n = 3^2$; (b) $2^n \times 2^3 = 2^8$; (c) $5 \times 5^n = 5^6$;

(d) $x \times a^4 = a^6$; (e) $x \times (a^2)^3 = a^7$; (f) $4 \times 2^n = 8^3$.

5. Simplify the following:

(a) $2x^3 \times x^2$; (b) $(2x^2)^3$; (c) $\dfrac{(3x)^2}{3x^2}$;

159

(d) $\dfrac{x^3 \times x^2}{x^4}$;

(e) $\dfrac{x^3 \times (x^2)^3}{x^4 \times x^5}$;

(f) $(x^2 \times y^3)(x^3 \times y^2)$;

(g) $\dfrac{x^3 \times y^4}{x^2 \times y^3}$;

(h) $\dfrac{x^2 \times (y^4)^3}{x^3 \times y^7}$. $\dfrac{x^2 \times y^{12}}{x^3 \times y^7} = x^{-1} \times y^5$

6. State whether the following are true or false:

(a) $2^4 \times 2^5 = 2^{20}$;

(b) $4^2 \times 5^2 = 20^2$;

(c) $(2x)^2 = 2x^2$;

(d) $\sqrt{36} = \sqrt{9} \times \sqrt{4}$;

(e) $\sqrt{2} \times \sqrt{50} = 10$;

(f) $x^a \times y^a = (xy)^a$.

7. Factorize, change to index form and simplify:

(a) $\dfrac{12^3 \times 3}{12^3 \times 3^2}$;

(b) $\dfrac{30^2 \times 5^3}{2^2 \times 3 \times 5^5}$;

(c) $\dfrac{100^4}{(10^3)^2 \times 1000}$.

8. Assuming that expressions like 2^{-3} have a meaning and that the laws of indices hold for such numbers, simplify the following:

(a) $2^4 \times 2^0$;

(b) $3^0 \times 3^5$;

(c) $3^{-1} \times 3^4$;

(d) $2^5 \times 2^{-3}$;

(e) $4^6 \div 4^{-1}$.

What values are suggested for 2^0, 3^0, 3^{-1}, 2^{-3}, 4^{-1}?

9. With the assumptions of Question 8, simplify:

(a) $2^{\frac{1}{2}} \times 2^{\frac{1}{2}}$;

(b) $(3^{\frac{1}{2}})^4$;

(c) $(10^2)^{\frac{1}{2}}$;

(d) $(2^{\frac{2}{3}})^2$;

(e) $2^{\frac{1}{3}} \times 2^{\frac{1}{3}} \times 2^{\frac{1}{3}}$;

(f) $(7^3)^{\frac{1}{3}}$.

What interpretation should be put upon the indices $\frac{1}{2}$, $\frac{3}{2}$, $\frac{1}{3}$?

10. In this question, use the answer to (i) to solve (ii). Simplify the following:

(a) (i) $(2^3)^4$, (ii) $\sqrt[4]{(2^{12})}$;

(b) (i) $(x^2)^3$, (ii) $\sqrt[3]{x^6}$;

(c) (i) $(3^2)^3$, (ii) $\sqrt{3^6}$;

(d) (i) $(x^5)^4$, (ii) $\sqrt[5]{(x^{20})}$.

1.1 The laws of indices. Exercise A illustrates the laws of indices, with which you are familiar, namely:

(1) $x^a \times x^b = x^{a+b}$;

(2) $x^a \div x^b = x^{a-b}$;

(3) $(x^a)^b = x^{ab}$.

In the above, x is called the *base*, a and b are *indices*, *powers* or *exponents*. The laws are easily explained where all the indices are natural numbers.

1.2 The extension of possible indices. As suggested in Exercise A, Questions 8 and 9, we define x^n, where n is a rational number, in such a way that the laws of indices still hold.

(i) *Negative index*

By division, $\qquad 2^4 \div 2^7 = 16 \div 128 = \frac{1}{8}$,

but, by law 2, $\qquad 2^4 \div 2^7 = 2^{-3}$.

We define 2^{-3} as $\dfrac{1}{2^3}$, and in general, x^{-a} as $\dfrac{1}{x^a}$.

160

(ii) *Zero index*

By division, $\qquad\qquad\qquad x^a \div x^a = 1,$

but, by law 2, $\qquad\qquad\quad x^a \div x^a = x^0.$

We define x^0 as 1 for all $x \neq 0$.

(iii) *Rational indices*

From $10^{\frac{1}{2}} \times 10^{\frac{1}{2}} = 10^1$, we see that we must define $10^{\frac{1}{2}}$ as the number which, when multiplied by itself, gives 10; as you know, this is called the square root of 10, and is written $\sqrt{10}$.

Also more generally $(x^{1/n})^n = x^1$ suggests that $x^{1/n}$ equals $\sqrt[n]{x}$, the nth root of x, meaning the positive real number whose nth power is x.

The equations $x^{m/n} = (x^{1/n})^m = (x^m)^{1/n}$ show that a number like $16^{\frac{3}{4}}$ can be interpreted and simplified in two equivalent ways:

$$16^{\frac{3}{4}} = (\sqrt[4]{16})^3 = 2^3 = 8 \quad \text{or} \quad 16^{\frac{3}{4}} = \sqrt[4]{(16^3)} = \sqrt[4]{4096} = 8.$$

In practice it is generally easier to reduce the size of the number by taking the root first.

1.3 Summary. We define, for $x > 0$,

(i) $\;x^{-n} = \dfrac{1}{x^n};$

(ii) $\;x^0 = 1;$

(iii) $\;x^{m/n} = (\sqrt[n]{x})^m = \sqrt[n]{(x^m)}, \quad n > 0.$

We should check that with these definitions the new exponential numbers do indeed combine according to the rules of Section 1.1, e.g. if a, b, c, d are natural numbers, $x^{a/b} \times x^{c/d} = x^{a/b+c/d}$.

We can also show that, if n is rational, $x^n \times y^n = (xy)^n$.

Exercise B

1. Express the following in index form, with a prime number base:

(*a*) 25;   (*b*) 64;   (*c*) $\sqrt[3]{7}$;

(*d*) $1/625$;   (*e*) $\sqrt{27}$.

2. Express the following as (i) powers of 2, (ii) powers of 4.

(*a*) 8;   (*b*) $\sqrt{2}$;   (*c*) $\frac{1}{4}$;

(*d*) 1024;   (*e*) $\sqrt{8}$;   (*f*) $\dfrac{1}{\sqrt[3]{2}}.$

3. Simplify

(*a*) 8^{-2};   (*b*) $8^{\frac{1}{3}}$;   (*c*) $8^{-\frac{1}{3}}$;

(*d*) 8^0;   (*e*) $9^{\frac{1}{2}}$;   (*f*) $9^{\frac{3}{2}}$;

(*g*) 9^0;   (*h*) $9^{-\frac{1}{2}}$;   (*i*) 9^{-3}.

4. Show that if m and n are natural numbers and x is positive, $[(\sqrt[n]{x})^m]^n = x^m$, i.e. that $(\sqrt[n]{x})^m = \sqrt[n]{(x^m)}$.

5. Simplify:

(a) $\sqrt[3]{64}$;   (b) $125^{\frac{1}{3}}$;   (c) $(1024)^{\frac{1}{5}}$;

(d) $(169)^{\frac{3}{2}}$;   (e) $(49)^{\frac{3}{2}}$;   (f) $(32)^{\frac{1}{5}}$;

(g) $(8)^{-\frac{2}{3}}$;   (h) $(100)^{-\frac{3}{2}}$.

6. Use a slide-rule to calculate the following, correct to two significant figures:

(a) $5^{-\frac{1}{2}}$;   (b) $8^{1\cdot5}$;   (c) $10^{\frac{1}{4}}$;

(d) $(0\cdot75)^{-2}$;   (e) $13^{-\frac{3}{4}}$.

7. Simplify:

(a) $x^{\frac{1}{3}} \times x^{-\frac{4}{3}}$;   (b) $\dfrac{x^2}{x^{\frac{1}{3}}}$;   (c) $\dfrac{x^{\frac{1}{2}}}{x^{-\frac{1}{2}}}$;   (d) $\dfrac{x^2\sqrt{x}}{x^{3\cdot5}}$.

8. Simplify:

(a) $\sqrt{12} \times \sqrt{3}$;   (b) $\dfrac{\sqrt{18}}{\sqrt{8}}$;   (c) $\dfrac{5\sqrt{2}}{\sqrt{50}}$;   (d) $\sqrt[3]{(8^5)}$.

9. Evaluate the following, given that $\sqrt{2} = 1\cdot4142$, $\sqrt{3} = 1\cdot7321$, $\sqrt{5} = 2\cdot2361$. [Examples:

$$\sqrt{75} = \sqrt{(25 \times 3)} = \sqrt{25} \times \sqrt{3} = 5\sqrt{3} = 8\cdot6605,$$

$$\frac{4}{\sqrt{2}} = \frac{2 \times 2}{\sqrt{2}} = 2\sqrt{2} = 2\cdot8284.]$$

(a) $\sqrt{48}$;   (b) $\sqrt{8}$;   (c) $\sqrt{50}$;

(d) $\sqrt{12}$;   (e) $\sqrt{18}$;   (f) $\sqrt{20}$;

(g) $\dfrac{8}{\sqrt{2}}$;   (h) $\dfrac{9}{\sqrt{2}}$;   (i) $\dfrac{50}{\sqrt{5}}$.

10. For what rational values of x is a^x defined if a is negative? Consider first $a = -64$ with (i) $x = \frac{1}{2}$, (ii) $x = \frac{1}{3}$, (iii) $x = -\frac{2}{3}$, (iv) $x = -\frac{3}{2}$.

2. DERIVATIVES

In Chapter 5 you will have differentiated the expression $\sqrt{x}$ from first principles to obtain $1/(2\sqrt{x})$. If we now write $\sqrt{x}$ in index form as $x^{\frac{1}{2}}$ and its derived function as $\frac{1}{2}x^{-\frac{1}{2}}$, we see that this is consistent with the rule

$$\frac{d(x^n)}{dx} = nx^{n-1},$$

which we have so far accepted only for natural numbers n. We now state that the above result is true for *all* rational n. Notice that this has not yet shown us a way of differentiating functions like $f: x \to a^x$; we shall return to that later.

162

Exercise C

1. Differentiate:

(a) $\dfrac{1}{x^3}$;   (b) $\dfrac{1}{\sqrt{x}}$;   (c) x^{-5};   (d) $3x^{-2}$;   (e) $\dfrac{5}{x}$;   (f) $\dfrac{3}{x^4}$;

(g) $x^{\frac{1}{4}}$;   (h) $x^{-\frac{3}{4}}$;   (i) $x^{\frac{3}{2}}$;   (j) $\sqrt[3]{x}$;   (k) $\dfrac{1}{\sqrt[3]{x}}$;   (l) $x^{-\frac{2}{5}}$.

2. Differentiate:

(a) x^{2n};   (b) $\dfrac{1}{x^{2n}}$;   (c) $(x^2)^n$;   (d) $\sqrt{x^n}$;

(e) $\dfrac{1}{\sqrt{x^n}}$;   (f) $\sqrt[n]{x}$;   (g) $x\sqrt{x}$.

3. Find $f(4)$ and $f'(4)$ if $f(x)$ is equal to

(a) x^{-2};   (b) $x^{\frac{3}{2}}$;   (c) $x^{-\frac{1}{2}}$;   (d) x^0.

Interpret your answers on sketch graphs.

4. Simplify, then differentiate:

(a) $\dfrac{1+x}{\sqrt{x}}$;   (b) $\dfrac{1+\sqrt{x}}{x}$;   (c) $\dfrac{x^{\frac{3}{4}}-x^{\frac{1}{4}}}{1-x^{\frac{1}{2}}}$.

3. THE GRAPH OF AN EXPONENTIAL FUNCTION

Suppose there is a thriving population of bacteria which doubles in number every day, and that on a certain day this population is estimated to be 1 million. When one day has passed, the number p (in millions) will be 2; after 2 days it will be 2^2; after seven days it will be 2^7. This suggests the formula

$$p = 2^t,$$

where t is the time measured in days.

Does this formula make good sense for rational values of t? Calculate the population size for $t = \frac{1}{2}$, $1\frac{1}{2}$, $-\frac{1}{2}$, -1, -2. Complete the following table and plot the values on a graph. Do the points lie on a smooth curve?

t	-3	-2	-1	$-\frac{1}{2}$	0	$\frac{1}{2}$	1	$1\frac{1}{2}$	2	3	4
2^t	$\frac{1}{8}$						2				16

We have defined 2^t for any rational t, and can calculate it to any desired accuracy (by trial and error, if need be, preferably with the aid of a computer or desk calculator). For example, to 3 significant figures we could obtain $2^{0\cdot1} = 1\cdot07$ ($1\cdot065^{10} < 2 < 1\cdot075^{10}$), $2^{0\cdot2} = 1\cdot15$, $2^{0\cdot3} = 1\cdot23$, ... Values so obtained will give further points on the graph of 2^t, all lying on the smooth curve of Figure 1. This is yet another satisfactory consequence of our choice of definition of 2^t for rational t.

163

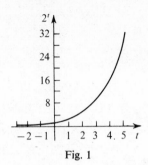

Fig. 1

Clearly, the graph of any function $x \to a^x$, with a positive, will also be a smooth curve.

Exercise D

1. A colony of bacteria is found to increase in number by 50 % every hour. If there are 3 million at noon, find their number at half-hourly intervals between 10.30 a.m. and 2.00 p.m., giving answers correct to two significant figures. Draw a graph and estimate from it the population at 11.20 a.m., 12.40 p.m. and 1.10 p.m. At what time is the population 4 million?

2. Write a flow chart for computing the number of bacteria in Question 1 at half-hourly intervals between 10.30 a.m. and 2.00 p.m.

3. A radio-active element has a mass of 50 grams and its decay reduces its mass by 20 % every year. Write down a formula for its mass after t years. By drawing the graph of m against t, estimate the time (to the nearest tenth of a year) when (a) the mass was 70 grams, (b) the mass will be 35 grams.

4. Draw the graphs of 2^x, 3^x, 4^x by taking a table of values of x thus:

x	-2	-1	0	1	2
2^x					
3^x					
4^x					

To this table add rows giving values of $(\frac{1}{2})^x$, $(\frac{1}{3})^x$, $(\frac{1}{4})^x$. How are these values related to the ones for 2^x etc? Draw all the graphs on the same diagram. Why is the graph of $(\frac{1}{2})^x$ a reflection in the line $x = 0$ of the graph for 2^x? Can you suggest a transformation mapping the graph of 2^x onto the graph of 4^x?

5. Given, to 3 significant figures, $\sqrt{3} = 1 \cdot 73$ and $\sqrt[3]{3} = 1 \cdot 44$, calculate approximate values of $3^{\frac{3}{2}}$, $3^{\frac{2}{3}}$ and $3^{-\frac{1}{2}}$. Do these give points on the graph of 3^x drawn in Question 4? Draw, as accurately as you can, the graph of $y = 3^x$ for $-2 \leqslant x \leqslant 2$.

6. Show, from the graph of Question 5, that $1 \cdot 7 \approx 3^{0 \cdot 48}$ and $2 \cdot 3 \approx 3^{0 \cdot 76}$. We can deduce that $1 \cdot 7 \times 2 \cdot 3 \approx 3^{0 \cdot 48 + 0 \cdot 76} = 3^{1 \cdot 24}$. What value do you obtain from the graph for $3^{1 \cdot 24}$? Is this equal to $1 \cdot 7 \times 2 \cdot 3$?

7. As in Question 6, use the graph of 3^x and the index laws to calculate (a) $1 \cdot 4 \times 4 \cdot 8$, (b) $5 \cdot 5 \times 0 \cdot 8$, (c) $7 \cdot 5 \div 1 \cdot 3$, (d) $1 \cdot 7^{1 \cdot 5}$, (e) $\sqrt[3]{7 \cdot 4}$, (f) $\sqrt{5 \cdot 9}$.

8. (a) Show that $(2^{\frac{7}{10}})^{20} < (2^{\frac{3}{4}})^{20}$. Does it follow that $2^{\frac{7}{10}} < 2^{\frac{3}{4}}$?

(b) If a and b are rational numbers with $a < b$, show that $2^a < 2^b$. What does this imply about the graph of 2^x?

9. Can you find a rational number n for which $2^n = 3$? In other words, can you find positive integers p and q for which $2^{p/q} = 3$?

4. LOGARITHMIC FUNCTIONS

In the bacteria example of Section 3, we obtained the formula $p = 2^t$ for the population after t days. From the graph of this function we could read off the value of the population for any given value of the time, t. If we are given the population and have to find the time, we simply read from the vertical to the horizontal axis instead of the usual way round. If we are given a value of p and have to find the corresponding value of t, we use the *inverse* of the exponential function $t \to 2^t$. This inverse mapping is a *logarithmic function*. It is written $p \to \log_2 p$, and its graph is, of course, a reflection of the graph of $t \to 2^t$.

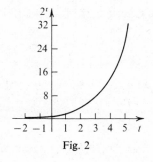

Fig. 2

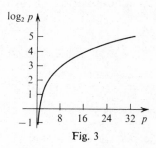

Fig. 3

The inverse of the exponential function to base a is the logarithmic function to base a:

$$y = a^x \Leftrightarrow \log_a y = x.$$

For example, $\qquad 64 = 2^6 \quad$ and $\quad \log_2 64 = 6.$

Explain why $\log_3 1 = 0$ and $\log_{10}(\sqrt{10}) = \frac{1}{2}$. What is $\log_2(\frac{1}{8})$?

From the graph of $y = 3^x$ (Exercise D, Question 5), write down approximate values for $\log_3 2$ and $\log_3 6$.

*4.1 Real number indices. As you know, one use of logarithms is as an aid to computation. Multiplication and division are replaced by the simpler operations of addition and subtraction. Exercise D, Questions 6 and 7, were in effect using logarithms to base 3 although the notation was avoided. In practice we use base 10 because our numeral system makes this the most convenient. We want every positive number to have a logarithm,

165

in other words we want to be able to express any number in exponential form with base 10. We should like the range of the function $x \to 10^x$ to be the set of all positive real numbers; this requires that we 'fill in' its graph by making appropriate definitions of $10^{\sqrt 2}$, 10^π etc., i.e. of 10^x for irrational x.

There is no special interpretation for x irrational (as negative powers indicate 'reciprocals' and denominators indicate 'roots'). It is nevertheless possible to find approximations to their values as follows:

π is an irrational number but we get closer and closer approximations by using rationals like 3·1, 3·14, 3·141, ... These values converge on (but never reach) π. 10^x is defined for any rational x and the numbers $10^{3·1}$, $10^{3·14}$, $10^{3·141}$..., converge on a number whose value is said to be 10^π.

We can now take the set of all real numbers as the domain of the function $x \to 10^x$. The graph is then complete and all positive numbers can consequently be written as powers of the base 10. Do you think the laws of indices hold with irrational indices?

All these issues are discussed more formally in a later chapter.

4.2 Combination of logarithms. Consider the following:

$$4 \times 32 = 2^2 \times 2^5 = 2^7 = 128;$$

$$\log_2 4 + \log_2 32 = 2 + 5 = 7 = \log_2 128.$$

An exponential function $f \colon x \to a^x$ converts addition into multiplication. The first law of indices, $a^{x+y} = a^x \times a^y$, can be written:

$$f(x+y) = f(x) \times f(y).$$

The inverse function $g \colon x \to \log_a x$ has the opposite effect, converting multiplication into addition:

$$g(x \times y) = g(x) + g(y),$$

i.e. $$\log_a (x \times y) = \log_a x + \log_a y.$$

This can be deduced from the first law of indices:

$$(\log_a x = p \text{ and } \log_a y = q) \Rightarrow (x = a^p \text{ and } y = a^q)$$

$$\Rightarrow x \times y = a^p \times a^q = a^{p+q}$$

$$\Rightarrow \log_a (x \times y) = p + q = \log_a x + \log_a y.$$

Write down alternative forms for $\log_a (x \div y)$ and $\log_a x^n$, and show how they can be derived from the laws of indices.

166

Exercise E

1. Draw the graph of $y = 5^x$ from $x = 0$ to $x = 2$, given that $\sqrt{5} = 2\cdot24$ and $\sqrt[3]{5} = 1\cdot71$. Read off the values of $\log_5 3$, $\log_5 4$, $\log_5 12$, $\log_5 16$ and $\log_5 20$. Comment on your answers.

2. Consider the following:

$$\log_{10} 100 = \log_{10} 10^2 = 2, \qquad \log_2 16 = \log_2 2^4 = 4.$$

Re-write the following, replacing the asterisks by appropriate numbers.

(a) $\log_2 \frac{1}{2} = \log_2 2^* = *$;   (b) $\log_2 1 = \log_2 2^* = *$;

(c) $\log_2 64 = \log_2 2^* = *$;   (d) $\log_3 \frac{1}{3} = \log_3 3^* = *$;

(e) $\log_3 27 = \log_3 3^* = *$;   (f) $\log_3 \frac{1}{81} = \log_3 3^* = *$;

(g) $\log_a \left(\dfrac{1}{a}\right) = \log_a a^* = *$;   (h) $\log_a(1) = \log_a a^* = *$;

(i) $\log_a a^2 = *$;   (j) $\log_a a^7 = *$.

3. State the value of x in each of the following:

(a) $\log_3 81 = x$;   (b) $\log_5 x = -2$;   (c) $\log_x 8 = 3$;

(d) $\log_4 64 = x$;   (e) $\log_{10} x = -\frac{1}{2}$;   (f) $\log_x 8 = \frac{1}{2}$.

4. In the following examples, insert the appropriate symbols in place of the asterisks:

(a) $\log_2(8 \times 32) = \log_2 8 * \log_2 32$;

(b) $\log_{10}(8 \times 32) = \log_{10} 8 * \log_{10} 32$;

(c) $\log_{10}(8 \div 32) = \log_{10} 8 * \log_{10} 32$;

(d) $\log_a(8 \times 8) = \log_a 8 * \log_a 8 = * \log_a 8$.

5. Given that, to some unspecified base, $\log 2 = 0\cdot69$ and $\log 3 = 1\cdot10$, find the values of:

(a) $\log 6$;   (b) $\log \frac{1}{2}$;   (c) $\log \frac{3}{2}$;

(d) $\log 27$;   (e) $\log 18$;   (f) $\log \frac{4}{3}$;

(g) $\log \sqrt{2}$;   (h) $\log \sqrt[3]{3}$;   (i) $\log \sqrt[3]{4}$;

(j) $\log \sqrt[4]{12}$.

6. Solve:

(a) $\log x = \log 7$;   (b) $\log 3x = \log 81$;   (c) $\log x + \log 5 = \log 30$;

(d) $\log x = 4 \log 2$;   (e) $\log 12 + 3 \log x = \log 96$; (f) $2 \log x + \log 5 = \log 1$.

Does it matter what the base of these logarithms is?

7. Show that $2^{10} \div 10^3 \approx 1$, and hence that $\log_{10} 2 \approx 0\cdot3$.

8. Given that $\log_{10} 2 = 0\cdot301$ and $\log_{10} 3 = 0\cdot477$, find the values of:

(a) $\log_{10} 30$;   (b) $\log_{10} 5$;   (c) $\log_{10} 2000$;   (d) $\log_{10} 3\frac{1}{3}$;

(e) $\log_{10} 0\cdot4$;   (f) $\log_{10} 2\cdot5$;   (g) $\log_{10} \sqrt{45}$.

9. Suppose the following mapping represents a logarithmic function:

$$1 \to 0$$
$$a \to 1$$
$$b \to 2$$
$$c \to 3$$
$$d \to 4$$

(a) Write down the values of log a and log b.
(b) What is the value of log a^2?
(c) Express b in terms of a (use your answer to (b)).
(d) Find c and d in terms of a.
(e) What is the base of these logarithms?
(f) If $k^2 = c$, find the value of log k.
(g) If $rd = 1$, find the value of log r.

4.3   Summary. Exercise E should have reminded you of the following.

   (i)   When multiplying two numbers, we add their logs.

   (ii) When dividing two numbers, we subtract their logs.

   (iii) When taking the power of a number, we multiply its log by that power.

   (iv) When finding the nth root of a number, we divide its log by n.

These follow immediately from the laws of indices, and may be written formally:

   (I) $\log_a (x \times y) = \log_a x + \log_a y.$

   (II) $\log_a (x \div y) = \log_a x - \log_a y.$

   (III) $\log_a (x^n) = n \log_a x.$

   (IV) $\log_a (\sqrt[n]{x}) = (\log_a x) \div n.$

5. COMPUTATION USING LOGARITHMS

5.1   Four figure tables. When doing calculations with logarithms, we normally use base 10 and for the rest of this chapter we shall drop the suffix 10, as is usual in everyday working.

At O-level we used tables rounded to three figures; for greater accuracy we shall now use four figure tables.

Example 1

Calculate $2 \cdot 168 \times 3 \cdot 086$ by logarithms.

$$
\begin{array}{cc}
 & x \qquad \log x \\
\times & \left(\begin{matrix} 2 \cdot 168 \to 0 \cdot 3361 \\ 3 \cdot 086 \to 0 \cdot 4895 \end{matrix} \right) +
\end{array}
$$

$$2 \cdot 168 \times 3 \cdot 086 = 6 \cdot 693. \qquad 6 \cdot 693 \leftarrow \overline{0 \cdot 8256}$$

168

Check this working to make sure you understand how to use four figure tables, then work out $1{\cdot}509 \times 5{\cdot}228$. You should get the answer $7{\cdot}889$.

When we work with four figures tables, the fourth significant figure of the answer is liable to slight error.

5.2 Negative characteristics. Tables only give the logarithms of numbers between 1 and 10. To cope with a number outside this interval, as you will remember, we first write it in Standard Form.

For example,
$$763{\cdot}1 = 10^2 \times 7{\cdot}631,$$
$$\log 763{\cdot}1 = \log 10^2 + \log 7{\cdot}631$$
$$= 2 + 0{\cdot}8826$$
$$= 2{\cdot}8826.$$

Also, $\qquad 0{\cdot}007631 = 10^{-3} \times 7{\cdot}631,$

giving $\qquad \log 0{\cdot}007631 = -3 + 0{\cdot}8826.$

The logarithm to the base 10 of a number between 1 and 10 must be included in the range $0 \leqslant l \leqslant 1$ because $\log 1 = 0$ and $\log 10 = 1$. This is called the *mantissa* of the logarithm. The integral part, corresponding to the integral power of 10, is called the *characteristic*.

In practice it pays to keep a logarithm with negative characteristic in this form, and to write for example $\log 0{\cdot}007631$ as $\bar{3}{\cdot}8826$ (read 'bar 3 point 8826'); not as $-3{\cdot}8826$, because this means that the $0{\cdot}8826$ as well as the 3 is negative, and not as $-2{\cdot}1174$ because this, though correct, generally increases the work.

Keeping to this notation, we must be careful when adding, subtracting, multiplying and dividing.

Adding:
$$\bar{2}{\cdot}8826$$
$$3{\cdot}9411$$
$$\overline{2{\cdot}8237} \quad (1 + 1{\cdot}8237)$$

Subtracting:

$3{\cdot}9411$	$\bar{2}{\cdot}8826$	$2{\cdot}8826$
$\bar{2}{\cdot}8826$	$3{\cdot}9411$	$3{\cdot}9411$
$\overline{5{\cdot}0585}$	$\overline{\bar{6}{\cdot}9415}$	$\overline{\bar{2}{\cdot}9415}$

The second and third of these subtractions may cause some difficulty. They may be re-written:

$\bar{3} + 1{\cdot}8826$	$1 + 1{\cdot}8826$
$3 + 0{\cdot}9411$	$3 + 0{\cdot}9411$
$\overline{\bar{6} + 0{\cdot}9415}$	$\overline{\bar{2} + 0{\cdot}9415}$

Multiplying: $\bar{2}\cdot8826$

$\underline{\qquad 3 \qquad}$

$\bar{4}\cdot6478$ $(\bar{6}+2\cdot6478)$

Dividing: $\bar{2}\cdot8826 \div 2 = \bar{1}\cdot4413$

$\bar{2}\cdot8826 \div 3 = ?$

The danger here is confusing the positive and negative parts. To avoid this, the following device is used:

$$\bar{2}\cdot8826 \div 3 = (\bar{3}+1\cdot8826) \div 3 = \bar{1}+0\cdot6275 = \bar{1}\cdot6275.$$

As you see, we have split the logarithm into two parts and have adjusted the characteristic part so that it is divisible by 3 and then redressed the balance by adding to the mantissa. We then divide and combine the two parts at the end.

Examples:

$$\bar{1}\cdot3421 \div 2 = (\bar{2}+1\cdot3421) \div 2 = \bar{1}+0\cdot6711 = \bar{1}\cdot6711.$$

$$\bar{1}\cdot3421 \div 5 = (\bar{5}+4\cdot3421) \div 5 = \bar{1}+0\cdot8684 = \bar{1}\cdot8684.$$

Exercise F

1. Assuming $\log 3\cdot142 = 0\cdot4972$, write down the logarithms of:

(a) 314·2;   (b) 314200;   (c) 0·3142;   (d) 0·003142.

2. Given $\log 2\cdot718 = 0\cdot4343$, write down the numbers with the following logarithms:

(a) 2·4343;   (b) $\bar{2}$·4343;   (c) 5·4343;   (d) $\bar{1}$·4343.

3. Find, from four figure tables, the logarithms of:

(a) 1·713;   (b) 292·6;   (c) 91·08;

(d) 0·0424;   (e) 0·5566.

4. Find x if $\log x$ is:

(a) 3·6062;   (b) 4·0472;   (c) $\bar{3}$·1423;   (d) $\bar{1}$·5991.

5. The following are all logarithms; combine them as in Section 5.2.

(a) $\bar{3}$·6614+2·5962;   (b) 1·7316+0·4267−$\bar{2}$·1659;

(c) 2·3477−3·5264;   (d) 4·6321−3·7291+$\bar{1}$·2163;

(e) $\bar{3}$·2164−$\bar{2}$·1926.

6. For each of the following, (i) multiply by 3, and (ii) divide by 3.

(a) 1·4673;   (b) $\bar{3}$·2181;   (c) $\bar{2}$·1766;

(d) 4·6014;   (e) $\bar{4}$·8101.

7. Assuming $\log 2 \cdot 2 = 0 \cdot 3424$ and $\log 5 \cdot 5 = 0 \cdot 7404$, find the values of the following:

(a) $\log (2 \cdot 2 \times 5 \cdot 5)$;   (b) $\log (22 \times 0 \cdot 55)$;   (c) $\log (2 \cdot 2 \div 5 \cdot 5)$;

(d) $\log (22 \div 0 \cdot 55)$;   (e) $\log 22^2$;   (f) $\log 0 \cdot 55^2$;

(g) $\log \sqrt{22}$;   (h) $\log \sqrt{0 \cdot 55}$;   (i) $\log (220 \sqrt{5 \cdot 5})$;

(j) $\log (0 \cdot 022^2 \div 5 \cdot 5)$.

5.3 Worked examples.

Example 2

Calculate $\dfrac{14 \cdot 67 \times 0 \cdot 112}{883 \cdot 6}$.

x	$\log x$	
14·67	1·1665	
0·112	$\bar{1}$·0492	
	0·2157	(adding)
883·6	2·9463	
0·001 860 ←	$\bar{3}$·2694	(subtracting)

$$\frac{14 \cdot 67 \times 0 \cdot 112}{883 \cdot 6} = 0 \cdot 001\,860$$

Example 3

Calculate $77^3 \div 9 \cdot 09^2$.

x	$\log x$
77	1·8865
77^3	$3 \times 1 \cdot 8865 = 5 \cdot 6595$
9·09	0·9586
$9 \cdot 09^2$	$2 \times 0 \cdot 9586 = 1 \cdot 9172$
5525	← 3·7423

$$77^3 \div 9 \cdot 09^2 = 5525$$

Example 4

Calculate $\sqrt{\dfrac{8 \cdot 647}{9 \cdot 173}}$.

x	$\log x$
8·647	0·9369
9·173	0·9625
	2) $\bar{1}$·9744
0·9710 ←	$\bar{1}$·9872

$$\sqrt{\frac{8 \cdot 647}{9 \cdot 173}} = 0 \cdot 9710$$

Exercise G

Find the values of the following, giving answers rounded to three significant figures.

1. $496 \times 0 \cdot 0371 \times 2 \cdot 15$.   **2.** $654 \div 361$.   **3.** $6 \cdot 14 \div 72^2$.

4. $\sqrt[3]{0 \cdot 1}$.   **5.** $\sqrt{0 \cdot 9}$.   **6.** $\sqrt{(94 \cdot 3/16)}$.

7. $\dfrac{462 \times \sqrt{(0\cdot253)}}{0\cdot0294}$.

8. $2\pi\sqrt{(34/981)}$.

9. $31\cdot4^7 \times 10^4$.

10. $0\cdot19^{13} \times 4\cdot739$.

11. $\sqrt[3]{6840}$.

12. $\sqrt[5]{(106/9380)}$.

13. $4\cdot609 \times 10^{-7} \times 8\cdot86 \times 10^{-3}$.

14. $\dfrac{5\cdot82 \times 10^{-7}}{8\cdot162 \times 10^{6}}$.

15. $\sqrt[3]{[(6\cdot31 \times 10^7 \times 304\cdot1 \times 10^{-3})/(1\cdot178 \times 10^{-6})]}$.

16. $1\cdot25/(7\cdot3 \times 10^4)^{\frac{2}{3}}$.

17. A light-year is the distance travelled by light in one year. How many kilometres is this if a year is taken as 365 days and light travels at 299 800 km/s?

18. The mean radius of the earth is 6400 km. What is its volume in km³ and area in km²? ($V = \frac{4}{3}\pi r^3$, $A = 4\pi r^2$.)

19. a is proportional to $1/d^2$. When $a = 2\cdot84$, $d = 7\cdot63$. What is d when $a = 7\cdot2$?

20. How many digits are there in 25^{25}?

5.4 The slide-rule. When using a slide-rule, we multiply, for example, using the rules of combination of logs, i.e. by addition, but without ever discovering the values of the logarithms we are combining.

The method can be seen from a graph of the function $x \to \log x$ for any base. Instead of marking the y-axis with the actual values of the logarithms (0 to 1, if the base is 10) it is labelled with the image-names of the domain (see Figure 4(a)).

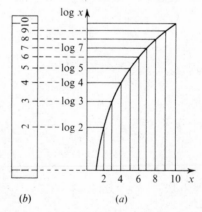

Fig. 4

A duplicate scale is put beside it, the word 'log' is eliminated and there is a slide-rule (see Figure 4(b)).

172

5.5 Compound interest. If a sum of money is invested at compound interest, then the interest is added to the investment. So, if the rate of interest is 6 % per annum, the sum remaining invested rises by 6 % each year. As usual, it will be best to think of this as the investments being *multiplied* by 106/100 or 1·06 each year.

Suppose £80 is the original sum.

After 1 year the investment is worth   £80 × 1·06,

after 2 years it is worth   £80 × 1·06², and so on.

The amount £A after t years is given by

$$A = 80 \times 1 \cdot 06^t.$$

To find the amount after 5 years, i.e. the value of A when $t = 5$, we may use logarithms.

	x	$\log x$
	80	1·9031
$A = 80 \times 1 \cdot 06^5 = 107 \cdot 0$	1·06⁵	$5 \times 0 \cdot 0253 = 0 \cdot 1265$
	107·0	2·0296

To find when the investment is worth £140, we must reverse this working. Again we use the relation

$$\log A = \log 80 + t \times \log 1 \cdot 06,$$

on this occasion to find t when $A = 140$.

$$t = \frac{\log 140 - \log 80}{\log 1 \cdot 06}$$

$$= \frac{\log 1 \cdot 75}{\log 1 \cdot 06}$$

$$= \frac{0 \cdot 2430}{0 \cdot 0253}.$$

We have used logarithms to simplify the original equation and isolate t. Now we are faced with a division sum, to which the answer is clearly between 9 and 10. After 9 years the amount is less than £140, and after 10 years it is greater. When money is invested at compound interest its value may increase steadily, and not by a jump each year. If that is the case here, we may wish to divide 0·2430 by 0·0253 more accurately, using slide-rule or logarithms.

	x	$\log x$
$t = \dfrac{0 \cdot 2430}{0 \cdot 0253} = 9 \cdot 605$	0·2430	1̄·3856
	0·0253	2̄·4031
	9·605	0·9825

5.6 The solution of equations where the unknown is an index.
We give another example of the type of equation which occurred in the second part of the last section.

Example 5

Solve
$$5^x = 0{\cdot}4.$$

Notice that $5^0 = 1$ and $5^{-1} = 0{\cdot}2$, so that the solution must lie between 0 and -1.
$$\log 5^x = \log 0{\cdot}4 \Leftrightarrow x \log 5 = \log 0{\cdot}4$$

$$\Leftrightarrow x = \frac{\log 0{\cdot}4}{\log 5} = \frac{\bar{1}{\cdot}6021}{0{\cdot}6990}.$$

We must now write the numerator as a single negative number:
$$\bar{1}{\cdot}6021 = -1 + 0{\cdot}6021 = -0{\cdot}3979.$$

Then

	n	$\log n$
	0·3979	$\bar{1}$·5998
$x = -\dfrac{0{\cdot}3979}{0{\cdot}6990} = -0{\cdot}5693$	0·6990	$\bar{1}$·8445
	0·5693	$\bar{1}$·7553

Notice that we have actually found $\log_5 0{\cdot}4$. Use this method to find $\log_2 3$.

Exercise H

1. Calculate the values of x when
   (a) $4^x = 8^3$; (b) $3^x = 10$; (c) $75{\cdot}3^x = 108$;
   (d) $1{\cdot}013^x = 0{\cdot}09$; (e) $x = \log_3 10$.

2. Use logarithms to base 10 to calculate:
   (a) $2^{0{\cdot}7}$; (b) $2^{4{\cdot}3}$; (c) $3^{-2{\cdot}1}$;
   (d) $\log_2 11$; (e) $\log_{11} 4$.

3. Arrange the following in order of magnitude; then use logarithms to evaluate the greatest and the least: $\log_{10} 9$, $\log_6 7$, $\log_6 7$, $\log_3 2$, $\log_9 80$.

4. £320 is invested at 2·5 % compound interest per annum. What is the value of the investment after 1 year? What is it after 3 years? After how many complete years will it have reached the value of £500?

5. Write a flow chart to find the value of the investment in Question 4 after each year, continuing until the value of the investment first exceeds £500.

6. After how many complete years will a sum of money be doubled if it is invested at compound interest at
   (a) 4·5 % per annum, (b) 5·5 % per annum, (c) 9 % per annum?

7. Write a flow chart for Question 6(c).

174

8. Suppose that the Government expects wages and salaries to rise by 4 % per annum. If the salaries in a particular profession are reviewed only every three years, by what percentage should they increase to keep up with the average rate of increase?

9. The rate of decay of a radio-active substance is usually measured in terms of its half-life. This is the time required for one-half of the material at any one time to decay.

Suppose that the formula for its mass at time t is $m = m_0 e^{-kt}$ where m_0 is the initial mass, $e = 2.718$ and k is a constant with a value particular to these circumstances.

If $m = 0.9 m_0$ when $t = 2$ show that $k = 0.0527$; hence find the value of t when $m = 0.5 m_0$.

10. Repeat Exercise D, Question 3, using logarithms rather than a graph.

11. The following readings arose in an experiment. It is known that $y = kb^x$, where k and b are constants.

x	1	2	3	4	5
y	2.9	6.2	12	25	46

Explain why the graph of log y against x should be a straight line. Draw the graph and obtain estimates for k and b.

From your graph, estimate the values of y when $x = 2.5$ and $x = 6$.

6. LOGARITHMS IN CONNECTION WITH EXPERIMENTAL RESULTS

Consider this table of results obtained from a pendulum-swinging experiment.

Length of pendulum (in metres)	l	0.6	1.0	1.4	1.8	2.2
Average time of swing (in seconds)	t	1.54	2.03	2.39	2.67	2.97

If we plot these results, we get the curve of Figure 5. This does not help us to predict a formula connecting t and l.

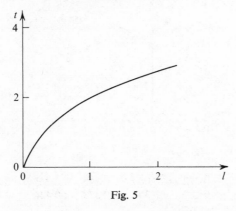

Fig. 5

175

If you suspected from the graph or from theoretical considerations that t is proportional to $\sqrt{l}$, you could plot t against $\sqrt{l}$ (as suggested in the O-level course) and hope to get a straight line.

$\sqrt{l}$	0·775	1·000	1·183	1·342	1·483
t	1·54	2·03	2·39	2·67	2·97

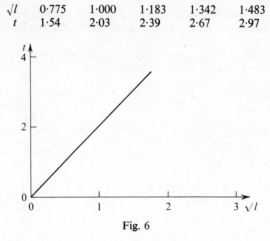

Fig. 6

What is the gradient of the line in Figure 6? What is the relation connecting t and $\sqrt{l}$?

There is an alternative method of testing to see whether any power law holds.

If $t = kl^n$, then $\log t = \log(kl^n)$

$$= \log k + n \log l.$$

Thus a graph of $\log t$ against $\log l$ will be a straight line of gradient n and with an intercept on the $\log t$ axis equal to $\log k$.

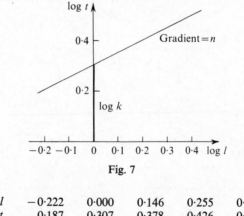

Fig. 7

$\log l$	−0·222	0·000	0·146	0·255	0·342
$\log t$	0·187	0·307	0·378	0·426	0·473

176

Draw the graph, find the value of k and show that $n = \frac{1}{2}$. Compare the value of k with that found from Figure 6.

A process similar to the above can be used if we have some growth function connecting the variables.

For example, if $y = kb^x$, where k is a constant, then taking logs of both sides of this equation,

$$\log y = \log kb^x$$

$$= \log k + x \log b.$$

What should we take for our axes here?

6.1 Use of logarithmic graph paper. Special graph paper can be obtained with one or both scales logarithmic instead of linear (equally spaced). This enables us to solve problems like that of Section 6 without looking up any logarithms.

It is instructive to compare the growth of a sum of money at different interest rates. To do this a graphical approach is to be preferred unless computing facilities are available. Using conventional graph paper would not reduce the work since we would have to plot many points to obtain the curves $y = (1 \cdot 04)^n$, $y = (1 \cdot 06)^n$ etc. (taking £1 as the investment). However, using log graph paper with a linear scale on one axis, we will obtain straight line graphs for each interest rate.

We label the linear axis in units of one year, and the log axis in units of £1. All the graphs will pass through the point (0, 1). Taking the line $y = (1 \cdot 04)^n$ as an example, we proceed as follows: when $n = 20$, say, $y = 1 \cdot 04^{20} = 2 \cdot 19$. We then have the point (20, 2·19) on our line and simply join it to (0, 1). Repeating this for other rates of interest we obtain a graph as in Figure 8.

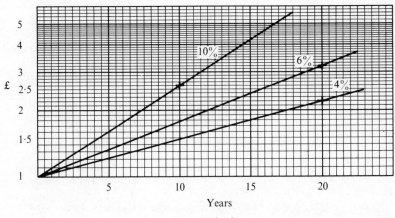

Years

Fig. 8

How much longer will it take for a sum of money to double at 4 % per annum compound interest than at 6 %? How many years will it take to double at 10 %? How much will it be worth after 10 years at 4 %, 6 %, 10 % per annum?

Exercise I

1.

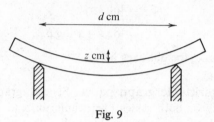

Fig. 9

In an experiment to determine how the sag of a beam varies with the distance between its supports, the following results were obtained.

d (in cm)	500	540	580	620	660	700
z (in cm)	1·1	1·3	1·7	2·0	2·4	2·8

where d is the distance between the supports and z is the sag.

By drawing the graph of log z against log d, determine the power of d to which z is proportional.

2. A simple experiment to determine Young's Modulus from the periodic vibration of a loaded cantilever can be carried out as follows:

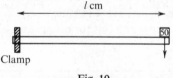

Fig. 10

A metre rule is fixed to a bench at one end and a mass of 50 g attached to the other.

The length, l cm, is varied and the time for 20 vibrations, T seconds, is measured, with the following results:

l	60	70	80	85	90	95
T	6·0	7·3	9·0	10·0	10·9	11·5

Assuming $T \propto l^n$, determine n by drawing a suitable log graph.

3. It is easy to obtain from a shop selling magnetic recording tapes a table showing, for a particular width of tape, the diameter of spool and approximate length of tape.

Investigate the proposition that the length of tape on a spool depends on the square of the diameter of the spool.

178

4. In an experiment with a tungsten filament lamp, the following readings were obtained of the current I (in amps) and the voltage, V.

V	1·3	2·0	2·8	4·4	5·7
I	1·5	1·8	2·1	2·5	2·9

Calculate the resistance R ohms (using Ohm's Law, $V = IR$) and the power P watts ($= VI$). Obtain a straight line graph by taking logarithms, given that $P = aR^n$, and use it to find the values of a and n.

5. A simple experiment to simulate radioactive decay can be performed as follows. Take 24 dice in a beaker. Throw them and remove any sixes that appear. Record the number of dice left. Repeat the experiment with the remaining dice. Plot the graph of log N against T, where N is the number left after T throws. What can you conclude from the graph? After how many throws was N first 12 or less? This corresponds to the half-life of the radio-active substance.

6.

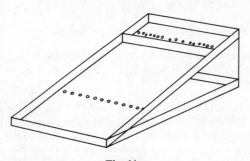

Fig. 11

In an attempt to simulate radio-active decay more convincingly, a large number of ball-bearings were weighed in a beaker and then allowed to roll down a board with a number of holes in it, into which some fell. The remainder were weighed and the experiment repeated. The following results were obtained for the mass M grams of the balls left after T turns.

T	M	T	M	T	M
0	200	7	112	14	59
1	184	8	104	15	52
2	170	9	95	16	48
3	156	10	85	17	45
4	145	11	77	18	42
5	135	12	72	19	40
6	122	13	65	20	37

Investigate the relation between T and M. Find the half-life of 'decay' of the ball bearings.

7. Repeat some of the questions of this exercise using logarithmic graph paper.

Miscellaneous Exercise

1. What is the value of a^b (i) when $a = 0$, $b \neq 0$, (ii) when $a \neq 0$, $b = 0$? How should 0^0 be defined?

2. Sketch the graphs of $y = 2^x$, $y = 2^{-x}$, $y = -2^x$, $y = \frac{1}{2}(2^x + 2^{-x})$.

3. Sketch the graphs of $y = \log 3x$, $y = \log (x-3)$, $y = \log x^3$. Under what transformations are these the images of the graph of $y = \log x$?

4. Use logarithms to evaluate the following:

(a) 3^{17};   (b) $\sqrt[3]{17}$;   (c) $\dfrac{473 \times 0 \cdot 0604}{6 \times 10^5}$;   (d) $\dfrac{13}{9!}$;

(e) $\pi h(R^2 - r^2)$ when $h = 14000$, $R = 0 \cdot 0565$, $r = 0 \cdot 0435$.

5. What is the relation between $\log_3 10$ and $\log_{10} 3$?

6. Show that $\log_a b \times \log_b c = \log_a c$.

7. Write a flow chart to produce a compound interest table, showing the value of an initial investment of £1 after 1, 2, ..., 20 years at many different rates of interest.

8. If there are 32 people in a knock-out tennis (singles) tournament, how many rounds must there be including the final? How many rounds if there were 61? (Some people may have a bye into the second round.) How many rounds if there were 237? Can you give a general rule? If there are 237 people in the tournament, how many matches will have to be played? Can you give a general rule?

9. (a) With paper, pencil and the piece of the D-scale of your slide-rule marked from 1 to 2·8, how could you reconstruct the integer points of the rest of the scale?

(b) Having obtained the integer points, the piece of the ruler was lost. So the middle points of the intervals between 1 and 2, and between 2 and 3, etc., were marked as 1·5, 2·5, etc. How should these first two midpoints have been marked?

10. The wavelength of a musical note is double the wavelength of the note which is one octave higher in pitch. So the wavelength is a growth function of its pitch. This relationship can be seen in the spacing of the frets of a guitar or in the curve formed by the pipes of an organ. Draw a graph of the distance from the bridge to fret against pitch for a guitar and check that the shape is a growth curve. (The notes are equally spaced in pitch.) In the equal tempered chromatic scale the octave is divided into 12 equal intervals, called semitones, which the ear recognises as equal steps in pitch. The notes which mark off these intervals are C, C#, D, D#, E, F, F#, G, G#, A, A#, B. On the piano they are sounded by successive keys: C, D, E, F, G, A, B (the diatonic scale of C Major) by the white keys, and C#, D#, F#, G#, A# by the black keys in between.

Find how many times greater the wavelength of any note is than the wavelength of a note one semitone higher.

180

SUMMARY

Zero, negative and rational indices

$$x^0 = 1,$$

$$x^{-a} = \frac{1}{x^a},$$

$$x^{m/n} = (\sqrt[n]{x})^m = \sqrt[n]{(x^m)}.$$

Laws of indices

(1) $x^a \times x^b = x^{a+b}$.

(2) $x^a \div x^b = x^{a-b}$.

(3) $(x^a)^b = x^{ab}$.

Logarithms

$$y = a^x \Leftrightarrow x = \log_a y.$$

Laws of logarithms

(1) $\log_a (x \times y) = \log_a x + \log_a y$.

(2) $\log_a (x \div y) = \log_a x - \log_a y$.

(3) $\log_a x^n = n \log_a x$.

Derivatives

If $f(x) = x^n$ and n is rational, then $f'(x) = nx^{n-1}$.

Graphing experimental data

$y = kx^n \Leftrightarrow \log y = \log k + n \log x$. Plot $\log y$ against $\log x$.

$y = kb^x \Leftrightarrow \log y = \log k + x \log b$. Plot $\log y$ against x.

9

SIGMA NOTATION AND SERIES

1. FLOW CHARTS FOR SERIES

Example 1

If a man saves £100 each year and it earns 6 % compound interest, find the value of the investment after

  (a) one year (i.e. just before the second payment),
  (b) five years,
  (c) thirty years.

The first two parts of the problem are quite easy. Part (c) is more difficult and very long. Can you suggest how you might shorten the working? The answer to part (c) is the sum

$$100 \times 1 \cdot 06 + 100 \times 1 \cdot 06^2 + 100 \times 1 \cdot 06^3 + \ldots + 100 \times 1 \cdot 06^{30}.$$

We could use logarithms to calculate each of the 30 terms and then add them all up, but this is rather tedious.

Notice that the sequence of terms is a geometric progression; the individual terms are the values $f(t)$ for the exponential function

$$f: t \to 100 \times 1 \cdot 06^t \quad \text{for} \quad t = 1, 2, \ldots, 30.$$

It is possible to write a flow chart to compute the sum of this sequence. For this we use the inductive definition of the sequence:

$$u_1 = 106,$$

$$u_{k+1} = u_k \times 1 \cdot 06.$$

Work through the flow chart of Figure 1 and check that it produces the correct sum. This would enable a computer to calculate the answer to the above problem; later in the chapter we shall find a method of solving this problem ourselves.

Example 2

Check that the flow chart in Figure 2 computes the sum

$$1^2 + 2^2 + 3^2 + \ldots + 8^2.$$

The counter C takes consecutive values from 1 to 8, and the term which in each loop is equal to C^2, is added to the accumulator, B. So we have used the function $i \to i^2$ defined on the natural numbers to produce the required sequence.

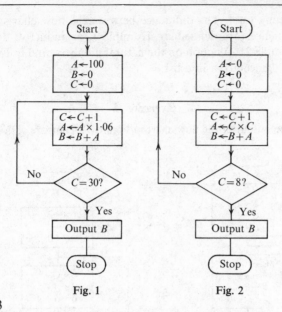

| Fig. 1 | Fig. 2 |

Example 3

If the data of Figure 3 are the daily takings, in pounds, of a taxi driver during one week, what does the flow chart compute?

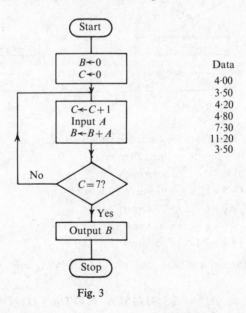

Fig. 3

From dry runs for the flow charts in Examples 1, 2 and 3, you will have noted the common features, the use of the store C for a counter and

B for a running total. The difference between the flow charts lies in the way the sequences are defined. In Example 1, an inductive definition is used, in Example 2 a function on the natural numbers, and in Example 3 a statistical sequence given in a list.

Exercise A

1. What is the output of the flow chart in Figure 4? Compare with Example 2.

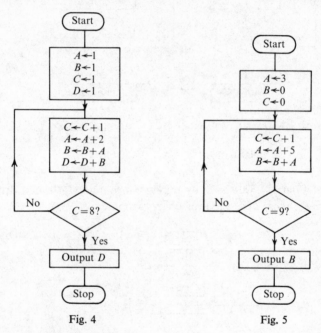

Fig. 4   Fig. 5

2. Write a flow chart for computing the sum of:

    (*a*) $8+14+20+26+...$to 12 terms;

    (*b*) $4+20+100+...$to 9 terms;

    (*c*) $1\times4+3\times12+5\times36+...$to 10 terms;

    (*d*) $1+\frac{1}{2}+\frac{1}{3}+\frac{1}{4}+...$to 20 terms;

    (*e*) $1-\frac{1}{2}+\frac{1}{3}-\frac{1}{4}+...$to 20 terms;

    (*f*) $\frac{1}{2}+\frac{3}{4}+\frac{5}{6}+\frac{7}{8}+...$to 13 terms.

3. Work through the flow chart of Figure 5. What series is being summed?

write it in the sigma form

2. SIGMA NOTATION

The terms of the expression in Example 1 are of the form

$$100\times1\cdot06^i,$$

184

where i takes the values 1, 2, 3, ..., 30. When the terms of a sequence are added together we have a *series*, in this case

$$100 \times 1 \cdot 06 + 100 \times 1 \cdot 06^2 + 100 \times 1 \cdot 06^3 + \ldots$$

The sum of the first 30 terms of this series may be written in shorthand form

$$\sum_{i=1}^{30} 100 \times 1 \cdot 06^i$$

instead of the cumbersome expression with the dots in the middle.

In general, any sequence $u_1, u_2, u_3, \ldots$ gives a series $u_1 + u_2 + u_3 + \ldots$ and the sum of the first n terms of this may be written

$$\sum_{i=1}^{n} u_i$$

in short for $u_1 + u_2 + u_3 + \ldots + u_n$.

Σ is the Greek capital letter 'sigma', which corresponds to 'S', the first letter of the English word 'Sum'. The whole symbol

$$\sum_{i=1}^{n} u_i$$

is read as 'Sigma, i equals 1 to n, of u_1'—or words to that effect. Sometimes we say 'the sum...' instead of 'sigma...'.

The symbol Σ indicates that a summation is to be carried out, and the terms to be added are u_i, where i is a counter to take *consecutive integral* values between the *limits* 1 and n. The lower limit of i is written *below* the Σ.

Example 4

Write out in full the sums

$$(a)\ \sum_{i=3}^{5} \frac{i-1}{i+1} \quad \text{and} \quad (b)\ \sum_{i=1}^{6} (2i+1).$$

(a) $\dfrac{3-1}{3+1} + \dfrac{4-1}{4+1} + \dfrac{5-1}{5+1} = \dfrac{2}{4} + \dfrac{3}{5} + \dfrac{4}{6} = 1\frac{23}{30}.$

(b) $(2 \times 1 + 1) + (2 \times 2 + 1) + (2 \times 3 + 1) + (2 \times 4 + 1) + (2 \times 5 + 1)$
$$+ (2 \times 6 + 1)$$
$$= 3 + 5 + 7 + 9 + 11 + 13$$
$$= 48.$$

The symbol may be abbreviated to

$$\sum_{1}^{6} (2i+1)$$

wherever there is no ambiguity as to which letter is the counter.

Note that
$$\sum_{i=1}^{6} (2i+1) = \sum_{j=1}^{6} (2j+1),$$

since the counting letter or counter does not appear in the final evaluation. We shall usually use the letter i.

Sigma notation is a simple shorthand, and like many simple shorthands it requires some practice at first. When mastered, it is a help in any work where 'families' of terms are to be added up. In particular it will be used in Chapter 10 on Integration and in Chapter 11 on Statistics.

Exercise ●B

1. Write out the following sums and evaluate them.

(a) $\displaystyle\sum_{2}^{4} i$; (b) $\displaystyle\sum_{1}^{7} 3i$; (c) $\displaystyle\sum_{1}^{4} i^2$;

(d) $\displaystyle\sum_{1}^{3} i^3$; (e) $\displaystyle\sum_{1}^{4} 2^i$; (f) $\displaystyle\sum_{-2}^{1} 2^{i+3}$;

(g) $\displaystyle\sum_{1}^{4} (-1)^i i^3$; (h) $\displaystyle\sum_{0}^{3} i(i+1)$.

2. (a) Write out in full the sum $\displaystyle\sum_{i=1}^{8} (3i+4)$.

(b) Give an inductive definition of the sequence involved.

(c) Draw a flow chart for computing the sum.

3. Repeat Question 2 for $\displaystyle\sum_{i=1}^{4} (2^i+3)$.

[*Hint.* For part (b) show that the inductive step amounts to 'double and subtract 3'.]

4. Given that $x_1 = 12$, $x_2 = 7$, $x_3 = 9$, $x_4 = 15$, $x_5 = 12$, $x_6 = 10$, $x_7 = 12$, $x_8 = 9$, evaluate:

(a) $\displaystyle\sum_{1}^{8} x_i$; (b) $\displaystyle\sum_{1}^{4} x_{2i}$; (c) $\displaystyle\sum_{1}^{4} 2x_i$;

(d) $\displaystyle\sum_{1}^{4} x_{2i-1}$; (e) $\displaystyle\sum_{1}^{4} (x_{2i}-1)$.

5. Express the following in Σ-notation:

(a) $7+12+17+22+27+32$;

(b) $3+6+12+24$; (c) $1+\frac{1}{2}+\frac{1}{3}+\frac{1}{4}+\frac{1}{5}+\frac{1}{6}$;

(d) $\frac{1}{3}+\frac{1}{4}+\frac{1}{5}+\frac{1}{6}+\frac{1}{7}$; (e) $\frac{1}{2}+\frac{2}{3}+\frac{3}{4}+\frac{4}{5}$.

2.1 Series in sigma form. To answer Question 5 of Exercise B we must express the general term of each sequence in terms of the counter. For example, in (a) the terms of the arithmetic progression are given by the function $i \rightarrow 2+5i$ defined on the natural numbers, and the sum $7+12+17+22+27+32$ may be written $\displaystyle\sum_{1}^{6} (2+5i)$.

Σ

You may have suggested a different, but equally correct, answer to this question, for example $\sum_{0}^{5}(7+5i)$ or even $\sum_{-2}^{3}(17+5i)$. Of the many possible forms, we shall usually prefer the one with lower limit 1.

In (b) of Question 5 the terms of the geometric progression are given by the function $i \rightarrow 1\cdot5 \times 2^i$, and the sum may be written

$$\sum_{1}^{4} 1\cdot5 \times 2^i \quad \text{or} \quad \sum_{1}^{4} 3 \times 2^{i-1}.$$

Example 5

Put $1 - \dfrac{1}{x} + \dfrac{1}{x^2} - \dfrac{1}{x^3} + \dfrac{1}{x^4}$ into Σ-form.

Notice that this may be written

$$\left(-\frac{1}{x}\right)^0 + \left(-\frac{1}{x}\right)^1 + \left(-\frac{1}{x}\right)^2 + \left(-\frac{1}{x}\right)^3 + \left(-\frac{1}{x}\right)^4.$$

So the sum is

$$\left(-\frac{1}{x}\right)^{1-1} + \left(-\frac{1}{x}\right)^{2-1} + \left(-\frac{1}{x}\right)^{3-1} + \left(-\frac{1}{x}\right)^{4-1} + \left(-\frac{1}{x}\right)^{5-1} = \sum_{i=1}^{5} \left(-\frac{1}{x}\right)^{i-1}.$$

Exercise ✏ C

1. Express the following in Σ-notation. Do each part twice, once beginning the summation at $i = 0$ and once at $i = 1$. In part (a), express the sum in a third way so that a term of zero value begins the expanded form.

(a) $1 \times 3 + 2 \times 4 + 3 \times 5 + \ldots + 10 \times 12$;

(b) $\frac{1}{4} + \frac{1}{5} + \frac{1}{6} + \ldots + \frac{1}{20}$;

(c) $64 + 64 \times (\frac{3}{4}) + 64 \times (\frac{3}{4})^2 + \ldots + \frac{243}{16}$;

(d) $x - 2x^2 + 3x^3 - 4x^4 + 5x^5$;

(e) $1 - x + x^2 - x^3 + \ldots + (-1)^n x^n$;

(f) $ar^p + ar^{p+1} + \ldots + ar^{p+q}$;

(g) $ar^{p-1} + ar^p + \ldots + ar^n$.

2. Express the following A.P.'s and G.P.'s in Σ-notation:

(a) $1 + 4 + 7 + 10 + \ldots + 61$;

(b) $3 + 8 + 13 + 18 + \ldots + 73$;

(c) $2 + 6 + 18 + \ldots + 162$;

(d) $5 + 15 + 45 + \ldots$(twelve terms in all).

3. Write flow charts to compute the sums of the series in Questions 1(a), 1(b), 2(a), 2(c).

4. Put each of the following into Σ-form and find the sum:

(a) $1 + 2 + 3 + \ldots + 9$;

(b) $1 + 2 + 3 + \ldots + 90$;

(c) $1 + 2 + 3 + \ldots + n$.

5. Given $s_n = \sum\limits_{1}^{n} i$, calculate s_n and s_n/n for $n = 1, 2, 3, 4, \ldots, 11$. Can you guess a formula for s_n?

6. Calculate $s_n = \sum\limits_{1}^{n} i^3$ for $n = 1, 2, 3, 4, 5$. Can you guess a formula for s_n?

7. How many terms are there in the sum $13 + 16 + 19 + \ldots + 91$? Express it in Σ-form. What is the middle term? What is the sum of the series? Explain your method.

8. Find the sums of the series in Question 2(*a*) and (*b*) without listing all the terms. Can you devise a simple method for summing the series of Question 2(*c*) and (*d*)?

9. Verify that $\qquad \sum\limits_{1}^{4} (8i+3) = \sum\limits_{3}^{6} (8i-13).$

Express this series in Σ-form (*a*) with lower limit 6, (*b*) with lower limit -2.

10. Investigate whether the following are true or false:

(*a*) $\sum\limits_{1}^{3} i^3 = \sum\limits_{0}^{5} (2i+1);$ (*b*) $\sum\limits_{1}^{8} (3i+4) = \sum\limits_{0}^{7} (28-3i);$

(*c*) $\sum\limits_{1}^{5} i^2 = \left(\sum\limits_{1}^{5} i\right)^2;$ (*d*) $\sum\limits_{1}^{6} (2i+8) = \left(\sum\limits_{1}^{6} 2i\right) + 8;$

(*e*) $\sum\limits_{1}^{n} (2i+8) = 2\sum\limits_{1}^{n} (i+4);$ (*f*) $\sum\limits_{1}^{n} (i^2+3i) = \sum\limits_{1}^{n} i^2 + \sum\limits_{1}^{n} 3i;$

(*g*) $\sum\limits_{1}^{n} (3i+4) = 3\sum\limits_{1}^{n} i + 4n;$ (*h*) $\sum\limits_{1}^{n} i . \sum\limits_{1}^{n} i^2 = \sum\limits_{1}^{n} i^3;$

(*i*) $\sum\limits_{-3}^{4} (x^i - x^{i-1}) = x^4 - x^{-4};$ (*j*) $\sum\limits_{0}^{6} (i+4)(i-2) = \sum\limits_{-3}^{3} (i+1)(i+7).$

11. Let f be the function $f: x \to 3x+1$ and u_1, u_2, u_3, u_4 be 4, 1, 3, 5. Find:

(*a*) $f(u_2);$ (*b*) $u_4 f(u_4);$ (*c*) $\sum\limits_{1}^{4} f(u_i);$

(*d*) $\sum\limits_{1}^{4} u_i f(u_i);$ (*e*) $\sum\limits_{1}^{4} (u_i - 3) f(u_i).$

What is the connection between your last three answers?

12. If $f(x) = 2x+3$, find $\sum\limits_{1}^{4} f(i^2), \sum\limits_{1}^{4} (f(i))^2, \left(\sum\limits_{1}^{4} f(i)\right)^2.$

13. In this question $x_i = x_0 + ih$, $g(x) = x^2$. Evaluate the sums concerned in each part. Show that the sum in (*a*) represents the shaded area in Figure 6, and illustrate the other sums similarly.

(*a*) $x_0 = 2, h = 1; \sum\limits_{i=0}^{3} g(x_i);$

(*b*) $x_0 = 2, h = \frac{1}{2}; \sum\limits_{0}^{7} (\frac{1}{2} g(x_i));$

(*c*) $x_0 = 3, h = 0{\cdot}1; \sum\limits_{0}^{9} (0{\cdot}1 g(x_i)).$

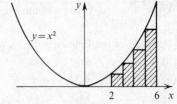

Fig. 6

2.2   Some useful general results. Parts of Questions 10 and 11 of Exercise C have illustrated the following general results:

$$\text{(i)} \quad \sum_1^n af(i) \equiv a \sum_1^n f(i);$$

$$\text{(ii)} \quad \sum_1^n (f(i)+b) \equiv \left(\sum_1^n f(i) \right) + nb;$$

$$\text{(iii)} \quad \sum_1^n (f(i)+g(i)) \equiv \sum_1^n f(i) + \sum_1^n g(i);$$

$$\text{(iv)} \quad \sum_1^n f(i) \equiv \sum_{1+k}^{n+k} f(i-k).$$

Each identity is proved by writing out in full the expressions implied by the sigma notation. The only one which looks surprising is (ii), and the proof of this is as follows.

$$\sum_1^n (f(i)+b) = (f(1)+b) + (f(2)+b) + (f(3)+b) + \ldots + (f(n)+b)$$

$$= (f(1)+f(2)+f(3)+\ldots+f(n)) + (b+b+\ldots+b)$$

$$= \left(\sum_1^n f(i) \right) + nb.$$

Identity (iv) formalizes the choice of ways of expressing a series in Σ-notation, as noted in Section 2.1.

3. SUMMATION OF FINITE SERIES

Having a shorthand way of writing a series is only a start. What we often require is the sum, and the rest of this chapter develops ways of procuring this economically. Working out all the terms and then adding them up is obviously one method, but this can be tedious, unless mechanized.

3.1   The sum of an arithmetic progression. Many of the series in the early part of this chapter have been arithmetic progressions, where each term is obtained from the previous one by adding a fixed number. These are the easiest series to sum, as you may have found already.

Example 6

A man's salary starts at £1600 p.a. and increases by £100 each year. How much has he earned altogether by the time his salary is £2300?

We require the sum of the A.P.

$$1600 + 1700 + \ldots + 2300.$$

The average of the first and last terms is $\frac{1}{2}(1600+2300) = 1950$. The sum £1950 is his average salary for the whole period. Each salary below this average is exactly balanced by an above-average salary in a later year.

Thus the total is $8 \times £1950 = £15600$.

In general, the sum of an A.P. is $\frac{1}{2}n(a+l)$, where n is the number of terms, a is the first term, and l the last term.

An important special case is $\sum_{1}^{n} i$. The method above gives the formula $\frac{1}{2}n(n+1)$ for the nth triangle number (see also Exercise C, Questions 4 and 5).

Example 7

Evaluate $\sum_{1}^{20} (12+7i)$.

This is the A.P. $19+26+33+\ldots+152$.

The method of Example 6 soon gives the sum as $\frac{1}{2} \times 20 \times 171 = 1710$, but we will also take this example to illustrate the use of the identities of Section 2.2.

$$\sum_{1}^{20} (12+7i) = 12 \times 20 + \sum_{1}^{20} (7i) \quad \text{from (ii),}$$

$$= 240 + 7\sum_{1}^{20} i \quad \text{from (i),}$$

$$= 240 + 7 \times \tfrac{1}{2} \times 20 \times 21$$

$$= 240 + 1470$$

$$= 1710.$$

Exercise D

1. Evaluate

    (*a*) $3+5+7+\ldots+47$,

    (*b*) $1+4+7+\ldots$ to 18 terms,

by both methods of Example 7.

2. How many terms need to be taken before the sum of the A.P. $12+17+22+\ldots$ exceeds 1000?

3. Evaluate:

    (*a*) $\sum_{1}^{15} (i+5)$;   (*b*) $\sum_{10}^{20} (2i+1)$;   (*c*) $\sum_{i=1}^{n} (r+3i)$;   (*d*) $\sum_{i=1}^{n} (n-i)$.

4. Find:

    (*a*) $\sum_{n+1}^{2n} i$;   (*b*) $\sum_{0}^{n-1} i$;   (*c*) $\sum_{n-k}^{n+k} i$.

5. Express the following in sigma notation, and find their sums:

    (*a*) $1+4+7+\ldots+94$;

    (*b*) $22+17+12+\ldots+(-28)$;

    (*c*) $12+14+16+\ldots$ to 39 terms;

    (*d*) $80+71+62+\ldots$ to 14 terms.

6. Express $\log x + \log x^2 + \log x^3 + \ldots + \log x^n$ in sigma form and find a formula for this sum.

7. Explain each step of the following proof.

$$\sum_1^n i = \sum_1^n (n+1-i) = \frac{1}{2}\left(\sum_1^n i + \sum_1^n (n+1-i)\right) = \frac{1}{2}\sum_1^n (i+n+1-i) = \tfrac{1}{2}n(n+1).$$

To what simple process is this method of proof equivalent?

8. Simplify:

(a) $\displaystyle\sum_1^4 (i^2+3) + \sum_5^7 (i^2+3)$;

(b) $\displaystyle\sum_1^5 (i+2)^2 - \sum_3^7 i^2$;

(c) $\displaystyle\sum_1^n i^2 + 2\sum_1^n i + n$;

(d) $\displaystyle\sum_1^n (i+1)^2 - \sum_1^n i^2$;

(e) $\displaystyle\sum_1^6 i^2 - \sum_1^5 i^2$;

(f) $\displaystyle\sum_1^{n+1} f(i) - \sum_1^n f(i)$.

9. (a) If $s_n = \displaystyle\sum_1^n u_i$, show that $s_n - s_{n-1} = u_n$.

(b) If $s_n = n^3$, what is u_n? Explain why $u_i = 3i^2 - 3i + 1$.

Deduce the formula for $\displaystyle\sum_1^n i^2$.

10. The populations of twelve villages, all very much the same size, are given in the frequency table.

i	Population x_i	Frequency $f(x_i)$
1	421	1
2	423	2
3	426	4
4	431	3
5	432	2

(a) Evaluate $\displaystyle\sum_{i=1}^5 f(x_i)$ and $\displaystyle\sum_{i=1}^5 x_i f(x_i)$ and explain what each answer represents. Deduce the mean population and write down a definition of the mean using Σ-notation.

(b) Calculate the mean using data zero 426, and then express what you have done in Σ-notation.

(c) Demonstrate algebraically that the two formulae are equivalent.

3.2 The difference method. Write out in full and simplify

$$\sum_1^4 (f(i+1)-f(i)).$$

Explain why the difference equation

$$\sum_1^n (f(i+1)-f(i)) = f(n+1)-f(1)$$

191

is true for any function f. As an example, take f as the function $x \to x^2$, and show that $\sum\limits_{1}^{n} (2i+1) = n^2 + 2n$.

Now this result is useful because from it we can obtain an expression for $\sum\limits_{1}^{n} i$. Further, it is an illustration of a general method which can be applied on a variety of occasions. In this case, the complete working is as follows.

From the difference equation,

$$\sum_{1}^{n} ((i+1)^2 - i^2) = (n+1)^2 - 1^2.$$

But
$$\sum_{1}^{n} ((i+1)^2 - i^2) = \sum_{1}^{n} (i^2 + 2i + 1 - i^2)$$

$$= \sum_{1}^{n} (2i+1) = 2\sum_{1}^{n} i + n,$$

and
$$(n+1)^2 - 1^2 = n^2 + 2n + 1 - 1$$

$$= n^2 + 2n,$$

so
$$2\sum_{1}^{n} i + n = n^2 + 2n$$

$$\sum_{1}^{n} i = \tfrac{1}{2}(n^2 + n).$$

In the next chapter, we shall need a formula for the sum of the first n square numbers, $\sum\limits_{1}^{n} i^2$. What function shall we use in the difference equation in order to get an expression containing $\sum\limits_{1}^{n} i^2$?

If we try $f: x \to x^3$, the difference equation gives

$$\sum_{1}^{n} ((i+1)^3 - i^3) = (n+1)^3 - 1^3.$$

But
$$\sum_{1}^{n} ((i+1)^3 - i^3) = \sum_{1}^{n} ((i^3 + 3i^2 + 3i + 1) - i^3)$$

$$= \sum_{1}^{n} (3i^2 + 3i + 1)$$

and it is now tempting to work out $(n+1)^3 - 1^3$. Do this and check that your answer for $\sum\limits_{1}^{n} i^2$ is the same as the one given by the following steps.

192

$$\sum_1^n (3i^2+3i+1) = (n+1)^3-1^3,$$

$$3\sum_1^n i^2+3\sum_1^n i+n = (n+1)^3-1,$$

$$3\sum_1^n i^2+3[\tfrac{1}{2}n(n+1)]+n = (n+1)^3-1,$$

$$3\sum_1^n i^2 = (n+1)^3-(n+1)-\tfrac{3}{2}n(n+1)$$
$$= (n+1)\,((n+1)^2-1-\tfrac{3}{2}n)$$
$$= (n+1)\,(n^2+\tfrac{1}{2}n).$$

Dividing by 3, $\qquad \sum_1^n i^2 = \tfrac{1}{6}n(n+1)\,(2n+1).$

In general, if this method is to be used to obtain $\sum_1^n u_i$, a function f has to be found so that the difference $f(i+1)-f(i)$ gives an expression involving u_i. Our experience in this section suggests that the function $f: x \to x^4$ would yield a formula for $\sum_1^n i^3$ (see Question 2 of Exercise E).

3.3 $\sum_1^n f(i)$, where $f(i)$ is a polynomial.

The formulae for $\sum_1^n i$, $\sum_1^n i^2$ and $\sum_1^n i^3$ are given in the summary at the end of this chapter and in the S.M.P. *Advanced Tables*. They enable us to sum series in which the ith term is a simple polynomial. For example,

$$\sum_1^n (i^3+6i^2-5) = \sum_1^n i^3+6\sum_1^n i^2-5n,$$

and now the standard results may be used.

Unfortunately, no pattern emerges in the results for $\sum_1^n i^k$, where k is any natural number: they would be hard to remember and clumsy to tabulate. Instead, another sequence of results is used which does have a very clear pattern and from which $\sum_1^n i^k$ can be calculated. We consider $\sum_1^n i$, $\sum_1^n i(i+1)$, $\sum_1^n i(i+1)\,(i+2),...$

Using the difference method to find these sums, we take $f(x)$ in turn as $(x-1)x$, $(x-1)x(x+1)$, $(x-1)x(x+1)\,(x+2)$,   ...

For instance, to find $\sum_1^n i(i+1)$ we use $f(x) = (x-1)x(x+1)$. Then the difference equation, $\sum_1^n (f(i+1)-f(i)) = f(n+1)-f(1)$, gives

$$\sum_1^n [i(i+1)\,(i+2)-(i-1)i(i+1)] = n(n+1)\,(n+2)-0.$$

193

But $\qquad i(i+1)(i+2)-(i-1)i(i+1) = i(i+1)[(i+2)-(i-1)]$

$$= 3i(i+1),$$

so $\qquad \sum_1^n i(i+1) = \tfrac{1}{3}n(n+1)(n+2).$

We now have the two results:

$$\sum_1^n i = \tfrac{1}{2}n(n+1),$$

$$\sum_1^n i(i+1) = \tfrac{1}{3}n(n+1)(n+2).$$

Guess a formula for $\sum_1^n i(i+1)(i+2)$. This will be established in Question 4 of Exercise E.

These formulae provide an alternative method of summing polynomial series and this can be illustrated with the series mentioned at the beginning of this section.

Since $\qquad i^3+6i^2-5 = i(i+1)(i+2)+(3i^2-2i-5)$

$$= i(i+1)(i+2)+3i(i+1)-5i-5,$$

$$\sum_1^n (i^3+6i^2-5) = \sum_1^n i(i+1)(i+2)+3\sum_1^n i(i+1)-5\sum_1^n i-5n.$$

Exercise E

1. Use the formulae for $\sum_1^n i$ and $\sum_1^n i^2$ to find

(a) $\sum_1^{10} i^2,$ (b) $\sum_1^{19} (i^2+7i),$ (c) $\sum_1^{12} (3i^2-1),$

(d) $\sum_1^{10} (i+2)^2,$ (e) $\sum_1^n (i+2)^2,$ (f) $\sum_1^n (n-i)^2.$

2. Use the method of Section 3.2 with $f(x) = x^4$ to find $\sum_1^n i^3.$

3. Find

(a) $\sum_1^9 (i^3+2i+1),$ (b) $\sum_1^{10} (i^3-i),$ (c) $\sum_1^n (4i^3-12i^2),$

(d) $\sum_1^n (i+1)^3.$

Check your answers to (c) and (d) by putting $n = 2$.

4. (a) Use the difference method with $f(x) = (x-1)x(x+1)(x+2)$ to find a formula for $\sum_1^n i(i+1)(i+2).$

(b) Fill in the missing steps in the following working:

$$\sum_1^n (i^3-i) = \sum_1^n i(i+1)(i+2)-3\sum_1^n i(i+1)$$

$$= \ldots = \tfrac{1}{4}n(n+1)(n+2)(n-1).$$

194

5. Given that i^3 may be written in the form $ai(i+1)(i+2)+bi(i+1)+ci$, find the values of a, b and c. Deduce the formula for $\sum_1^n i^3$, using the results of Section 3.3 and Question 4(a).

6. Show that both methods of Section 3.3 give

$$\sum_1^5 (i^3+6i^2-5) = 530.$$

7. Find a, b, c such that

$$i^3+12i^2+17i = ai(i+1)(i+2)+bi(i+1)+ci \quad \text{for all } i.$$

Hence find

$$\sum_1^n (i^3+12i^2+17i).$$

8. For $f: x \to 1/x$, find $f(i+1)-f(i)$, and use this to sum

$$\tfrac{1}{2}+\tfrac{1}{6}+\tfrac{1}{12}+\tfrac{1}{20}+\tfrac{1}{30}+\tfrac{1}{42}.$$

9. Find a function f for which $f(i+1)-f(i) = (i-1)i(i+1)$.
Deduce that

$$\sum_1^n (i-1)i(i+1) = \tfrac{1}{4}(n-1)n(n+1)(n+2).$$

10. If f is a polynomial function of degree k, what can you say about $f(i+1)-f(i)$?

3.4 The sum of a geometric progression.

Let us return to the problem of Example 1, finding the sum $100 \sum_1^{30} 1\cdot06^i$. This is a geometric progression, each term being obtained from the previous one by multiplying by a fixed number.

Since the terms are increasing exponentially we shall try the difference method with an exponential function

$$f: x \to r^x.$$

Then

$$\sum_1^n (f(i+1)-f(i)) = f(n+1)-f(1)$$

gives

$$\sum_1^n (r^{i+1}-r^i) = r^{n+1}-r$$

and

$$\sum_1^n (r-1)r^i = (r^n-1)r$$

$$\Rightarrow (r-1)\sum_1^n r^i = (r^n-1)r$$

$$\Rightarrow \sum_1^n r^i = \frac{r(r^n-1)}{r-1}.$$

Thus

$$100 \sum_1^{30} 1\cdot06^i = \frac{100 \times 1\cdot06(1\cdot06^{30}-1)}{1\cdot06-1}$$

$$= \frac{106(5\cdot74-1)}{0\cdot06}$$

$$= 8360 \text{ (to 3 sf).}$$

x	$\log x$
1·06	0·0253
	× 30
5·74	0·759

The total investment in Example 1 is worth approximately £8360 after 30 years.

It is easy to modify this result for the sum of the first n terms of the G.P. with first term a and common ratio r.

$$a + ar + ar^2 + \ldots + ar^{n-1} = a \sum_1^n r^{i-1} = a \left(\frac{r^n - 1}{r - 1} \right).$$

Example 8

Find the sum of the first 10 terms of the G.P.

$$8 + 12 + 18 + 27 + \ldots$$

Putting $a = 8$, $r = 1\frac{1}{2}$, $n = 10$ in the formula, we obtain

$$8 \left(\frac{1 \cdot 5^{10} - 1}{1 \cdot 5 - 1} \right) = 16(1 \cdot 5^{10} - 1)$$

$$= 16 \times 56 \cdot 68$$

$$= 907 \quad \text{(to 3 SF)}.$$

x	$\log x$
1·5	0·1761
	× 10
57·68	1·761

Exercise F

1. Show, by long division, that

$$\frac{r^5 - 1}{r - 1} = r^4 + r^3 + r^2 + r + 1.$$

2. Write down the sums of the following G.P.s. Simplify but do not evaluate your answers.

 (a) $7 + 14 + 28 + 56 + \ldots$, to 10 terms;

 (b) $2 + \frac{1}{2} + \frac{1}{8} + \frac{1}{32} + \ldots$, to 12 terms;

 (c) $3 - 6 + 12 - 24 + \ldots$, to 19 terms;

 (d) $-3 + 1 - \frac{1}{3} + \frac{1}{9} - \ldots$, to 16 terms.

3. Find the smallest natural number n for which the first n terms of the sequence 1, 1·1, 1·21, 1·331, ... have a sum greater than 20.

4. A chess board has 64 squares. If 1p is put on the first square, 2p on the second, 4p on the third, 8p on the fourth and so on for the 64 squares, calculate the total sum required.

5. If I invest £40 each year on 1 January for ten years and my money earns a steady 5 % compound interest, what is my total investment worth exactly ten years after the first instalment?

Investigate what difference it makes if interest is compound every six months (at $2\frac{1}{2}$ %) and I invest £20 every six months, for the same period of ten years.

6. (a) A mortgage of £4000 on a house is paid off in 20 equal annual instalments of £y. Interest of 6 % is charged each year on the remaining part of the debt. Show that after two years the amount owed is £$(4000x - y)x - y$ where $x = 1 \cdot 06$. Find an expression for the amount owed after 20 years, and by equating this with zero evaluate y.

(b) Using your answer to (a), find how much was still owing after ten years. How would you check whether or not your answer is reasonable?

196

7. If you can afford to pay £300 p.a. for 20 years and interest is charged at 8 % p.a., what size of mortgage will this provide?

8. Let $s_n = 1 + \frac{1}{2} + \frac{1}{4} + \frac{1}{8} + \dots$. Draw the graph of s_n against n for $n = 1, 2, 3, 4, 5$. (The graph will be a set of isolated points, of course.) Write down the formula for s_n and consider what happens as n tends to infinity. Does your graph suggest this?

9. Repeat Question 8 for the series (a) $1 - \frac{1}{2} + \frac{1}{4} - \frac{1}{8} + \dots$ and (b) $\frac{1}{2} + \frac{1}{3} + \frac{2}{9} + \frac{4}{27} + \dots$.

10. When a certain ball is dropped from a height of 3 metres the first bounce takes 1 second (this is the interval between the instants when the ball hits the ground for the first and second times). Each subsequent bounce take two-thirds of the time of the previous bounce. Find the total times taken (a) by the first 3 bounces, (b) by the first 10 bounces (use logarithms), and (c) until bouncing stops.

11. Find the sum of n terms of the G.P.

$$0 \cdot 23 + 0 \cdot 0023 + 0 \cdot 000023 + \dots.$$

What fraction is equivalent to the recurring decimal $0 \cdot 232323\dots$?

12. Denote the sum of the first n terms of the G.P., $\sum_{0}^{n-1} x^i$, by s_n. Explain why s_{k+1} can be written either as $s_k + x^k$ or as $1 + xs_k$.

Hence derive a formula for s_k.

Miscellaneous Exercise

1. Evaluate

(a) $\sum_{1}^{20} i + \sum_{1}^{20} (5 - i)$, (b) $\sum_{1}^{20} 2i + \sum_{1}^{20} (2i - 1) - \sum_{1}^{40} i$, (c) $\sum_{1}^{20} i^2 + \sum_{1}^{20} (21 - i)^2$.

2. Show that $n(n+1)(2n+1)$ is divisible by 6 for all natural numbers n.

3. Assuming $x_1 = 15$, $x_2 = 8$, $x_3 = 7$, $x_4 = 11$, $x_5 = 18$, $x_6 = 10$, $x_7 = 12$, $x_8 = 9$, $x_9 = 10$, evaluate:

(a) $\sum_{1}^{9} x_i$; (b) $\sum_{1}^{3} x_{3i}$; (c) $\sum_{1}^{3} 3x_i$;

(d) $\sum_{1}^{3} x_{3i-2}$; (e) $\sum_{1}^{3} (x_{3i} - 2)$.

4. Let a_{ij} denote the element in the ith row and jth column of the matrix

$$\begin{pmatrix} 1 & 4 & 6 & 3 \\ 2 & 0 & 7 & 1 \\ 8 & 3 & 2 & 0 \end{pmatrix}.$$

Write down the values of $\sum_{i=1}^{3} a_{ij}$ when $j = 3$, and $\sum_{j=1}^{3} \left(\sum_{i=1}^{3} a_{ij} \right)$.

5. If a_{ij} and b_{ij} are the elements in the ith row and jth column of two 3×3 matrices A and B, show that the element in the second row and third column of the product AB is $(a_{21}b_{13} + a_{22}b_{23} + a_{23}b_{33})$. Express this in sigma notation, and write down an expression for the element in the ith row and jth column of the product.

197

6. If $x_i = x_0 + ih$, $x_0 = 2$, $h = 4/n$, $g(x) = x^2$, display $\overset{n-1}{\underset{i=0}{\Sigma}} h \times g(x_i)$ as in Exercise C, Question 13, and carry out the summation.

What is the limit of this sum as n tends to infinity? What does this represent?

7. Repeat Question 6 with $x_0 = a$, $h = (b-a)/n$.

8. Show that

$$\sin \left(ih + \frac{h}{2}\right) - \sin \left(ih - \frac{h}{2}\right) = 2 \cos (ih) \sin \frac{h}{2}.$$

By taking $h = 0.2$ and summing both sides from $i = 1$ to $i = 5$ evaluate

$$\cos 0.2 + \cos 0.4 + \ldots + \cos 1.0.$$

9. By the method of Question 8 obtain expressions for

$$\overset{n}{\underset{1}{\Sigma}} \cos ih \quad \text{and} \quad \overset{n}{\underset{1}{\Sigma}} \sin ih.$$

10. A mortgage of £3000, with interest charged at 6 % p.a., is paid off in equal annual instalments of £200.

(a) Find how much is still owing after 10 years.

(b) For how many more years must the instalments be paid to complete the repayment?

(c) Write a flow chart to answer (a), and modify it to answer (b).

11. What is the annual payment for a 25 year mortgage of £5000 at 7 % p.a. interest?

12. A car, valued at £600, is bought on hire purchase and paid for by equal monthly instalments of £17. Interest is charged at 9 % p.a., but this means that 9 % of £600 is charged every year until the whole debt is repaid. Find how long this takes.

Show that at a real rate of interest of 1 % per month (charged on the outstanding loan only, as in a mortgage), four fewer equal monthly payments of £17 would be required.

13. Simplify $\overset{n+1}{\underset{2}{\Sigma}} i^3 - \overset{n}{\underset{1}{\Sigma}} i^3$, and explain why this expression is equivalent to $\overset{n}{\underset{1}{\Sigma}} [(i+1)^3 - i^3]$.

14. When the sum of the first n terms of a series, s_n, tends to a limit s as $n \to \infty$, the series is said to be convergent and s is called the sum of the infinite series.

Find the sum of the infinite G.P.s:

(a) $1 + \frac{1}{3} + \frac{1}{9} + \frac{1}{27} + \ldots$;

(b) $10 + 5 + 2.5 + 1.25 + \ldots$;

(c) $0.4 + 0.04 + 0.004 + \ldots$.

15. Denoting the sum of the infinite series $1 + \frac{1}{2} + \frac{1}{4} + \frac{1}{8} + \ldots$ by s, $s_5 = \overset{5}{\underset{1}{\Sigma}} (\frac{1}{2})^{i-1}$ is an approximation to s. How much nearer to s is s_{15}?

SUMMARY

A shorthand for $u_1 + u_2 + u_3 + \ldots + u_n$ is

$$\sum_{i=1}^{n} u_i \quad \text{or} \quad \sum_{1}^{n} u_i.$$

$$\sum_{1}^{n} [af(i) + bg(i) + c] = a \sum_{1}^{n} f(i) + b \sum_{1}^{n} g(i) + cn.$$

$$\sum_{1}^{n} f(i) = \sum_{1+k}^{n+k} f(i-k) \text{ for any integer } k.$$

Some finite series

$$\sum_{1}^{n} i = \tfrac{1}{2}n(n+1),$$

$$\sum_{1}^{n} i^2 = \tfrac{1}{6}n(n+1)(2n+1),$$

$$\sum_{1}^{n} i^3 = \tfrac{1}{4}n^2(n+1)^2,$$

$$\sum_{1}^{n} i(i+1) = \tfrac{1}{3}n(n+1)(n+2), \quad \sum_{1}^{n} i(i+1)(i+2) = \tfrac{1}{4}n(n+1)(n+2)(n+3).$$

Arithmetic progression

sum $= \tfrac{1}{2}n$ (first term + last term).

Geometric progression

$$a + ar + ar^2 + \ldots + ar^{n-1} = a\left(\frac{r^n - 1}{r - 1}\right).$$

10

AREA AND INTEGRATION

1. INTRODUCTION

You know that the area under a graph may represent a physical quantity such as distance or speed. Consequently, we should like to develop a quick and accurate method of calculating such areas. So far, the only methods at our disposal are counting squares and the trapezium rule.

We shall need to consider *upper* and *lower bounds*. An upper bound is a value that a given quantity could not possibly exceed. Similarly a lower bound is a value demonstrably less than the given quantity.

As usual, the functions in our mathematical models have sets of real numbers as domain and codomain. The area under the graph of a function is also a real number. It is the number of square centimetres if 1 cm is used as the unit for both axes.

Many of the ideas that we shall need for the chapter are introduced in Exercise A.

Exercise A

1.

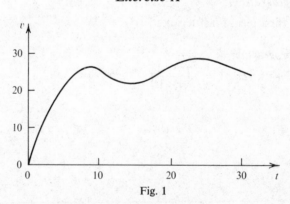

Fig. 1

The diagram, Figure 1, shows how the speed, v m/s, of a go-kart starting from rest variés with time, t seconds, during the first 30 seconds of its run. What does the area under the curve represent? Roughly how far did the go-kart travel in the 30 seconds? Give a quick answer to the question. Now, keeping the edge of a set-square or geoliner parallel to the time axis, move it so as to estimate upper and lower bounds for the distance the go-kart travelled.

2.

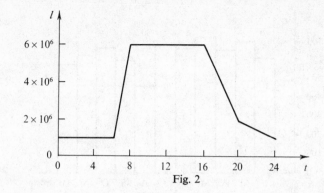

Fig. 2

The diagram shows an approximation to the water consumption, l litres/hour, of a small town during a typical day. Is the area under the graph significant? As in Question 1, make quick estimates of upper and lower bounds for the quantity of water used during the day.

Do you think that the average of your two answers would be a good estimate for the amount of water used?

Check this by dividing the area into rectangles or trapezia and calculating the total area. A quick rough estimate is always a good idea.

3. An accelerometer is a device for measuring the acceleration of a moving object; an aircraft 'black box' will contain one and Figure 3 shows the record of such a box during take-off. What does the area under the graph represent? Make a quick estimate of upper and lower bounds to this area and, by drawing a single line parallel to the time axis, try to make a more accurate estimate of the actual area.

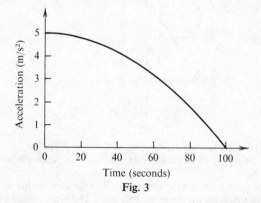

Fig. 3

The equation of this curve is $y = 5 - t^2/2000$, and later in this chapter we shall discover how to calculate the area exactly and more quickly than you have done above.

201

4.

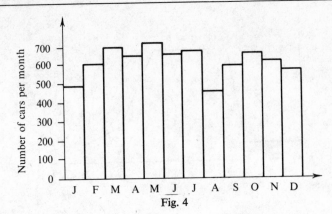

Fig. 4

Figure 4 shows the number of cars produced per month by a motor company. Estimate quickly the annual production.

In this chapter we shall be concerned with continuous functions. Though area can be calculated usefully from this graph, it can only be done for discrete periods, i.e. integer numbers of months. For example, we could not say that 300 cars were produced in the first half of September.

5. Figure 5 shows the speed of a motor-cyclist starting from rest and accelerating so that his speed, v m/s, after t seconds is given by $v = 10t - \frac{1}{2}t^2$.

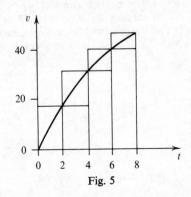

Fig. 5

(a) What is the significance of the area under the graph?

(b) Estimate mentally as accurately as you can the area under the curve for the interval [0, 8].

(c) Use 4 trapezia to estimate the area. Would this be an upper or lower bound? Can you estimate the error in this bound? What would be the effect of doubling the number of trapezia?

(d) Instead of trapezia we can fit rectangles, the sum of the areas of which give upper and lower bounds. In the diagram this is done with sets of 4 rectangles (one of zero height!). Use these to calculate upper and lower bounds for the area under the curve.

(*e*) Now determine upper and lower bounds using, in turn, rectangles of width, 8, 4, 1. Tabulate the results and also, in each case, the average of the upper and lower bounds.

To aid you, the actual speeds are tabulated below:

Time (s)	0	1	2	3	4	5	6	7	8
Speed (m/s)	0	$9\frac{1}{2}$	18	$25\frac{1}{2}$	32	$37\frac{1}{2}$	42	$45\frac{1}{2}$	48

(*f*) Discuss the effect of increasing the number of rectangles. Do you consider that the areas would approach a limit?

(*g*) Determine the total area taking 8 trapezia, and compare with the average of the upper and lower bounds using 8 rectangles. Would the result be generally true?

6. Taking 8 intervals, obtain upper and lower bounds for the area between the graph of $y = 8x - x^2$ and the x-axis. Average these results. (You will need to draw the graph.)

1.1 Summary. The following points should have emerged:

(1) The trapezium method gives a good approximation to the area under a curve.

(2) The rectangle method gives upper and lower bounds to the area under a curve, and hence bounds for the error from the trapezium method. The average of these upper and lower bounds is the sum of the areas of the trapezia.

(3) For a function whose values at all points in the domain can be calculated, increased accuracy in the estimate of the area can be obtained by increasing the number of rectangles or trapezia.

1.2 Flow chart for finding areas under graphs. Figure 6 on p. 204 shows a flow chart to determine the upper bound to the area under the graph of an increasing function using the rectangle method. It is assumed that the required ordinates ('y-values') are already known, or have been calculated.

Exercise B

1. Modify the flow chart of Figure 6 to determine a lower bound.

2. What would happen if the function were (*a*) decreasing, (*b*) increasing for part of the interval and decreasing for the rest? (It might help to draw a graph.)

3. Assuming an increasing function, write a flow chart to estimate the area using a set of trapezia. Is it necessary to assume the function to be increasing?

4. If you have computer facilities, write a program to evaluate v for $t = 0.4, 0.8, 1.2, \ldots, 8$ where $v = 10t - \frac{1}{2}t^2$ (see Exercise A, Question 5), and compute corresponding upper and lower rectangle sums and their average.

5. Modify the program of Question 4 so that after printing out answers, the calculations are repeated with the step length halved until the step length reaches 0·025.

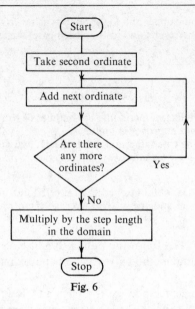

Fig. 6

2. RECTANGLE SUMS

Figure 7 shows the speed in m/s of the accelerating motor-cycle of Exercise A, Question 5 with sets of rectangles drawn in to give upper and lower bounds for the area.

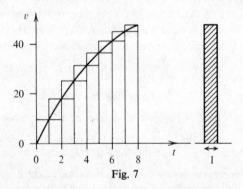

Fig. 7

Why is the difference between the upper and lower bounds equal to the area of the shaded rectangle? What is the effect on this difference of area when the width of the rectangles is halved? Can this process be continued repeatedly? What can you say about the limits of the sequences of upper and lower bounds?

204

We see that rectangle sums giving upper and lower bounds to an area under a continuous graph can come as close as we like to the actual area. Indeed, this gives us a way of *defining* the area of a region with a curved boundary.

2.1   Systematic calculation of rectangle sums. The process of calculating more and more ordinates in order to increase the accuracy of our answer is tedious and time consuming. We shall now seek to short-circuit this problem so that, as in differentiation, we are able to write down an answer rather than work from first principles each time. Consider first an easy example.

Example 1

Find the area under the graph of $y = x$ from $x = 0$ to $x = 8$ by using rectangle sums.

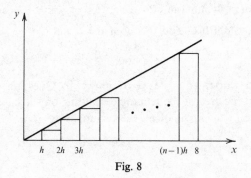

Fig. 8

We begin by considering the lower bound to the area (see Figure 8). Let the width of each rectangle be h, chosen so that there are exactly n rectangles and $nh = 8$.

The sum of the area of the rectangles

$$= 0 + h^2 + 2h^2 + 3h^2 + 4h^2 + \ldots (n-1)h^2$$

$$= h^2 \sum_{1}^{n-1} i.$$

In the last chapter we found that $\sum_{1}^{n} i = \tfrac{1}{2}n(n+1)$, so $\sum_{1}^{n-1} i = \tfrac{1}{2}(n-1)n$. Hence the lower bound area is

$$h^2 \times \tfrac{1}{2}(n-1)n = \frac{64}{n^2} \times \tfrac{1}{2}(n-1)n \quad \left(\text{replacing } h \text{ by } \frac{8}{n} \right)$$

$$= 32 \left(\frac{n-1}{n} \right) = 32 \left(1 - \frac{1}{n} \right).$$

What is the effect on this area of letting n increase more and more? Try $n = 10, 100, 1000, 10^6$.

Exercise C

1. Repeat Example 1 but for the upper bound.

2. Find the area enclosed by the graph of $y = x$, the x-axis and the ordinate $x = b$, by writing down both upper and lower rectangle sums and proceeding to a limit.

3. Draw the graph of $y = x^2$ from $x = 0$ to 6, and draw two sets of rectangles of unit width, one enclosing and one enclosed by the curve and bounded by the x-axis and the ordinate $x = 6$. Calculate the total area of each set.

4. Sketch the graph of $y = x^2$ and consider the area enclosed by the x-axis, $x = b$ and the curve. Divide the base into n intervals of width h and write down the areas of the rectangles enclosed by the curve. How many rectangles are there? What is the area standing on the base from ih to $(i+1)h$ as shown in Figure 9? What is the relation between n, h and b?

5. Repeat Question 3 but using 20 rectangles of width 0·3, and again with 30 rectangles of width 0·2. You will need the result $\sum\limits_{1}^{n} i^2 = \tfrac{1}{6}n(n+1)(2n+1)$ developed in the last chapter.

2.2   The area under the graph of $y=x^2$. In Question 4 you should have found that the area of the rectangle standing on the base ih to $(i+1)h$ is i^2h^3. The sum of the areas of all the rectangles is

$$A_n = h^3 \sum_{1}^{n-1} i^2.$$

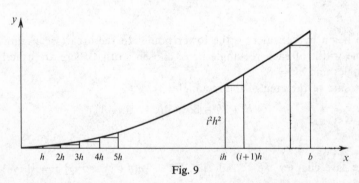

Fig. 9

Using the result $\sum\limits_{1}^{n} i^2 = \tfrac{1}{6}n(n+1)(2n+1)$ and replacing n by $(n-1)$ gives

$$\sum_{1}^{n-1} i^2 = \tfrac{1}{6}(n-1)(n)(2n-1)$$

and so $A_n = h^3 \times \tfrac{1}{6}(n-1)n(2n-1).$

206

But $$h = \frac{b}{n}, \quad \text{so} \quad A_n = \frac{b^3}{6}\left(\frac{n-1}{n}\right)\left(\frac{n}{n}\right)\left(\frac{2n-1}{n}\right)$$

$$= \frac{b^3}{6}\left(1-\frac{1}{n}\right)\left(2-\frac{1}{n}\right).$$

What is the value of this expression as n takes the values 10, 100, 1000 in turn? What would be the effect of letting n tend to infinity?

Do you agree that the limit is $\frac{1}{3}b^3$?

Exercise D

1. Determine upper and lower bounds for the areas under the graphs of the following from $x = 0$ to $x = 4$, taking rectangles of width $h = 4/n$.

(a) $y = x$; (b) $y = x^2$.

Evaluate these bounds for $n = 10, 100, 1000$.

2. Show, by taking n rectangles of width h, that $\frac{1}{6}b^3\left(1+\frac{1}{n}\right)\left(2+\frac{1}{n}\right)$ is an upper bound for the area under the graph of $y = x^2$ from $x = 0$ to $x = b$. What is the limiting value of this as n tends to infinity?

3. Find upper and lower bounds for the area under the graph of $y = x^3$ from $x = 0$ to 4, and also from $x = 0$ to b, taking n rectangles of equal width. (It was proved in Chapter 9 that the sum of the cubes of the first n natural numbers is $\frac{1}{4}n^2(n+1)^2$.)

Discuss what happens when n is made larger and larger.

4. Sketch the graphs of $x \to x^2$ and the inverse function $x \to x^{\frac{1}{2}}$. Use the result of Section 2.2 to write down the area under the graph of $y = x^2$ from $x = 0$ to 4, and deduce the area under the graph of $y = x^{\frac{1}{2}}$ from $x = 0$ to 16. Similarly use the result for the area under the graph of $y = x^2$ from $x = 0$ to b, to determine the area under the graph of $y = x^{\frac{1}{2}}$ from $x = 0$ to a, where $a = b^2$.

5. Draw the graph of $y = 2^x$ from $x = 0$ to $x = 6$.

(a) Draw two sets of rectangles of unit width enclosed by and enclosing the curve, and calculate the total area of each set.

(b) Repeat (a) with rectangles of width $\frac{1}{2}$.

(c) Repeat again, but with width h, simplifying your answer by using the formula for the sum of a geometrical progression. Hence try to find the area under the curve by making h smaller and smaller.

3. SUMMATION METHOD

The summation method used to find the areas in Section 2 is in essence due to Archimedes (born 287 B.C.). He anticipated the development of integral calculus by Newton and Leibnitz by about 2000 years! He made the well known discovery that an immersed body loses weight by an amount equal to the weight of the fluid displaced; he was also a great applied mathematician and used his knowledge to design huge and highly successful catapults, cranes and grappling irons in defence of his native Syracuse. But he regarded his discovery that the area of a sphere was equal to the area of the circumscribing cylinder as his most satisfying.

3.1 Definite integral. From this summation method we derive an important piece of mathematical notation. In Figure 10 is one of the rectangular regions whose area forms part of the sum. The height of such a region is equal to the value of the function f for some number x in the interval $[0, a]$, which we denote by $f(x)$; the width is a small portion of the x-axis, denoted by δx. The area of the rectangle is then denoted by $f(x)\delta x$, and the sum of all the areas, which makes up the area of one of the bounding regions, is written

$$\underset{x=0}{\overset{x=a}{S}} f(x)\delta x.$$

This is a vague notation (unlike the Σ-notation) giving no indication of how the rectangles are to be drawn.

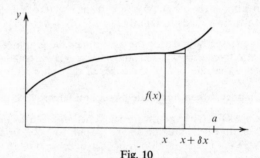

Fig. 10

In the notation for the area under the curve itself, i.e. for the value of the limit of the rectangle sum, δx is replaced by dx (just as $\delta y/\delta x$ became dy/dx in the limiting process of differentiation). At the same time the letter S is 'straightened out' into the symbol which is known as the '*integral sign*'. The final form of the notation is then given by the following:

Definition

The area under the graph of $y = f(x)$ over the interval $[0, a]$ is denoted by the symbol

$$\int_0^a f(x)\,dx.$$

We call this, the *definite integral* of the function f over the interval $[0, a]$. Thus we could write the results of Section 2 and Exercise D as

$$\int_0^b x\,dx = \tfrac{1}{2}b^2, \qquad \int_0^b x^2\,dx = \tfrac{1}{3}b^3, \qquad \int_0^b x^3\,dx = \tfrac{1}{4}b^4.$$

208

1. Draw the graph of $y = x$ and use it as a check on the values of $(a) \int_0^1 x\,dx$,

$(b) \int_0^3 x\,dx$. What is the area enclosed between the ordinates at $x = 1$ and $x = 3$, the x-axis, and the graph itself? Suggest a definite integral to represent this area.

2. Sketch the graph of $y = x^2$, determine the area under the curve from $x = 1$ to $x = 3$, and suggest a definite integral to represent the area.

3. Repeat Question 2 but for the interval from $x = a$ to $x = b$.

3.2   The definite integral over any interval

Definition

The definite integral of $f(x)$ over the interval $[a, b]$, where $b > a$, is

$$\int_a^b f(x)\,dx$$

and it equals

$$\int_0^b f(x)\,dx - \int_0^a f(x)\,dx.$$

It represents the area shaded in Figure 11.

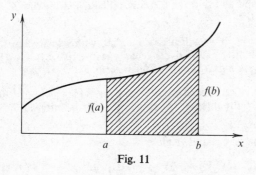

Fig. 11

Exercise F

1. Draw graphs to illustrate the following definite integrals and find their values:

$(a) \int_1^2 (x+2)\,dx;$ $(b) \int_1^2 (3x-1)\,dx;$ $(c) \int_1^2 2x\,dx;$

$(d) \int_1^2 x^2\,dx;$ $(e) \int_1^2 3x^2\,dx;$ $(f) \int_1^2 2x^3\,dx;$

$(g) \int_1^b x^2\,dx;$ $(h) \int_1^2 |3x-4|\,dx.$

2. Show that $\qquad \int_a^b (px+q)\,dx = (\frac{1}{2}pb^2+qb)-(\frac{1}{2}pa^2+qa),$

given that $a < b$ and

$$px+q > 0 \quad \text{for} \quad a \leqslant x \leqslant b.$$

3. Draw a graph of $y = 3x^2$ and mark on it the areas representing $\int_1^4 3x^2\,dx$ and $\int_4^{12} 3x^2\,dx$. Deduce the value of $\int_1^{12} 3x^2\,dx$ and simplify the expression

$$\int_a^b f(x)\,dx + \int_b^c f(x)\,dx.$$

4. Sketch the graphs of $y = kx$ and $y = kx^2$ and mark on them the areas represented by $\int_1^2 kx\,dx$ and $\int_1^2 kx^2\,dx$. Determine the values of these definite integrals. (*Hint*. What transformation maps the region with area $\int_a^b f(x)\,dx$ onto the region with area $\int_a^b kf(x)\,dx$?)

5. It was found in Exercise D, Question 3, that $\int_0^b x^3\,dx = \frac{1}{4}b^4$. Draw the graph of $y = x^{\frac{1}{3}}$ and use this result to establish $\int_0^a x^{\frac{1}{3}}\,dx = \frac{3}{4}a^{\frac{4}{3}}$.

6. A body falls freely from rest so that its velocity after t s is $10t$ m/s. Sketch the velocity-time graph and find the distance fallen (*a*) in the first 4 seconds, (*b*) in the fifth second (i.e. from $t = 4$ to $t = 5$).

7. A stone is thrown down a disused mine shaft with velocity 5 m/s. It accelerates at 10 m/s² so that after t seconds its velocity is $(5+10t)$ m/s. How far does it fall (*a*) in the first 3 seconds, (*b*) in the fourth second?

8. The output, p, of an oil well after t days is given by $p = (\frac{9}{10})^t \times 10^6$ barrels/day. Write down a definite integral to represent the production in the first 100 days of the well.

9. Shade, on separate graphs, regions with areas

(*a*) $\displaystyle\int_1^8 x^{\frac{1}{3}}\,dx$; \quad (*b*) $\displaystyle\int_1^4 y^{\frac{3}{2}}\,dy$; \quad (*c*) $\displaystyle\int_0^1 10^x\,dx$; \quad (*d*) $\displaystyle\int_2^{10} \log_{10} y\,dy$.

Indicate regions congruent to those in (*b*) and (*d*) on the graphs of (*a*) and (*c*) respectively.

Describe $\int_a^b f^{-1}(y)\,dy$ as an area associated with the graph of $y = f(x)$.

10. Given the function $f: x \to 2^x$, show that

$$\int_1^3 f(x)\,dx = \int_1^3 f(t)\,dt = \int_1^3 f(y)\,dy.$$

Would it be ambiguous to write $\int_1^3 f$?

210

4. INTEGRAL FUNCTIONS

From the results of the previous sections, we could calculate

$$\int_1^2 x^2\,dx = 2\tfrac{1}{3}, \quad \int_1^3 x^2\,dx = 8\tfrac{2}{3}, \quad \int_1^4 x^2\,dx = 21, \quad \int_1^5 x^2\,dx = 41\tfrac{1}{3}.$$

These values represent areas of various regions under the graph of $f\colon x \to x^2$, each with the fixed left hand boundary 1. They depend therefore only upon the right hand boundary numbers. We have here a functional relationship and we may write

$$F(2) = 2\tfrac{1}{3}, \quad F(3) = 8\tfrac{2}{3}, \quad F(4) = 21, \quad F(5) = 41\tfrac{1}{3}.$$

Now we have seen that $\int_1^b x^2\,dx = \tfrac{1}{3}b^3 - \tfrac{1}{3}$, so that $F(b) = \tfrac{1}{3}b^3 - \tfrac{1}{3}$ and F is defined by $F\colon x \to \tfrac{1}{3}x^3 - \tfrac{1}{3}$.

F is called an *integral function* of f. Clearly, if we chose a different left hand boundary, we should obtain a different integral function of f.

This idea may be generalized. Suppose that the definite integral of any function f is known over an interval from L to b, where L is some fixed left hand boundary. Then for each value of b this integral has a specific value, so that an integral function F is established which maps the number b onto the integral $\int_L^b f(x)\,dx$. We can then write $F(b) = \int_L^b f(x)\,dx$; this is illustrated in Figure 13.

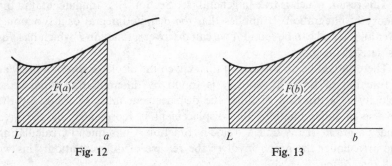

Fig. 12   Fig. 13

It follows at once (compare Figures 12 and 13) that

$$\int_a^b f(x)\,dx = F(b) - F(a).$$

The expression on the right of this last equation is of sufficiently common occurrence to warrant the introduction of a special notation. We write

$$F(b) - F(a) = \Big[F(x) \Big]_a^b.$$

211

Thus $$\int_{9}^{12} x^2\,dx = \left[\tfrac{1}{3}x^3 - \tfrac{1}{3}\right]_{9}^{12} = (\tfrac{1}{3} \times 12^3 - \tfrac{1}{3}) - (\tfrac{1}{3} \times 9^3 - \tfrac{1}{3}).$$
$$= 333.$$

In the general case, we have similarly

$$\int_{a}^{b} f(x)\,dx = \left[F(x)\right]_{a}^{b},$$

where F is any integral function defined from f.

4.1 Some special integral functions. The problem of evaluating definite integrals comes down to the determination of an integral function F. This has already been done for a number of functions f by special methods, and it will be helpful at this stage to make a list of the results obtained. In these examples the left hand boundary is taken as zero, but this is not essential.

$f(x)$	$F(x)$	Reference
x^2	$\tfrac{1}{3}x^3$	Section 2.2
x^3	$\tfrac{1}{4}x^4$	Exercise D, Question 3
$px+q$	$\tfrac{1}{2}px^2+qx$	Exercise F, Question 2
$x^{\frac{1}{2}}$	$\tfrac{2}{3}x^{\frac{3}{2}}$	Exercise D, Question 4
$x^{\frac{1}{3}}$	$\tfrac{3}{4}x^{\frac{4}{3}}$	Exercise F, Question 5

Careful study of this table will reveal an important relation between the functions f and F: *in each case, f is the derived function of F.*

This result, which is true in general (see Section 7), is fundamental in the theory of integration. It implies that the definite integral of a function f over an interval can be found if we can discover a function F which has f as its derived function.

There should be no surprise in this. Given the displacement of a body as a function of time, its velocity is found by differentiation. Given the velocity as a function of time, the displacement must be found by the reverse of differentiation. But displacement is represented by the area under a graph of the time → velocity function. Consequently, calculating the area under the graph involves the reverse of differentiation; this we call *integration*.

Example 2

In Exercise A, Question 3, the final velocity of an aircraft accelerating from rest was given by the area under the graph of $y = 5 - t^2/2000$ over the interval [0, 100].

We can now write this as

$$v = \int_{0}^{100} \left(5 - \frac{t^2}{2000}\right) dt.$$

An integral function is found easily and we proceed:

$$v = \left[5t - \frac{t^3}{6000} \right]_0^{100}$$

$$= \left(500 - \frac{10^6}{6000} \right) - (0-0)$$

$$= 333.$$

The final velocity is 333 m/s.

Exercise G

1. The integral function for $f: x \to x^2$ with $L = 1$ was shown in Section 4 to be $F: x \to \frac{1}{3}x^3 - \frac{1}{3}$. Find integral functions for f corresponding to values $-1, 0, 2, 5$ for L.

2. Evaluate

(a) $\left[x^2 + 3x \right]_1^2$;   (b) $\left[x^2 + 3x + 7 \right]_1^2$;   (c) $\left[1 - \cos x \right]_0^{\frac{1}{2}\pi}$;

(d) $\left[x + \frac{1}{x} \right]_2^3$.

3. Use the results of the last section to find

(a) $\int_4^6 x^3 \, dx$;   (b) $\int_0^2 (-2x + 5) \, dx$;   (c) $\int_9^{25} \sqrt{x} \, dx$;

(d) $\int_0^1 (x^3 - x^2 + 6x + 4) \, dx$.

4. (i) Differentiate

(a) x^5;   (b) $3x^2 + 2x - 7$;   (c) $\frac{1}{4}x^8$;

(d) $\frac{1}{x^2}$;   (e) $\sin x + \cos x$;   (f) $\sin 2x$.

(ii) Deduce integral functions F for the following functions f:

(a) $f: x \to 5x^4$;   (b) $f: x \to 6x + 2$;   (c) $f: x \to x^7$;

(d) $f: x \to \frac{1}{x^3}$;   (e) $f: x \to \cos x - \sin x$;   (f) $f: x \to \cos 2x$.

5. Write down integral functions for

(a) $x \to x^5$;   (b) $x \to x^{-\frac{1}{3}}$;   (c) $x \to px^3 + qx^2 + rx + s$;

(d) $x \to x^n (n \neq -1)$;   (e) $x \to \sin x$.

6. Explain why, with the notation of the last sections, $F(L) = 0$. State the value of L for the following pairs of functions and integral functions. In each case work out $F(2)$ and illustrate as an area on a sketch graph.

(a) $f: x \to 3x^2 + 1$, $F: x \to x^3 + x$;   (b) $f: x \to 3x^2 + 1$, $F: x \to x^3 + x + 2$;

(c) $f: x \to \frac{1}{x^2}$, $F: x \to 1 - \frac{1}{x}$;   (d) $f: x \to x^{-\frac{1}{2}}$, $F: x \to 2x^{\frac{1}{2}}$.

7. Evaluate the following definite integrals. In each case check the reasonableness of your answer by drawing a graph and examining the corresponding area.

(a) $\int_3^4 6x^2\,dx$;   (b) $\int_0^2 (4-x^2)\,dx$;   (c) $\int_0^{\frac{1}{2}\pi} \sin x\,dx$;

(d) $\int_0^{\frac{1}{4}\pi} 2\cos 2x\,dx$;   (e) $\int_1^4 \frac{1}{x^2}\,dx$;   (f) $\int_1^2 \frac{1}{x^3}\,dx$;

(g) $\int_1^8 x^{\frac{1}{3}}\,dx$;   (h) $\int_{0\cdot2}^{0\cdot5} \cos x\,dx$.

8.

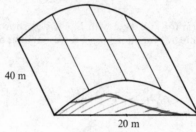

40 m

20 m

Fig. 14

A swimming pool is covered by a roof 40 m long and 20 m wide, with vertical ends and uniform cross-section with height $6\sin(\frac{1}{20}\pi x)$ metres, where x is the distance from one side. Find the volume enclosed.

9. The Severn Bore takes the form of a half sine wave 2 m high and 5 m across. What is its cross-sectional area? If the wave from bank to bank is 100 m long, what volume of water does it contain?

5. INDEFINITE INTEGRALS

Any function F whose derived function is f is called a *primitive* or an *indefinite integral* of f. The notation used to describe this relationship is

$$\int f(x)\,dx = F(x).$$

Thus we may write $\int x^2\,dx = \frac{1}{3}x^3+k$, whatever numerical value is assigned to k.

The ambiguity in specifying the indefinite integral of a function is linked with the fact that in Section 4 the integral function was assigned an arbitrary left hand boundary L. By giving different values to L, we obtain different integral functions F, all of which have the property that $F' = f$.

In evaluating a definite integral, it is immaterial which of the primitives is used.

214

Thus the shaded area in Figure 15 is

$$\int_2^3 \frac{1}{x^2}\,dx = \left[-\frac{1}{x}+k\right]_2^3$$

$$= (-\tfrac{1}{3}+k)-(-\tfrac{1}{2}+k)$$

$$= \tfrac{1}{6}.$$

In such examples, we usually choose the simplest formula and take $k = 0$.

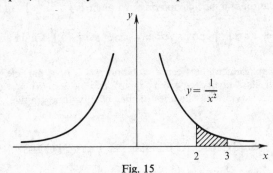

Fig. 15

Example 3

Suppose we know that the acceleration of a particle moving in a straight line is given by $a = 2\sin t$ and that when $t = 0$, $v = 3$ and $x = 1$.

Then the formula for v is given by an indefinite integral of $2\sin t$, i.e. $v = -2\cos t+k$. In this context, different values of k correspond to different starting velocities. When $t = 0$, $\cos t = 1$, so k must be 5 to comply with the given initial velocity of 3.

Integrating again, $x = -2\sin t+5t+k'$. But $x = 1$ when $t = 0$; hence $k' = 1$ and $x = -2\sin t+5t+1$.

Exercise H

1. Write down indefinite integrals of

(a) $x \to x^{\frac{1}{2}}$;   (b) $x \to x(x^2+1)$;   (c) $x \to ax^2+bx+c$;

(d) $x \to \cos 4x$.

2. Write down expressions for

(a) $\displaystyle\int \sin 3x\,dx$;   (b) $\displaystyle\int \frac{1}{x^m}\,dx$ $(m \neq 1)$;   (c) $\displaystyle\int \frac{x+4}{x^3}\,dx$.

3. The gradient at any point of the graph of a function f is given by

$$f'(x) = 6x^2-18.$$

Give the equations of three such functions, and sketch their graphs.

4. The velocity of a particle (in m/s) moving along the x-axis is given by $v = 5t - 3t^2$. Find an equation for x in terms of t given that $x = 2$ when $t = 0$. Find the values of x, v and the acceleration a when $t = 1, 2, 3, 4$. When is x greatest? When is v greatest?

5. The acceleration (in m/s²) of a particle moving in a straight line is given by $a = \cos 2t$. If its velocity is 3 m/s when $t = 0$, find its velocity when $t = 0.6$. What is its greatest velocity?

6. The acceleration of a particle moving in a plane is $\begin{pmatrix} 3\sin t \\ 4\cos 2t \end{pmatrix}$, and when $t = 0$ its position vector $\mathbf{r}$ is $\begin{pmatrix} 0 \\ 0 \end{pmatrix}$ and its velocity vector $\mathbf{v}$ is $\begin{pmatrix} -3 \\ 0 \end{pmatrix}$. Find $\mathbf{r}$ and $\mathbf{v}$ at time t.

7. Find the displacement between $t = 1$ and $t = 2$ of a particle moving in a straight line if its velocity is given by (a) $v = t - 3t^2$, (b) $v = (t-1)(t-2)$. Illustrate your answers with sketches of the velocity–time graphs.

6. SOME GENERALIZATIONS

So far, the definite integral $\int_a^b f(x)\,dx$ has been defined only when $a < b$ and when $f(x)$ is positive or zero throughout the interval $[a, b]$. It is convenient to extend the definition to cover other cases, and we now consider generalizations for functions with negative values over the interval, and to integrals for which $a > b$. In both cases we define the integrals by the formal processes of Section 4, and accept the consequences.

6.1 The integral $\int_a^b f(x)\,dx$ when $f(x)$ takes negative values

Example 4

Evaluate the definite integrals $\int_0^2 (x^2 - 2x)\,dx$ and $\int_0^3 (x^2 - 2x)\,dx$, and interpret the results.

A primitive for the function to be integrated is given by

$$F(x) = \tfrac{1}{3}x^3 - x^2,$$

so that formal evaluation gives

$$\int_0^2 (x^2 - 2x)\,dx = \left[\tfrac{1}{3}x^3 - x^2\right]_0^2 = (2\tfrac{2}{3} - 4) - (0 - 0)$$
$$= -1\tfrac{1}{3}.$$

Similarly $\int_0^3 (x^2 - 2x)\,dx = \left[\tfrac{1}{3}x^3 - x^2\right]_0^3 = (9 - 9) - (0 - 0)$
$$= 0.$$

216

The graph of $y = x^2 - 2x$ is shown in Figure 16. It crosses the x-axis at $x = 2$, and so makes two regions over the interval $[0, 3]$; their areas are denoted by A_1 and A_2.

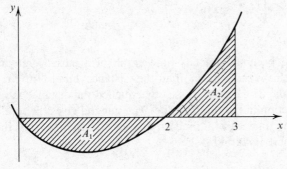

Fig. 16

The first of our definite integrals shows that $A_1 = 1\frac{1}{3}$, and the minus sign indicates that the region is below the x-axis. (It would be wrong to think of A_1 as a negative area; there is no such thing.)

To justify the assertion above, we shall consider a general function f taking negative values over the interval $[a, b]$. The graph of $y = -f(x)$ is the reflection in the x-axis of the graph of $y = f(x)$, and the areas in the two diagrams are clearly equal (see Figures 17 and 18).

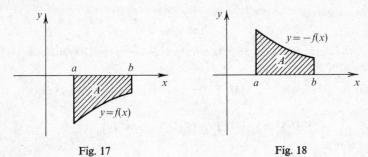

Fig. 17   Fig. 18

Each shaded area (A) equals $\displaystyle\int_a^b (-f(x))\,dx$

$$= \left[-F(x)\right]_a^b \quad \text{where} \quad F(x) \text{ is a primitive of } f(x),$$

$$= -\left[F(x)\right]_a^b = -\int_a^b f(x)\,dx \quad \text{by definition.}$$

Thus $\displaystyle\int_a^b f(x)\,dx = -A$, so that the integral measures *minus* the area bounded

217

by parts of the graph of $y = f(x)$, the x-axis, and the lines $x = a$ and $x = b$.

The second definite integral in Example 4 shows that $A_1 = A_2$ since

$$0 = \int_0^3 (x^2 - 2x)\,dx = \int_0^2 (x^2 - 2x)\,dx + \int_2^3 (x^2 - 2x)\,dx$$

$$= -A_1 + A_2.$$

If this had been the velocity-time graph of a particle moving in one dimension, this would mean that the distance moved in the negative direction in the first 2 seconds exactly equalled the distance moved in the positive direction in the third second. The integral gives the total displacement over the time interval, and an answer of 0 signifies that the particle ended up where it started.

6.2   The integral $\int_a^b f(x)\,dx$ when $a > b$.

We define $\qquad \int_a^b f(x)\,dx \quad$ as $\quad \left[F(x)\right]_a^b = F(b) - F(a)$

$$= -(F(a) - F(b))$$

$$= -\int_b^a f(x)\,dx.$$

This last integral has a well-understood meaning if $a > b$.

Exercise I

1. Evaluate the following definite integrals, and interpret their meaning with the aid of graphs.

(a) $\int_0^1 (x^3 - x)\,dx;$ $\qquad$ (b) $\int_0^\pi \cos x\,dx;$ $\qquad$ (c) $\int_{-4}^2 (x+1)\,dx;$

(d) $\int_0^{-\frac{1}{2}\pi} \sin x\,dx;$ $\qquad$ (e) $\int_{-2}^{-3} x\,dx;$ $\qquad$ (f) $\int_{-2}^{-3} \frac{1}{x^2}\,dx;$

(g) $\int_{-2}^2 (x^2 - 3)\,dx.$

2. If $F(a) = \int_1^a x^3\,dx$, find $F(0)$, $F(1)$, $F(2)$, $F(3)$, and sketch the graph of F over the interval $[0, 3]$.

Explain why $\int_a^a f(x)\,dx = 0$.

3. What is the connection between

(a) $\int_{-1}^{-2} \frac{1}{x^2}\,dx$ and $\int_1^2 \frac{1}{x^2}\,dx;$ $\qquad$ (b) $\int_{-a}^{-b} \frac{1}{x}\,dx$ and $\int_a^b \frac{1}{x}\,dx?$

218

4. Sketch the graphs of the following and determine the value of the definite integral of each over the interval $[1, a]$. If a limit exists as a tends to ∞, give its value.

(a) $x \to x^{-\frac{1}{2}}$;   (b) $x \to x^{-3}$;   (c) $x \to x^{\frac{1}{2}}$;

(d) $x \to x^{-\frac{4}{3}}$;   (e) $x \to x^{\frac{4}{3}}$.

5. For the same functions as are defined in Question 4, determine the definite integrals over the interval $[a, 1]$ where $0 < a \leqslant 1$. If a limit exists as a tends to 0, give its value.

6. Use the results of Questions 4 and 5 to determine for what values of m a meaning can be given to

(a) $\displaystyle\int_1^{\infty} x^{-m}dx$;   (b) $\displaystyle\int_0^1 x^{-m}dx$.

7. Prove that $\displaystyle\int_a^b f(x)dx = \int_b^a (-f(x))dx.$

7. PROOF OF THE FUNDAMENTAL THEOREM OF ANALYSIS

The important result introduced in Section 4.1 may be stated formally as follows:

If f is a continuous function, and a function F is defined by the equation $F(x) = \displaystyle\int_L^x f(x)dx$, then $F' = f$ (L is some fixed left hand boundary).

We recall that $F'(p)$, the derivative of a function F at a value p of the domain, is defined as the limit of the expression

$$\frac{F(q)-F(p)}{q-p}, \quad \text{as } q \text{ tends to } p.$$

(In the proof that follows we consider the case $q > p$. It is left as an exercise to consider what modifications are needed for $q < p$.)

In the present context, we have seen that

$$F(q)-F(p) = \int_p^q f(x)dx,$$

and this measures the area under the graph of $y = f(x)$ from p to q, the shaded region in Figure 19.

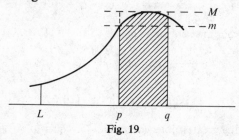

Fig. 19

Suppose that over this interval the upper and lower bounds of the values of the function f are M and m. Then the region is contained completely within a rectangle of area $M(q-p)$, and includes one of area $m(q-p)$, so that

$$m(q-p) \leqslant F(q)-F(p) \leqslant M(q-p).$$

It follows that

$$m \leqslant \frac{F(q)-F(p)}{q-p} \leqslant M.$$

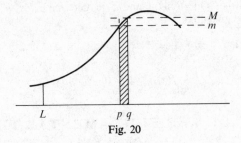

Fig. 20

We now consider the effect of varying q. Figure 20 shows the situation when q is much closer to p than in Figure 19. It is clear that since f is continuous, M and m must both tend to the value $f(p)$ as q tends to p. It follows that

$$\frac{F(q)-F(p)}{q-p}$$

must also tend to $f(p)$, so that the desired limit exists and (since similar considerations apply to the case $q < p$)

$$F'(p) = f(p).$$

Since this holds for each separate value of p, we can assert that the functions F' and f are in fact the same.

Miscellaneous Exercise

1. (*a*) Determine the values of

$$\int_2^5 x^2\,dx \quad \text{and} \quad \int_1^4 (x^2+2x+1)\,dx,$$

and explain why your answers are related.

(*b*) Find

$$\int_2^5 \frac{1}{(x+3)^2}\,dx \quad \text{and} \quad \int_3^6 \sqrt{(x-2)}\,dx.$$

2. Find

$$\int_0^a [x]\,dx \quad \text{and} \quad \int_0^a (x-[x])\,dx.$$

where $[x]$ means the greatest integer less than or equal to x.

3. If $f(x) < g(x)$, what relationship exists between

$$\int_L^x f(x)\,dx \quad \text{and} \quad \int_L^x g(x)\,dx?$$

Use the result to show that $\cos x > 1 - \tfrac{1}{2}x^2$ for $x > 0$ by integrating from 0 to x the two expressions x and $\sin x$. Try continuing the process to find other inequalities for $\sin x$ and $\cos x$; generalize the results.

4. For the areas under the graphs of the following, find (i) upper and lower rectangle sums, taking 6 rectangles in each case, (ii) the trapezium sum, taking 6 trapezia, (iii) the correct area by integration.

(a) $y = 10x - x^3$ from $x = 0$ to $x = 3$;

(b) $y = 30 + 2x - x^2$ from $x = 1$ to $x = 4$;

(c) $y = 30 + 4x - x^2$ from $x = 1$ to $x = 7$.

5. Find the areas of the regions bounded by the x-axis and the graphs of the following:

(a) $y = x^2 - 3x$;　(b) $y = (5-x)(2-x)$;　(c) $y = (x+1)(6-x)$;

(d) $y = x^2(6-x)$;　(e) $y = x(6-x)^2$;　(f) $y = x^3 - 8x^2 + 13x - 6$.

6. Find the areas bounded by parts of the graphs of

(a) $y = 3x + 5$ and $y = x^2 + 1$;

(b) $y = 15\sqrt{x}$ and $y = x^2 + 14$.

7. The following definite integrals clearly have a meaning, yet their values cannot be found by methods we have used so far. Find approximate values.

(a) $\displaystyle\int_1^2 \frac{1}{x}\,dx$;　(b) $\displaystyle\int_{-1}^1 \frac{1}{1+x^2}\,dx$;　(c) $\displaystyle\int_0^3 2^{-x}\,dx$.

8. From the formulae of Chapter 6, it can be shown that

$$2\cos\frac{ib}{n}\sin\frac{\tfrac{1}{2}b}{n} = \sin(i+\tfrac{1}{2})\frac{b}{n} - \sin(i-\tfrac{1}{2})\frac{b}{n}.$$

Use this result to sum the series

$$1 + \cos\frac{b}{n} + \cos\frac{2b}{n} + \ldots + \cos\frac{(n-1)b}{n}$$

and

$$\cos\frac{b}{n} + \cos\frac{2b}{n} + \ldots + \cos b.$$

Now use the rectangle sum method to prove that $\displaystyle\int_0^b \cos x\,dx = \sin b$. (To simplify the argument, assume that $b < \tfrac{1}{2}\pi$.)

SUMMARY

The area under a velocity–time graph over an interval represents the displacement in that time interval. The area under an acceleration–time graph represents the change in velocity.

Areas may be found approximately by the trapezium rule, or exactly as the limit of sequences of upper and lower bounds obtained from rectangle sums.

Areas are more often found by integration, the inverse process of differentiation.

Notation and terminology

The area under the graph of $y = f(x)$ from $x = a$ to $x = b$ is written as the definite integral $\int_a^b f(x)\,dx$. It may be evaluated from $\left[F(x)\right]_a^b$, where F is any primitive of f.

The indefinite integral $\int f(x)\,dx$ equals $F(x) + k$, where k is any constant.

REVISION EXERCISES

6. CIRCULAR FUNCTIONS

1. (*a*) Write down the values of

$$\sin \tfrac{1}{4}\pi, \quad \cos \tfrac{5}{6}\pi, \quad \tan \tfrac{3}{4}\pi, \quad \sin \tfrac{4}{3}\pi, \quad \tan \left(-\tfrac{1}{6}\pi\right).$$

(*b*) Without using trigonometrical tables, but given that $\sqrt{2} = 1\cdot414$ and $\sqrt{3} = 1\cdot732$, find the value of $\cos 105°$.

(*c*) Express the following in the form $\pm \sin x$ or $\pm \cos x$:

$$\sin (\pi - x), \quad \cos(\tfrac{1}{2}\pi + x), \quad \cos (-x), \quad \sin (\tfrac{1}{2}\pi - x).$$

2. Sketch the graph of $y = \sin x$ in the interval $-2\pi \leqslant x \leqslant 2\pi$. Using the same axes, sketch the graph of $y = \tfrac{1}{2} \sin 2x$, and $y = \sin (x + \tfrac{1}{4}\pi)$. Find the gradient of each graph at the point where $x = \tfrac{1}{3}\pi$.

3. Differentiate

(*a*) $\sin 5x$; (*b*) $\sin (5x + \tfrac{1}{4}\pi)$; (*c*) $\cos 2x$;

(*d*) $3 \cos 2x$; (*e*) $6 \sin x + 7$; (*f*) $10 \cos (\tfrac{1}{3}\pi - x) + 4$.

4. The length of the night (the time between sunset and sunrise) at Walrus Island varies between 2 hours on Midsummer day and 22 hours on Midwinter day. Obtain an algebraic model for the function

$$f: \text{months after Midwinter} \to \text{length of night},$$

assuming that its graph is similar to that of a cosine function.

When is the night 6 hours long? For how many months in each year is the night shorter than 14 hours?

Find the values of $f(2)$ and $f'(2)$, and interpret your answers. What is the length of the night 2 months and 6 days after Midsummer?

(You may assume that a year consists of 12 months each of exactly 30 days.)

5. (*a*) Define a radian and explain the advantages of introducing this unit of angle measure.

(*b*) If $f(x) = \sin x$, evaluate $\dfrac{f(1\cdot3) - f(1\cdot1)}{1\cdot3 - 1\cdot1}$ and compare with $f'(1\cdot2)$.

(*c*) If $g(x) = \sin x°$, evaluate $\dfrac{g(67) - g(63)}{67 - 63}$ and compare with $g'(65)$.

6. A sector of a circle with radius 30 cm and angle 2·5 radians is cut out of thin card and bent into the shape of a cone. Find the radius and curved surface area of the cone.

7. Given that both x and y lie between 0 and $\tfrac{1}{2}\pi$, and that $\cos x = \sqrt{5}/3$, $\cos y = \sqrt{7}/4$, find (without using tables) the values of $\sin x$, $\sin y$, $\sin (x+y)$, $\cos (x+y)$. Is $(x+y)$ greater or less than $\tfrac{1}{2}\pi$?

8. (*a*) Show that

$$\left(\frac{1 - \cos h}{h}\right) = \left(\frac{\sin h}{1 + \cos h}\right)\left(\frac{\sin h}{h}\right),$$

223

and hence find

$$\lim_{h \to 0} \left(\frac{1 - \cos h}{h} \right).$$

(b) Show that

$$\lim_{h \to 0} \left(\frac{\cos(a+h) - \cos a}{h} \right) = -\sin a,$$

making use of the result in (a).

7. KINEMATICS

In Questions 1–5, all distances are in metres, all times are in seconds.

1. The diagram (Figure 1) shows the path of a ball struck from (0, 0) with a velocity $\begin{pmatrix} 14 \\ 19\cdot6 \end{pmatrix}$ m/s as recorded on film exposed at intervals of 0·2 s.

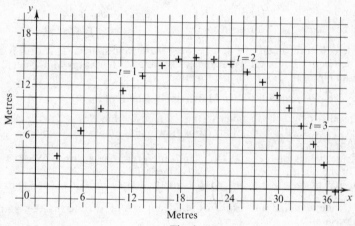

Fig. 1

(a) Use the formula

$$f'(a) \approx \frac{f(a+h) - f(a-h)}{2h}$$

to estimate the velocity at $t = 1$ and $t = 2$.

(b) Hence estimate the average acceleration from $t = 1$ to $t = 2$.

(c) Find approximately the acceleration at $t = 2$.

(d) Find the theoretical answers to (a), (b) and (c) if the motion were given by

$$\mathbf{r} = t \begin{pmatrix} 14 \\ 19\cdot6 \end{pmatrix} + \tfrac{1}{2}t^2 \begin{pmatrix} 0 \\ -9\cdot8 \end{pmatrix}$$

and comment on the discrepancies.

224

2. An object is thrown in the air and its position at time t is given by

$$\begin{pmatrix} kt \\ 25t - 5t^2 \end{pmatrix}.$$

Find the heights when the times are 1 s and 3 s.

If the object were thrown vertically upward what would be the value of k? In that case, what is the average speed over the interval $1 \leqslant t \leqslant 3$? What is the average velocity over the same interval?

What is the average velocity over that interval, in the situation when $k = 2$?

3. The path of a projectile is given by the equation

$$\mathbf{r} = t\mathbf{i} + (2t - t^2)\mathbf{j}.$$

(a) What is the magnitude and direction of the velocity when $t = \frac{1}{2}$? What is the magnitude and direction of the acceleration at this time?

(b) At what time is the velocity parallel to the x-axis?

(c) At what time is the velocity perpendicular to that at $t = \frac{1}{2}$?

(d) Is the acceleration constant?

4. A point moves so that its position vector at time t referred to rectangular axes is
$$\mathbf{r} = (t - \sin t)\mathbf{i} + (1 - \cos t)\mathbf{j}.$$

(a) When is its velocity parallel to $\mathbf{j}$? To $\mathbf{i}$? To $\mathbf{i} + \mathbf{j}$? To $\mathbf{i} - \mathbf{j}$?

(b) Find the magnitude and direction of the acceleration at each of these times.

(c) Sketch the path of the point in the interval $0 \leqslant t \leqslant 2\pi$, and mark on your sketch arrows representing the velocities and accelerations at the times you have considered.

5. The position vector $\mathbf{r}$ of a particle can be expressed in terms of the constant orthogonal unit vectors $\mathbf{i}$, $\mathbf{j}$ by means of the relation

$$\mathbf{r} = \mathbf{i} \cos nt + \mathbf{j} \sin nt.$$

Find the speed of the particle at time t.

Show that its acceleration at time t is the vector $-n^2\mathbf{r}$.

What is the path of the particle? (OC)

6. A car C is rounding a corner, which is a circular arc with centre O and radius 300 m, at a steady 25 m/s. Find the angular velocity of OC and the acceleration of the car.

7. The radius of the wheel and tyre of a Mini is 25 cm. What is the angular velocity of the wheel when the car is travelling at 80 km/h? At that speed, what is the acceleration (in m/s²) of a point on the tread?

8. An electrical turbine is driven by water from a dam. It is rotating at 2000 rev/min. When the sluice gates are opened the turbine increases its speed to 2500 rev/min in 2 minutes.

(a) What is the angular acceleration (assumed constant) during this interval?

(b) Some blades are 2 m from the axis of rotation. What is the rate at which the speed of these blades is increasing?

(c) How are the answers to (a) and (b) related?

(d) What is the magnitude of the total acceleration of the blades immediately after the sluice gates are opened?

225

8. INDICES AND LOGARITHMS

1. Simplify:

(a) $x^2 \times x^5 \times x^4$;   (b) $x^3 \times x \times (x^2)^2$;   (c) $\dfrac{x^5 \times x^2}{x^8}$.

2. Simplify:

(a) $8^{\frac{2}{3}}$;   (b) $9^{\frac{3}{2}}$;   (c) $64^{\frac{5}{6}}$;   (d) 4^{-3};   (e) $\dfrac{1}{10^{-2}}$.

3. Simplify:

(a) $x^{\frac{1}{2}} \times x^{-1}$;   (b) $x^{\frac{2}{3}} \times x^{-\frac{1}{3}}$;   (c) $\dfrac{x \times x^{\frac{2}{3}}}{x^{\frac{1}{3}}}$;

(d) $\dfrac{(xy)^2 \times x^{\frac{1}{2}}}{x^3 y^4}$;   (e) $\dfrac{4x^2 y^3 \times 3x^{\frac{1}{2}} y^{\frac{1}{2}}}{(6x^{\frac{1}{2}} y)^3}$.

4. Draw a graph of the function $f: x \to 1 \cdot 5^x$ and estimate the values of x to 2 significant figures for which
$$0 \cdot 5 < f(x) < 3.$$

5. What are the values of the elements a, b, c, e, f of the domain of the logarithmic mapping diagram shown in Figure 2, if the base d is (i) 4, (ii) 9, (iii) $\frac{1}{25}$?

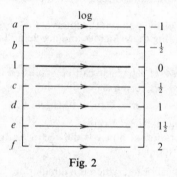

Fig. 2

6. If $\log_e 2 \cdot 718 = 1$, what is the value of e? Given that $\log_e 10 = 2 \cdot 303$, work out the values of the following. Where they are negative, write them a second time with positive mantissa and negative characteristic.

(a) $\log_e 27 \cdot 18$;   (b) $\log_e 0 \cdot 2718$;   (c) $\log_e (2 \cdot 718)^3$;

(d) $\log_e \sqrt{10}$;   (e) $\log_e 1000 \sqrt{(2 \cdot 718)}$;   (f) $\log_e \sqrt[5]{(2 \cdot 718/100)}$;

(g) $\log_e \frac{1}{10}$;   (h) $\log_e \sqrt{(0 \cdot 02718/0 \cdot 1)}$.

7. Solve the following equations:

(a) $4^x = 64$;   (b) $4^x = 8$;   (c) $4^x = 5$;   (d) $1 \cdot 06^x = 3$.

Make up a problem which would lead to the equation of part (d).

8. A population increases by a tenth every 10 years. By how much does it increase each year? How long does it take to double itself?

226

9. If $\log_{10} y = \log_{10} b + c \log_{10} x$ can be condensed into the form

$$\log_{10} y = \log_{10} A,$$

express A in terms of b, c and x and hence find the relation between x and y.

If $\log_{10} y = cx + \log_{10} b$ can be condensed into the form $\log_{10} A = cx$, express A in terms of y and b and hence find the exponential relation between x and y.

The scales on each axis of Figure 3 have equal intervals. Find the relation between y and z in exponential form, and work out the value of y when $t = 3.7$ for:

(a) $z = \log_{10} t,$ \qquad\qquad (b) $z = t.$

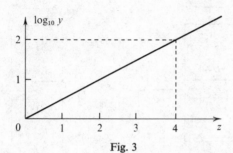

Fig. 3

The following questions provide practice in computation using logarithms to the base 10. Give your answers to as many figures as you consider warranted by the data and the tables you use. All working should be shown.

Calculate:

10. (a) $\dfrac{57.04 \times 368}{248.6}$; \qquad\qquad (b) $\dfrac{4386 \times 0.34}{0.949}$;

(c) $\dfrac{8293}{17.69 \times 492.6}$; \qquad\qquad (d) $\dfrac{0.04702 \times 0.316}{7.045 \times 0.6774}$.

11. (a) $\sqrt{14}$; \qquad\qquad (b) $(86.31)^3$;

(c) $\sqrt[5]{4783}$; \qquad\qquad (d) $29 \times 3643 \times \sqrt{(71/9.6)}$.

12. (a) $\sqrt{0.4}$; \qquad\qquad (b) $(0.847)^5$;

(c) $14\sqrt{(0.067)}$; \qquad\qquad (d) $72.9 \times 0.43 \times \sqrt{(0.87/0.977)}$.

13. (a) $\dfrac{4.37 \times 10^6}{9.47 \times 10^{-3}}$; \qquad\qquad (b) $\sqrt{(8.647 \times 10^{-7})}$;

(c) $\left(\dfrac{5.409 \times 10^{-3}}{9.4 \times 10^{-5}}\right)^3$; \qquad\qquad (d) $\sqrt{\left(\dfrac{2 \times 10^{10}}{4.9 \times 10^7 \times 9.64 \times 10^7}\right)}$.

14. (a) $\dfrac{49.3 \times \sqrt{(1.104 \times 10^{-5})}}{3698}$; \qquad\qquad (b) $\dfrac{2486 \times 3700}{5849 \times 41 \times 10^4}$;

(c) $\sqrt[3]{\left(\dfrac{3.16 \times 10^4}{944 \times 717}\right)}$; \qquad\qquad (d) $\left(\dfrac{49.3^4 \times 67.14^3}{71.05 \times 10^{-6}}\right)^{\frac{1}{8}}$.

15. Find the value of x in the following:

(a) $2 \cdot 13^x = 4931$; (b) $2 \cdot 86^x = 7949$;

(c) $\dfrac{7423^x}{4907} = \sqrt{942\,600}$; (d) $0 \cdot 073^x = 0 \cdot 0313$.

9. SIGMA NOTATION AND SERIES

1. Carry out a dry run for the following flow diagrams.

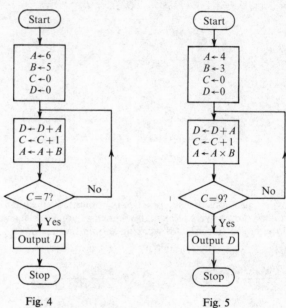

Fig. 4   Fig. 5

2. Draw flow diagrams to sum the following series to 50 terms:

(a) $5+8+11+14+\ldots$;

(b) $5+6+8+11+15+20+\ldots$;

(c) to find the total saved in 12 years if, each year, £50 is put into a bank at 5% per annum interest.

3. Use the sigma notation to express the following:

(a) $20+25+30+35+\ldots$ to 25 terms;

(b) $10000+1000+100+10+\ldots$ to 10 terms;

(c) $1+1\cdot1+1\cdot21+1\cdot331+\ldots$ to 15 terms;

(d) $\dfrac{1}{1+2}+\dfrac{1}{2+3}+\dfrac{1}{3+4}+\dfrac{1}{4+5}+\ldots$ to 8 terms;

(e) $3+2\times3^2+3\times3^3+4\times3^4+\ldots$ to 20 terms;

(f) the number of oranges in a pyramid consisting of 12 layers of oranges, the pyramid being (i) square based and (ii) triangle based.

228

4. Write out the following sums in full:

(a) $\sum\limits_{1}^{6} i^2(i+1)$;

(b) $\sum\limits_{0}^{4} (-1)^i(i+1)$;

(c) $\sum\limits_{0}^{5} x^i$;

(d) $\sum\limits_{0}^{4} \dfrac{i}{i+1}$;

(e) $\sum\limits_{1}^{6} f(x_i)$.

5. Work out the sum in each of the following:

(a) $\sum\limits_{1}^{5} 3i$;

(b) $\sum\limits_{1}^{5} (2^i+3i)$;

(c) $\sum\limits_{1}^{4} i^2$;

(d) $\sum\limits_{1}^{4} (i^2+3i+2)$.

6. Put in simpler form:

(a) $\sum\limits_{1}^{n} i+2\sum\limits_{1}^{n-1} (i+1)$;

(b) $\sum\limits_{1}^{7} i^5+\sum\limits_{7}^{10} i^5$;

(c) $\sum\limits_{1}^{n} i^2-\sum\limits_{1}^{n} (i-1)^2$;

(d) $\sum\limits_{1}^{n+1} i-\sum\limits_{1}^{n} (n-i)$;

(e) $\sum\limits_{1}^{n} 2i-\sum\limits_{1}^{2n} i$.

7. Which of the following statements are true?

(a) $\sum\limits_{1}^{n} (2i^2+i) = \sum\limits_{1}^{n} (2j^2+j)$;

(b) $\sum\limits_{1}^{n} (3i^2+1) = 3\sum\limits_{1}^{n} i^2 +1$;

(c) $\sum\limits_{1}^{n} i = \sum\limits_{1}^{n} (n-i)$;

(d) $\sum\limits_{1}^{9} i^3 = \sum\limits_{1}^{9} (10-i)^3$;

(e) $\sum\limits_{i=1}^{n} n = n^2$;

(f) $\sum\limits_{1}^{n} i^2(i+1)^2 = \sum\limits_{1}^{n-1} i^2(i-1)^2$.

8. Give the last term and the sum of the following progressions:

(a) $20+25+30+35\ldots$to 12 terms;

(b) $7+14+28+56\ldots$to 10 terms;

(c) $2+\frac{1}{2}+\frac{1}{8}+\frac{1}{32}+\ldots$to 20 terms;

(d) $1-\frac{1}{2}+\frac{1}{4}-\frac{1}{8}+\ldots$to 100 terms.

9. (a) Write down the nth term and the sum to n terms of the arithmetic progression whose first term is 12 and whose difference is 5.

(b) Write down the nth term and the sum to n terms of the geometric progression whose first term is 4 and whose common ratio is 1·5.

(c) Insert 4 terms between 32 and 243 so that (i) all 6 terms are in arithmetic progression, (ii) all 6 terms are in geometric progression.

(d) a, b and c are in arithmetic progression. What is the relation between a, b and c? What would it be if they were in geometric progression?

10. (*a*) Check that the terms of the following series can be expressed as $\left(\dfrac{1}{r}-\dfrac{1}{r+1}\right)$ where r is the number of the term.

$$\tfrac{1}{2}+\tfrac{1}{6}+\tfrac{1}{12}+\tfrac{1}{20}+\tfrac{1}{30}+\ldots.$$

By expressing each term in this way, find the sum of the first 6 terms, 50 terms, n terms.

(*b*) Using the difference relation

$$\sum_{1}^{n}(f(i+1)-f(i)) = f(n+1)-f(1),$$

what functions f do you choose to find the sums

$$\sum_{1}^{n} i, \quad \sum_{1}^{n} i^2, \quad \sum_{1}^{n} i^3, \quad \sum_{1}^{n} i(i+1), \quad \sum_{1}^{n} i(i+1)(i+2)?$$

(*c*) (i) Express $3i^3-2i^2+7i$ in terms of $i(i+1)(i+2)$, $i(i+1)$ and i and hence find $\displaystyle\sum_{1}^{n}(3i^3-2i^2+7i)$.

(ii) Express $\displaystyle\sum_{1}^{9}(3i^3-2i^2+7)$ in terms of $\displaystyle\sum_{1}^{9}i^3$, $\displaystyle\sum_{1}^{9}i^2$ and $\displaystyle\sum_{1}^{9}i$ and so obtain an expression for the original sum. Check your answer from the result of part (i).

10. AREA AND INTEGRATION

1. The graph of Figure 6 shows the time $\rightarrow$ speed graph of a train moving between stations. Estimate the distance travelled. This estimate may be inaccurate: state upper and lower bounds that *must* contain the area.

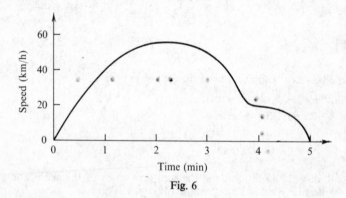

Fig. 6

The following table refers to the above journey. Use the trapezium rule to calculate the distance between stations.

Time (min)	0	1	2	3	4	5
Velocity (km/h)	0	40	55	50	20	0

230

2. The sum of the fourth powers of the first n natural numbers is

$$\tfrac{1}{30}n(n+1)\,(6n^3+9n^2+n-1).$$

Draw n rectangles over the graph of $y = x^4$ from $x = 0$ to $x = b$. Use the above result to calculate an upper bound for the area between these limits. By increasing n, confirm that the area under the graph is $b^5/5$.

3. Draw graphs to illustrate the following definite integrals and find their values. Also, in each case, find the area bounded by the given limits for x, the curve and the x-axis.

(a) $\displaystyle\int_{-1}^{2} (5x+2)\,dx;$ (b) $\displaystyle\int_{-2}^{2} \tfrac{1}{2}x^3\,dx;$ (c) $\displaystyle\int_{-\frac{2}{3}}^{1} (3x^2-x-2)\,dx.$

4. Write down integral functions for the following:

(a) $x \rightarrow x^3+6x-7;$ (b) $x \rightarrow \dfrac{1}{x^2}+x^2;$ (c) $x \rightarrow 3\cos x+\sin x;$

(d) $x \rightarrow \sin 3x-x^5;$ (e) $x \rightarrow x^{\frac{1}{2}}-x^{-3}.$

5. Evaluate the following definite integrals:

(a) $\displaystyle\int_0^1 (1-2x^2)\,dx;$ (b) $\displaystyle\int_0^{\frac{1}{4}\pi} \cos x\,dx;$ (c) $\displaystyle\int_2^4 \left(1-\dfrac{1}{x^3}\right)dx;$

(d) $\displaystyle\int_0^\pi (1-\sin x)\,dx.$

6. A graph passes through the point $(2, 5)$ and its gradient at any point is given by

$$\frac{dy}{dx} = x^2+5x-1.$$

Express y in terms of x and find the value of y when $x = 1$.

7. The velocity (in m/s) of a particle moving along a straight line is given by $v = 4-3t+t^3$. At what times is the acceleration zero? In between these times, is the velocity increasing or decreasing? What is the distance travelled in that period?

8. A particle moves with an acceleration given by

$$\ddot{\mathbf{r}} = \mathbf{i}+2t\mathbf{j}.$$

When $t = 0$, $\dot{\mathbf{r}} = 3\mathbf{i}$ and $\mathbf{r} = 2\mathbf{j}$. Write down expressions for the velocity and position. What are the velocity and position when $t = 2$? What is the displacement over the time interval $0 \leqslant t \leqslant 2$?

9. What is the area of the region enclosed by the curve $y = 3\sqrt{x}$ and the line $y = x$?

10. The lengths (in cm) of some leaves in a sample are measured and the results are shown on a histogram. A curve that roughly fits the histogram is

$$f(x) = 40+40\cos(x-5),$$

over the interval $2 \leqslant x \leqslant 8$. Sketch the curve. Use integration to estimate how many leaves were less than (i) 4 cm in length, (ii) the mean length.

REVISION PAPERS

(These papers cover approximately the first term's work.)

A1

This is a multiple choice paper. Some questions have more than one correct answer.

1. $\dfrac{48 \times 27^{\frac{2}{3}}}{81^{\frac{1}{4}} \times 12^{\frac{1}{2}} \times 16^{\frac{1}{4}}}$. This expression is equal to

(a) $9\sqrt{3}$;   (b) $\sqrt{27}$;   (c) $9/\sqrt{3}$;

(d) $3^{\frac{3}{2}}$;   (e) $\frac{16}{27}$.

2. $\sqrt{48} + \sqrt{50}$ is equal to

(a) 14;   (b) $4\sqrt{3} + 5\sqrt{2}$;   (c) $\sqrt{98}$;

(d) $9\sqrt{6}$;   (e) $9\sqrt{5}$.

3. $\dfrac{\sqrt{5}+1}{2}$ is equal to

(a) $\frac{5}{3}$;   (b) $\frac{1}{2}\sqrt{6}$;   (c) $\dfrac{2}{\sqrt{5}-1}$;

(d) $\sqrt{3}$;   (e) $1\cdot6$.

4. Which of the following statements are correct?

(a) $2^4 = 16 \Leftrightarrow \log_2 4 = 16$;   (b) $3^2 = 9 \Leftrightarrow \log_3 9 = 2$;

(c) $\dfrac{\log_2 5}{\log_2 10} = \log_{10} 5$;   (d) $\log_2 1024 = 10$;

(e) $\log_a 1024 = 10 \log_a 2$.

5. In how many years will an investment of £P double its value if the compound interest rate is 8%?

(a) 9;   (b) 10;   (c) 11;

(d) 12;   (e) 13.

6. If **a** and **b** are two vectors which are equal in magnitude, then the pair of vectors $\mathbf{a}+\mathbf{b}$ and $\mathbf{a}-\mathbf{b}$ are always (a) parallel, (b) perpendicular, (c) both zero, (d) such that one is zero, (e) equal in length.

7. In the diagram, O is the origin and $\mathbf{OA} = \mathbf{a}$, $\mathbf{OB} = \mathbf{b}$. Which of the following are correct?

(a) $\mathbf{QP} = \mathbf{a}-\mathbf{b}$;

(b) $\mathbf{OQ} = 2\mathbf{a}+3\mathbf{b}$;

(c) $\mathbf{OR} = -(3\mathbf{b}+\mathbf{a})$;

(d) $\mathbf{OS} = 2\mathbf{b}+3\mathbf{a}$;

(e) $\mathbf{OT} = \mathbf{b}-\mathbf{a}$.

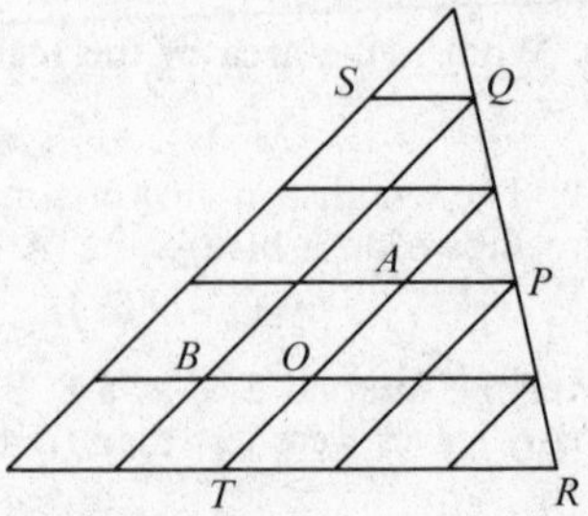

Fig. 1

8. Which of the following are factors of $2x^3 - x^2 - 2x + 1$?

(a) $x-1$;   (b) $x+1$;   (c) $x-2$;

(d) $x+2$;   (e) $2x+1$.

9.

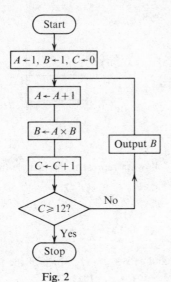

Fig. 2

Which of the following statements are true about the above flow diagram?
(a) When the stop instruction is reached, the number in store C is 12.
(b) The flow chart computes the sum of the first 12 integers.
(c) The print-out is 12! only.
(d) The first 12 factorials from 1! to 12! are printed.
(e) 2 is the first number printed.

10. $K(n)$ is defined to be the sum of the cubes of the three consecutive integers $n, n+1, n+2$. Indicate which of the following statements are correct.

(a) $K(0) = 9$;   (b) $K(2) = 100$;   (c) $K(n)$ is divisible by 9;

(d) $K(n) = (n+3)^3$;   (e) $K(n)$ is a perfect square.

11. Which of the following are functions, if the domain is to be the set of real numbers?

(a) $x \to \sin^2 x$;   (b) $x \to 1/\sin x$;   (c) $x \to \pm \sqrt{x}$;

(d) $x \to [x]$, where $[x]$ means the greatest integer not greater than x;

(e) $x \to \dfrac{1}{x-1}$.

12. If $f(x) = 1 - x^2$, which of the following are correct?

(a) $ff(3) = 3^2$;   (b) $f^{-1}(5) = 2$;   (c) $f^{-1}f(2) = 2$;

(d) $f''(-2) = -2$;   (e) $f(x)$ has a minimum value of 1.

13. Which of the following functions could be represented by the mapping diagram in Figure 3?

(a) $x \to x^{\frac{1}{2}}$;   (b) $x \to \sin \frac{1}{2}\pi x$;   (c) $x \to x^3$;

(d) $x \to x$;   (e) $x \to \tan \frac{1}{2}\pi x$.

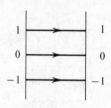

Fig. 3

14. Which of the following represent the inverse function of $f: x \to \dfrac{1}{3x-2}$?

(a) $x \to \dfrac{1}{3} + 2x$;   (b) $x \to \dfrac{1}{3x} - \dfrac{2}{3}$;   (c) $y \to \dfrac{1+2y}{3y}$;

(d) $x \to \dfrac{1}{3x} + \dfrac{2}{3}$;   (e) $x \to \dfrac{3}{x+2}$.

15. For $f: x \to x^3$ and $g: x \to 2x-1$, which of the following is the function fg?

(a) $x \to (2x-1)^3$;   (b) $x \to (8x^3-1)$;   (c) $x \to (2x^4-x^3)$;

(d) $x \to (2x^3-1)$;   (e) $x \to 8x^3-12x^2+6x-1$.

16. Which of these represents the graph of $y = x^{\frac{2}{3}}$ near the origin?

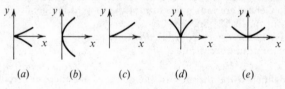

(a)   (b)   (c)   (d)   (e)

Fig. 4

17. Which equation is represented by the graph of Figure 5?

(a) $y = \dfrac{1}{(x-1)(x-2)}$;

(b) $y = \dfrac{x}{(x-1)(x-2)}$;

(c) $y = \dfrac{(x-1)(x-2)}{x^3}$;

(d) $y = \dfrac{1}{(x-2)(x-1)^2}$;

(e) $y = \dfrac{1}{(x-1)(x-2)^2}$.

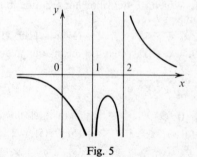

Fig. 5

18. For which of the following values of x does the function f attain a maximum value, given that $f(x) = x^3 - x^2 - x + 1$?

(a) 1;   (b) $\frac{1}{2}$;   (c) $\frac{1}{3}$;

(d) $-\frac{1}{3}$;   (e) -1.

19. Which of the following equal $\cos 2x$?

(a) $1 - \sin^2 x$;   (b) $2 \cos^2 x - 1$;   (c) $\cos x + \cos x$;

(d) $(\cos x - \sin x)^2$;   (e) $(\cos x - \sin x)(\cos x + \sin x)$.

20. Which of the following will produce a rotation of the plane equivalent to a third of a complete rotation in the positive direction?

(a) $\begin{pmatrix} \cos 120° & -\sin 120° \\ \sin 120° & \cos 120° \end{pmatrix}$;   (b) $\frac{1}{2} \begin{pmatrix} \sqrt{3} & -1 \\ 1 & \sqrt{3} \end{pmatrix}$;

(c) $\begin{pmatrix} \cos 240° & \sin 240° \\ -\sin 240° & \cos 240° \end{pmatrix}$;   (d) $\begin{pmatrix} \frac{2}{3}\pi & -\frac{2}{3}\pi \\ \frac{2}{3}\pi & \frac{2}{3}\pi \end{pmatrix}$;

(e) $\begin{pmatrix} 0 & -1 \\ 1 & 0 \end{pmatrix} \begin{pmatrix} \frac{1}{2} & \frac{1}{2}\sqrt{3} \\ \frac{1}{2}\sqrt{3} & \frac{1}{2} \end{pmatrix}$.

21. In Figure 6, A is the graph of $y = \sin x$. Which transformation maps A into B?

(a) A stretch parallel to Ox of factor 2 and a stretch parallel to Oy of factor -1;

(b) $\begin{pmatrix} x \\ y \end{pmatrix} \to \begin{pmatrix} \frac{1}{2}x \\ -y \end{pmatrix}$;   (c) $\begin{pmatrix} x \\ y \end{pmatrix} \to \begin{pmatrix} -\frac{1}{2}x \\ y \end{pmatrix}$;   (d) $\begin{pmatrix} x \\ y \end{pmatrix} \to \begin{pmatrix} 2x \\ -y \end{pmatrix}$;

(e) the transformation given by $\begin{pmatrix} -\frac{1}{2} & 0 \\ 0 & 1 \end{pmatrix}$.

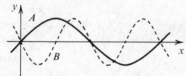

Fig. 6

22. Indicate which of the following functions have maximum values in the interval $0 \leqslant x \leqslant 1$:

(a) $x \to \dfrac{1}{x(x-1)}$;   (b) $x \to 3 \sin \frac{1}{2}x$;

(c) $\begin{cases} (x, y): y = x & \text{if } 0 \leqslant x \leqslant \frac{1}{2} \\ y = 1 - x & \text{if } \frac{1}{2} \leqslant x \end{cases}$;

(d) $x \to x^3 - 4x$;   (e) $x \to 2x^3 - 3x^2 - 12x$.

A2

1. For each of the following functions, the domain D and the codomain are real numbers (except that in (iii) and (v), 2 is omitted from the domain). For each function, state (*a*) the elements which map onto 1; (*b*) the inverse function, if it exists without restriction of D.

(i) $f: x \to x^2 - 3$; (ii) $g: x \to x^2 + 3$;

(iii) $h: x \to \dfrac{1}{x-2}$; (iv) $i: x \to \sin x$;

(v) $j: x \to \dfrac{2x-1}{x-2}$.

2. Consider the function $f: x \to \dfrac{x^2}{(x+1)(x^2+2)}$. State the numbers a and n, given that the function behaves like ax^n

(i) when x is small; (ii) when x is large.

For what value or values of x is the function discontinuous? Sketch the graph of the function.

3. (*a*)

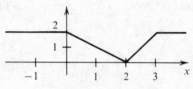

Fig. 7

Figure 7 shows the shape of the graph of the function $x \to \text{myst}(x)$.
Copy the diagram five times and sketch on the same axes the graphs of:

$x \to \text{myst}(x) + 2$; $x \to \text{myst}(x+2)$;

$x \to \text{myst}(2x)$; $x \to 2\,\text{myst}(x)$;

$x \to 2\,\text{myst}(2x+2) + 2$.

(*b*)

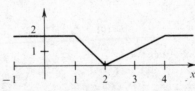

Fig. 8

Express, in a form similar to the above, the function whose graph is shown in Figure 8.

236

4.

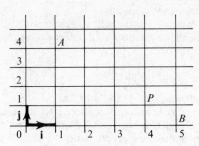

Fig. 9

(a) **i** and **j** are unit vectors: **p**, **a** and **b** are the position vectors of the points P, A and B.

Express **p** in terms of (i) **i** and **j**, and (ii) **a** and **b**.

In what ratio $r:1$ does P divide the segment AB?

(b) P', A' and B' are the images of P, A and B under the transformation given by $\begin{pmatrix} 1 & 0 \\ 2 & 1 \end{pmatrix}$. Express **p'** in terms of **a'** and **b'** and hence find the ratio in which P' divides the segment A'B', if it lies on that line.

5. Express the following as single fractions:

(i) $\dfrac{2}{x-3}+\dfrac{x}{3}$; (ii) $\dfrac{2}{x-3}-\dfrac{x}{x^2-9}$.

From the fact that the following equation is true for all values of x, prove that $a = 3$, $b = 1$ and $c = -2$.

$$ax^3+bx^2+c = 3x^3+x^2-2.$$

Use this principle to find a and b where, for all values of x,

$$\frac{x}{(x-1)(x-3)} = \frac{a}{x-1}+\frac{b}{x-3}.$$

6.

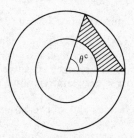

Fig. 10

Show that the area of the shaded part of Fig. 10 is given by

$$A = (2 \sin \theta - \tfrac{1}{2}\theta) \text{ cm}^2,$$

if the radii are 1 cm and 2 cm and $\theta < \tfrac{2}{3}\pi$. What value of θ gives the greatest possible area?

7. (*a*) Use logarithms to work out $50 \times 1 \cdot 1^8$ to 3 SF.

(*b*) The quantities x and y are thought to be connected by an equation of the form $y = ka^x$. To find the constants k and a, some measurements were taken for x and y and they were:

x	1	2	3	4
y	18	27	40	61

Use this information to estimate k and a to 2 SF.

(*c*) The cost of a picture was proportional to its age and was given by $c = 1250t$. (Cost in £ and time in years.) For an advertisement, this function had to be shown on a piece of graph paper 28 cm × 18 cm with the special restriction that the cost over the first 10 years should cover a space of at least 2 cm. What sort of scales would you suggest? Outline them on a sheet of graph paper and sketch in the shape very roughly.

8. The pressure at the bottom of a conical tank is $1000 h$ newtons per square metre where h is the depth of the liquid in the tank in metres. The tank is such that the radius of the top is equal to the height. Liquid is pumped in at a constant rate of $\frac{1}{4}\pi \times 10^{-3}$ cubic metres per second. Express as functions of t, the volume, the height and the pressure at the bottom. (t is the time, in seconds, after pumping begins.) Write down the derived functions, state what each represents and the units in which it is measured. Estimate the rise in pressure in the time interval from $t = 72$ to $t = 74$.

9. Show that if $\cos 2\theta$ is irrational, then $\cos \theta$ is also irrational. Is the converse also true? Prove your conclusion or provide a counter example.

A 3

1. If f and g are the functions $f: x \to 2x - 1$, $g: x \to 3x^3$, what are (i) $fg(2)$, (ii) $gf(2)$, (iii) $ff(2)$, (iv) $f^{-1}(6)$, (v) $g^{-1}f^{-1}(-7)$? Express as single functions (vi) ff, (vii) $f^{-1}g$.

2. (i) Work out by logarithms $\dfrac{63 \cdot 2 \times 0 \cdot 08416}{1 \cdot 61}$. Check your answer using a slide-rule.

(ii) Write down a rough approximation for x if $(2 \cdot 9)^x = 73$. Use logarithms to find x to 3 SF.

3. Consider the graph of the function $f: x \to x + 4/x^2$.

(i) What happens when x is very small (positive and negative)?

(ii) What happens when x is very large (positive and negative)?

(iii) Sketch the graph.

(iv) With the same axes, sketch and label carefully the graph of the function $x \to (x - 3) + 4/(x - 3)^2$.

(v) Find the coordinates of any maximum or minimum point on the graph of f.

4. Simplify (i) $64^{\frac{2}{3}}$, (ii) 4^{-2}, (iii) 8^0, (iv) $a^{\frac{1}{3}} \times a^{\frac{1}{2}}$, (v) $b^2 \div b^{-3}$.

Express in index form as simply as possible (vi) $x\sqrt{x}$, (vii) $7/x^4$.

(viii) If $\log_p q = r$, which of the following is true

(*a*) $q = p^r$, \qquad\qquad (*b*) $p = q^r$, \qquad\qquad (*c*) $q = r^p$?

Express the following in index form and hence find s and t:

(ix) $\log_5 s = 2$, (x) $\log_4 8 = t$.

5. If f, g are the functions $f: x \to 3x^2 + 5$, $g: x \to x(1 + x)$, write down the derived functions f' and g'.

What are (i) $g'f'$, (ii) gf, (iii) $(gf)'$?

6. (i) Explain the purpose of the flow chart in Figure 11.

(ii) Use logarithms to find exactly what answer a computer, programmed in accordance with this flow chart, would print out. Show all your working.

7. The position vector of a particle at time t is given by $\mathbf{r} = 3 \sin t\mathbf{i} + 4 \sin 2t\mathbf{j}$. Sketch the path of the particle and find its position, velocity and acceleration when $t = 1 \cdot 2$.

8. A triangle has sides 10, 10, $2x$ centimetres. Show that if S cm⁴ denotes the square of the area of the triangle, then $S = 100x^2 - x^4$.

Find the maximum value of S, and hence give the maximum area of the triangle.

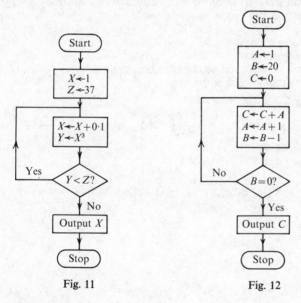

Fig. 11   Fig. 12

A 4

1. The flow chart shown in Figure 12 was intended to sum the series $1 + 3 + 5 + \ldots$ to 20 terms. It contains a mistake.

(a) Say what it will actually print.

(b) Say which is the wrong instruction and write a correct version.

(c) Write down the new print-out.

2. Functions f, g, h, s are defined as $f: x \to x^2$, $g: x \to 1/x$, $h: x \to 3x$, $s: x \to \sin x$.

(a) What are the functions fg, gf, gh, hg?

(b) What are the images of $x = \frac{1}{6}\pi$ under the functions hs and sh?

3. Give the inverses of the following functions:

$$x \to \tfrac{4}{3}\pi x^3, \quad x \to \frac{1}{x+2}, \quad x \to \frac{2x-3}{x-2}.$$

239

4. (*a*) $f: x \rightarrow a+bx$ is a linear function. Find the linear function f such that $f(0) = 7$, whose graph is parallel to the graph of g where $g(x) = 2-5x$.

(*b*) The function h is such that $h(-8) = 19$, $h(2) = 4$ and $h(10) = -9$. Can it be a linear function? Explain.

5. Define the meaning of *odd* and *even* functions in both algebraic and geometric terms. State whether the following functions are odd, even or neither:

$$x \rightarrow x+x^2, \quad x \rightarrow \sin x, \quad x \rightarrow \frac{1}{1+x^3}, \quad x \rightarrow \sin^2 x \cos x.$$

6. Differentiate from first principles $f: x \rightarrow x^2 - 1/x$.

7. Without using differentiation, find the minimum value of $(x+3)^2+4$, and find the maximum and minimum values of $3 \cos (x+\frac{1}{3}\pi)+1$.

8. The time (in seconds) since the start of motion of a car maps onto the speed (in metres per second) by the mapping $t \rightarrow 2t - \frac{1}{30}t^2$.

Find
(i)   the acceleration at $t = 0$,
(ii) the acceleration at $t = 20$,
(iii) the time at which the acceleration becomes zero,
(iv) the maximum speed of the car.

9. Sketch the graphs of

$$y = x^3 - x, \quad y = \frac{1}{x-3} \quad \text{and} \quad y = \frac{1}{(x+1)(x-3)}$$

on separate diagrams.

10. Differentiate

(i) $3x^3 + 7x^2 - \dfrac{2}{x}$,   (ii) $\dfrac{7x^3+1}{x}$,   (iii) $x(x-1)(x+2)$.

11

POSITION AND SPREAD

1. INTRODUCTION

With what kinds of problem can the study of statistics assist?

A city has to plan for several years ahead the provision of schools, hospitals, housing etc. What information is required when forecasting the numbers in the first forms of secondary schools in five years time? The number of six-year-olds now is obviously a guide, but migration to and from the city must be taken into account even though it may be difficult to quantify. The siting of new factories, housing policy, possible redundancies in existing factories are all relevant. Judgement is called for, but statistical information can reduce the inevitable uncertainties.

Comprehensive information is provided by the national census taken every ten years, but in most fields we have to be content with samples.

How would you find out whether taking glucose an hour before the start improves your performance in a cross-country run? How can an agricultural research centre abroad evaluate new types of rice which are being considered for introduction into the region?

Difficult questions arise. How can we avoid bias in our sampling methods? What are the chances of getting a thoroughly unrepresentative sample? How large should the sample be?

Torch batteries are being mass-produced in a factory. How can the management ensure that the quality of the product is being maintained?

'20 560 000 people watched the finals of the 'Miss Earth' competition on television last week.' On what information might this newspaper statement be based? How accurate would you expect it to be?

The essential feature common to all these examples is that information from the past and present is to be used in making decisions for the future. The first stage is to gather data. The O-level course was concerned with this, together with the subsequent sorting and presentation in various graphical forms; also the calculation of numbers—such as the mean, median and quartiles—which for certain purposes may provide an adequate summary of the relevant information. In this chapter, we shall make a more thorough study of some of these basic ideas, including the introduction of a more complicated but more useful measure of spread. Later chapters will develop probability theory which will be necessary before the above questions can be answered satisfactorily.

Exercise A

1. The table shows the age distribution of the inhabitants of the U.K. in 1959, 1964, 1969. Figures are given in hundred thousands. For each year, calculate the approximate proportion of the population (*a*) over the age of 65, (*b*) under the age of 15. Comment on the trends. Can you make predictions for 1974 and 1979?

	0–10	10–20	20–30	30–40	40–50	50–60	60–70	70–80	80–
1959	79	77	67	74	70	68	48	29	10
1964	87	81	70	68	71	70	53	30	11
1969	93	78	79	67	72	66	58	32	12

2. Articles though manufactured by the same machine, nevertheless vary in size. Measurements were made of one batch and the frequency diagram of Figure 1 gives the results.

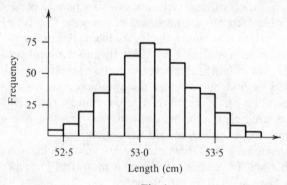

Fig. 1

The specification stated that articles greater than 53·5 cm or less than 52·5 cm were unacceptable. What proportion of the batch is acceptable? The machine setting can be adjusted so that the lengths are increased or decreased slightly in future, though the variation in length cannot be avoided. What proportion of articles produced by this machine should be acceptable after adjustment?

2. POPULATIONS. SORTING NUMERICAL DATA

In an investigation to find an appropriate amount to be fixed as a minimum weekly wage, enquiries were made from 100 households about the amount spent on food per person per week. The data received (in pence) were as shown on page 243.

In statistics, we shall call a collection of numbers of this kind a *population*. The word 'set' is not appropriate as an element may well be repeated, and that is not acceptable in the definition of sets.

190	180	170	200	170	180	210	240	160	190
220	330	200	240	210	240	220	170	190	210
260	210	270	220	260	150	180	230	230	290
290	200	160	180	210	160	190	200	180	250
190	270	230	300	220	200	240	250	260	180
190	170	250	180	180	230	220	270	170	260
280	230	180	220	240	190	160	200	190	180
220	170	200	190	200	180	180	170	220	150
240	250	160	210	170	170	240	190	200	170
280	190	200	230	190	260	180	220	250	290

The numbers in this population are all rounded to the nearest 10 pence. If a family of three spent $4453\frac{1}{2}$ pence over an observed period of 8 weeks, what figure would be recorded? Do you think the data should be recorded more accurately? Should the average for a household of 7 carry more weight in the investigation than that for a household of 3? Suggest other issues which should be decided before proceeding.

Suppose that all families spending less than 170 pence per head are to be considered for a Family Income Supplement. How many of these are there in the sample? Such questions are answered easily when we have carried out the usual sorting procedure.

Make out a table, and using tally marks find how many times each number occurs in the population. You should find, for example, that 200 has frequency 10, meaning that 10 households spent on average between 195 and 205 pence per person per week.

The information is perhaps best conveyed by a diagram. Check that your frequencies agree with those in the frequency diagram of Figure 2.

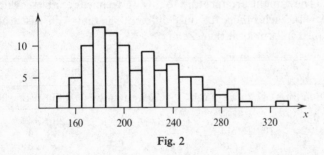

Fig. 2

The way such data are recorded is a matter of choice. If each amount had been rounded to the nearest 20p the following frequency table might have resulted, giving the frequency diagram of Figure 3.

Amount spent	140	160	180	200	220	240	260	280	300	320
Frequency	1	12	25	18	14	14	7	6	2	1

243

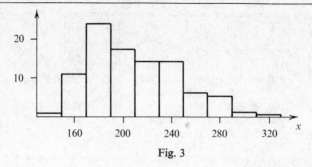

Fig. 3

The same survey has given rise to two different populations. In the first we found the number of elements in the intervals 145–155, 155–165 etc., while in the second the intervals chosen have been 130–150, 150–170 etc. Had we chosen intervals of length 20 starting with 145–165, 165–185, the corresponding frequencies would have been 7, 23, and the *midmarks* (or representative numbers) would have been 155, 175....

The choice of interval length is a matter of judgement, and no hard and fast rules can be laid down, but taking between 7 and 10 intervals nearly always proves satisfactory. The actual intervals may be chosen to give convenient midmarks.

2.1 Frequency density and histograms. There is a problem of interpretation of frequency diagrams which leads to some new ideas.

Suppose that, to judge the use that is being made of the cheap rate times, two girls, Ann and Zena, were asked independently to record the lengths of the first 100 calls after 6 p.m. to pass through their manual telephone exchange. They might produce the following frequency tables, which are consistent with each other; the only difference is that Ann has produced more detailed information than Zena.

Ann		Zena	
Duration (min)	Number of calls	Duration (min)	Number of calls
0–1	18	0–1	18
1–2	14	1–2	14
2–3	26	2–3	26
3–4	12	3–6	33
4–5	6	6–12	9
5–6	15		
6–7	2		
8–9	2		
9–10	3		
11–12	2		

Figure 4 shows the frequency diagrams corresponding to the two frequency tables. Why is the second one misleading? What impression does it give you of the proportion of calls between 3 and 6 minutes?

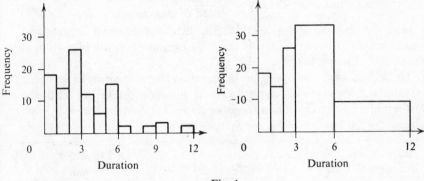

Fig. 4

Diagrams that are easier to interpret are obtained by representing the frequency corresponding to each interval by the *area* of the rectangle with the interval as base, and not by the height of the rectangle. The axis up the page in our example will then represent the number of calls per minute interval.

From Zena's information, 33 of the calls lasted between 3 and 6 minutes. On average this is 11 calls for each minute interval.

The new diagrams are then as in Figure 5.

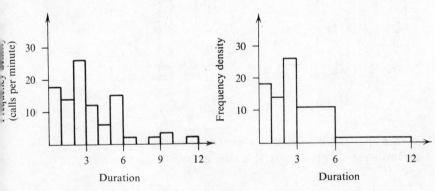

Fig. 5

Such diagrams are called *histograms*. These two convey broadly the same impression as, of course, they should.

Instead of the *frequency* (i.e. the number of times an element appears in a population or the number of elements in an interval) we are considering the *frequency density* (i.e. the number of elements per unit measure of interval). Notice that the frequency density is a rate:

$$\text{frequency density} = \frac{\text{frequency in the class}}{\text{length of class interval}}.$$

If all the intervals are of equal length, then the frequency diagram and histogram differ only in scale. If the class lengths vary, the histogram is more easily interpreted.

The second way of analysing the information from the survey of Section 2 is tabulated below and displayed in a histogram, together with the histogram arising from the previous analysis. The frequency density now represents the number of households per penny interval.

Amount spent	Midmark	Frequency	Frequency density
130–150	140	1	0·05
150–170	160	12	0·6
170–190	180	25	1·25
190–210	200	18	0·9
210–230	220	14	0·7
230–250	240	14	0·7
250–270	260	7	0·35
270–290	280	6	0·3
290–310	300	2	0·1
310–330	320	1	0·05

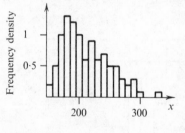 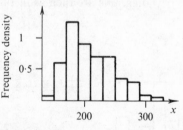

Fig. 6

Notice that the vertical scales are the same; in Figures 2 and 3, the diagrams were only of comparable size because different scales were used.

Exercise B

1. From the two populations of Section 2, state how many households spent on average (*a*) less than 185p, (*b*) less than 190p, (*c*) between 190 and 195p.

2. Find the total areas of the histograms of Figure 6 to the left of the line $x = 220$. What do these numbers represent?

3. Group the data of Section 2 in different ways, e.g. with intervals of length 20 starting 145–165 or intervals of length 20 starting 135–155 or intervals of length 30 starting 135–165. Draw the corresponding histograms, using the same scales on each occasion.

4. What are the disadvantages of grouping data with (a) too few, (b) too many class intervals?

5. What is d if the line $x = d$ divides the first histogram of Figure 6 into two parts of equal area? What do we call this number?

6. A batsman's scores during a season when grouped were as follows:

No. of runs	0	1–9	10–29	30–49	50–59	60–99
No. of innings	9	9	15	10	8	4

Draw a histogram to show these figures. What are the units of the frequency density?

7. Figure 7 arose from measuring a large sample of stalks of wheat 8 weeks after sowing. Calculate the approximate number of stalks (a) less than 10 cm tall, (b) between 10 and 15 cm tall.

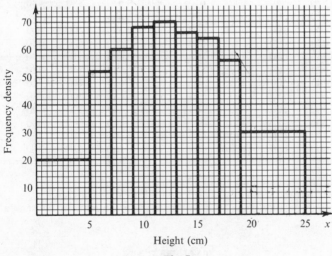

Fig. 7

8. On a copy of Figure 7, draw the graph of $y = 12x - \frac{1}{2}x^2$. Find, by integration, the area under this graph (a) between $x = 0$ and $x = 10$, (b) between $x = 10$ and $x = 15$. Compare with your answers to Question 7.

Find also the approximate number of stalks for which $a < x < b$.

9. In a game of billiards between novices, the number of shots in each 'break' was noted.

Number of shots in break	1	2	3	4	5	6	7	8	9	10
Frequency	120	30	13	7	4	4	2	1	0	1

Draw the histogram and superimpose on it the graph of $g(x) = 100/x^2$.

Find $\displaystyle\int_{\frac{1}{2}}^{10\frac{1}{2}} g(x)\,dx$, $\displaystyle\int_{1\frac{1}{2}}^{2\frac{1}{2}} g(x)\,dx$ and $\displaystyle\int_{2\frac{1}{2}}^{7\frac{1}{2}} g(x)\,dx$

and comment on your answers.

10. In connection with the survey of Section 2, the weekly rents of 200 households selected at random were found, and provided the following data (in pence).

600	500	500	780	230	480	680	780	320	200
500	450	160	460	720	390	520	200	700	350
490	600	500	520	540	660	380	600	420	200
500	400	180	240	500	660	290	550	240	420
740	220	250	640	300	450	680	880	540	480
800	500	660	280	500	590	250	520	490	520
320	640	300	700	580	380	500	640	800	350
340	530	400	470	500	900	590	200	300	490
440	520	560	190	560	360	620	380	480	300
400	520	300	500	290	520	600	560	390	440
620	400	700	560	480	500	390	500	600	800
580	480	600	280	390	640	490	160	450	600
520	260	600	440	300	360	400	410	480	640
460	520	490	440	580	480	280	440	480	640
500	480	500	320	360	320	460	400	540	700
690	400	380	550	620	540	480	400	480	520
580	560	500	300	560	500	420	520	390	360
380	600	390	480	400	700	340	500	500	590
400	320	400	280	420	260	400	380	460	280
440	600	440	600	400	370	500	620	360	260

(a) Arrange the data into about 10 classes.
(b) Work out the frequency densities and draw the histogram.
(c) Without detailed calculation, estimate the mean rent per household.

3. THE MEAN

3.1 Representative statistics. When statistical data has been collected and sorted, it may be that all the information needed is available. On most occasions, though, some further analysis is required, such as the calculation of proportions and averages. Any single number produced from the mass of data comprising a population is called a *statistic*. There are very many different statistics devised to represent different facets of a population, but in the next sections we limit ourselves to the two most important ones, the mean and standard deviation.

3.2 The mean. There is a wide variety of practical examples in which the mean is useful in the general process of advancing from a situation of uncertainty to a position where a decision can be made. One category of such problems has not yet been introduced.

Many situations involve flow, the flow of people into a dining room or past a shop counter, the flow of ships through a dock, of goods through a market, of cars through a crossing, of components in a manufacturing process, of patients through a doctor's surgery. In each case there is uncertainty, the time taken to choose a meal, to unload and load etc., but in each case a minimum requirement is that the organization should be able to cope with the total of the times of the operations.

Exercise C

1. As part of a manufacturing process, two routines follow each other: a series of transistors has to be fitted and then they have to be tested and perhaps replaced. The times to the nearest minute for each process have been noted on 200 occasions.

Times (min)	2	3	4	5	6	7	8	9	10	11	12
1st process	0	0	0	0	10	40	80	52	9	5	4
2nd process	30	120	28	0	0	0	0	10	8	4	0

How many people should be at each work bench if an average of 40 an hour is required?

2.

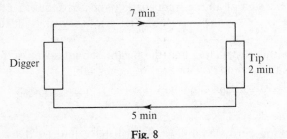

Fig. 8

As part of a large scale construction process, a mechanical digger scoops up material and loads it into a series of lorries. These then transport it to the site of a new embankment and return to the digger. It has been observed that the times are fairly constant (as given in the diagram) except at the digger, where the following table was drawn up.

Time at digger (min)	2	3	4	5	6	7	8	9
Frequency	3	18	35	20	12	2	6	4

What is the best number of lorries to employ? What criterion are you adopting?

3. A dentist used an appointment system in which each patient was given 30 minutes. Examining his records, he classed 20 % of his patients as children, 50 % as adults, and 30 % as elderly. Further, he noted that on average it took 30 minutes to treat each child, 20 minutes for each adult, and 45 minutes for each elderly person. Would you consider his present appointment system satisfactory? Do you think a 4 hour session (e.g. 9 a.m.–1 p.m.) will often over-run by more than half an hour? Would you consider it best to keep to his present system or change? If the latter, how should he organize his appointments?

4. Examine some situations involving flow which are within your experience. (Are there enough towels in the washroom? Are enough people serving in the shop at break time? Are there enough sugar buns? Are there enough coffee urns? Precisely what changes should be made?)

4. CALCULATION OF THE MEAN

Exercise C has given some examples of the use of the mean in decision making. In these the calculations are straightforward, as in the following example.

The ages, in months, of the members of a fifth form are:

Age x	192	193	194	195	196	197	198	199	200
Frequency f	1	2	0	5	5	3	6	2	6

What is the number, N, of members of this form?
What is the total age of all those in the form?
What is their mean age m?

We may write $m = \dfrac{1}{N} \Sigma xf$, where $N = \Sigma f$.

Here the symbol Σ is used in a less precise manner than in Chapter 9. Σf means 'the sum of all the frequencies', and Σxf requires us to multiply each value of x by the corresponding frequency and add up all such terms.

Now use this formula to find the mean amount spent on food by the households of Section 2, using the frequency table:

Amount x	140	160	180	200	220	240	260	280	300	320
Frequency f	1	12	25	18	14	14	7	6	2	1

4.1 Working zero. Doubtless you will have noticed that everyone in the fifth form is aged 16, the youngest being 16.0 and the oldest 16.8. The amounts, d, by which their ages deviate from 16 are:

Deviation d (months over 192)	0	1	2	3	4	5	6	7	8
Frequency f	1	2	0	5	5	3	6	2	6

What is the total deviation, in months, from 16.0? What is the average deviation from 16.0?

250

Hence write down the mean age of the form.

Here we have taken 192 months as our working zero, k, in order to simplify the arithmetic.

Using the symbols d, f, N, k and Σ, write down your method for calculating m.

Now apply your formula with $k = 140$ to verify your result for the mean amount the households spent on food.

Of course, any number may be chosen as working zero and a rough approximation to the mean is often a convenient choice. Some values of d will then be negative ($d = x - k$).

Example 1

Calculate the mean amount spent on food using working zero $k = 200$.

	x	d	f	df	
	140	-60	1	-60	
	160	-40	12	-480	
	180	-20	25	-500	Average deviation $= \dfrac{1020}{100}$
$k = 200$	200	0	18	0	(from $k = 200$)
	220	20	14	280	$= 10\cdot2$
	240	40	14	560	
	260	60	7	420	$m = k + 10\cdot2$
	280	80	6	480	$= 210\cdot2$
	300	100	2	200	
	320	120	1	120	
			100	1020	

4.2   Change of scale. Finally, it is helpful to realize that the deviations can be measured in any units, regardless of the units chosen for x. In the food example, we might count in twenties. In the working below, t stands for the deviation from 200 measured in twenties.

x	t	f	tf
140	-3	1	-3
160	-2	12	-24
180	-1	25	-25
200	0	18	0
220	1	14	14
240	2	14	28
260	3	7	21
280	4	6	24
300	5	2	10
320	6	1	6
		100	51

Here the average deviation is $\frac{51}{100}$ twenties, i.e. $20 \times 0.51 = 10.2$ pence. The mean is therefore $m = 200 + 10.2 = 210.2$ as before.

Call the scale factor c, so that $d = c \times t$. Now express the method of this section concisely, writing m in terms of t, f, N, c and k.

You will appreciate that the scale factor we have used is the length of the intervals into which the original data were grouped. This shows the merit of grouping with equal length intervals.

4.3   Accuracy. The mean calculated in the preceding sections should be quoted to 2 or 3 significant figures only. The process of grouping data reduces accuracy, but even more serious errors usually occur in gathering the original recorded values.

4.4   Formulae for mean. Using a working zero k is equivalent to the transformation $d = x - k$. The effect of introducing a scale factor c is equivalent to the further transformation $t = d/c$, so that $x = k + ct$.

We now introduce the notation $\bar{d}$ to represent the average deviation d, and $\bar{t}$ for the average deviation in the new units. The mean m may then be written alternatively as $\bar{x}$.

The formulae of the preceding sections are now summarized:

(1) $m = \bar{x} = \dfrac{1}{N}\Sigma xf$,   where $N = \Sigma f$.

(2)   With a working zero k, $x = k + d$,

$$\bar{d} = \frac{1}{N}\Sigma df \quad \text{and} \quad \bar{x} = k + \bar{d}.$$

(3)   With a change of scale, $x = k + ct$,

$$\bar{t} = \frac{1}{N}\Sigma tf \quad \text{and} \quad \bar{x} = k + c\bar{t}.$$

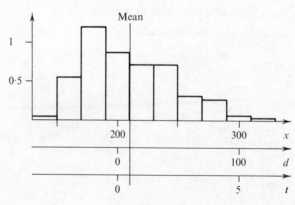

Fig. 9

Figure 9 shows the histogram for the expenditures on food. The simplifying transformations are equivalent to replacing the x-axis first by the d-axis and then by the t-axis. The line drawn at the mean passes through the balance point of the histogram. You may like to test this, first drawing the histogram on card and cutting it out.

Exercise D

1. Repeat the calculation of Example 1 in Section 4.1 using a different working zero.

2. Find the mean of the amounts spent on food using the table below. Employ a working zero and change of scale.

Amount spent	Frequency
145–175	17
175–205	35
205–235	21
235–265	17
265–295	8
295–325	1
325–355	1

3. The packaging department of a tea company employs an automatic filling and weighing machine. A check was made of the net weights (in grams) of a random sample of 50 packets.

Net weight	98–100	100–102	102–104	104–106	106–108
No. of packets	5	9	16	14	6

(a) Find the mean net weight of the sample.

(b) Would it be sensible to print on the packets 'Net weight 100 grams'?

(c) A new machine gives mean weight 102·3 grams when set so that 10 % of the packets are marginally underweight. How much tea could the company save per box of 200 packets by using this machine?

4. Find the mean of the population of Exercise B, Question 7.

5. A supermarket sells fresh bread at 10p a loaf. On the last 200 weekdays, 500 loaves have been bought each day and sales have followed the pattern given in the table.

No. of loaves sold	321–350	351–380	381–410	411–440	441–470	471–500
No. of days	11	19	40	52	41	37

The loaves cost 5p each. Bread not sold in the shop goes to a pig farm each day and brings in 2p a loaf.

Calculate approximately the average profit per day on bread over this period.

Now suppose only 450 loaves had been bought each day; what effect would this have had on profits? What side-effects might result from a reduction in the amount of bread stocked?

253

6. A newsagent wishes to know how many copies of a particular weekly magazine he should take in order to obtain the greatest profit. As a first order approximation to the real problem, let us assume (a) that the magazines cost him 10p each and that he sells them for 15p each, (b) that if he fails to sell them, he can make no money out of them.

Consider the problem now and decide what extra information you would require and how you would advise him.

Suppose that the record of sales over the last 54 weeks was:

Number sold	7	8	9	10	11	12	13	14
Frequency	6	10	11	9	5	8	4	1

Assuming that future demand follows the pattern of the recent past, estimate his average weekly gain if he took (a) 8, (b) 9, (c) 10, (d) 11 magazines each week. What number would you now advise him to take?

7. If the management of the supermarket of Question 5 decided to switch to wrapped bread (which need not be sold on the day it arrives in the shop), what quantity should be ordered each day?

5. SPREAD

The mean, though important, does not supply all the information required in the situations described in the questions of the earlier exercises. For example, the dentist of Exercise C, Question 3, only has a problem because the times taken up by different patients *vary*. If every patient took exactly the same time, the simplest appointment system would function perfectly and the dentist would know exactly when he would finish work each day.

Exercise E

1. Two types of wheat are tested extensively under identical conditions. Why might one not prefer the type giving the greater mean yield?

2. Look back at Question 3 on page 253. What is the characteristic of a good filling machine? Can you devise a statistic to represent this?

3. For the smooth running of the factory of Question 1 on page 249, there must be a stock of items for which the first process has been completed but the second process not yet begun. Explain why the size of this stock will fluctuate. Why will the management wish to keep this stock as small as possible? What factors affect the best mean stock level?

4. In Questions 5 and 6 on pages 253 and 254, the optimum number of articles to stock is somewhat greater than the mean demand. What factors determine how much greater?

5. Two continental customs posts adopt different approaches when clearing cars through. One officer, Carl, has a standard procedure for all cars. Another, Bertrand, is either very thorough or else very brief. They both take the same mean time, 5 minutes, as is seen from the table below. This shows the proportion of cars taking various inspection times (to the nearest minute).

Time (min)	1	2	3	4	5	6	7	8	9
Proportion (Carl)	0	0	0	0·2	0·6	0·2	0	0	0
(Bertrand)	0·3	0·2	0	0	0	0	0	0·2	0·3

Simulate 2 hours work by Carl, assuming cars arrive regularly at exactly 5 minute intervals. Use a table of random digits, and associate 0, 1 with 4 minutes, 2–7 with 5 minutes and 8, 9 with 6 minutes. Then if 8, 2, 9, 1, 0 were the first five digits they would represent checking times of 6, 5, 6, 4, 4 minutes with the following results.

Car number	Arrival time	Random number	Checking time	From	To	Waiting time
1	0	8	6	0	6	0
2	5	2	5	6	11	1
3	10	9	6	11	17	1
4	15	1	4	17	21	2
5	20	0	4	21	25	1

The sixth car will not be kept waiting at all.

Simulate 2 hours at Bertrand's customs post and comment on the respective merits of the two systems.

6. With the data of Question 2 on page 249, the mean time at the digger is 4·7 minutes. This suggests that $14/4\cdot7 \approx 3$ lorries could be filled during the 14 minute period while a particular lorry was driving to the tip and back. Why should more than 4 lorries be used? Carry out a simulation, assuming that 5 lorries are operating and an 8 hour day is worked. What is the mean waiting time of a lorry? Allocate two digit random numbers in the obvious way and set your work out as follows:

Lorry No.	Random No.	Time at digger	From	To	Time of return
1	31	4	8.30	8.34	8.48
2	19	3	8.34	8.37	8.51
3	84	6	8.37	8.43	8.57

7. To compare two new machines designed to do the same job, 20 operators each had half an hour's practice on each machine, then were timed. The results were:

Average time (in seconds)	120	130	140	150	160	170
Frequency (Machine A)	1	2	6	6	4	3
Frequency (Machine B)	0	0	7	8	5	0

Find the mean job time on each machine. Which machine would you prefer to install, other things being equal?

5.1   Measures of spread. All the examples of Exercise E were concerned with the amount quantities vary. It is clearly desirable to have a single number, a statistic, to describe this feature of a population.

In the O-level course, we found the quartiles (the elements one quarter and three quarters of the way through the population) and the inter-quartile range (the difference between the quartiles). Is this a 'good' measure of spread? What criteria do we adopt in choosing one measure rather than another?

When quoting a measure of central position, we may reckon on many occasions that the mean and median are equally suitable. There are two reasons, though, why the mean is often strongly preferred.

(i) The analytical treatment of the mean in probability models provides powerful ideas for more advanced work.

(ii) The mean takes into account every member of the population, and reflects to some extent the 'shape' of the corresponding histogram.

The first point will only be appreciated as the course develops, but the second should have immediate appeal. Accordingly, we shall now consider deviations from the mean, and devise a statistic to represent in some way the average deviation for the whole population. We could equally well choose to consider deviations from some other central measure of x (the median perhaps), but the choice of the mean in this context has advantages which will soon emerge.

5.2   Standard deviation. For the form of Section 4, the deviations from the mean age of 197 months are:

Deviations from mean d	-5	-4	-3	-2	-1	0	1	2	3
Frequency $\quad\quad\quad f$	1	2	0	5	5	3	6	2	6

What is the total deviation from the mean age? You should find that Σdf comes to zero, and so the average deviation is zero. Will this always be the case?

x	f	d (from 197)	df	d^2f	
192	1	-5	-5	25	
193	2	-4	-8	32	
194	0	-3	0	0	
195	5	-2	-10	20	Average (deviation)$^2 = \dfrac{150}{30} = 5$
196	5	-1	-5	5	
$m = $ 197	3	0	0	0	
198	6	1	6	6	
199	2	2	4	8	
200	6	3	18	54	
	$\overline{30}$		$\overline{0}$	$\overline{150}$	

The average deviation is clearly not a measure of spread. To overcome the difficulty caused by the negative deviations, the square of the deviations is taken:

The two aged 193 months, for example, each have (deviation)^2 of 16, and so contribute 32 to the total square deviation of 150.

The average (deviation)^2, or *variance*, is 5, corresponding to a deviation of $\sqrt{5}$ months per person. This measure of spread, the square root of the variance, is called the *standard deviation* (S.D. for short).

Using the symbols x, f, m and the sigma notation, write down a formula for calculating the standard deviation.

5.3   Working zero. What happens if the deviations are measured from some working zero k instead of from the mean m? Find $\overline{d}$ and the average (deviation)^2 for the fifth form, taking $k = 192$.

We show the calculation for $k = 199$.

x	f	$d = x - k$	df	d^2f	
192	1	-7	-7	49	
193	2	-6	-12	72	
194	0	-5	0	0	$\overline{d} = \dfrac{-60}{30} = -2.$
195	5	-4	-20	80	
196	5	-3	-15	45	
197	3	-2	-6	12	Average (deviation)$^2 = \dfrac{270}{30} = 9.$
198	6	-1	-6	6	
$k = 199$	2	0	0	0	
200	6	1	6	6	
	30		-60	270	

You should now have the information tabulated below:

Working zero k	192	193	194	195	196	197	198	199	200
$\overline{d}$		5	4	3	2	1	0	-1	-2	-3
Average (deviation from k)^2	30						5		9

Complete this table (dividing the work among the class), and look for a pattern in the results.

Notice that when k is 2 away from m, the average (deviation)^2 is 4 more than the variance. When k is 5 away from m, the average (deviation)^2 is 25 more than the variance.

Suggest a formula for calculating the variance (and hence the standard deviation) using a working zero k. This will be proved later.

5.4   Collected formulae for variance and standard deviation. The variance is defined by
$$v = \frac{1}{N}\Sigma(x-m)^2 f.$$

257

With a working zero k, $x = k+d$, $\bar{x} = k+\bar{d}$

and
$$v = \frac{1}{N}\Sigma d^2 f - \bar{d}^2.$$

Notice that the second formula for v reduces to the first when $k = m$, for then $\bar{d} = 0$.

The standard deviation $s = \sqrt{v}$.

A useful special case arises from taking $k = 0$:

$$s = \sqrt{\left[\frac{1}{N}\Sigma x^2 f - \bar{x}^2\right]}.$$

5.5   Areas on a histogram. The following example demonstrates the calculation of the standard deviation from the last formula of Section 5.4.

x	f	xf	$x^2 f$
1	10	10	10
2	10	20	40
3	20	60	180
4	40	160	640
5	50	250	1250
6	20	120	720
	150	620	2840

$$m = \bar{x} = \frac{620}{150} = 4\cdot133;$$

$$s = \sqrt{\left(\frac{2840}{150} - 4\cdot133^2\right)}$$

$$= 1\cdot36.$$

Note that the fourth column in the table is most easily found by multiplying each number in the third column by the corresponding number in the first column.

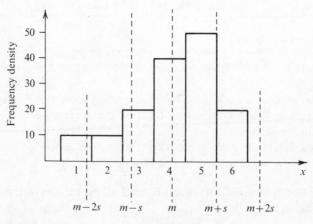

Fig. 10

258

Some idea of the meaning of standard deviation is given by the lines superimposed on the histogram of Figure 10 at $x = m$, $m-s$, $m+s$, $m-2s$, and $m+2s$. Thus the area of the histogram between the lines $x = m-s$ and $x = m+s$ gives an estimate of the number in the population between these values. In this example it is about

$$\tfrac{7}{10} \times 20 + 40 + 50 = 104,$$

or 69 % of the population size. Between $m-2s$ and $m+2s$ the corresponding figure is 141, representing 94 % of the population. These are typical results for fairly symmetrical well-humped histograms.

Exercise F

1. The ages of the children at a Christmas party were 2, 3, 3, 4, 5, 5, 5, 6, 7, 8, 8, 9, 9, 10 years. Find the mean and standard deviation.

2. 15 sacks were taken from a merchant's lorry and their weights checked. These were 49, 52, 47, 53, 55, 48, 50, 50, 54, 52, 51, 52, 49, 50, 53 kg.
Show that the mean weight was 51 kg, and calculate the standard deviation.

3. The numbers 1, 2, 3, 4, 5, 6, 7 occur with the following frequencies in 6 different populations.

x	Frequency					
	(i)	(ii)	(iii)	(iv)	(v)	(vi)
1	1	20	10	50	10	10
2	6	50	20	40	50	10
3	15	40	30	30	20	10
4	20	20	30	10	60	10
5	15	10	40	30	30	10
6	6	10	70	40	20	10
7	1	5	0	50	10	0

Find the mean and standard deviation for each population. Draw the histograms, and mark in the lines $x = m-2s$, $m-s$, m, $m+s$, $m+2s$. Find in each case what percentage of the area lies (a) within one standard deviation of the mean, (b) within two standard deviations of the mean.
Cut out one of the unsymmetrical histograms and show (by driving a compass point or drawing pin through a point on the line $x = m$) that the balance point is at the mean.

4. (a) Construct a frequency function for another population having the same size, mean, and s.d. as the first one in Question 3.
(b) Construct an unsymmetrical frequency function for a population with mean 10 and s.d. 4.

259

5. (*a*) Part of a flow chart for calculating the mean and variance of a population is given. Copy and complete it.

(*b*) Modify your flow chart for a population given in the form of a frequency table.

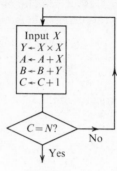

Fig. 11

6. AIDS TO CALCULATION

6.1 'Two-standard-deviation' check. It is clear that if we take intervals

$$m-s < x < m+s, \quad m-2s < x < m+2s,$$

$$m-3s < x < m+3s, \quad \text{and so on,}$$

then an increasing fraction of the total population will be included. Chebyshev (1821–94) showed, in a famous inequality that bears his name, that if we take an interval $m-\lambda s < x < m+\lambda s$, then less than $1/\lambda^2$ of the population can lie outside this interval, however eccentric the frequency function may be.

Very often, however, we shall be dealing with populations whose histograms are humped. If they are not too unsymmetrical, the figures will approximate to those of Normal populations,† which we shall discuss in later chapters. For these it is possible to be more precise about the proportion of the population lying within various intervals. The relevant figures are:

	Normal populations	Chebyshev
Within 1 S.D. either side of the mean	68 % of the population	*Not* none of the population
Within 2 S.D. from the mean	95 %	At least $\frac{3}{4}$
Within 3 S.D. from the mean	Effectively all	At least $\frac{8}{9}$

The population of Section 5·5 gave figures very similar to those for Normal populations, even though its histogram was by no means sym-

† 'Normal' is a technical term here.

metrical, and the examples of Question 3 on page 259 should have done so too with the notable exceptions of the fourth and last populations.

The 'two-standard-deviation' check is a quick way of ensuring that our answer for a standard deviation is reasonable. This involves seeing that about 5% of the population lies outside the interval $m - 2s < x < m + 2s$.

6.2 Working zero and change of scale. We shall now give a complete worked example of the calculation of mean and standard deviation, demonstrating all the techniques of the last few sections.

Example 2

In a certain year percentages obtained in O-level mathematics at one school were distributed as follows:

Marks	10–19	20–29	30–39	40–49	50–59	60–69	70–79	80–89	90–99
No. of pupils	1	4	11	25	41	29	37	14	3

Since the midmarks are 14·5, 24·5 etc., we shall use a working zero to avoid tiresome arithmetic. If we choose 54·5 as working zero, the deviations are -40, -30 etc.; we see that it will be convenient to work in units of 10. The working zero and change of scale are together equivalent to the transformation $t = \frac{1}{10}(x - 54\cdot5)$ applied to all the midmarks. The calculations are then carried out with the population of t's.

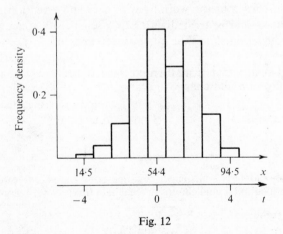

Fig. 12

The histogram in Figure 12 can be regarded as applying to the t-population by replacing the x-axis by the t-axis. It is clear at once from the diagram that $\bar{x} = 54\cdot5 + 10\bar{t}$, and, if s_x and s_t denote the standard deviations, that $s_x = 10s_t$.

261

The full working is now given:

Class interval	x	t	f	tf	t^2f
10–19	14·5	−4	1	−4	16
20–29	24·5	−3	4	−12	36
30–39	34·5	−2	11	−22	44
40–49	44·5	−1	25	−25	25
50–59	54·5	0	41	0	0
60–69	64·5	1	29	29	29
70–79	74·5	2	37	74	148
80–89	84.5	3	14	42	126
90–99	94·5	4	3	12	48
			165	94	472

The mean : $\bar{t} = \dfrac{94}{165} = 0\cdot57$.

The standard deviation: $s_t = \sqrt{\left(\dfrac{472}{165} - (0\cdot57)^2\right)} = 1\cdot59$.

For the original population, the mean and standard deviation are:

$$\bar{x} = 54\cdot5 + 10 \times 0\cdot57 = 60\cdot2,$$

$$s_x = 10s_t = 15\cdot9.$$

Two-standard-deviation check: $\bar{x} - 2s_x = 28\cdot4$, $\bar{x} + 2s_x = 92\cdot0$.

About 7 out of 165, i.e. 4%, of the candidates scored less than 29 or more than 92; the check is therefore satisfied.

It is good to carry out the working with care and attention to detail, but the answers should be treated with strong scepticism. Here, the mean and standard deviation should be quoted as 60 and 16.

6.3 General results for transformed data. With our standard notation for working zero and change of scale,

$$\text{if} \quad x = k + ct, \quad \text{then} \quad \bar{x} = k + c\bar{t} \quad \text{and} \quad s_x = cs_t.$$

Exercise G

This exercise should be supplemented by questions based, for example, on topical data from national publications or local data from school records.

1. Repeat the example of Section 6.2, using a working zero of 64·5.

2. Measurements of the height (in cm) of a species of thistle are as follows:

Height	116–124	124–132	132–140	140–148	148–156	156–164
Frequency	4	18	26	31	15	6

Find the mean and standard deviation, and apply the two-standard-deviation check.

262

3. The number of live births in England and Wales per 1000 women in various age ranges (*a*) in 1961, (*b*) in 1966, were as follows:

Age of mother	15–19	20–24	25–29	30–34	35–39	40–44	45–49
(*a*)	37	172	177	103	48	14	1
(*b*)	48	174	172	96	46	12	1

Thus on average 172 out of every 1000 women over 25 and under 30 in 1966 gave birth that year.

Calculate the mean and standard deviation for each year. Comment on your answers. Would you expect the average age of all mothers giving birth in England and Wales in those years to be greater or less than the means calculated?

4. Two methods of analysing quantitatively the impurity in a certain chemical are being tested. Each was used with 100 samples, and the results (in arbitrary units) were:

Method *A*

Dial reading, x	6–7	7–8	8–9	9–10	10–11	11–12	12–13
Frequency	3	11	23	29	20	10	4

Method *B*

Weight of precipitate, y	2·0–2·2	2·2–2·4	2·4–2·6	2·6–2·8	2·8–3·0	3·0–3·2
Frequency	2	16	28	30	19	5

Calculate the mean and standard deviation for each population. Suggest how the *x* numbers should be transformed for comparison with the *y* numbers.

Devise an alternative (better) way of setting up an experiment to compare the two methods.

5. The weights of packets of raisins filled by a machine have standard deviation 20 grams. The packets are marked 'Net weight 400 grams.' What should be the mean net weight of the packets if the proportion of underweight packets is to be about 1 in 40?

6. Two brands of car batteries have been tested. Brand *A* batteries have a mean life of 29 months and standard deviation 5 months. Brand *B* batteries have a mean life of 27 months and standard deviation 2 months. Which brand would you recommend (*a*) for a private motorist, (*b*) for the owner of a fleet of taxis?

7. Obtain the data from the Annual Abstract of Statistics for the most recent distribution of personal incomes before tax. Draw the histogram and, without detailed calculation, estimate from it the mean and standard deviation. Compare with a previous year, and/or the distribution of incomes after tax.

8. Look up in the Annual Abstract of Statistics the numbers of private households in England and Wales at the last Census occupying dwellings of 1, 2, 3, ... rooms. Round off the figures to the nearest hundred thousand, and calculate the mean and standard deviation. If possible, repeat with the corresponding figures from the previous census.

7. FORMAL NOTATION AND PROOFS

So far we have relied on intuition and experiment to bring out the various alternative formulae for the mean and standard deviation. They can be proved formally by algebra, and that is the purpose of this section.

Example 3

Prove that, with our usual notation,

$$x = k + ct \Rightarrow \bar{x} = k + c\bar{t}.$$

By definition, $\quad \bar{x} = \dfrac{1}{N}\Sigma xf, \quad$ where $\quad N = \Sigma f;$

then $\qquad\qquad \bar{x} = \dfrac{1}{N}\Sigma(k+ct)f$

$$= \dfrac{1}{N}[\Sigma kf + \Sigma ctf].$$

The result of multiplying each frequency by k and then summing is denoted by Σkf. The same number is obtained by adding up the frequencies and multiplying by k afterwards. We proceed:

$$\bar{x} = \dfrac{1}{N}[k\Sigma f + c\Sigma tf]$$

$$= \dfrac{1}{N}(kN) + c\dfrac{1}{N}\Sigma tf$$

$$= k + c\bar{t}.$$

This is reminiscent of the work carried out in Chapter 9, but the notation is not ideal since it is not easy to distinguish constants from variables.

7.1 Notation. When data have been arranged into a frequency table, a *frequency function* is defined. In the example of Section 2, we had:

Amount spent	140	160	180	200	220	240	260	280	300	320
Frequency	1	12	25	18	14	14	7	6	2	1

The domain of the function is the set of different amounts spent listed in the table. If x denotes an element from this set, $f(x)$ denotes its frequency and f is now the frequency function. Thus $f(260) = 7$.

We write n for the number of different values of x that occur in the domain, and represent the size of the population by N, as before. Then

$$N = f(x_1) + f(x_2) + \dots + f(x_n) = \sum_{i=1}^{n} f(x_i),$$

where $x_1, x_2, \dots, x_n$ are the particular elements of the domain.

264

The mean. Since x_i either occurs (or is representative of a class of elements which occurs) $f(x_i)$ times in the population, it contributes $x_i f(x_i)$ to the total. This total is then

$$\sum_{i=1}^{n} x_i f(x_i).$$

So the mean is

$$m = \frac{1}{N} \sum_{1}^{n} x_i f(x_i).$$

Now that suffix notation is being employed, the Σ-notation is used in exactly the same way as in Chapter 9, i taking consecutive integral values between the specified limits.

The proof of the result of Example 3 now starts

$$\bar{x} = \frac{1}{N} \sum_{1}^{n} x_i f(x_i)$$

$$= \frac{1}{N} \sum_{1}^{n} (k + ct_i) f(x_i)$$

and follows exactly the same lines as before. Write it out in full. It is now clear which factors are dependent upon i and which are not.

7.2   Standard deviation formulae.

The definition of standard deviation is

$$s = \sqrt{\left[\frac{1}{N} \sum_{1}^{n} (x_i - m)^2 f(x_i) \right]},$$

and the main alternative version of the formula is

$$s = \sqrt{\left[\frac{1}{N} \sum_{1}^{n} x_i^2 f(x_i) - m^2 \right]}.$$

The derivation of this second form is typical of algebraic proofs which occur elsewhere in the study of Statistics.

$$s = \sqrt{\left[\frac{1}{N} \Sigma (x_i - m)^2 f(x_i) \right]}$$

$$\Leftrightarrow s^2 = \frac{1}{N} \Sigma (x_i^2 - 2mx_i + m^2) f(x_i)$$

$$= \frac{1}{N} [\Sigma x_i^2 f(x_i) - 2m\Sigma x_i f(x_i) + m^2 \Sigma f(x_i)]$$

$$= \frac{1}{N} [\Sigma x_i^2 f(x_i) - 2m \times mN + m^2 N] \quad \text{since } m = \frac{1}{N} \Sigma x_i f(x_i)$$

$$= \frac{1}{N} [\Sigma x_i^2 f(x_i) - m^2 N].$$

So

$$s = \sqrt{\left[\frac{1}{N} \Sigma x_i^2 f(x_i) - m^2 \right]}.$$

Exercise H

1. If
$$N = \Sigma f(x_i) \quad \text{and} \quad m = \frac{1}{N}\Sigma x_i f(x_i),$$
show that

(a) $\dfrac{1}{N}\Sigma(x_i - m) f(x_i) = 0$;

(b) $\dfrac{1}{N}\Sigma(x_i - k) f(x_i) + k = m$, where k is any constant;

(c) $\dfrac{1}{N}\Sigma(x_i - k)^2 f(x_i) - (m - k)^2 = \dfrac{1}{N}\Sigma x_i^2 f(x_i) - m^2$.

Interpret these results in terms of a population, frequency function f, and working zero k.

2. Given that
$$x_i = k + ct_i, \quad \bar{x} = \frac{1}{N}\sum_1^n x_i f(x_i) \quad \text{and} \quad \bar{t} = \frac{1}{N}\sum_1^n t_i f(x_i),$$
show that
$$\sqrt{\left[\frac{1}{N}\sum_1^n (x_i - \bar{x})^2 f(x_i)\right]} = c\sqrt{\left[\frac{1}{N}\sum_1^n (t_i - \bar{t})^2 f(x_i)\right]}.$$

8. RELATIVE FREQUENCY AND PROBABILITY

Suppose a single die is thrown 600 times, with the following results:

Score	1	2	3	4	5	6
Frequency	95	112	103	106	94	90

What answer would you give to the question 'What is the probability that the next two throws will both be sixes?'? You might argue 'Before the experiment I would have said $\frac{1}{6} \times \frac{1}{6}$, basing my answer on the apparent symmetry of the die, and the experiment has not shaken by confidence in this symmetry.' An alternative approach might be 'The observed relative frequency is $\frac{90}{600} = \frac{3}{20}$, suggesting a small amount of bias. Taking this as the probability that any subsequent throw is a six gives an answer of $\frac{3}{20} \times \frac{3}{20}$ for the original question.' These are both respectable arguments, and could form a basis for action (betting, perhaps). Either attitude might require revision if more evidence were accumulated.

Now consider the newsagent of Exercise D, Question 6. The demand for the magazine under discussion was 12 or more in 13 weeks out of the 54 in the sample, giving a relative frequency of $\frac{13}{54}$. He might be inclined to take this figure as the probability of such a demand in any one future week, and certainly he has no other obvious guide.

To sum up:

(i) the relative frequency (called experimental probability in the O-level course) of an event is the proportion of occasions on which this event has been observed in the past;

266

(ii) the relative frequency is useful in setting up a probability model as a guide to the future.

These ideas have been implicit in much of the previous work in this chapter.

8.1   Algebraic models. Looking at the histogram (Figure 13) for the newsagent's data, one might be struck by the frequencies for $x = 11, 12$. The histogram would have had a more regular pattern if these frequencies had been interchanged. Perhaps this new pattern would provide a better model for the future.

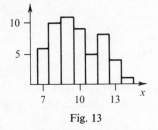

Fig. 13

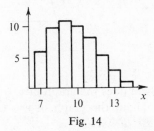

Fig. 14

Figure 14 shows the histogram for the frequency density function $g(x) = \frac{1}{10}(x-6)(x-15)^2$ with the same domain. This gives very much the same impression as Figure 13, and we shall find that a simple algebraic description is a great advantage in a probability model.

Strictly g could not be a frequency density function as $g(8) = 9.8$, for example, suggesting a frequency of 9.8. But frequencies must be integers. However, one could envisage a frequency of 98 in a population ten times the size of the original one.

With the original data, it was easy in Exercise D to find the number of magazines to stock in order to maximize profits; trial and error was the only method available, though. With more complicated problems, an algebraic method will be preferable.

8.2   Constructing algebraic models. The model of the last section was produced like a rabbit out of a hat. How do we set about constructing such models? The first stage is to draw a continuous curve (see Figure 15) whose outline more or less follows that of the histogram.

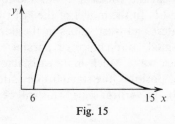

Fig. 15

Then we select from our armoury of simple functions one with a graph
of the right basic shape. On this occasion, we need look no further than a
simple polynomial. Figure 16 shows a typical cubic polynomial graph;
we take the arc ABC, and stretch and translate as required.

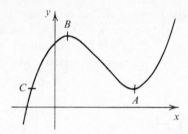

Fig. 16

Where does the graph of $y = (x-a)(x-b)(x-c)$ intersect the x-axis?
How about the graph of $y = (x-a)(x-b)^2$? Sketch these graphs, with
$0 < a < b < c$.

Show that $(-\frac{2}{3}a, \frac{4}{27}a^3)$ is a maximum point on the graph of $y = x^2(x+a)$.

Take $a = 9$ and apply the translation $\begin{pmatrix} 15 \\ 0 \end{pmatrix}$ to the graph. Is the equation of

the image curve $y = (x-6)(x-15)^2$? What are the coordinates of its
maximum point? What are the coordinates of the maximum point on the
graph of $y = \frac{1}{10}(x-6)(x-15)^2$?

8.3   Parameters. One of the central tasks of mathematical statisticians
over the last 250 years has been the development of theoretical functions
which in some ways mirror real situations. We see that there are two stages
on any particular occasion:

(i) selecting a family of functions with the right characteristics,

(ii) choosing the appropriate member of the family.

The members of a family of functions are distinguished by having different
values for various constants, which we call *parameters*.

The equation $y = k(x-a)(x-b)^2$ represents a family of cubic polynomials whose graphs cut the x-axis at $x = a$ and touch it at $x = b$; the
parameters are k, a and b. In the model of the last two sections, we have
in effect used the greatest and least values in the domain and the modal
frequency density to guide our choice of parameters. These are often
unreliable. Can you see why? Much more satisfactory is to employ the
mean to fix the central position, the standard deviation to fix the spread,
and the total area to fix the vertical scale. This will be developed in a later
chapter.

Exercise I

1. A graph (Figure 17) passes through $(2, 0)$ and $(5, 0)$ and bounds with the x-axis a region of area 10. Find k, a, b if its equation is $y = k(x-a)(x-b)$.

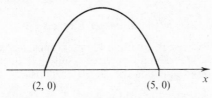

$(2, 0)$ $(5, 0)$ x

Fig. 17

2. Practical measurements (in degrees) of a certain terrestrial angle were taken and it was found that $g(\theta) = -100(15 - 8\theta + \theta^2)$ gave a good approximation to the frequency densities.

(*a*) Taking the discrete domain 3·1, 3·3, 3·5, ..., 4·9, work out the approximate number of measurements which were between $4°$ and $4\cdot4°$.

(*b*) Compare your answer to (*a*) with $\displaystyle\int_4^{4\cdot4} g(\theta)\, d\theta$.

(*c*) Approximately how many measurements were made altogether?

3. It is apparently true that customers in supermarkets are affected by the height of the shelves on which goods are displayed, buying more of the conveniently placed goods, that is those which are just a few centimetres above or below their eye-height. A supermarket manager has to decide upon the best height to fix his main display shelf.

The first task is obviously to find the distribution of eye heights of customers. Suppose the frequency densities calculated from observations made (in cm) conformed roughly to the function $g(x) = \frac{1}{100}(x-140)(200-x)^2$, with domain $\{x: 140 \leqslant x \leqslant 200\}$. With the transformation $x = 200 - t$, this is equivalent to the model $h(t) = \frac{1}{100} t^2(60-t)$ with domain $\{t: 0 \leqslant t \leqslant 60\}$.

(*a*) Sketch the graphs of the functions g and h, with the given domains.

(*b*) To what eye heights do the values $t = 10$, 20 correspond?

(*c*) Evaluate $\displaystyle\int_{10}^{20} h(t)\, dt$ and interpret your answer.

(*d*) Assuming that displays are noticed by customers if they are within 10 cm above or below eye level, show that the manager's problem is equivalent to finding the value of a for which $\displaystyle\int_{a-10}^{a+10} h(t)\, dt$ is a maximum. Solve the problem.

4. (i) Sketch the graphs of $g(x) = k(a^2 - x^2)^2$ and $h(x) = k'(1 + \cos(\pi x/a))$ for $-a \leqslant x \leqslant a$. Find in terms of a the values of k, k' which make the total areas under each graph equal to 100. Show that for each, the area under the graph from $x = -2b$ to $x = 2b$ is approximately 95 % of the total area under the graph when $b = 0\cdot35a$. (Slide-rule accuracy is sufficient.)

(ii) Find the mean (m) and standard deviation (s) for the sample given by the following frequency table:

x_i	1·7	2·0	2·3	2·6	2·9	3·2	3·5	3·8
$f(x_i)$	2	9	19	27	24	13	5	1

269

(iii) Set b equal to s and plot the graph of g translated so that $x = m$ is its axis of symmetry. Draw the histogram for the sample with the same axes.

(iv) Repeat (iii) for the function h.

(v) Which of the functions g and h would form the better basis for a probability model in this instance?

Miscellaneous Exercise

1. Sort the data of Exercise B, Question 10 into groups in a variety of ways. Find the mean and standard deviation from each resulting frequency table, and comment on the effect of grouping on the calculated statistics.

2. Carry out a simulation, equivalent to a period of several weeks, for the problem of the dentist, of Exercise C, Question 3, if he makes appointments for 9.00, 9.30, 10.00, ..., 12.30 and 2.30, 3.00, ... 5.00. Assume that his patients are booked in randomly and independently. Is this realistic? Use a table of random numbers and associate 0, 1 with children, 2–6 with adults, 7–9 with elderly people. Then if 0, 2, 7, 5 were the first 4 digits, they would represent patients being attended for 30, 20, 45, 20 minutes, i.e. from 9.00 to 9.30, 9.30 to 9.50, 10.00 to 10.45 and 10.45 to 11.05, assuming every patient arrives exactly at his appointment time. The dentist has been kept waiting from 9.50 to 10.00.

Find at what time, on average, he finishes his morning sessions. Is he often kept waiting when there are no patients to see? State the assumptions you make, and suggest ways in which the mathematical model could be improved.

3. A greengrocer mixes a batch of 100 apples of mean weight 150 g and standard deviation 30 g with another batch of 400 apples of mean weight 150 g and standard deviation 20 g. What is the standard deviation for the combined batch of 500 apples?

4. Two populations are to be combined to give a single larger population. If the sizes, means and S.D.s of the two separate populations are as given below, find in each case the mean and S.D. of the combined population.

	First population			Second population		
	N	m	s	N	m	s
(a)	10	15	4	10	15	6
(b)	10	12	4	10	16	4
(c)	10	12	4	30	16	6

5. A measure of spread which may be used instead of the standard deviation is the *mean absolute deviation*. This is the average of the moduli of the deviations from the mean,

i.e.
$$\frac{1}{N}\Sigma|x_i - m|f(x_i).$$

Take any simple population (like those in Exercise F, Question 3) and calculate the mean and mean absolute deviation. Investigate with this population the result of averaging the absolute deviations from some number other than the mean. Can a working zero be used conveniently when calculating the mean absolute deviation?

270

SUMMARY

For a population in which $x_1, x_2, ..., x_n$ occur with frequency $f(x_1)$, $f(x_2), ..., f(x_n)$,

the population size is
$$N = \sum_{i=1}^{n} f(x_i),$$

the mean is
$$m = \bar{x} = \frac{1}{N} \sum_{i=1}^{n} x_i f(x_i),$$

the standard deviation is
$$s = \sqrt{\left[\frac{1}{N} \sum_{i=1}^{n} (x_i - m)^2 f(x_i) \right]}$$
$$= \sqrt{\left[\frac{1}{N} \sum_{i=1}^{n} x_i^2 f(x_i) - m^2 \right]}.$$

Working zero and change of scale

If
$$x_i = k + ct_i, \quad \text{then} \quad \bar{x} = k + c\bar{t} \quad \text{and} \quad s_x = cs_t.$$

Simplified notation

$$N = \Sigma f, \quad m = \frac{1}{N} \Sigma xf, \quad s = \sqrt{\left[\frac{1}{N} \Sigma (x - m)^2 f \right]} = \sqrt{\left[\frac{1}{N} \Sigma x^2 f - m^2 \right]}.$$

Histograms

A histogram is a frequency density diagram; frequencies are represented by areas. For fairly symmetrical humped histograms, about two thirds of the area lies within 1 standard deviation from the mean, and about 95 % within 2 standard deviations from the mean.

Probability models

In a sample, the relative frequency of an event is

$$\frac{\text{frequency of that event}}{\text{total of all the frequencies}}.$$

In subsequent calculations, the relative frequency is often taken as the probability of this event.

With 'continuous' models, areas and hence probabilities are found by integration.

The mean and standard deviation are the most usual parameters used when fitting a model.

12

MECHANICS OF A PARTICLE

1. FORCE

1.1   Motion. In Chapter 7 (Kinematics) we investigated the behaviour of particles and looked at ways of describing their motion. No attempt was made to say what *caused* the motion and it is this problem that we take up in this chapter.

In the early days of science it was natural for people to make the 'obvious' assumptions when describing the world about them—the sun moves round a stationary earth, heat flows like a liquid from one body to another, and the normal behaviour of objects is for them to come to rest. It is easier for us today to appreciate a more sophisticated set of postulates. We have all seen films of spacemen tumbling about inside their space capsules and objects, barely touched, are seen to move readily from rest across the spacecraft until they bang against the side of the capsule. On the other hand, if the space engineer releases his spanner it stays where he leaves it, and, if his assistant wants to borrow it, the engineer simply pushes it in his direction and it will float across until caught. However, if a girder has to be manoeuvred into position on a space platform, it requires more than just a little push to get it moving quickly.

The following exercise provides an opportunity for you to think about motion and its causes.

Exercise A

1. Describe what is likely to happen to a passenger on the left hand side of the back seat of a car in each of the following situations:

(*a*) the car swerves violently round a left hand bend;

(*b*) the car is moving steadily along when suddenly the road drops away sharply downhill;

(*c*) the driver suddenly jams on the brakes;

(*d*) the car is accelerated suddenly from rest.

2. A boy whirls a conker on a string around his head. The conker moves at a constant speed.

(*a*) What is the direction of the acceleration?

(*b*) What happens to the conker if the string breaks?

(*c*) What do you think causes the acceleration in (*a*)?

(*d*) Would the string be more likely to break if a heavier conker were whirled at the same speed?

272

3. (*a*) Two tugs are pulling a liner steadily into port. The tow ropes are equally inclined either side of the direction of motion of the liner when one of the ropes breaks. Describe what happens if the skipper of the remaining tug is unaware of the accident.

(*b*) Two huskies of unequal strength are pulling a sled and both are working as hard as they can. Is the angle made by the connecting harness of the more power-ful husky with the direction of the sled smaller or greater than the angle made by the other harness? (Assume that the huskies are abreast of one another and are connected to the sled by separate harnesses.)

4. A spaceman A pushes a steel girder and discovers that it accelerates at $\frac{1}{2}$ m/s^2. What do you think would be the acceleration in the following cases:

(*a*) two men, both pushing as hard as A, try to move a similar girder;

(*b*) three men, all pushing as hard as A in the same direction try to move a steel girder having twice the volume of the original.

5. A stone is sliding across a frozen pond and its position at time t is given by

$$\mathbf{r} = (8t - t^2)(\mathbf{i} + \mathbf{j}) \quad \text{for} \quad 0 \leqslant t \leqslant 4$$

(*t* in seconds, distances in metres).

What are its velocity and position when $t = 2$?

What is its acceleration at time t?

Describe the motion of the stone as t increases from zero.

What do you think is causing the stone to act in this way?

6. You are holding a parcel on your lap in the car of Question 1. Describe the forces you must exert on the parcel in each of the circumstances of that question.

1.2   Newton's laws. The results of Section 1.1 and Exercise A can be summarized as follows:

(i) It is change of motion (and not motion itself) which requires a cause. Newton† named such causes *forces* and propounded as his First Law:

> Every body remains stationary or in uniform motion in a straight line unless it is made to change that state by external forces.

(ii) Associated with each body there is a constant which will be called its *mass*. Whatever the position or time, the same mass will be associated with a given body. We think of mass as representing in some way the quantity of matter belonging to the body. It can be thought of also as a measure of a body's 'resistance to acceleration'.

(iii) The acceleration caused by a force is in the same direction as the force. Furthermore, the more massive a body the greater the force needed

---

† Sir Isaac Newton (1642–1727) was one of the greatest ever mathematicians. His major contributions to mathematics were in the realms of dynamics and cal-culus but his interests ranged from alchemy to medicine and also to money—he was made Master of the Mint in 1696.

to impart the same acceleration. These ideas are contained in the vector statement of Newton's Second Law:

The force acting on a body is proportional to its mass and to its acceleration and has the direction of the acceleration.

Thus, if the force acting on a body is represented by a vector **F** and it gives rise to an acceleration **a** we have

$$\mathbf{F} \propto m\mathbf{a} \quad (m \text{ being the mass of the body}).$$

1.3 Units. It is usual to define units of force in terms of the standard units of mass and acceleration. We adhere exclusively to the internationally agreed S.I. units in which the unit of force is the *newton* and is defined to be that force which will impart an acceleration of 1 m/s² when acting on a mass of 1 kg.

Using these units, the vector form of Newton's Second Law becomes:

$\mathbf{F} = m\mathbf{a}$, where **F** is measured in newtons (N),

m is measured in kilograms,

a is measured in metres per second per second.

Example 1

A force is causing a 2 kg mass to move in a circle of radius 0·2 m with an angular velocity of 3 rev/s. What is the magnitude of the force?

In Chapter 7 we showed that the acceleration required to maintain circular motion with an angular velocity ω was $r\omega^2$ towards the centre. Here $r = 0·2$ m and $\omega = 6\pi$ rad/s.

Hence
$$\text{force towards centre} = 2 \times 0·2 \times (6\pi)^2 \text{ N}$$

$$\approx 142 \text{ N}.$$

Exercise B

Unless otherwise stated the action takes place in space away from any gravitational field.

1. What is the acceleration of a particle of mass 100 kg when pushed with a force (*a*) of 10 N, (*b*) of 100 N?

2. What force must be exerted on a particle of mass 2000 kg in order to give it an acceleration of (*a*) 1 m/s², (*b*) 10 m/s², (*c*) $\frac{1}{2000}$ m/s²?

3. Figure 1 is a graph of the velocity of a particle of mass 200 kg moving in a straight line over a period of 20 seconds. From the sketch, estimate the force that is being exerted upon the particle when (*a*) $t = 1$, (*b*) $t = 10$, (*c*) $t = 18$.

274

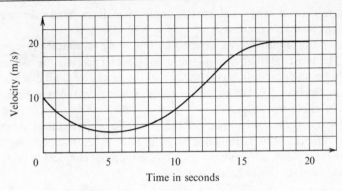

Fig. 1

4. A particle of mass 25 kg is moving with a constant velocity of magnitude 10000 m/s and is then pushed with a force of 100 N.

   (*a*) Does the initial velocity make any difference to the change of velocity?

   (*b*) Can any information about the change of velocity be deduced if the initial velocity is not given?

   (*c*) What is the magnitude of the change in velocity, if the force is exerted for 1 s? What can be stated about its direction?

5. The position vector of a particle of mass 5 kg at time *t* is given by

   (*a*) $\mathbf{r} = t(\mathbf{i}+\mathbf{j})$;   (*b*) $\mathbf{r} = t\mathbf{i}+t^2\mathbf{j}$;

   (*c*) $\mathbf{r} = \mathbf{i}+t^3(\mathbf{i}+\mathbf{j})$;   (*d*) $\mathbf{r} = t\mathbf{i}+(\sin t)\,\mathbf{j}$.

What forces must be acting on the particle in each case at the moments when $t = 0, 1, \frac{1}{2}$?

6. A particle of mass 1 kg is moving with constant velocity of 5 m/s when it is pulled by a constant force.

   (*a*) If the force is of magnitude 1 N making an angle of 45° with the original path, what will the new velocity be after (i) 1 s, (ii) 3 s?

   (*b*) If the final velocity after 1 s is 5 m/s at right angles to the original path, what was the magnitude and direction of the force exerted?

7. What force must be exerted on a particle of mass 5 kg to cause it to move in a circle of radius 12 m at a speed of 5 m/s?

2. TYPES OF FORCE

2.1   Contact and non-contact forces. Forces give rise to accelerations and it is common experience that accelerations are achieved in a variety of ways: a car engine provides the thrust needed to accelerate from 0 to 100 km/h in 10 s, a wall provides the force necessary to bring the car to rest in 1s; a cricket ball hit along the ground towards the boundary is decelerated by long grass or a fielder's foot. Even when no motion is occurring we experience forces; push against the desk with your hand and the desk seems to push back; somebody pulls your chair from under you

275

and you fall downwards and so the chair must have been exerting an upward force on you previously.

All these are *contact forces*, applied by one body to another in contact with it. The most familiar example of a *non-contact force* is the weight of an object, i.e. the gravitational attraction of the earth (we shall discuss this further in Section 3). Other non-contact forces are those exerted by magnetic and electric fields.

Apart from these exceptions, all the forces in a mechanical problem are contact forces. When drawing a diagram to show the forces acting on a body one must insert a force from each of the material contacts in addition to the non-contact forces (usually gravity).

Example 2

An aircraft is diving at an angle of 30° to the horizontal. Show the forces acting on it.

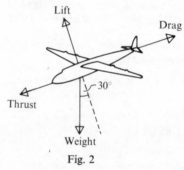

Fig. 2

There are different forces acting on each part of the aircraft. A simple and useful model is given by combining these into four main forces, the weight, the forward thrust of the engines, the lift force provided by the wings and the drag force due to air resistance. These are shown in Figure 2; note the type of arrow we adopt for forces.

2.2 Resultant forces. Experiment shows that two forces acting on a single particle cause an acceleration in the direction of the vector sum of vectors representing the forces. Force is thus a *vector quantity* and we assume that two forces represented by F_1, F_2 may be replaced by a single force, called the *resultant*, without altering the effect on the particle. The resultant is represented by a vector R where $R = F_1 + F_2$, the vector sum of the vectors representing the original forces.

(We have been careful here to distinguish between forces and the vectors which represent them. In what follows we shall not maintain the distinction and will simply say 'the force F', etc.)

Example 3

If a mass of 4 kg is acted on by forces of 5, 10 and 8 newtons in directions north, east and S 60° W, find the resultant force.

The simplest way to find the vector sum is by drawing, as shown in Figure 3. The resultant force, represented by **AD**, is found by measurement to be 3·2 units in a direction N 72° E.

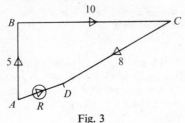

Fig. 3

Note. In this example we have extended the result to three forces. We may argue simply:

$$(AB+BC)+CD = AC+CD,$$

$$= AD.$$

The argument can clearly be extended to any number of forces acting on a particle.

If the resultant force has magnitude 3·2 newtons, the acceleration has magnitude $3·2 \div 4$ m/s². So the acceleration is approximately 0·8 m/s² in a direction N 72° E.

Exercise C

1. Two children are pushing a stubborn donkey with horizontal forces of 60 N and 80 N. If the directions of the forces are perpendicular and if their resultant is due north find (i) the resultant and (ii) the directions of the forces.

2. Two more children come along to help with the donkey in Question 1. If one of them pushes N.E. with a force of 50 N with what force must the other push in order to give a resultant for the two of 100 N in a northerly direction?

3. Three coplanar forces act on a particle. They are inclined at 120° to each other and have magnitudes 2, 2 and 3 newtons. If the magnitude of the resultant acceleration is ½ m/s², what is the mass of the particle?

4. A particle of mass 10 kg, in position *A*, is acted on by forces of 6, 6, 1 N in directions which make angles of 0°, 120°, 210° with a fixed direction **AB**. What is its acceleration?

5. A moving particle of mass 6 kg is acted on by a force of 5 newtons in a direction of 40° from the direction of its velocity.

(*a*) What additional force at 90° to its velocity will keep the particle moving in a straight line?

(*b*) In what direction should an additional force of 4 N be applied to keep the particle moving in a straight line?

(*c*) What additional force will give the particle an instantaneous acceleration of 2 m/s² in a direction of 70° from the direction of its velocity?

6. Three forces acting on a body of mass 12 kg are represented by the vectors $5\mathbf{i}+\mathbf{j}$, $2\mathbf{i}-8\mathbf{j}$, $\mathbf{i}+4\mathbf{j}$. Show these and their resultant on a diagram and state the acceleration of the body.

7. Express each of the forces in Question 4 in terms of its components parallel and perpendicular to **AB**. Give the resultant force and the acceleration in the same form.

8. A satellite of mass 500 kg moves in a circular orbit around the earth's centre. It is at a height of 250 km and takes 90 minutes to complete one circuit. Find the force necessary to cause this motion. (Take the radius of the earth to be 6400 km and ignore the effects of air resistance.)

9. A spacecraft is returning to earth and during re-entry into the earth's atmosphere, when its speed is v, it experiences a downward force of 1000 N, a lift force perpendicular to its path and a drag force of magnitude $\frac{1}{2}v^2$ N. Find, in terms of v, the resultant *retarding* force along the path when the spacecraft is moving at 80° to the downward vertical. If the acceleration of the craft is instantaneously zero when the path makes an angle of 60° with the downward vertical, find its speed and the lift force at this instant.

10. An electron, charge e, is moving between two parallel plates which are charged, the top one positively and the bottom one negatively. It can be shown that the field strength E is a constant everywhere between the plates and that the electron experiences a force $Ee\hat{\mathbf{n}}$ towards the upper plate, where $\hat{\mathbf{n}}$ is a unit vector perpendicular to the plates. When $t = 0$ the electron is halfway between the plates and moving parallel to them with speed u. Sketch the path of the electron until the instant that it arrives at the top plate.

3. GRAVITY

3.1 Newton's universal law of gravitation. Galileo's name is associated with the discovery (in 1589) that, when a body falls vertically near the earth's surface (air resistance being ignored), it falls with a constant acceleration. In some famous experiments conducted whilst he was at Pisa he showed that bodies near the earth's surface fall with the same acceleration whatever their mass. Newton's First Law tells us that we cannot have acceleration in the absence of force and we must therefore postulate the existence of a *force of gravity*.

' One of the most beautiful laws of Newton's model takes this concept of terrestrial gravity and incorporates it into the *universal* law of gravitation. In fact it was from astronomic data that Newton was able to postulate the laws of his model and the main confirming tests of his hypotheses were to be found in observations of the moon and planets.

278

In the early part of the seventeenth century, Kepler (1571–1630) announced three kinematical laws of planetary motion which he unfolded after many years of arduous calculation based on the observational data provided by the astronomer Tycho Brahe.

From his laws of motion Newton showed that Kepler's empirical laws required that the sun should exert an attractive force on the planets which varied as their mass and inversely as the square of their distance from the sun at any point in their orbit. Furthermore, he showed that the acceleration of the moon towards the earth as she pursues her almost circular orbit, compared with the acceleration of a body falling freely near the earth's surface, was in the inverse ratio of the square of the distance of the moon and the terrestrial body from the earth's centre. So the law of attraction which accounted for the motion of the planets around the sun could also be applied to the gravitational force which the earth exerts on any object at its surface and on the moon.

It appeared to be a law of nature that an attracting body exerts a force of km/d^2, where m is the mass of the attracted body and d its distance away, while k is a constant depending on the attracting body.

On the assumption that the gravitational attraction between two bodies is a mutual force, the role of attracting and attracted bodies are interchangeable. So Newton was led to propound his universal law of gravitation. Effectively this states that *between any two particles of masses m and m', at a distance d apart, there is a mutual attractive force of Gmm'/d²*, where G is a universal constant depending only on the system of units employed. It can be deduced from this law, as Newton showed, that the gravitational force between spherical bodies of masses m and m' (of any radius) is given by the same formula where d is the distance between their centres.

It is a remarkable fact that similar inverse square laws occur in models used in electrostatics, magnetism and photometry. Einstein said that 'our actual experience confirms belief in the mathematical simplicity of nature' and Newton that 'nature is pleased with simplicity, and affects not the pomp of superfluous causes'. It is certainly true that Newton's laws of motion, together with his law of gravitation, form a firm foundation for a vast branch of mathematics that has come to be known as classical mechanics; the ramifications of this subject are far removed from the simplicity of these original laws!

3.2   Weight. Near the earth's surface, the gravitational force on a body of mass m is $m\left(\dfrac{GM}{R^2}\right)$, where M is the mass of the earth and R is the radius of the earth. This, the weight of the body, is approximately $9{\cdot}8m$ newtons if the mass is measured in kilograms. If allowed to fall freely, the body will have acceleration GM/R^2, which is independent of the mass.

Since the earth is not an exact sphere, the magnitude of this acceleration (usually denoted by the letter g) varies slightly over the earth's surface, from 9·83 m/s² at the North pole to 9·78 m/s² at the equator. Unless otherwise stated we will take the value of g to be constant at 9·8 m/s². (The magnitude also varies with height, but in most of our examples this will be negligible.) The direction of this acceleration is towards the centre of the earth and usually defines what we mean by 'vertically downwards'. This is not strictly accurate because of some small effects due to the rotation of the earth.

We have seen that the weight of a body is not an absolute property of the body (as is the mass) since it lessens as the body moves further from the earth's centre. The term 'weight' is sometimes used in relation to other heavenly bodies; in fact it may prove useful anywhere that a constant gravitational attraction is experienced. On the moon, for example, a man has a 'weight' that is about one sixth of his earth weight.

If the mass of a body is m kg, its weight (on earth) has magnitude mg newtons. This force acts whether or not the body is free to fall.

Example 4

A large crate of mass 1 tonne (1000 kg) is suspended from the cable of a crane. Find the tension in the cable if the crate is

    (*a*) in equilibrium;

    (*b*) being accelerated upwards at 2 m/s²;

    (*c*) being accelerated downwards at 3 m/s².

Figure 4 shows the forces on the crate, namely the tension in the cable and the weight.

Let $\mathbf{j}$ be a unit vector in the downward vertical direction.

Newton's second law gives:

$$\mathbf{T}+\mathbf{W} = 1000\mathbf{a},$$

where $\mathbf{a}$ is the acceleration of the crate.

In the three different cases we have:

    (*a*) in equilibrium $\mathbf{a} = \mathbf{0}$ and so $\mathbf{T} = -\mathbf{W} = -1000g\mathbf{j}$; i.e. the tension is 9800 N upwards.

    (*b*) Here $\mathbf{a} = -2\mathbf{j}$ and we have $\mathbf{T} = -1000g\mathbf{j}-1000\times 2\mathbf{j}$, giving an upward tension of 11 800 N.

    (*c*) $\mathbf{a} = 3\mathbf{j}$, leading to an upward tension of 6800 N.

3.3 Measurement of mass. We have a simple, practical way of measuring mass. For two bodies in the same locality, their weights will be proportional to their masses; so that, for instance, if one has three times the weight of the other, it will have three times the mass. Hence we can determine the mass of any other body by comparing its weight (as shown on a weighing machine) with the weight of the unit mass.

The kilogram is defined as the mass of a platinum–iridium standard, a solid cylinder of height equal to its diameter, which is preserved at the International Bureau of Weights and Measures at Paris.

3.4   Units and dimensions. Throughout Chapter 7, we used the metre as the standard unit of length and the second as a unit of time. The units of area, volume, rate of change of volume, speed, acceleration are all derived from our basic units of length and time.

The idea of a length multiplied by a length giving an area is formalized as $L \times L = L^2$, where the symbol L denotes the *dimension* of length and the notation follows convention. Extensions are immediately suggested. For example $L \div T = LT^{-1}$ can be interpreted as length $\div$ time $=$ speed, the dimension of speed being LT^{-1}. Similarly, we say that the dimension of volume is L^3 and that of acceleration LT^{-2}.

Now the units of mass and force clearly cannot be expressed in terms of our basic units of length and time, so we will need to take another basic dimension. Because of the constant nature of the mass of a body, we take mass itself as the third basic dimension and assign the letter M to denote it.

We shall denote the dimension of a quantity by enclosing it in square brackets; e.g. $[\text{acceleration}] = LT^{-2}$.

From Newton's second law, we immediately obtain the dimensions of force:

$$[\text{Force}] = [\text{mass} \times \text{acceleration}]$$

$$= [\text{mass}] \times [\text{acceleration}]$$

$$= MLT^{-2}.$$

The dimensions of all other quantities used in mechanics can be expressed in terms of these three basic dimensions. Formulae can then be checked by considering the dimensions.

Exercise D

In Questions 1–3, take the radius of the earth as 6400 km.

1. What is the weight at the earth's surface of a body of mass 10 kg? With what acceleration would it move in free fall when its height above the surface of the earth is

(a) 320 km;   (b) 3200 km;   (c) 6400 km?

2. If a man moves from sea level to the top of a mountain 5 km high, by approximately what ratio has his weight decreased?

3. The height of a body is 1200 km above the surface of the earth. If its mass is 2000 kg, what is its weight? What is the mass of another body that has this weight when at the surface of the earth?

4. In an experiment similar to the original one by Cavendish in 1798, two spheres of mass 1 g placed with their centres at a distance 1 cm apart were found to attract each other with a force of 6.66×10^{-8} dynes. (A dyne is the unit of force used when the units of mass and length are gram and centimetre, respectively.)

Find the value of G in metre-kilogram-second units.

If R is the radius of the earth and M is its mass, show by considering the weight of a particle of mass m near the earth's surface that $g = GMR^{-2}$. Hence, taking $g = 9.81$ m/s² and $R = 6.38 \times 10^6$ m, find an approximate value for the mass of the earth.

5. Sketch graphs showing the general way in which the gravitational forces to the earth and the moon vary with position during a rocket flight directly to the moon. Sketch also the way in which the acceleration varies with position, and from this deduce the graph of the speed against position, assuming the rocket quickly attains its maximum speed away from the earth and then the propulsive force ceases.

6. If a man of mass 60 kg were to stand on the surface of the moon, what would his weight be, relative to the moon, given that the mass of the moon is approximately $\frac{1}{80}$ the mass of the earth and that its radius is $\frac{3}{11}$ the radius of the earth?

7. Suppose that a small spherical planet has a radius of 10 km and a mean density of 5 tonnes/m³.

(a) What would be the acceleration due to gravity at its surface?

(b) What would a man weigh on this planet if his weight on earth were 700 N?

8. (a) If the acceleration due to gravity on the surface of a spherical planet P is g_p, prove that
$$g_p = \tfrac{4}{3}\pi G R_p \sigma_p,$$
where R_p is the radius,

σ_p the mean density of P,

and G the universal constant of gravitation.

(b) Taking Mars to be a sphere of radius 3400 km, mean density 3900 kg/m³, and the Earth to be a sphere of radius 6400 km, mean density 5500 kg/m³, calculate the acceleration due to gravity on the surface of Mars.

9. A body of mass 10 kg is falling with a downward acceleration of a m/s². What is the value of a, if the resisting force is 13 N?

10. A metal canister of mass 3 kg is released underwater. If the buoyancy is 60 N, what is its initial acceleration? If, later on when it is moving, the water offers a resistance of 15 N, what is its acceleration then?

11. A crane is lifting a mass of 1 tonne. How quickly can the mass be accelerated upwards if the coupling must not bear a strain of more than 1.1×10^4 N?

12. A parachutist, of total mass 90 kg, at the end of a free fall has a constant speed of 40 m/s. What is the air resistance? When the parachute opens there is an additional resistance of 2000 N for the next $1\frac{1}{2}$ s. What is his speed at the end of this time? If instead of opening, the parachute had broken free, would his speed have increased or decreased?

13. Find the dimensions of the universal constant of gravitation G.

14. Find the dimensions of pressure.

15. Instead of taking mass, length and time as our basic dimensions we could take force (**F**), velocity (**V**) and acceleration (**A**). Find in terms of **F**, **V**, **A**, the dimensions of (*a*) mass, (*b*) length, (*c*) time, (*d*) density, (*e*) pressure.

Why cannot force, mass and acceleration be taken as the three basic dimensions?

*16. (*a*) A projectile fired with initial velocity **V** falling under a constant acceleration **g** has a velocity given by $\mathbf{v} = \mathbf{V} + \mathbf{g}t$. If a projectile starts from the origin O at $t = 0$ guess an expression for the position vector **r** and check it by ensuring that $\dot{\mathbf{r}} = \mathbf{v}$.

(*b*) **i** is a unit vector along the horizontal and **j** a unit vector in the direction of the upward vertical and the projectile in (*a*) is fired at an angle θ to **i** (in the plane of **i** and **j**). Use your answer to (*a*) to show that the position vector of the projectile at time t is

$$\mathbf{r} = Vt\cos\theta\,\mathbf{i} + (Vt\sin\theta - \tfrac{1}{2}gt^2)\,\mathbf{j},$$

g being the magnitude of **g**.

*17. Use the result of Question 16(*b*) to find out the time at which the projectile lands on the horizontal plane. Find the distance of the projectile from O at this instant. (This distance is called the range and it will be a maximum when $\theta = \tfrac{1}{4}\pi$.)

4. APPLICATIONS

4.1 Summary of Newton's model.

Whenever we attempt to apply mathematics to real situations, we have to make assumptions, approximations and abstractions. We have done this in setting up algebraic models in earlier chapters; for example, in the model for finding the best shape for a cylindrical oil-drum (page 25), it was sensible to ignore the thickness of the metal and assume that there were no seams. The solution of the idealized problem is a good basis for a decision.

In mechanics, we have one model which we apply to the motion of bodies large and small. The rules which govern our calculations are basic assumptions or *postulates*. A model is considered to be a good one if events predicted in the model turn out to agree with observations. When a model has been well tested (as Newton's has been over the last three hundred years), then the postulates are often called *laws*.

The concept of a particle is of fundamental importance in Newton's model. Whenever we ignore the extension of a body in space and just consider it as matter concentrated at a point, we are treating it as a particle. A planet in its motion round the sun may be considered as a particle as can a falling parachutist, provided that we are not concerned with their movements about their own centres.

Newton's first and second laws are other basic postulates of the system. In the first instance they apply only to particles. We defer to later chapters

283

the extensions to systems of interacting particles and rotating bodies. We shall then require Newton's Third Law, the Interaction Principle:

> Forces arise only when bodies are acting on one another; when a body A exerts a force on a body B, then body B exerts an equal and opposite force on body A. (The two forces act along the same straight line.)

If you stand still, you push downwards onto the ground, and, to keep you there, the ground has to push upwards with the same force. If you whirl a dancing partner round, a force must be exerted on her to make her move in a circle; an equal but opposite force pulls you towards her. When a rifle is fired a force acts on the bullet while an equal and opposite force is exerted on the rifle; in turn, the rifle is prevented from moving in the opposite direction to the bullet by your shoulder, which experiences a force from the gun. All these are instances of the two-ended nature of force; no body can exert a force in one direction on another body without the second body exerting an equal force in the opposite direction. This principle, which is embodied in Newton's model as a postulate, holds whether the bodies are at rest, moving uniformly, or being accelerated.

Another postulate of the model (see Section 2.2) is that where several forces act on a single particle, the acceleration is that which would be caused by a single force equal to the vector sum (resultant) of the individual forces.

In this section, Newton's model will be used for various examples. In each case, the aircraft, person or cable-car will be considered as a particle and the weight, pressure forces and tensions will be the forces acting upon it.

The method of solution will be to equate the sum of the force vectors to the sum of the 'mass × acceleration' vectors (which will in future be written mass-acceleration). In most of the examples, several forces are combined and equated to a single mass-acceleration vector.

Always draw diagrams showing each of the forces acting on the body, and its mass-acceleration. The problems may be tackled in two ways: directly from the vector polygon or by means of components.

4.2 Vector polygons

Example 5

The aircraft of Example 2 has weight 15000 units, the drag force is 20000 units and the forward thrust of the engines is 25000 units. Find the lift force and the resultant forward force.

We start by drawing **AB**, **BC**, **CD** in the vector polygon. Then knowing that the acceleration and hence the resultant force are in the direction of **BA** and that the lift is at right angles to this direction, we can construct the point E.

284

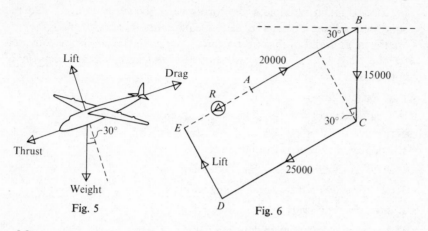

Fig. 5   D   Fig. 6

Measurement (or calculation by trigonometry) then gives the magnitude of the lift force to be 13 000 units and the resultant forward force to be 12 500 units.

Example 6

A cable-car of total mass 1 tonne is supported by two stays inclined at 30° and 60° to the vertical. Find the tensions in the stays if the car is accelerating at 2 m/s² up a 20° slope.

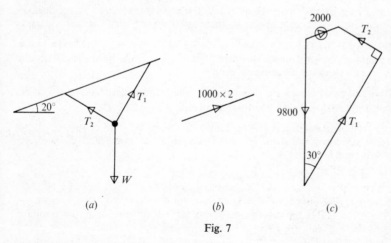

Fig. 7

Figure 7(a) shows the forces on the cable-car, Figure 7(b) shows its mass-acceleration vector, and Figure 7(c) gives the force polygon with the mass-acceleration vector replacing the resultant. Notice that the weight W has magnitude $1000 g = 9800$ N.

By measurement, $T_1 \approx 10000$ N, $T_2 \approx 3600$ N.

285

Notice that in example 4 the forces were shown as vectors, and the equations written down were vector equations. In example 6, T_1 and T_2 are the magnitudes of the tension forces, and their directions are conveyed by the diagram. In future we shall use whichever form seems more convenient.

Exercise E

In Questions 1–12 draw diagrams showing the forces acting on the bodies in italics.

1. The *seat* of a swing with a boy sitting on it.

2. A *ladder* standing on level ground leaning against a wall.

3. An *astronaut* on the moon standing on the ladder up to his spacecraft.

4. An *aircraft* in steady flight.

5. A *boy* on a sledge sliding down a slope.

6. A *hovercraft* moving forward at steady speed.

7. A *golf-ball* standing on a tee at the instant it is struck by the golf club.

8. A *horse* pulling a cart up a hill.

9. A *garden rake* being pulled steadily across a lawn.

10. A *paint roller* being pushed steadily up a wall.

11. A *packing case* being pushed by a horizontal force up a slope.

12. A *car* being towed by a pick-up truck, the car's front wheels being clear of the ground and the tow cable being inclined at 60° to the horizontal.

In Questions 13–26 draw one diagram showing all the forces on the body, and a second diagram showing the mass-acceleration vector; in Questions 16–26 obtain the answers by drawing a vector polygon to scale.

13. A buoy of mass 2000 kg is supporting a length of cable of weight 10000 N, when it breaks free. What is its initial acceleration?

14. A conker of mass 10 g is swung round in a vertical circle of radius 60 cm. What is the tension in the string when the mass is at the lowest point if the speed there is 120 cm/s?

15. A stone of mass 1 kg is sinking at 2 m/s towards the sea bed. What is its acceleration if the buoyancy is 5 N and the water offers a resistance of 4 N?

What will be the water resistance later on when the stone is sinking at a steady speed, and what is this speed if the water resistance is proportional to the square of the speed?

16. A toboggan of mass 50 kg is pulled by a force of 40 N at an angle of 40° above the horizontal. Assuming the snow surface to be horizontal and the reaction of the snow on the toboggan to be at right angles to the surface, find the acceleration of the toboggan.

17. Repeat Question 16 with the toboggan accelerating up a surface inclined at 10° to the horizontal, and the pull increased to 120 N.

18. An aircraft of mass 10^5 kg is climbing along a straight flight path at 30° to the horizontal with an acceleration of 2 m/s². The engines exert a thrust of 8×10^5 N along the flight path. Show in one clearly labelled vector polygon the weight, the thrust and the total aerodynamic force together with the mass-acceleration vector.

19. Two wires are clipped to a ring in the top of a block of stone of mass 1000 kg. The wires are each inclined to the vertical at an angle of 15°. What is the tension in each wire? What would the new tension be, if the wires gave the stone an upward acceleration of 1 cm/s²?

20. A stage 'fairy' is supported by two wires and moves horizontally across the stage. Her mass is 50 kg, and when she is accelerating at 3 m/s² across the stage, the wires are inclined at 60° and 150° to the direction of motion. What are the tensions in the wires?

21. A pendulum, consisting of a 3 kg mass on the end of a light rod, hangs from the roof of a car. If it is inclined at a constant backward angle of 10° from the vertical, what is the car's acceleration? What would be the behaviour of the pendulum if the car accelerated at this rate from rest?

22. Two boys are dragging a 50 kg friend by the legs. They pull with forces of 40 N and 60 N in horizontal directions 50 ° apart. If the victim's total resistance is entirely frictional and of amount 75 N, what is his acceleration?

23. A car of mass 500 kg is freewheeling down a slope of 16° to the horizontal. What is its acceleration if the total resistance to motion is 800 N?

24. A car of mass 600 kg is travelling at 30 m/s on the banked surface of a circular track of radius 300 m. At what angle to the horizontal is the surface banked if the car has no tendency to sideslip?

25. An aircraft of mass 3000 kg is flying at a constant speed in a horizontal circle of radius 3000 m, banked over at 30 ° from the horizontal. If there is no tendency to sideslip, at what speed is it flying and what is the lift force? (Take the lift force to lie in the plane of symmetry of the aircraft at right angles to the direction of motion.)

26. A hemispherical bowl is fixed with its rim in a horizontal plane. A small ball-bearing rolls steadily around the smooth inside surface of the bowl in a horizontal plane half-way between the plane of the rim and the bottom of the bowl. What is the speed of the ball-bearing?

4.3   Components. In all our work with vectors, we have the choice between using vector triangles and polygons (as in the last exercise) or expressing each vector in terms of components (as we usually did in Chapter 7). The following examples show how the component method can be used in problems involving Newton's second law.

Example 7

A bead of mass m is threaded on a smooth horizontal straight wire and a force **P** is applied to it in a direction making a constant angle α with the wire. Find the acceleration of the bead.

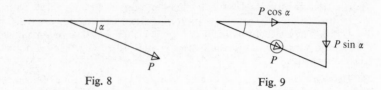

Fig. 8   Fig. 9

We can replace **P** by a force of magnitude $P \cos \alpha$ along the wire and a force $P \sin \alpha$ perpendicular to it without altering the vector sum of the force system. The only other forces are the weight **W** and a contact force, **Q** say. When a particle pushes against a surface, there is a force of equal magnitude which opposes it. Since the wire is smooth, this force will neither help nor hinder the motion, and must act at right angles to the wire. It is called a *normal contact force*; such forces will be discussed more fully in Chapter 24.

The mass-acceleration, $m\mathbf{a}$, is in the direction of the wire. All the forces are perpendicular to the wire except for the component of magnitude $P \cos \alpha$. Hence the vector polygon must give

$$P \cos \alpha = ma,$$

and the required acceleration has magnitude $(P \cos \alpha)/m$.

Example 8

For the cable-car of Example 6 determine the tensions in the stays by (i) replacing T_1, T_2 and W by components along and perpendicular to the cable, and (ii) replacing W and the mass-acceleration vector by components along the directions of T_1 and T_2.

(i) Figure 11 shows T_1 resolved into components along and perpendicular to the cable. Draw diagrams showing the components of T_2 and W in these directions.

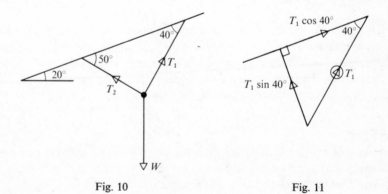

Fig. 10   Fig. 11

Newton's second law then gives

$$T_1 \cos 40° - T_2 \cos 50° - 9800 \cos 70° = 1000 \times 2,$$

and $T_1 \sin 40° + T_2 \sin 50° - 9800 \sin 70° = 0.$

These equations can be solved simultaneously.

(ii) Figure 12 shows (with different scales) the components of the weight and the mass-acceleration vector in the directions of T_1 and T_2.

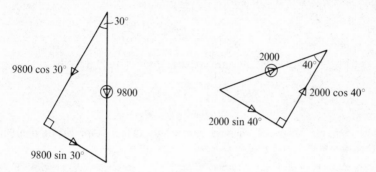

Fig. 12

Newton's second law gives

$$T_1 - 9800 \cos 30° = 2000 \cos 40°,$$

and $9800 \sin 30° - T_2 = 2000 \sin 40°.$

These equations are more convenient than those in (i). Show that they give the same answers as in Example 6.

Example 9

If a mass of 12 kg is acted on by forces of 5 N, 10 N, 8 N in directions 000°, 070° and 220°, calculate the resultant force and hence the acceleration.

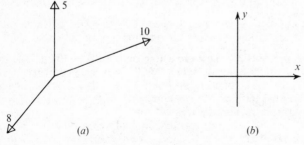

Fig. 13

Taking coordinate axes as in Figure 13(*b*), the force vectors can be written in component form:

$$\begin{pmatrix} 0 \\ 5 \end{pmatrix}, \quad \begin{pmatrix} 10 \sin 70° \\ 10 \cos 70° \end{pmatrix}, \quad \begin{pmatrix} 8 \sin 220° \\ 8 \cos 220° \end{pmatrix}.$$

Their resultant is
$$\begin{pmatrix} 0+9·40-5·14 \\ 5+3·42-6·13 \end{pmatrix} = \begin{pmatrix} 4·26 \\ 2·29 \end{pmatrix}.$$

The acceleration vector is therefore

$$\begin{pmatrix} 4·26 \\ 2·29 \end{pmatrix} \div 12 = \begin{pmatrix} 0·35 \\ 0·19 \end{pmatrix}.$$

Show that this represents an acceleration of 0·40 m/s² in the direction 062°.

Exercise F

The ideas of this section should be used to answer some of the questions of Exercise E. The following offer some further practice.

1. A mass of 3 kg is constrained to slide on a smooth vertical wire. If a force of 50 N is applied to the mass at an angle of 30° from the upward vertical, calculate the acceleration of the mass and the normal contact force from the wire.

2. A body of mass m is sliding down a smooth plane inclined at an angle θ to the horizontal. Find the acceleration of the body and the normal contact force from the plane.

3. Using the method of Example 9, find the resultant of the following sets of coplanar forces acting at a point O, where the directions are measured from some fixed direction **OA**:

    (*a*) 9 N at 0°;   6 N at 60°;   3 N at 270°;

    (*b*) 5 N at 0°;   4 N at 125°;   3 N at 320°;

    (*c*) 2 N at 0°; 10 N at 170°; 12 N at 250°.

4. A box is being pulled along a horizontal board by a rope. The tension in the rope is 60 N. Resisting forces parallel to the board are 15 N. What will be the sum of the components of all the forces acting on the box parallel to the board given that the angle between the board and the rope is (*a*) 60°, (*b*) 30°, (*c*) 0°?

    If the mass of the box is 8 kg, what will the acceleration be in each case?

5. Answer the questions in Question 4, given that the board is inclined at 10° to the horizontal and that the rope tends to pull the box *up* the slope.

6. Three forces in a vertical plane are acting on a mass of 10 kg. One force of 50 N is acting vertically downward. One of 100 N is inclined at 60° to the upward vertical. One of 80 N is inclined at 20° on the opposite side of the upward vertical. Find the sum of the components of these forces in:

    (*a*) the vertical and the horizontal directions;

    (*b*) directions parallel and perpendicular to the force of 80 N.

Check that the resultant forces obtained from these two pairs are equal. What is the final acceleration of the mass?

7. A mass of 10 kg is swinging at the end of a string 1·2 m long as though it were a pendulum. When the string is inclined at 20° to the vertical, the mass is moving at 0·3 m/s.

(a) What are the components of the weight of the particle, along and perpendicular to the line of the string?

(b) What is the acceleration component of the mass along the line of the string?

(c) What is the tension of the string?

(d) What are the components of the forces acting on the mass in the vertical and horizontal directions?

5. PATHS

Newton's second law occupies a central position in the classical model of dynamics. In this final section we investigate more situations in which the law is used to determine the motion of particles.

5.1 Variable acceleration. Situations in which the acceleration varies with time are commonplace occurrences.

Example 10

A man pushes an 800 kg car from rest with a force that decreases linearly with time from 250 N to 50 N in 20 seconds. The resistance to motion is a constant 50 N. How fast is the car going after 20 s and how far has he pushed it?

The force F exerted by the man decreases by 200 N in 20 s, i.e. at a rate of 10 N/s.

Hence $F = 250 - 10t$. The resultant force on the car is thus

$$250 - 10t - 50 \text{ newtons,}$$

and we have

$$200 - 10t = 800 \frac{dv}{dt}.$$

Hence $v = \frac{1}{800}(200t - 5t^2)$ since $v = 0$ when $t = 0$. This gives a speed of $2\frac{1}{2}$ m/s when $t = 20$.

Further integration gives $x = \frac{1}{800}(100t^2 - \frac{5}{3}t^3)$, taking x as 0 when $t = 0$, and the displacement when $t = 20$ is thus $33\frac{1}{3}$ m.

5.2 Projectiles. An important example of accelerated motion is the motion of a projectile. The two forces acting are:

(i) the weight **W** of the particle, and

(ii) the air resistance **R**.

Newton's second law gives

$$\mathbf{W} + \mathbf{R} = m\frac{d\mathbf{v}}{dt}.$$

In general the magnitude of **R** varies according to the height and speed of the particle, and its direction lies approximately along the tangent to the path. The problem of the general motion of a resisted particle is complicated and we therefore simplify the model in two ways:

   (a) by neglecting air resistance i.e. $\mathbf{R} = \mathbf{0}$,

and   (b) by assuming that the weight of the body is constant,

i.e. $\mathbf{W} = m\mathbf{g}$ for *constant* $\mathbf{g}$, m being the mass of the particle. With these simplifications, the equation of motion is

$$mg = m\frac{d\mathbf{v}}{dt},$$

i.e.
$$\frac{d\mathbf{v}}{dt} = \mathbf{g}.$$

Integration with respect to t gives

   (1) $\mathbf{v} = \mathbf{u} + t\mathbf{g}$ where $\mathbf{u}$ is the velocity when $t = 0$.

Furthermore, since $\mathbf{v} = d\mathbf{r}/dt$, we may integrate again:

$$\mathbf{r} = \mathbf{r}_0 + t\mathbf{u} + \tfrac{1}{2}t^2\mathbf{g},$$

where $\mathbf{r}_0$ is the position vector of the particle when $t = 0$.

   Normally the position of the particle will be taken relative to the point of projection (i.e. $\mathbf{r}_0 = \mathbf{0}$) giving

   (2) $\mathbf{r} = t\mathbf{u} + \tfrac{1}{2}t^2\mathbf{g}$.

Substitution for $t\mathbf{g}$ from (1) in (2) gives:

   (3) $\mathbf{r} = \tfrac{1}{2}t(\mathbf{u} + \mathbf{v})$.

   Equation (1) is illustrated by means of the velocity diagram of Figure 14(b) and equations (2) and (3) by the displacement diagram of Figure 14(c).

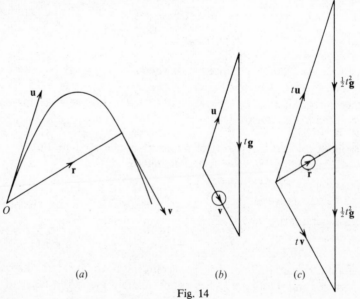

(a)   (b)   (c)

Fig. 14

It is often convenient to use the above equations in component form using horizontal and vertical axes.

Thus, if
$$\mathbf{r} = \begin{pmatrix} x \\ y \end{pmatrix}, \quad \mathbf{u} = \begin{pmatrix} u_1 \\ u_2 \end{pmatrix} \quad \text{and} \quad \mathbf{g} = \begin{pmatrix} 0 \\ -g \end{pmatrix},$$
the equations give

(1a) $\dot{x} = u_1,$

(1b) $\dot{y} = u_2 - tg;$

(2a) $x = tu_1,$

(2b) $y = tu_2 - \frac{1}{2}t^2 g.$

Substitution for t from (2a) in (2b) gives
$$y = \left(\frac{x}{u_1}\right) u_2 - \frac{1}{2}\left(\frac{x}{u_1}\right)^2 g$$

which is the equation of a parabola.

Motion of a projectile under gravity is thus seen to be parabolic if air resistance is ignored.

Example 11

A golf-ball is hit with velocity 33 m/s in a direction making an angle 30° with the horizontal ground. If its path takes it over the edge of a cliff, how far will it have gone horizontally and vertically when it strikes the sea after 5 s? What will be its greatest height?

We choose the origin to be at the initial position of the ball and the x and y axes to be horizontal and vertically upwards. The units will be metres and seconds.

The initial velocity is
$$\mathbf{u} = \begin{pmatrix} 33 \cos 30° \\ 33 \sin 30° \end{pmatrix} = \begin{pmatrix} 28·6 \\ 16·5 \end{pmatrix},$$

and the acceleration is
$$\begin{pmatrix} 0 \\ -9·8 \end{pmatrix}.$$

In the x-direction we have $\quad x = 28·6t$

and in the y-direction $\quad y = 16·5t - 4·9t^2.$
When $t = 5$, we calculate

$$x = 143 \quad \text{and} \quad y = -40.$$

The sea is therefore 40 m below the golf course. To find the maximum height we first find the time taken to reach this height.

When $\dot{y} = 0$, Equation (1b) gives $16·5 - 9·8t = 0$, i.e. $t = 1·68$. Then $y = 16·5 \times 1·68 - 4·9 \times 1·68^2 \approx 14$, so the ball reaches a maximum height of 14 m.

Exercise G

1. A car of mass 1000 kg is stationary at time $t = 0$ and then accelerates so that after t seconds the net tractive force (resistance included) is $250(5+t)$ newtons. Find how long it takes to reach a speed of 54 km/h.

In Questions 2–4, a particle of mass m kg moves along Ox starting from the origin O at $t = 0$ with a speed of u m/s. After t s it is at a distance x metres from O moving with a speed v m/s. All forces are in newtons.

2. Find (i) v in terms of t, and (ii) x in terms of t, if the particle is acted on by a force $m(2-t)$ *towards O*.
Find for what values of u the particle is

    (*a*) never stationary;
    (*b*) stationary for only one value of t.

In case (*a*) find the minimum speed and in (*b*) find how far the particle is from O when it stops.

3. The particle moves under a force $8m \sin 2t$ towards O. Find v and x in terms of t.
For what values of u is the particle never stationary?
If $u = 1$, find by means of a graph, or otherwise, the value of t when the particle first returns to O.

4. The particle is repelled from O by a force $m/(t+4)^{\frac{3}{2}}$. By putting $t+4 = t'$, find v in terms of t.
What happens to v as $t \to \infty$?

5. A particle is projected at 20 m/s at an angle of 50° above the horizontal. Find by drawing and measurement (or by calculation) the velocity and displacement after 3 s, giving the magnitude and direction of both vectors. (Take $g = 10$ m/s².)

6. A stone is thrown horizontally at a speed of 20 m/s from the top of a vertical cliff 100 m high. How long will it take to fall into the sea and how far from the foot of the cliff will it fall? At what speed and in what direction would it have to be thrown back from this position in order to reach the top of the cliff with a horizontal velocity of 20 m/s?

7. How far away (horizontally) from his target should a bomb-aimer release a bomb when he is flying horizontally at 1000 km/h at 2000 m?

8. A fielder catches a cricket ball 80 m from the place where it was hit and 5 s after it left the bat. What was the initial velocity of the ball and how high did it rise?

9. A particle of mass m starts from the origin at $t = 0$ with a velocity $\begin{pmatrix} 0 \\ 2a \end{pmatrix}$ and is acted on by a constant force $\begin{pmatrix} 2am \\ 0 \end{pmatrix}$. Show that the path of the particle is a parabola with the origin as vertex. Find the coordinates of the point at which the particle is moving parallel to the line $y = x$.

10. A particle moves under a force towards the origin proportional to its distance from the origin. Show that $\ddot{x} = -n^2x$ and $\ddot{y} = -n^2y$ where n is a constant. Show further that

$$\mathbf{r} = \begin{pmatrix} a \cos nt \\ b \sin nt \end{pmatrix}$$

satisfies these equations and find a, b, n if the particle is at $(3, 0)$ when $t = 0$, $(0, 2)$ when $t = 1$ and $(-3, 0)$ when $t = 2$.

Find the position and velocity of the particle when $t = 4\frac{1}{2}$. What sort of path do you think the particle would have under this law of force if its position and velocity at $t = 0$ were $\begin{pmatrix} 2 \\ 4 \end{pmatrix}$, $\begin{pmatrix} -1 \\ -2 \end{pmatrix}$?

11. A particle, moving at 6×10^6 m/s in the direction of the x-axis of a system of Cartesian coordinates, enters an electric field which gives it a constant acceleration in the direction of the y-axis of 10^{15} m/s^2. After 2×10^{-9} s it is deflected through a right angle in a clockwise direction without change of speed. After how long will it next be moving in the direction of the x-axis and what will be its speed then? Find its total displacement up to this instant.

Miscellaneous Exercise

1. The force of gravitational attraction due to the earth on a rocket standing on the earth's surface is 10^6 N. Find the force of attraction it will experience from the earth when its distance from the earth's *surface* is (i) 320 km, (ii) 3200 km, (iii) 32000 km. (Take the earth's radius to be 6400 km.)

2. The moon is approximately 380 000 km from the earth and 150000000 km from the sun. The magnitude of the force of gravity between sun and moon is about 2·2 times that of the force between earth and moon. Find the ratio of the mass of the sun to the mass of the earth.

Assuming that the moon moves in circular orbits relative to both the earth and the sun, show that there are approximately 13 lunar months in a year.

3. A rock of mass 2 kg is to be given an acceleration of 3 m/s^2. What force must be exerted upon it if the direction of the acceleration is to be (*a*) vertically upward, (*b*) vertically downward?

4. A glider of weight W glides at 10° to the horizontal at constant speed. Find the lift and drag forces. (Assume that the lift force is perpendicular to the line of flight and the drag force is along the line of flight.)

5. A ski-lift chair is supported by two stays making angles of 40° and 50° with the lift cable. The combined weight of the chair and passenger is 1000 N.

(i) Draw a diagram showing the forces when the chair is travelling at a steady speed in the case where the lift cable runs (*a*) horizontally, (*b*) at 20° down from the horizontal.

(ii) Find the tensions in the stays in (*a*) and (*b*).

6. Repeat Question 5(ii) for a ski-lift accelerating at 2 m/s^2.

7. A particle of mass 5 kg is moving on a circular course of radius 2 m. If at some instant its speed is 1 m/s, and its speed is decreasing at $\frac{1}{4}$ m/s^2, what is the total force exerted on the particle?

8. A particle of mass 1 kg is moving in a circle of radius 1 m. Its angular velocity is 1 rad/s. What force is being exerted on it?

If the angular velocity is increased by 1 rad/s in 1 second, what force is being exerted along the tangent? What is now the total force acting upon the particle?

9. A tip-up truck contains a heavy packing case of weight 3 W. A constant horizontal force of magnitude $\sqrt{3}W$ is applied to the case. The tipper is inclined at an angle θ to the horizontal. The magnitude of the normal reaction is N and of the friction force is F.

Draw the force polygon which takes the forces in the order $3W, N, F, \sqrt{3}W$. Use this diagram to find:

   (i) the value of F when $N = 3W$;

   (ii) the angle θ at which equilibrium would be possible if the floor of the truck were smooth;

   (iii) the angle at which F and N become equal (assuming that F does not reach a limiting value).

10. When an electrified particle, of mass m, carrying a charge e, is moving with velocity **v** at right angles to a magnetic field **H**, it experiences a force of magnitude Hev in a direction which is perpendicular to both **H** and **v**.

If the velocity of such a particle at time t is given by $\begin{pmatrix} \dot{x} \\ \dot{y} \\ 0 \end{pmatrix}$ and $\mathbf{H} = \begin{pmatrix} 0 \\ 0 \\ H \end{pmatrix}$

is the magnetic field (H being constant), write down in component form the force **F** on the particle in terms of $\dot{x}, \dot{y}, e$ and H.

Newton's second law gives $\mathbf{F} = m\ddot{\mathbf{r}}$ where **r** is the position vector of the particle. Show that

$$\mathbf{r} = \begin{pmatrix} a \cos \omega t \\ a \sin \omega t \\ 0 \end{pmatrix}$$

is a possible solution, and find ω in terms of m, e and H.

Describe the path given by this solution given that

$$\mathbf{v} = \begin{pmatrix} 0 \\ u \\ 0 \end{pmatrix} \quad \text{when} \quad t = 0,$$

and show that the period is independent of u.

11. A boy jumps into a swimming pool from the top diving board and causes a splash in which particles of water move in all directions with speeds up to 9 m/s. Show that a spectator on the side of the pool 3 m away is liable to be hit by water from the splash for a period of about $1\frac{1}{2}$ seconds.

12. A projectile of mass m, fired from a point A on the top of a mountain, moves under gravity and is subject to a resistive drag (along the tangent to the path) of magnitude mkv where v is its speed. Show that the coordinates (x, y) of the projectile (at time t) relative to horizontal and vertical axes through A satisfy the equations: $\ddot{x}+k\dot{x} = 0$ and $\ddot{y}+k\dot{y}+g = 0$ (g being the acceleration due to gravity). The velocity of projection is $\begin{pmatrix} u \\ v \end{pmatrix}$. Assuming that x is never negative, show that the projectile cannot pass beyond the line $x = u/k$.

SUMMARY

Newton's laws of motion

(I) Every body remains stationary or in uniform motion in a straight line unless it is made to change that state by external forces.

(II) The force acting on a particle is proportional to its mass and to its acceleration and has the direction of the acceleration, i.e. $\mathbf{F} \propto ma$ where $\mathbf{F}$ is the force, m the mass and $\mathbf{a}$ the acceleration. Or $\mathbf{F} = ma$ if $\mathbf{F}$ is measured in newtons, m in kg and $\mathbf{a}$ in m/s². (1 newton is that force required to impart an acceleration of 1 m/s² to a particle of mass 1 kg.)

(III) Forces arise only when bodies are acting on one another; when a body A exerts a force on a body B, then body B exerts an equal and opposite force on body A. These two forces act along the same straight line.

Newton's law of universal gravitation

Two bodies of mass m, m' at a distance d apart attract each other with a gravitational force of magnitude Gmm'/d^2 where G is the universal constant of gravitation. (If masses are measured in kg, distance in metres, and the force in newtons, $G \approx 6.7 \times 10^{-11}$.)

Weight

Near the earth's surface bodies fall with an approximately constant acceleration, $\mathbf{g}$, of magnitude 9·8 m/s². The weight (on earth) of a body of mass m is the force $m\mathbf{g}$.

Projectiles

The motion of a projectile fired from the origin when $t = 0$ with an initial velocity $\mathbf{u}$ is described by the equations:

$$\mathbf{v} = \mathbf{u} + t\mathbf{g} \quad \text{and} \quad \mathbf{r} = t\mathbf{u} + \tfrac{1}{2}t^2\mathbf{g} = \tfrac{1}{2}t(\mathbf{u} + \mathbf{v}).$$

13

THE CHAIN RULE AND INTEGRATION BY SUBSTITUTION

1. COMPOSITE FUNCTIONS

Consider a particle moving in a plane so that its Cartesian coordinates at time t seconds are $x = \sin 2t$, $y = \cos t$ (measured in metres). The motion of such a particle was discussed in Chapter 7, Section 4; Figure 1 shows the path of the particle and its velocity and acceleration at four points on the path.

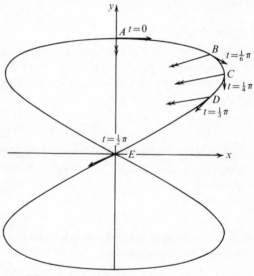

Fig. 1

At A, the speed is 2 m/s; at B it is $\sqrt{(1+(\frac{1}{2})^2)} = 1\cdot12$ m/s and the diagram shows that the particle is still slowing down because the acceleration arrow makes an angle of more than a right angle with the velocity arrow. At C and D, on the other hand, the particle is speeding up until, at E, the speed is $\sqrt{5}$ m/s. Somewhere between B and C it reaches a minimum speed and we now set out to find the time when this happens.

Since $\dot{x} = 2\cos 2t$ and $\dot{y} = -\sin t$, the speed v is given by

$$v^2 = f(t) = 4\cos^2 2t + \sin^2 t.$$

In order to find when this is a minimum we shall want to differentiate it
and this will involve differentiating $\cos^2 2t$ which, we notice, is a composite
function using the square function and the cosine function. So far, our
investigation of differentiation has been limited to basic functions; we
now extend this investigation to include composite functions. We shall
return to complete the solution of the problem of the particle later, in
Section 2.1.

Exercise A

1. Differentiate each of the following functions, by first removing the brackets,
and express the derived functions in factorized form. For example, for the function $f: x \to (x+2)^3$, $f(x) = x^3 + 6x^2 + 12x + 8,$

$$f'(x) = 3x^2 + 12x + 12 = 3(x+2)^2.$$

The factorized form of the answer shows its relationship to the form in which f
is given.

(a) $x \to (x-1)^2$;   (b) $x \to (3x+2)^2$;   (c) $x \to (x-3)^3$;

(d) $x \to (2x+5)^3$;   (e) $x \to (x^2+3)^2$;   (f) $x \to (2x^2-1)^3$.

2. Differentiate from first principles, i.e. by finding

$$\lim_{b \to a} \frac{f(b)-f(a)}{b-a}:$$

(a) $x \to \dfrac{1}{x+3}$;   (b) $x \to \dfrac{1}{2x-1}$;

(c) $x \to \dfrac{1}{x^2+1}$;   (d) $x \to \sqrt{(1-x^2)}$.

[*Hint for* (d). Multiply top and bottom by $\sqrt{(1-b^2)} + \sqrt{(1-a^2)}$.]

3. A good numerical approximation to the value of the derivative of $f(t)$ at
$t = a$ can usually be obtained by using the average scale factor

$$\frac{f(a+h)-f(a-h)}{2h}$$

for a small value of h. Taking $f(t) = \sin^2 t$, find the values of $f'(t)$ for $t = 0$,
$0.3, 0.6, ..., 1.5$; it is suggested that you use circular function and square tables
and work in tabular form as follows:

t	$\sin t$	$\sin^2 t$	$\delta(\sin^2 t)$	$f'(t)$	t
$\begin{cases} -0.05 \\ +0.05 \end{cases}$					0
$\begin{cases} 0.25 \\ 0.35 \end{cases}$	0.2474 0.3429	0.0612 0.1176	0.0564	0.564	0.3

Plot the graph of the function $t \to f'(t)$ and, from its shape, suggest a formula for
$f'(t)$.

Verify your suggestion by expressing $f(t)$ in terms of $\cos 2t$ and differentiating
directly.

299

4. Write down flow diagrams which show how the functions of Questions 1 and 2 are built up from simpler functions. For example, $x \to \sin(x^2-1)$ may be expressed by the flow diagram:

$$\boxed{\text{Take } x} \longrightarrow \boxed{\text{Square it}} \longrightarrow \boxed{\text{Subtract 1}} \longrightarrow \boxed{\text{Find its sine}}$$

5. Write down flow diagrams for the following functions and then, from your experience of Questions 1 and 2, *write down* what you think will be the derived functions.

(a) $x \to (2x-1)^3$;   (b) $x \to (4x+1)^4$;   (c) $x \to \dfrac{1}{(x+3)^2}$;

(d) $x \to \dfrac{1}{(x^2+1)^2}$;   (e) $x \to \sin 4x$;   (f) $x \to (\sin x)^3$.

Check your answers to parts (d) and (f) by applying a numerical method to find the value of the derivative at $x = 1$.

6. By considering the graphs of $y = x^2, y = x^3, y = 1/x$, and transforming them by translations and stretches as appropriate, confirm the answers to Questions 1(a)–(d) and 2(a), (b).

[*Hint.* If the graph G is transformed into G_1 by a stretch of factor $\frac{1}{2}$ parallel to Ox, so that $y = f(x)$ is transformed into $y = f(2x)$, how is the gradient of G_1 at $\frac{1}{2}a$ related to the gradient of G at a?]

1.1   Composite function mapping diagrams. The questions of Exercise A will have suggested the way in which composite functions can be differentiated by differentiating the component functions. Consider, for example, the function

$$f: x \to (\tfrac{1}{2}x-3)^3.$$

A flow diagram

$$\boxed{\text{Take } x} \longrightarrow \boxed{\text{Halve it}} \longrightarrow \boxed{\text{Subtract 3}} \longrightarrow \boxed{\text{Cube it}}$$

shows that it is composed of the three functions

$$p: x \to \tfrac{1}{2}x, \quad q: x \to x-3, \quad r: x \to x^3$$

so that $f = rqp$.

What follows is more clearly understood if we introduce new letters to describe the functions:

$$p: x \to \tfrac{1}{2}x, \quad q: u \to u-3, \quad r: v \to v^3.$$

Then, if $u = \frac{1}{2}x$, $v = u-3$ and $y = v^3$, we have

$$y = v^3 = (u-3)^3 = (\tfrac{1}{2}x-3)^3.$$

The mapping diagrams for the separate functions can then be combined into one composite diagram (Figure 2) in which the broken lines show the composite function $f = rqp$.

300

Consider now the interval [10, 12] which maps, as shown, into the interval [8, 27]. The average scale factor of the function f over this interval is

$$\frac{27-8}{12-10} = \frac{19}{2} = 9\tfrac{1}{2}$$

and this is clearly the product of the three separate scale factors $\tfrac{1}{2} \times 1 \times 19$.

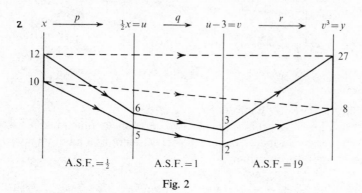

Fig. 2

The same result would hold for any interval, however small, so we conclude that it holds for the local scale factors. Figure 3 shows the situation at $x = 10$. (The L.S.F of the final stage is $r'(2) = 12$, calculated from $r': v \to 3v^2$.)

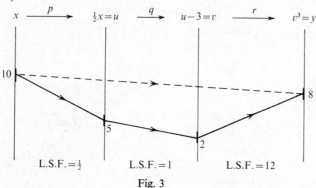

Fig. 3

The overall scale factor is thus $\tfrac{1}{2} \times 1 \times 12 = 6$.

To generalize this result, consider the value $x = a$ shown in Figure 4. Here $b = \tfrac{1}{2}a$, $c = b - 3 = \tfrac{1}{2}a - 3$ and $d = c^3 = (\tfrac{1}{2}a - 3)^3$. The overall scale factor is

$$f'(a) = p'(a) \times q'(b) \times r'(c)$$
$$= \tfrac{1}{2} \times 1 \times 3c^2$$
$$= \tfrac{3}{2} \times (\tfrac{1}{2}a - 3)^2.$$

Thus the derived function is $f': x \to \tfrac{3}{2}(\tfrac{1}{2}x - 3)^2$.

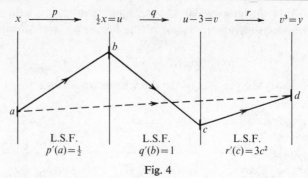

$$x \xrightarrow{\quad p \quad} \tfrac{1}{2}x = u \xrightarrow{\quad q \quad} u - 3 = v \xrightarrow{\quad r \quad} v^3 = y$$

L.S.F.   L.S.F.   L.S.F.
$p'(a) = \tfrac{1}{2}$ $q'(b) = 1$ $r'(c) = 3c^2$

Fig. 4

Example 1

Find the derived function of $f: x \to \sqrt{(3x^2 + 2)}$.

Figure 5 shows this split into two component functions, p and q; p is itself a composition of more elementary functions but nothing is gained by breaking it down further.

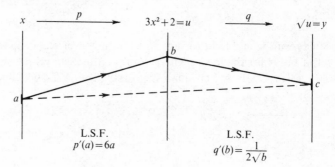

$$x \xrightarrow{\quad p \quad} 3x^2 + 2 = u \xrightarrow{\quad q \quad} \sqrt{u} = y$$

L.S.F.   L.S.F.
$p'(a) = 6a$ $q'(b) = \dfrac{1}{2\sqrt{b}}$

Fig. 5

$$f'(a) = p'(a) \times q'(b) = 6a \times \frac{1}{2\sqrt{b}} = \frac{6a}{2\sqrt{(3a^2 + 2)}},$$

i.e. the derived function is

$$f': x \to \frac{3x}{\sqrt{(3x^2 + 2)}}.$$

Exercise B

1. As in Example 1, split each of the given functions into component functions p and q so that $u = p(x)$ and $y = q(u)$ giving $y = qp(x)$; sketch a composite mapping diagram and so find the derived function f'.

(a) $x \to (3x + 4)^4$;   (b) $x \to (x^2 + 1)^2$;

(c) $x \to (\sin x)^2$ (which is usually written $\sin^2 x$);

(d) $x \to \sin(x^2)$ (which is usually written $\sin x^2$);

(e) $x \to \sqrt{(1 + \cos x)}$.

2. For each of the following sets of functions, draw the composite mapping diagram and find the function $f = rqp$ and its derived function f'.

(a) $p : x \to x^2$, $\quad q : x \to 4x + 2$, $\quad r : x \to x^4$;

(b) $p : x \to 4x + 5$, $\quad q : x \to \sin x$, $\quad r : x \to 5x + 4$;

(c) $p : x \to x - 1$, $\quad q : x \to \sqrt{x}$, $\quad r : x \to 1/x$.

3. The function g is such that $g'(x) = 3/x$ and a is the number such that $g(a) = a$. If $h = gg$ and $k = ggg$, find (in terms of a) $h(a)$, $k(a)$, $h'(a)$ and $k'(a)$. (Draw mapping diagrams to illustrate your answers.)

2. THE CHAIN RULE

The Chain Rule, for differentiating composite functions, can now be stated as follows:

The local scale factor of a composite mapping is equal to the product of the local scale factors of the component mappings.

Figure 6 illustrates the composite function $h = fg$ where $g(a) = b$ and $f(b) = c$ so that $h(a) = c$.

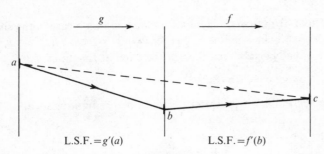

L.S.F. $= g'(a)$ $\qquad$ L.S.F. $= f'(b)$

Fig. 6

Then

$$h'(a) = g'(a) \times f'(b) = g'(a) \times f'(g(a))$$
$$= g'(a) \times f'g(a).$$

Thus we can state the chain rule as follows:

$$h'(x) = f'g(x) \times g'(x).$$

It is probably simpler to think of this rule informally as the rule for differentiating a function of a bracket in which case it could be stated as:

Derivative of f (bracket) $= f'$ (bracket) $\times$ derivative of bracket.

This enables us to apply the rule mentally as the following examples show.

Example 2

Differentiate $h : x \to (1 - \cos x)^2$.

Think: differentiate *square* of bracket to get *twice* bracket, differentiate *bracket* to get *sin x*; this gives

$$h' : x \to 2(1 - \cos x) \sin x.$$

303

2.1 Conclusion of the particle problem. We can now find the solution to the problem posed at the beginning of the chapter. To find where the speed of the particle is a minimum, differentiate $f(t) = 4 \cos^2 2t + \sin^2 t$. This gives

$$f'(t) = 4 \times 2 \cos 2t \times (-2 \sin 2t) + 2 \sin t \times \cos t$$

$$= -16 \cos 2t \times \sin 2t + \sin 2t$$

$$= \sin 2t(1 - 16 \cos 2t).$$

For maximum or minimum values, $f'(t) = 0$, and hence

$$\sin 2t = 0, \quad \text{i.e.} \quad t = 0, \quad \tfrac{1}{2}\pi, \pi, \text{ etc.}$$

or $\quad\quad \cos 2t = 0.0625, \quad \text{i.e.} \quad t = 0.754, \quad 2.388, \text{ etc.}$

Between B and C of Figure 1 the speed is a minimum when $t = 0.754$. This is just before C, where $t = 0.785$.

Alternative approaches are suggested in Exercise C, Question 7.

2.2 Linear functions. An important and common case of the chain rule is when the 'bracket' is linear, e.g. $f(x) = (3x+5)^4 \Rightarrow f'(x) = 12(3x+5)^3$. We have already considered this for the circular functions, e.g.

$$g(x) = \sin (2x-3) \Rightarrow g'(x) = 2 \cos (2x-3).$$

This application is obvious and it should be used automatically.

Exercise C

1. Find the derivative at a for each of the following functions:

(a) $x \to (2x+3)^4$;

(b) $x \to (x^2-1)^5$;

(c) $x \to \dfrac{1}{2x+1}$;

(d) $x \to \dfrac{1}{2x^2+5x+1}$;

(e) $x \to \sqrt{(3-2x)}$;

(f) $x \to (2x^2+3)^{-\frac{1}{2}}$;

(g) $x \to \sin 4x$;

(h) $x \to \sin^3 \tfrac{1}{2}x$.

2. Find dy/dx for the following relations:

(a) $y = (x^2-2x+4)^3$;

(b) $y = (1-2x^3)^4$;

(c) $y = (1+x^2)^{-1}$;

(d) $y = (1-x^2)^{\frac{1}{2}}$;

(e) $y = \dfrac{1}{1-x^2}$;

(f) $y = \sin^4 x$;

(g) $y = \cos^2 3x$;

(h) $y = \sin^2 x + \cos^2 x$;

(i) $y = (\cos x + \sin x)^3$.

3. Find the values of x for which $x - \sqrt{(3x+1)}$ is a minimum.

304

4. Find any maximum and minimum points on the graphs of

(a) $y = x\sqrt{(3-x)}$;   (b) $y = x\sqrt{(x-3)}$.

[*Hint.* Before differentiating, take the factor x inside the square root sign.]

Sketch separately the graphs of these two relations. Also sketch the graph of $y = x\sqrt{|x-3|}$.

5. The function $x \to \sec x$ is defined by the relation $\sec x = 1/\cos x$. Use the chain rule to differentiate

(a) $x \to \sec x$;   (b) $x \to \sec^2 x$;   (c) $x \to \sqrt{(\sec^2 x - 1)}$.

From the relation $\sin^2 x + \cos^2 x = 1$ deduce that $\sec^2 x - \tan^2 x = 1$. What result emerges from applying this result to (c)?

6. Use the chain rule to show that if $g = f^{-1}$ (i.e. gf is the identity function) and $b = f(a)$, then $g'(b) = 1/f'(a)$.

Assuming that the derivative of x^2 is $2x$, deduce that the derivative of $\sqrt{x}$ is $1/(2\sqrt{x})$.

There is a function f such that $f'(x) = f(x)$. If g is the inverse of this function, express $g'(x)$ in terms of x.

7. (i) Solve the particle problem of Section 1 by first expressing $f(t)$ as $4u^2 - \frac{1}{2}u + \frac{1}{2}$, where $u = \cos 2t$.

(ii) Intuitively, the speed will be least at a point where the acceleration vector is perpendicular to the velocity vector. Use this as an alternative method of solving the original problem.

2.3 Alternative statement of the chain rule. Using the notation shown in Figure 7, the average scale factor of the function $f: x \to y$ over the interval of length δx is

$$\frac{\delta y}{\delta x} = \frac{\delta y}{\delta u} \times \frac{\delta u}{\delta x}.$$

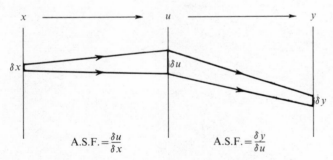

$$\text{A.S.F.} = \frac{\delta u}{\delta x} \qquad\qquad \text{A.S.F.} = \frac{\delta y}{\delta u}$$

Fig. 7

To find the value of the derived function, dy/dx, we have to consider the limit as $\delta x \to 0$; $\delta y/\delta x \to dy/dx$, $\delta y/\delta u \to dy/du$ and $\delta u/\delta x \to du/dx$ so it would be reasonable to conclude that

$$\frac{dy}{dx} = \frac{dy}{du} \times \frac{du}{dx}.$$

305

To prove the result formally, which we shall not attempt here, we have to cope with the limit of a product and also the possibility that δu might be zero even if $\delta x \neq 0$. (What difficulty would this create?)

It is important to realize that we could not have proved the result by 'cancelling' du in the same way that we can cancel δu in the expression for the average scale factor, because the symbol du has been given no meaning on its own. However, the du part of dy/du does act as a visual 'link' in the chain which could clearly be extended by further links, if necessary, to deal with more complicated functions, e.g.

$$\frac{dy}{dx} = \frac{dy}{du} \times \frac{du}{dv} \times \frac{dv}{dw} \times \frac{dw}{dx}.$$

Example 3

Differentiate
$$y = \frac{1}{(3x^2+4)^2}.$$

Put
$$y = \frac{1}{u^2} = u^{-2}, \quad \text{where} \quad u = 3x^2+4;$$

then
$$\frac{dy}{du} = -2u^{-3} \quad \text{and} \quad \frac{du}{dx} = 6x,$$

so
$$\frac{dy}{dx} = \frac{dy}{du} \times \frac{du}{dx} = \frac{-2}{u^3} \times 6x = \frac{-12x}{(3x^2+4)^3}.$$

2.4 Inverse functions. The result of Question 6 in the last exercise is of considerable importance and it is worth restating it here. If f and g are inverse functions so that $y = g(x) \Leftrightarrow x = f(y)$ then $g'(x) = 1/f'(y)$.

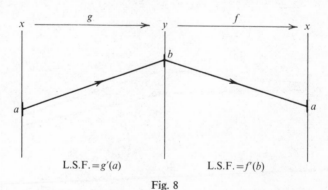

Fig. 8

This looks more obvious if it is expressed in Leibnitz notation. If x and y are connected by a relation so that y is a function of x and x is a function of y (that is, the relation is one–one), then

$$\frac{dy}{dx} = 1 \div \frac{dx}{dy}.$$

The graphical interpretation of the result is interesting. Figure 9 shows the graph of a function and its inverse; the graphs are reflection images of each other in the line $x = y$ so the gradient at P is the reciprocal of the gradient at Q, that is $g'(a) = 1/f'(b)$.

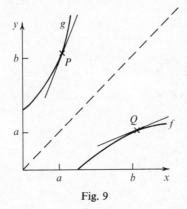

Fig. 9

As an example of the use of this result, consider how we can find the derivative of the cube root function from that of the cube function. For if

$$y = \sqrt[3]{x} \quad \text{then} \quad x = y^3$$

so
$$\frac{dx}{dy} = 3y^2;$$

thus
$$\frac{dy}{dx} = \frac{1}{3y^2} = \frac{1}{3\sqrt[3]{x^2}}.$$

2.5 Application of the chain rule to rates of change

Example 4

The radius of a circular puddle is growing at the rate of 1 centimetre per second. At what rate is the area growing when the radius is 1·4 metres?

Expressing the data symbolically we are told that

$$\frac{dr}{dt} = 0\cdot01 \quad \text{(units: metres, seconds)}$$

and we are asked to find dA/dt when $r = 1\cdot4$.

We have three related variables—t, r, A. We know the scale factor of the $t \to r$ function and wish to know the scale factor of the $t \to A$ function. But we know that A and r are connected by the relation $A = \pi r^2$. So $dA/dr = 2\pi r$, and by the chain rule,

$$\frac{dA}{dt} = \frac{dA}{dr} \times \frac{dr}{dt}$$

$$= 2\pi r \times 0\cdot01.$$

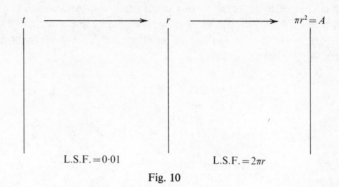

Fig. 10

When $r = 1.4$,

$$\frac{dA}{dt} = 2\pi \times 1.4 \times 0.01$$

$$= 0.088,$$

so the area is increasing at 0.088 m²/s.

Notice in this example that, since the radius is growing at a constant rate, it would be easy to express the radius in terms of the time and so to get the area explicitly in terms of the time (try this and show that you get the same answer); but the above method holds even if the radius is not growing at a constant rate – the essential information is the relation connecting the radius and the area. Notice also how, once we have proposed a mathematical model of the situation by expressing the data of the question symbolically, the chain rule answers the question for us.

Example 5

A slag heap has the shape of a cone with its radius roughly equal to its height. If slag is dropped onto it at the rate of 8 cubic metres per hour, find the rate of growth of the height when it is 10 m tall.

Data: $r = h$, $dV/dt = 8$ (units: cubic metres, hours).
Find: dh/dt when $h = 10$.

Because the slag heap is conical,

$$V = \tfrac{1}{3}\pi r^2 h = \tfrac{1}{3}\pi h^3,$$

which gives $dV/dh = \pi h^2.$

Show all the information so far on a mapping diagram.
By the chain rule,

$$\frac{dV}{dt} = \frac{dV}{dh} \times \frac{dh}{dt};$$

308

substitution gives $\qquad\qquad 8 = \pi h^2 \times \dfrac{dh}{dt}.$

When $h = 10$, $\qquad\qquad\qquad 8 = 100\pi \dfrac{dh}{dt},$

and so $\qquad\qquad\qquad\quad \dfrac{dh}{dt} = \dfrac{8}{100\pi} = 0\cdot025,$

i.e. the heap is growing taller at a rate of $2\cdot5$ cm per hour.

Exercise D

1. Find dy/dx for the following relations:

(a) $y = (3x+5)^3$; $\qquad\qquad\qquad$ (b) $y = (2-3x)^7$;

(c) $y = \surd(1-x)$; $\qquad\qquad\qquad$ (d) $y = \sin(4x+5)$;

(e) $y = \dfrac{1}{(3x-2)}$; $\qquad\qquad\qquad$ (f) $y = 4-3\cos 2x$;

(g) $y = \dfrac{3}{(6-4x)^2}.$

2. Differentiate

(a) $x \to \left(x - \dfrac{1}{x}\right)^4$; $\qquad\qquad$ (b) $x \to \dfrac{1}{x(x+1)}$;

(c) $x \to (x^3-1)^{\frac{1}{3}}$; $\qquad\qquad\qquad$ (d) $x \to \dfrac{1}{\surd(a^2+x^2)}.$

3. Find the x-coordinates of the points of the graph of $y = \cos^2 x$ for which $dy/dx = 0$ and find the corresponding values of y. Hence sketch the curve.

4. Find the gradient of the curve $y = \surd(25-x^2)$ at $(4, 3)$. Sketch the graph and explain the significance of the result.

5. Water is being poured into a conical glass of which the top diameter is equal to the height. If the depth is increasing at 2 cm per second when it is 8 cm deep, find the rate at which the water is being poured in.

6. The volume of a large balloon (assumed spherical) being blown up by a pump is increasing at a rate of $0\cdot2$ m³/s. Find the rate at which the radius is expanding when it is 3 m and also when it is 6 m. Discuss the assumptions that have been made in proposing your mathematical model.

7. The slag heap in Example 5 is growing taller at a rate of around 20 cm per 8-hour shift. Will it grow 200 cm in 10 shifts?

8. A solid cube of metal, mass 5 kg, has edges $0\cdot1$ m long which are expanding at the rate of 3×10^{-8} m/s because it is being heated. Find the rates at which the volume and the density are changing.

9. A ladder 13 metres long is resting against a wall with its foot on the ground x metres from the wall. If the top reaches h metres up the wall, obtain h as a function of x. If the foot is pulled away at a speed of $0\cdot4$ m/s, find the speed of the top when the bottom has been pulled out 5 m.

10. A wine glass is shaped so that, when the depth of wine is y cm, it contains roughly V cm³ of wine where $V = 20y^{\frac{3}{2}}$. Explain geometrically the significance of dV/dy and make a sketch of the wine glass.
[*Hint.* Try the same problem first with a cylindrical tumbler and with a conical glass.]

11. A particle moves round an ellipse so that its position at time t is given by $x = a \cos t$, $y = b \sin t$. Show that the points where the speed is greatest and least are at the ends of the axes of symmetry.

3. INTEGRATION BY THE CHAIN RULE

The work of the first part of this chapter has introduced a large variety of functions which can now be differentiated at sight or by formal application of the chain rule. Consequently, we can reverse the process and integrate many functions which previously we could not have tackled. It is worth realizing from the outset, however, that whereas we now have a method for differentiating any composite function (if we can differentiate the component functions), no such general method exists for integration.

Example 6

(i) Differentiate $f(x) = \sqrt{(x^2+1)^3}$.
(ii) Integrate $g(x) = x\sqrt{(x^2+1)}$.

(i) At sight, by the chain rule,

$$f'(x) = \tfrac{3}{2}(x^2+1)^{\frac{1}{2}} \times 2x = 3x\sqrt{(x^2+1)}.$$

(ii) We notice that $f'(x) = 3g(x)$, so

$$\int x\sqrt{(x^2+1)}\, dx = \frac{1}{3} \int 3x\sqrt{(x^2+1)}\, dx.$$

$$= \tfrac{1}{3}\sqrt{(x^2+1)^3} + k.$$

Exercise E

1. Find dy/dx for each of the following; write the answer down directly if you can.

(a) $y = (2x-1)^3$; (b) $y = \dfrac{1}{\sqrt{(3x-2)}}$; (c) $y = (3x^5-4)^4$;

(d) $y = \sin^3 x$; (e) $y = \dfrac{1}{1+x^2}$; (f) $y = \sqrt{(ax^2+bx+c)}$;

(g) $y = \dfrac{1}{\sin x}$.

Use the results to find the following integrals:

(a') $\displaystyle\int 2(2x-1)^2\, dx$; (b') $\displaystyle\int \frac{1}{\sqrt{(3x-2)^3}}\, dx$; (c') $\displaystyle\int x^4(3x^5-4)^3\, dx$;

(d') $\int \sin^2 x \cos x \, dx;$ $\qquad$ (e') $\int \dfrac{x}{(1+x^2)^2} \, dx;$ $\qquad$ (f') $\int \dfrac{x}{\sqrt{(x^2+1)}} \, dx;$

(g') $\int \dfrac{\sin x}{\cos^2 x} \, dx.$

2. Differentiate each of the following functions and then express the result in the form of an integral.

(a) $x \to (3x^2+1)^{10};$ $\qquad$ (b) $x \to \sqrt[3]{(1+x^3)};$ $\qquad$ (c) $x \to \sin(1/x);$

(d) $x \to \cos^4 x;$ $\qquad$ (e) $x \to \sqrt{(\sin x)};$ $\qquad$ (f) $x \to (2 - \cos x)^3.$

3. Make a guess at each of the following integrals. Then check your guess by differentiating it using the chain rule, and amend it if necessary.

(a) $\int 3x^2(x^3+2) \, dx;$ $\qquad$ (b) $\int x(x^2-7)^5 \, dx;$ $\qquad$ (c) $\int 3\sin^3 x \cos x \, dx;$

(d) $\int x\sqrt{(1-3x^2)} \, dx;$ $\qquad$ (e) $\int \dfrac{\cos x}{\sin^3 x} \, dx;$ $\qquad$ (f) $\int \cos x \sin x \, dx;$

(g) $\int \dfrac{x}{(1-x^2)^2} \, dx;$ $\qquad$ (h) $\int (\cos x + \sin x)(\cos x - \sin x)^2 \, dx.$

4. We know that
$$y = (2x+1)^3 + k \iff \frac{dy}{dx} = 6(2x+1)^2.$$

Does it follow that $\int (2x+1)^2 \, dx = \frac{1}{6}(2x+1)^3 + k$? Why?

We also know that
$$y = (x^2+1)^3 + k \iff \frac{dy}{dx} = 6x(x^2+1)^2.$$
Why does it not follow that
$$\int (x^2+1)^2 \, dx = \frac{1}{6x}(x^2+1)^3 + k?$$

5. Evaluate the following definite integrals:

(a) $\int_1^8 \dfrac{1}{\sqrt[3]{x^2}} \, dx;$ $\qquad$ (b) $\int_{-1}^1 \dfrac{x}{1+x^2} \, dx \cdot$ (use symmetry);

(c) $\int_0^1 x(2x^2+3)^3 \, dx.$

6. Find the following indefinite integrals:

(a) $\int (3x+5)^4 \, dx;$ $\qquad$ (b) $\int \sin(3x+\frac{1}{5}\pi) \, dx;$

(c) $\int \dfrac{1}{(1-5x)^3} \, dx;$ $\qquad$ (d) $\int \sqrt{(4+5x)} \, dx.$

7. Find the following indefinite integrals:

(a) $\int x^2 \cos(x^3) \, dx;$ $\qquad$ (b) $\int x^3(x+2) \, dx;$

(c) $\displaystyle\int x(x+2)^3\,dx;$

(d) $\displaystyle\int \frac{2x-3}{x^4}\,dx;$

(e) $\displaystyle\int \frac{1}{\sqrt{(6x-5)}}\,dx;$

(f) $\displaystyle\int (x+2)\sqrt{x}\,dx.$

8. Evaluate:

(a) $\displaystyle\int_0^4 x^{-\frac{1}{2}}\,dx;$

(b) $\displaystyle\int_0^{0\cdot3} x(1-x^2)^2\,dx;$

(c) $\displaystyle\int_0^3 x\sqrt{(x^2+16)}\,dx;$

(d) $\displaystyle\int_0^{\frac{1}{2}\pi} \sin x\cos^3 x\,dx;$

(e) $\displaystyle\int_0^{\frac{1}{2}} (4x+1)^3\,dx;$

(f) $\displaystyle\int_{-\pi}^{\pi} \sin^2 2x\cos 2x\,dx;$

(g) $\displaystyle\int_{1\cdot25}^{2\cdot60} x(x^2-1)^{-\frac{1}{2}}\,dx;$

(h) $\displaystyle\int_0^{0\cdot6} \frac{x}{\sqrt{(1-x^2)^3}}\,dx.$

4. INTEGRATION BY SUBSTITUTION

The method used in Section 3 depends on our ability to make an informed guess as to the answer and then use the chain rule to verify that guess by differentiation. An integral like $\int x(3x+1)^{\frac{1}{2}}\,dx$ cannot be found in this way, but there is another method also based upon reversing the chain rule. We first demonstrate this technique with definite integrals so that the main stage in the argument can be illustrated in terms of areas under graphs. In each example, we aim to replace a complicated integral by a simpler one which can be evaluated easily.

4.1 Transformation of areas. In Exercise A, Question 6, derivatives of composite functions were obtained by applying simple linear transformations to graphs of standard functions. The same method can be used to illustrate a method of finding the integrals of some composite functions.

Example 7

Evaluate
$$\int_1^2 \frac{1}{\sqrt{(3x-2)^3}}\,dx.$$

A primitive for this function has already been found in Exercise E, Question 1, but here we adopt a different approach. The function to be integrated is clearly composite, being of the form $u^{-\frac{3}{2}}$ where $u = 3x-2$, and this suggests the transformation to apply to the graph of

$$y = \frac{1}{\sqrt{(3x-2)^3}},$$

which is $\qquad (x, y) \to (u, y) \quad$ where $\quad u = 3x-2.$

312

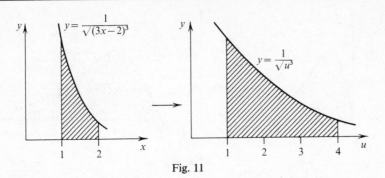

Fig. 11

Note especially that the interval [1, 2] maps onto the interval [1, 4]. Geometrically, the transformation is equivalent to a stretch with scale factor 3 away from the y-axis followed by a translation of 2 units to the left.

Thus, the area shaded (which represents the integral) has been trebled and we can therefore write

$$3 \int_1^2 \frac{1}{\sqrt{(3x-2)^3}} \, dx = \int_1^4 u^{-\frac{3}{2}} \, du.$$

The latter integral can be evaluated easily, so

$$\int_1^2 \frac{1}{\sqrt{(3x-2)^3}} \, dx = \frac{1}{3} \int_1^4 u^{-\frac{3}{2}} \, du$$

$$= \frac{1}{3} \left[-2u^{-\frac{1}{2}} \right]_1^4$$

$$= \tfrac{1}{3}(-2 \times \tfrac{1}{2} + 2 \times 1)$$

$$= \tfrac{1}{3}.$$

Example 8

Evaluate
$$\int_0^2 \frac{x}{(2x+1)^4} \, dx.$$

Although this is not expressible simply as a composite function, the same method can be applied. Putting $u = 2x+1$, i.e. inversely, $x = \frac{1}{2}(u-1)$, the graph of the function is transformed as in Figure 12. This transformation is a stretch with scale factor 2 and a translation so that the area has been doubled and hence

$$\int_0^2 \frac{x}{(2x+1)^4} \, dx = \frac{1}{2} \int_1^5 \frac{\frac{1}{2}(u-1)}{u^4} \, du$$

$$= \frac{1}{4} \int_1^5 (u^{-3} - u^{-4}) \, du$$

$$= \frac{1}{4} \left[-\tfrac{1}{2}u^{-2} + \tfrac{1}{3}u^{-3} \right]_1^5$$

$$= \tfrac{14}{375}.$$

313

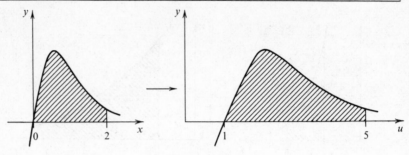

Fig. 12

Notice again how the limits of the integral are changed as the interval [0, 2] maps onto the interval [1, 5].

Exercise F

1. Why does $\int_5^6 \dfrac{x+2}{(x-4)^4}\,dx$ equal $\int_1^2 \dfrac{u+6}{u^4}\,du$?

Find the value of the latter integral.

2. Use the method of Example 8, with rough sketches of the graphs, to evaluate

$$\int_0^1 x\sqrt{(3x+1)}\,dx.$$

3. Sketch the ellipse given by the relation $\dfrac{x^2}{9}+\dfrac{y^2}{4}=1$.

What linear transformation on x (express this algebraically as well as geometrically) will change the ellipse into a circle? Find the area enclosed by the ellipse. Generalize this result to find a formula for the area of an ellipse with greatest diameter $2a$ and least diameter $2b$.

From the original relation, express y as a function of x (restricting consideration to positive values of x and y only). What integral can then be evaluated from the first result?

4. What geometric transformations change $\displaystyle\int_2^3 \sin \pi(x-2)\,dx$ into $\displaystyle c\int_a^b \sin u\,du$ for suitable values (to be stated) of a, b and c? Evaluate the integral.

5. What geometric transformations change $\displaystyle\int_{-1}^1 \dfrac{x}{(4-3x)^3}\,dx$ into $\displaystyle c\int_a^b \dfrac{4-u}{3u^3}\,du$? State the values of a, b and c and evaluate the integral.

6. Sketch the graph of $y=\dfrac{1}{x^2+4}$. Given that $\displaystyle\int_0^3 \dfrac{1}{x^2+4}\,dx=0\cdot49$, find

(a) $\displaystyle\int_0^1 \dfrac{1}{9x^2+4}\,dx$; (b) $\displaystyle\int_0^{1\cdot5} \dfrac{1}{x^2+1}\,dx$;

(c) $\displaystyle\int_{-1}^2 \dfrac{1}{(x+1)^2+4}\,dx$; (d) $\displaystyle\int_1^4 \dfrac{1}{x^2-2x+5}\,dx$.

Sketch graphs to illustrate the transformation involved in each case.

314

7. Given that $\int_0^1 \dfrac{x}{1+x}\,dx = 0\cdot307$, find other integrals by the following transformations; in each case state the new integral and its value.

(a) Translation 1 to the right.
(b) Stretch with scale factor 2 from the y-axis.
(c) (a) followed by (b).
(d) (b) followed by (a).
(e) Reflection in $x = \frac{1}{2}$.

4.2 Deductions from the chain rule. In each of the examples of Section 4.1, we have in effect used the chain rule in reverse, and an alternative way of illustrating the process is on a mapping diagram. The method applies equally well to definite or indefinite integrals.

Example 9

Find the indefinite integral

$$\int \frac{x}{(2x+1)^4}\,dx.$$

(i) We have the derived function of some unknown function. This we choose to consider as the combination of two simpler functions, the first of which is $x \to 2x+1$. We write $2x+1 = u$, as in Example 8.

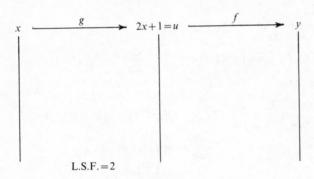

L.S.F. = 2

Fig. 13

We are given the derivative, $x/(2x+1)^4$, for the composite function fg, and since by the chain rule this is equal to $2 \times f'(u)$, we obtain

$$f'(u) = \frac{1}{2} \times \frac{x}{(2x+1)^4} = \frac{1}{2} \times \frac{\frac{1}{2}(u-1)}{u^4}$$

$$= \tfrac{1}{4}(u^{-3} - u^{-4}).$$

Hence f maps u onto $\ \tfrac{1}{4}(-\tfrac{1}{2}u^{-2} + \tfrac{1}{3}u^{-3}) + k,\ $ for some k. It follows that fg maps x onto $\ \tfrac{1}{4}(-\tfrac{1}{2}(2x+1)^{-2} + \tfrac{1}{3}(2x+1)^{-3}) + k.\ $ Compare the ways $du/dx = 2$ enters the working here and in Example 8.

315

(ii) We might prefer a more abstract format using the alternative notation:

$$y = \int \frac{x}{(2x+1)^4}\, dx \Leftrightarrow \frac{dy}{dx} = \frac{x}{(2x+1)^4}.$$

If we put $u = 2x+1$, $\dfrac{du}{dx} = 2$.

Also, by the chain rule, $\dfrac{dy}{dx} = \dfrac{dy}{du} \times \dfrac{du}{dx}$,

so that $\dfrac{dy}{du} \times 2 = \dfrac{x}{(2x+1)^4} = \dfrac{\frac{1}{2}(u-1)}{u^4}.$

Hence $\dfrac{dy}{du} = \frac{1}{4}(u^{-3} - u^{-4}),$

$$y = \tfrac{1}{4}(-\tfrac{1}{2}u^{-2} + \tfrac{1}{3}u^{-3}) + k$$
$$= \tfrac{1}{4}(-\tfrac{1}{2}(2x+1)^{-2} + \tfrac{1}{3}(2x+1)^{-3}) + k.$$

More complicated substitutions can be carried out in the same way.

Example 10

Find $\displaystyle\int x^3\sqrt{(x^2-1)}\, dx.$

If we put $u = x^2 - 1$, then $du/dx = 2x$.

Now $y = \displaystyle\int x^3\sqrt{(x^2-1)}\, dx \Leftrightarrow \dfrac{dy}{dx} = x^3\sqrt{(x^2-1)}.$

It follows that

$$\frac{dy}{du} \times \frac{du}{dx} = \frac{dy}{du} \times 2x = x^3\sqrt{(x^2-1)} = \tfrac{1}{2}x^2\sqrt{(x^2-1)} \times 2x,$$

and hence $\dfrac{dy}{du} = \tfrac{1}{2}(u+1)\, u^{\frac{1}{2}}$

$$= \tfrac{1}{2}u^{\frac{3}{2}} + \tfrac{1}{2}u^{\frac{1}{2}}.$$

Therefore $y = \tfrac{1}{5}u^{\frac{5}{2}} + \tfrac{1}{3}u^{\frac{3}{2}} + k$

$$= \tfrac{1}{5}(x^2-1)^{\frac{5}{2}} + \tfrac{1}{3}(x^2-1)^{\frac{3}{2}} + k.$$

Our first aim is to obtain an expression for dy/du in terms of u. It usually pays, as on this occasion, to extract a factor equal to du/dx before proceeding with the substitution.

Exercise G

1. Use the method of Section 4.2 with the suggested substitutions to evaluate the following integrals. The final answers should, of course, be functions of x, not of u.

(a) $\int x(x+4)^3 \, dx, \quad u = x+4;$ (b) $\int x\sqrt{(2x+3)} \, dx, \quad u = 2x+3;$

(c) $\int x(5-x^2)^3 \, dx, \quad u = 5-x^2;$ (d) $\int 4x^3(x^2+1)^3 \, dx, \quad u = x^2+1;$

(e) $\int \dfrac{\sin\sqrt{x}}{\sqrt{x}} \, dx, \quad u = \sqrt{x};$ (f) $\int x^3\sqrt{(1-x^2)} \, dx, \quad u = 1-x^2;$

(g) $\int \dfrac{\sin x}{\cos^2 x} \, dx, \quad u = \cos x.$

4.3   Shortened form of presentation. The original integral in Example 10 could be written as

$$\int \tfrac{1}{2}x^2\sqrt{(x^2-1)} \times 2x \, dx.$$

After the substitution $u = x^2-1$, the problem was changed to that of finding

$$\int \tfrac{1}{2}(u+1) \sqrt{u} \, du.$$

The substitution method seems to be equivalent to replacing the expression $(du/dx) \, dx$ by du and writing the rest of the integrand in terms of the new variable u.

This is quite general. Suppose we are trying to find $y = \int f(x) \, dx$ where we can express $f(x)$ in the form

$$g(u) \times \frac{du}{dx} \quad (u \text{ being a function of } x),$$

then
$$y = \int g(u) \times \frac{du}{dx} \, dx;$$

so
$$\frac{dy}{dx} = g(u) \times \frac{du}{dx}.$$

But
$$\frac{dy}{dx} = \frac{dy}{du} \times \frac{du}{dx}.$$

Comparing these, we find
$$\frac{dy}{du} = g(u),$$

so
$$y = \int g(u) \, du.$$

That is,
$$\int f(x) \, dx = \int g(u) \frac{du}{dx} \, dx = \int g(u) \, du.$$

If therefore we can recognize an appropriate u, we may replace the expression $(du/dx)\,dx$ by du and carry out the integration with respect to u.

Example 11

Find
$$\int \sin^4 x \cos^3 x \, dx.$$

Substitute $u = \sin x$, giving $du/dx = \cos x$. Replace $\cos x\, dx$ by du. This leaves $\sin^4 x \cos^2 x$ which can be written entirely in terms of u if we recollect that $\sin^2 x + \cos^2 x = 1$.

$$\int \sin^4 x \cos^3 x \, dx = \int \sin^4 x \cos^2 x \cos x \, dx$$

$$= \int \sin^4 x (1 - \sin^2 x) \cos x \, dx$$

$$= \int u^4 (1 - u^2) \, du$$

$$= \tfrac{1}{5} u^5 - \tfrac{1}{7} u^7 + k$$

$$= \tfrac{1}{5} \sin^5 x - \tfrac{1}{7} \sin^7 x + k.$$

This example demonstrates the most concise format for the working. If you are in doubt as to how and why the method works, it is better to return to the earlier ways of writing out the intermediate steps.

It should be realized that the method does not of itself evaluate the integral—it replaces the integral by another integral so that it is only valuable if the substitution was such that the second integral is more tractable than the first. Picking an appropriate u for substitution is a matter of experience; the thing to look for is the occurrence of a function together with its derivative.

4.4 Substitution in definite integrals. The work of Section 4.1 on transformation of areas showed that when a definite integral is transformed by making a substitution the interval of integration is also transformed.

Example 12

Find
$$\int_0^1 \frac{6x}{(2x+1)^3} \, dx.$$

Put
$$u = 2x+1, \quad \text{so} \quad \frac{du}{dx} = 2.$$

Replace $2dx$ by du.

318

The interval $0 \leqslant x \leqslant 1$ maps onto the interval $1 \leqslant u \leqslant 3$.

$$\int_0^1 \frac{6x}{(2x+1)^3}\,dx = \int_1^3 \frac{3 \times \frac{1}{2}(u-1)}{u^3}\,du \quad (\text{since } x = \tfrac{1}{2}(u-1))$$

$$= \frac{3}{2}\int_1^3 (u^{-2}-u^{-3})\,du$$

$$\frac{3}{2}\left[-u^{-1}+\tfrac{1}{2}u^{-2}\right]_1^3$$

$$= \tfrac{3}{2}(-\tfrac{1}{3}+\tfrac{1}{18})-\tfrac{3}{2}(-1+\tfrac{1}{2})$$

$$= \tfrac{1}{3}.$$

Notice in this example that, for a definite integral, there is no need to substitute back to the original variable after the integration has been carried out: the value of the integral is a function of the limits of the interval of integration, not of the variable.

Exercise H

1. Use the given substitutions to evaluate the following integrals.

   (a) $\int x\sqrt{(1+3x)}\,dx$, $u = 1+3x$;

   (b) $\int 4x(x^2+1)^3\,dx$, $u = x^2+1$;

   (c) $\int (1+x)(4-3x)^2\,dx$, $u = 4-3x$;

   (d) $\int 6x^3(x^2-2)\,dx$, $u = x^2-2$;

   (e) $\int 6x^2\sqrt{(x^3-2)}\,dx$, $u = x^3-2$.

2. Evaluate

   (a) $\int (x+3)(5-2x)^4\,dx$;   (b) $\int x\sqrt[3]{(2x-1)}\,dx$;

   (c) $\int x\sqrt[3]{(2x^2-1)}\,dx$;   (d) $\int \sin 2x \cos^3 2x\,dx$;

   (e) $\int (a\cos x + b\sin x)(b\cos x - a\sin x)\,dx$.

3. Evaluate the following integrals:

   (a) $\displaystyle\int_0^{\frac{1}{4}\pi} \cos^3 x \sin x\,dx$;   (b) $\displaystyle\int_0^{0\cdot6} \frac{x^3}{\sqrt{(1-x^2)}}\,dx$;

   (c) $\displaystyle\int_0^1 x^5(1-x^3)^4\,dx$;   (d) $\displaystyle\int_{\frac{1}{4}\pi}^{\frac{1}{2}\pi} \frac{\cos^3 x}{\sqrt{(\sin x)}}\,dx$.

4. Evaluate the following integrals:

   (a) $\displaystyle\int_0^2 x\sqrt{(1+2x^2)}\,dx$;   (b) $\displaystyle\int_{\frac{1}{2}}^1 \frac{x-1}{(x^2-2x)^2}\,dx$;

   (c) $\displaystyle\int_0^1 \sin x \cos x\,dx$;   (d) $\displaystyle\int_{-2}^{-1} x(3+2x)^7\,dx$;

   (e) $\displaystyle\int_{-2}^{-1} (2+3x)(3+2x)^7\,dx$.

319

5. Use the substitution $u = \sin x$ to evaluate $\int \cos x \sin x \, dx$.
Evaluate the same integral by using the substitution $v = \cos x$. Can you explain the discrepancy between the answers?

6. Discover which of the following integrals you can simplify by a suitable substitution and evaluate them. (Leave the others alone!)

(a) $\int \dfrac{x+3}{\sqrt{(2x+1)}} \, dx;$ (b) $\int \sin x \sqrt{(\cos x)} \, dx;$ (c) $\int x^2 \sin x \, dx;$

(d) $\int \dfrac{x^3}{\sqrt{(1+x^2)}} \, dx;$ (e) $\int \dfrac{x^2}{\sqrt{(1+x^2)}} \, dx;$ (f) $\int x \sqrt{(x^3+1)} \, dx.$

(The fact that the method of substitution does not help does not imply that the integrals cannot be found by other methods.)

7. Use whatever method you consider most appropriate to evaluate the following integrals.

(a) $\displaystyle\int_{-1}^{1} (x^3+1)^2 \, dx;$ (b) $\displaystyle\int_{-1}^{1} x(1+x)^5 \, dx;$

(c) $\displaystyle\int_{-1}^{1} x^2(x^3+1)^4 \, dx;$ (d) $\displaystyle\int_{-1}^{1} \sin x \, dx;$

(e) $\displaystyle\int_{-1}^{1} x^2 \sin x \, dx;$ (f) $\displaystyle\int_{0}^{3} x^2 \sqrt{(4-x)} \, dx;$

(g) $\displaystyle\int_{0}^{\frac{1}{2}\pi} \sin 2x \sqrt{(1-\cos 2x)} \, dx;$ (h) $\displaystyle\int_{0}^{\frac{1}{2}\pi} \sqrt{(1-\cos 2x)} \, dx.$

4.5 Substituting $x = f(u)$

Example 13

Find
$$\int_{0}^{\frac{1}{2}} \frac{1}{\sqrt{(1-x^2)}} \, dx.$$

The substitution $u = 1-x^2$ fails on this occasion (see Exercise I, Question 9). An alternative is suggested by the fact that $1 - \sin^2 u = \cos^2 u$.

Put $x = \sin u$, where $0 \leqslant u \leqslant \frac{1}{2}\pi$. The restriction on the values of u makes the transformation one–one, and the interval $0 \leqslant x \leqslant \frac{1}{2}$ then maps onto the interval $0 \leqslant u \leqslant \frac{1}{6}\pi$.

In previous examples we have obtained du/dx in terms of x, and this has played an important role in the substitution method. Here we can more easily start by writing dx/du in terms of u. In fact $dx/du = \cos u$.

We proceed by adapting the original way of reversing the chain rule.

$$\frac{dy}{dx} = \frac{1}{\sqrt{(1-x^2)}},$$

$$\frac{dy}{du} = \frac{dy}{dx} \times \frac{dx}{du} = \frac{1}{\sqrt{(1-\sin^2 u)}} \times \cos u.$$

320

Hence
$$y = \int_0^{\frac{1}{6}\pi} \frac{1}{\cos u} \times \cos u \, du$$

$$= \int_0^{\frac{1}{6}\pi} 1 \, du$$

$$= \left[u \right]_0^{\frac{1}{6}\pi}$$

$$= \tfrac{1}{6}\pi.$$

In general, when a substitution is more conveniently expressed in the form $x = f(u)$, the correct transformed integral is given by replacing dx by $(dx/du) \, du$.

Example 14

Find
$$\int x\sqrt{(x+1)} \, dx.$$

In order to eliminate the square root, substitute $x+1 = u^2$, i.e. $x = u^2 - 1$ (where we may stipulate $u \geqslant 0$ for a one-one transformation). Then $dx/du = 2u$, so replace dx by $2u \, du$. This gives

$$\int x\sqrt{(x+1)} \, dx = \int (u^2 - 1) \, u 2u \, du$$

$$= \int (2u^4 - 2u^2) \, du$$

$$= \tfrac{2}{5}u^5 - \tfrac{2}{3}u^3 + k$$

$$= \tfrac{2}{15}u^3(3u^2 - 5) + k$$

$$= \tfrac{2}{15}(3x - 2) \sqrt{(x+1)^3} + k.$$

4.6 Formal derivation of the method. The method is best understood by its use in examples but it can be derived (as in Section 4.3) from the chain rule. For if

$$y = \int g(x) \, dx \quad \text{where} \quad x = f(u),$$

then
$$\frac{dy}{dx} = g(x)$$

$$= gf(u).$$

But
$$\frac{dy}{du} = \frac{dy}{dx} \times \frac{dx}{du} \quad \text{(chain rule)}$$

$$= gf(u) \times \frac{dx}{du}$$

$$\Rightarrow \quad y = \int gf(u) \times \frac{dx}{du} \, du.$$

There are thus, in effect, two forms of the method of integration by substitution:

(a) substitute $u = f(x)$, replacing $\dfrac{du}{dx}\, dx$ by du;

(b) substitute $x = f(u)$, replacing dx by $\dfrac{dx}{du}\, du$.

In both cases, for a definite integral, also replace the limits of the interval of integration.

The following exercise is mostly concerned with method (b).

Exercise I

Throughout this exercise, it should be assumed that the domain of u is restricted so that the transformation $x \leftrightarrow u$ is one–one.

1. Evaluate the following integrals, using the suggested substitutions:
   (a) $\int x(x+1)^3\, dx$; $x = u-1$;   (b) $\int x\sqrt{(1-x)}\, dx$; $x = 1-u^2$;
   (c) $\int (x+1)\sqrt{(x+2)}\, dx$; $x = u^2-2$.

2. Evaluate the following definite integrals, using the suggested substitutions:
   (a) $\displaystyle\int_0^{\frac{1}{2}} \frac{1}{\sqrt{(1-x^2)}}\, dx$; $x = \cos u$;   (b) $\displaystyle\int_0^1 \frac{1}{\sqrt{(4-x^2)}}\, dx$; $x = 2\sin u$;

   (c) $\displaystyle\int_{\frac{1}{2}}^{\frac{3}{4}} \frac{1}{\sqrt{(x-x^2)}}\, dx$; $x = \frac{1}{2}(1+\sin u)$;   (d) $\displaystyle\int_0^{\frac{1}{4}} \frac{1}{\sqrt{(1-4x^2)}}\, dx$; $x = \frac{1}{2}\sin u$.

3. Evaluate $\displaystyle\int_0^1 \frac{x}{\sqrt{(9-x^2)}}\, dx$ by two methods,
   (i) by substituting $x = $ a suitable trigonometric function of u;
   (ii) by substituting $u = $ a suitable algebraic function of x.

4. Show that $\int \cos^2\theta\, d\theta = \frac{1}{2}\theta + \frac{1}{4}\sin 2\theta + k$. Use this result and the given substitutions to evaluate the following integrals:

   (a) $\displaystyle\int_0^1 \sqrt{(1-x^2)}\, dx$; $x = \sin u$;   (b) $\displaystyle\int_0^{\frac{1}{2}} \sqrt{\left(\frac{x}{1-x}\right)}\, dx$; $x = \cos^2 u$;

   (c) $\displaystyle\int_0^{\frac{1}{2}} \sqrt{\left(\frac{1+x}{1-x}\right)}\, dx$; $x = \cos 2u$ (use the double angle formulae).

5. Evaluate the following integrals:
   (a) $\displaystyle\int_0^{\frac{1}{2}} \frac{1}{\sqrt{(1-x^2)}}\, dx$;   (b) $\displaystyle\int_0^2 \frac{2}{\sqrt{(9-x^2)}}\, dx$;   (c) $\displaystyle\int_0^{\frac{1}{2}} \frac{x^2}{\sqrt{(1-x^2)}}\, dx$;

   (d) $\displaystyle\int_0^{\frac{1}{2}} \frac{1}{\sqrt{(1-2x^2)}}\, dx$;   (e) $\displaystyle\int_0^2 \sqrt{(4-x^2)}\, dx$;   (f) $\displaystyle\int_0^1 \frac{1}{\sqrt{(4-3x^2)}}\, dx$.

6. Why are the following meaningless:

   (a) $\displaystyle\int_0^2 \frac{1}{(1-x)^2}\, dx$;   (b) $\displaystyle\int_2^3 \frac{1}{\sqrt{(1-x^2)}}\, dx$?

7. Use the substitution $x = 8\cos^2 u + \sin^2 u$ to evaluate $\displaystyle\int_3^5 \frac{1}{\sqrt{((8-x)(x-1))}}\,dx.$
Use a similar method to evaluate

(a) $\displaystyle\int_3^4 \frac{1}{\sqrt{((5-x)(x-2))}}\,dx;$ (b) $\displaystyle\int_2^4 \frac{1}{\sqrt{(6x-x^2-5)}}\,dx.$

8. Use the substitution $x+1 = \sin u$, i.e. $x = \sin u - 1$, to evaluate

$$\int \frac{1}{\sqrt{(1-(x+1)^2)}}\,dx.$$

Use a similar method to evaluate

(a) $\displaystyle\int \frac{1}{\sqrt{(1-(1-x)^2)}}\,dx;$ (b) $\displaystyle\int \frac{1}{\sqrt{(4-(3x+1)^2)}}\,dx;$

(c) $\displaystyle\int \frac{1}{\sqrt{(6x-x^2-5)}}\,dx.$

9. The substitution used in Example 13 is hardly obvious at first sight. Try to evaluate the integral using the apparently more elementary substitution $u = 1-x^2$. Also try $u = \sqrt{(1-x^2)}$. Are these substitutions helpful in evaluating

(a) $\displaystyle\int_0^1 \sqrt{(1-x^2)}\,dx;$ (b) $\displaystyle\int_0^1 x\sqrt{(1-x^2)}\,dx;$

(c) $\displaystyle\int_0^1 x^2\sqrt{(1-x^2)}\,dx;$ (d) $\displaystyle\int_0^1 x^3\sqrt{(1-x^2)}\,dx?$

4.7 Transformation of areas with variable scale factor. In Section 4.1, the method of integration by substitution was illustrated by considering linear transformations, i.e. those with constant scale factors, graphically. This section illustrates the method where the scale factor is variable, but it should not be taken as a proof of the method.

The notation for the definite integral $\displaystyle\int_a^b f(x)\,dx$ was introduced from considering the area under the graph of $y = f(x)$ as the limit of the sum of the areas of rectangular regions. If this graph is transformed by a substitution such as $(x, y) \to (u, y)$ where $u = x^2$, with inverse form $x = \sqrt{u}$, the transformation could be considered as a stretch parallel to the x-axis with a *variable* scale factor $du/dx = 2x.$

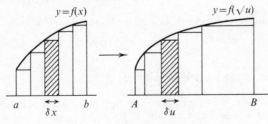

Fig. 14

323

Each interval is enlarged by a factor which will be the local scale factor of the transformation at some point within that interval, so

$$\delta u = \frac{du}{dx} \times \delta x;$$

or, from the inverse transformation,

$$\delta x = \frac{dx}{du} \times \delta u.$$

The shaded rectangular areas are clearly changed by the same factor, that is

$$f(x) \times \delta x = f(\sqrt{u}) \times \frac{dx}{du} \times \delta u.$$

Taking the sum of the rectangular regions over the interval $[a, b]$

$$\overset{x=b}{\underset{x=a}{\mathrm{S}}} {}' f(x) \times \delta x = \overset{u=B}{\underset{u=A}{\mathrm{S}}} f(\sqrt{u}) \times \frac{dx}{du} \delta u,$$

where $A = a^2$ and $B = b^2$. (Strictly, here, $f(\sqrt{u})$ and dx/du are calculated for different but approximately equal values of u.)

This suggests a limiting form which is the integral result

$$\int_a^b f(x)\, dx = \int_A^B f(\sqrt{u}) \frac{dx}{du}\, du.$$

In general, for the transformation given by $x = g(u)$,

$$\int_a^b f(x)\, dx = \int_A^B fg(u) \frac{dx}{du}\, du.$$

Miscellaneous Exercise

1. Find the points where a particle whose coordinates are $x = \cos 2t$, $y = \sin t$ is furthest from the origin.

2. The position vector of a particle at time t is $\begin{pmatrix} a\cos t \\ a\sin t \end{pmatrix}$.

What is the velocity vector and the direction of motion?

3. Repeat Question 2 for particles with position vectors

(a) $\begin{pmatrix} a\cos^2 t \\ a\sin^2 t \end{pmatrix}$;   (b) $\begin{pmatrix} a\cos^3 t \\ a\sin^3 t \end{pmatrix}$.

Sketch the path of the particle for all three cases.

4. If the path of the particle in Question 3(b) is stretched parallel to the y-axis, it is given by $x = a\cos^3 t$, $y = b\sin^3 t$. Find the point of this curve which is closest to the origin when $a = 9$, $b = 16$.

5. Figure 15 shows the path of a particle with position vector $\begin{pmatrix} t - \sin t \\ 2(1 - \cos t) \end{pmatrix}$ at time t. Write down the velocity and acceleration vectors of the particle and mark them on a copy of the figure at time intervals of $\frac{1}{4}\pi$. Find the points where the speed is greatest and mark on the diagram the parts of the path where the particle is slowing down.

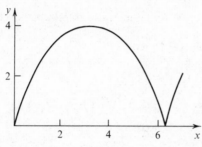

Fig. 15

6. What is $\displaystyle\lim_{b \to a} \frac{\sin b - \sin a}{b - a}$?

Find the derivative of $\sin^2 x$ at $x = a$ from first principles.
[*Hint.* Factorize $\sin^2 b - \sin^2 a$ as $(\sin b - \sin a)(\sin b + \sin a)$.]

7. Generalize the method of Question 6 to show that the derivative of $(f(x))^2$ is $2f(x)f'(x)$. Show that this is a special case of the chain rule.

8. What is $\displaystyle\lim_{b \to a} \frac{f(b^2) - f(a^2)}{b^2 - a^2}$?

Use the chain rule to differentiate $g(x) = f(x^2)$. Obtain the same result from first principles.

9. (*a*) Differentiate $\cos 8x$ with respect to x.
   (*b*) Differentiate $1/2y^2$ with respect to y.
   (*c*) Differentiate $\sqrt{(p^2 + 2)}$ with respect to p.
   (*d*) Discuss differentiating x^2 with respect to y.
   (*e*) If $y^2 = 1 + x^2$, find dy/dx in terms of x and y without taking any square roots.

10. Use a diagram to show that

$$\int_0^{\frac{1}{2}\pi} \sin^2 x \, dx = \int_0^{\frac{1}{2}\pi} \cos^2 x \, dx$$

and hence find the value of each of these integrals by adding them together.

11. Apply suitable stretch and translation transformations to simplify

$$\int_0^{2\pi} (x - \pi) \cos \frac{x - \pi}{2} \, dx$$

and illustrate by sketches. Write down the value of the simplified integral and hence evaluate

$$\int_0^{2\pi} x \cos \frac{x - \pi}{2} \, dx.$$

325

12. The Beta function is defined as $B(m, n) = \int_0^1 x^{m-1}(1-x)^{n-1}\, dx$. What transformation shows that $B(m, n) = B(n, m)$?

What similar integral can be related to $B(m, n)$ by the stretch $x \to kx$?

13. Use a sketch to show that $\int_0^{\frac{1}{2}\pi} \sin x\, dx = \int_0^{\frac{1}{2}\pi} \cos x\, dx$. What transformation demonstrates this? Apply the same transformation to $\int_0^{\frac{1}{2}\pi} x \sin^2 x\, dx$ and hence find the value of $\int_0^{\frac{1}{2}\pi} \cos^2 x\, dx$.

[*Hint.* $\sin^2 x + \cos^2 x = 1$.]

14. Integrate

(a) $\int f(x) f'(x)\, dx$;   (b) $\int f'(x) \sqrt{(f(x))}\, dx$.

15. Integrate $\int \cos x f'(\sin x)\, dx$.

Evaluate:

(a) $\int_0^{\frac{1}{2}\pi} \cos x(1 + \sin x + \sin^2 x)\, dx$;

(b) $\int_0^{\frac{1}{2}\pi} \cos x \sqrt{(1 - \sin x)}\, dx$.

16. The road from Ayton to Beevill is 2 km long, straight across the moor. A man who lives at a cottage 1 km from the road on a track which crosses the road (at right angles) at Beevill goes to work in Ayton. He can push his bike over the moor at 5 km/h and he can cycle at 16 km/h. Where should he join the road in order to get to work in the least time?

SUMMARY

Chain rule for differentiating a composite function

   (i) If $h = gf$ and $b = f(a)$,

then $h'(a) = g'(b) \times f'(a)$.

   (ii) If $x \overset{f}{\to} u \overset{g}{\to} y$,

then $\dfrac{dy}{dx} = \dfrac{dy}{du} \times \dfrac{du}{dx}$.

Inverse functions

If $g = f^{-1}$ and $f(a) = b$,

then $g'(b) = \dfrac{1}{f'(a)}$.

This may be written $\dfrac{dx}{dy} = 1 \div \dfrac{dy}{dx}$.

326

Integration by substitution

   (*a*) Substitute $u = f(x)$,   replacing $\dfrac{du}{dx}\, dx$ by du;

   (*b*) Substitute $x = f(u)$, replacing dx by $\dfrac{dx}{du}\, du$.

In both cases, for a definite integral, also replace the limits of the interval of integration.

14

VECTOR GEOMETRY

1. THREE DIMENSIONAL GEOMETRY

We have already used vectors to describe displacements, velocities, accelerations and forces. Vector methods are also effective for solving some geometrical problems concerning lines, planes, curves and surfaces.

Exercise A

All the questions of this exercise refer to Figure 1 in which **a**, **b** and **c** are vectors from the origin *O*. They form three edges of the parallelepiped *OADBCGFE*.

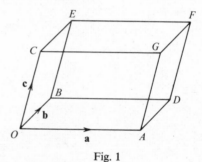

Fig. 1

1. Write down in terms of **a**, **b**, **c** the position vectors of the points *D*, *E*, *F* and *G*. Also write down the position vectors of the midpoints of *OA*, *OD*, *OE*, *AD*, *CF* and *EG*.

2. Identify the points with position vectors given by:

(*a*) $\mathbf{a} + \frac{1}{3}\mathbf{b}$; (*b*) $\mathbf{b} + \frac{2}{3}\mathbf{c}$; (*c*) $\mathbf{a} + \mathbf{c} + \frac{1}{3}\mathbf{b}$; (*d*) $\frac{1}{3}\mathbf{a} + \frac{2}{3}\mathbf{b}$.

3. Write down the position vectors of three points along *OA*. Does the point with position vector 56**a** lie on *OA*? Suggest a general form for all points on *OA*.

4. Suggest a general form for the position vectors of points along the line *AD*. [*Hint.* Look at the points you already know lie on the line, make up a few more and see the pattern that emerges.]

5. Repeat Question 4 for the lines *OD*, *BE*, *AC*.

6. List the position vectors of six points that lie in the plane *OADB*; suggest a general form for the position vector **r** of a point lying in the plane *OADB*.

328

7. Repeat Question 6 for the planes *OBEC*, *ADFG*. How is the fact that these planes are parallel accounted for in your general forms for the planes?

8. List the position vectors of several points in the plane *BAGE*. Can you suggest the general form of the position vector of a point in this plane? Does the point with position vector $\frac{2}{3}\mathbf{a} + \frac{1}{2}\mathbf{b} + 75\mathbf{c}$ lie in this plane?

2. PLANES THROUGH THE ORIGIN

Suppose we now simplify the situation and begin by looking at just two vectors, **a** and **b** as in Figure 2. In Exercise A, we discovered that points in the plane *OAB* had position vectors of the form $\lambda\mathbf{a} + \mu\mathbf{b}$ (where λ and μ are real numbers). We should be able to reach every point in the plane *OAB* by starting from *O* and taking multiples of **a** and **b**.

Copy Figure 2, marking in the points *D*, *E*, *F* and *G* approximately as in the figure. Now obtain the position vector of each point as the sum of two vectors in the directions of **a** and **b** and finally calculate the corresponding values of λ and μ.

In which of these cases is (i) λ negative, (ii) μ negative? Can you say in which part of the plane a point lies if you know that λ is positive and μ negative?

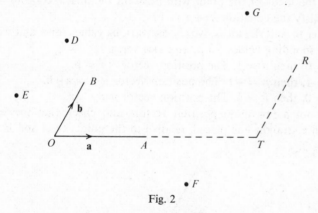

Fig. 2

We find that we can reach any point *R* in the plane *OAB* simply by drawing lines *OT* along *OA* and *TR* parallel to *OB* (see Figure 2). So we can say that, in general, a point *R* in the plane must have a position vector **r** such that
$$\mathbf{r} = \lambda\mathbf{a} + \mu\mathbf{b},$$
where λ and μ are two real numbers called *scalar parameters*. This is the *vector equation* of the plane through *O* 'containing' the vectors **a** and **b**. Referring back to Figure 1, write down the equations of the planes *OAC* and *OBC* in the form
$$\mathbf{r} = \lambda(\text{some vector}) + \mu(\text{some vector}).$$

(We shall use λ, μ and ν (lambda, mu and nu) as general symbols like x, y and z. As before, we shall usually write **p** as the position vector of P relative to an origin O, **q** as the position vector of Q, etc.)

2.1 Relations between the scalar parameters.

With the expression $\mathbf{r} = \lambda\mathbf{a} + \mu\mathbf{b}$, we obtain all points of the plane OAB. What happens, however, if there is some restriction on the values of λ or μ, or a relation between them?

Draw two vectors **a** and **b** and mark in several points with position vector **r** in each of the following cases: (i) $\lambda = 1$ while μ ranges over the real numbers; (ii) λ and μ are connected by the equation $\lambda + \mu = 1$; (iii) $\lambda = \mu^2$. Sketch the locus in each case, and describe it.

If there is a relation between λ and μ, we should expect to get only some of the points of the plane OAB. Instead of two free choices giving us a two dimensional plane, we now have only one free choice and that usually gives us a line of points (not necessarily a straight line).

Example 1

What is the locus of the point with position vector $\mathbf{r} = \lambda\mathbf{a} + \mu\mathbf{b}$ where λ and μ satisfy the equation $2\lambda + \mu = 1$?

In order to find the locus, we choose various values for λ and work out the corresponding values for μ, and vice versa.

If $\lambda = 0$, then $\mu = 1$. The position vector is $\mathbf{r} = \mathbf{b}$.
If $\lambda = 1$, then $\mu = -1$. The position vector is $\mathbf{r} = \mathbf{a} - \mathbf{b}$.
If $\mu = 0$, then $\lambda = \frac{1}{2}$. The position vector is $\mathbf{r} = \frac{1}{2}\mathbf{a}$.

Work out a few more position vectors and check that they all give points on a straight line placed, relative to the points O, A and B, as m is in Figure 3.

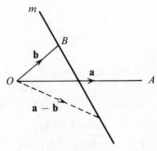

Fig. 3

Did you guess that the locus would be a straight line? Write down some other relations between λ and μ that would give straight lines.

Since $\mu = 1 - 2\lambda$, we can write the equation of the line as

$$\mathbf{r} = \lambda\mathbf{a} + (1 - 2\lambda)\mathbf{b}.$$

Such an equation (containing a single parameter) is called a *vector equation* of the locus. There were plenty of examples in the Kinematics chapter, where the scalar parameter was the time t. Using the relations between λ and μ that you have just written down, give vector equations of the lines.

Exercise B

For this exercise, draw any two vectors $\mathbf{a}$ and $\mathbf{b}$ different in length and direction.

1. Sketch the locus of points with position vector $\mathbf{r} = \lambda\mathbf{a} + \mu\mathbf{b}$ in the following cases (plot half a dozen or so points and sketch the resulting curve):

(i) $\lambda = 3$, μ unrestricted;
(ii) $\lambda = -1$, μ unrestricted;
(iii) $\mu = 2$, λ unrestricted;
(iv) $\lambda + 4\mu = 1$;
(v) $\lambda\mu = 1$;
(vi) $2\lambda + 8\mu = 21$;
(vii) $\lambda^2 + \mu^2 = 4$.

What is the connection between the loci in (i) and (ii)? Which loci are not straight lines? Write down the equations involving λ and μ that give parallel straight lines.

2. Is the locus of points given by $\mathbf{r} = \lambda\mathbf{a} + \mathbf{b}$ (i.e. $\mu = 1$) a straight line? How is this locus related to that of $\mathbf{r} = \lambda\mathbf{a}$? What would you say was the 'direction' of the line $\mathbf{r} = \lambda\mathbf{a} + 4\mathbf{b}$?

3. Draw the lines with the following vector equations, and in each case write down the equation of a parallel line through the point with position vector $5\mathbf{a}$.

(i) $\mathbf{r} = 3\mathbf{a} + 4\lambda\mathbf{b}$,　　(ii) $\mathbf{r} = 2\lambda\mathbf{a} + \lambda\mathbf{b}$,　　(iii) $\mathbf{r} = \lambda(\mathbf{a} + \mathbf{b})$.

4. You may have noticed that all the loci in Question 1 to some extent resemble those you have sketched in earlier chapters using x, y coordinates and rectangular axes. What vectors $\mathbf{a}$ and $\mathbf{b}$ were you using then?

5. Sketch the locus given by $\mathbf{r} = \lambda\mathbf{a} + \mu\mathbf{b}$ in each of the following cases (*a*) taking $\mathbf{a}$ and $\mathbf{b}$ of unequal length and inclined at an acute angle, and (*b*) taking $\mathbf{a} = \mathbf{i}$ and $\mathbf{b} = \mathbf{j}$:

(i) $\mu = \lambda^3$,　　(ii) $\lambda^2\mu = 1$,　　(iii) $\lambda = \mu^2$.

6. Take any three points O, A, B (not on a straight line) and construct the points C, D, E, F, G with position vectors $\mathbf{c} = \frac{1}{2}\mathbf{a} + \frac{1}{2}\mathbf{b}$, $\mathbf{d} = \frac{1}{4}\mathbf{a} + \frac{3}{4}\mathbf{b}$, $\mathbf{e} = 2\mathbf{a} - \mathbf{b}$, $\mathbf{f} = \frac{2}{3}\mathbf{a} + \frac{1}{3}\mathbf{b}$, $\mathbf{g} = \frac{1}{4}\mathbf{a} + \frac{1}{2}\mathbf{b}$.

What can you say about a point with position vector

$$\mathbf{r} = \lambda\mathbf{a} + \mu\mathbf{b} \quad \text{if} \quad \lambda + \mu > 1?$$

Describe as accurately as you can the positions of C, E and F in relation to A and B.

7. (i) Explain why $\mathbf{AB} = \mathbf{b} - \mathbf{a}$.

(ii) Where are P and Q if $\mathbf{p} = \mathbf{a} + \frac{1}{2}(\mathbf{b} - \mathbf{a})$ and $\mathbf{q} = \mathbf{a} - (\mathbf{b} - \mathbf{a})$?

3. THE RATIO THEOREM

Copy Figure 4, and find in the form $\lambda\mathbf{a}+\mu\mathbf{b}$ the position vector of the point P which lies one quarter of the way from A along AB. What do you notice about the values of λ and μ? Repeat for Q and T where $\mathbf{AQ} = \frac{1}{3}\mathbf{AB}$ and $\mathbf{BT} = \frac{2}{7}\mathbf{BA}$. Describe a general rule for the position vectors of points between A and B. Where is the point with position vector $\frac{3}{10}\mathbf{a}+\frac{7}{10}\mathbf{b}$?

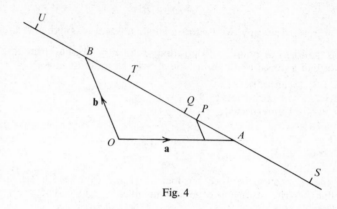

Fig. 4

These are all examples of a result known as the *ratio theorem*.

If R is a point on the line AB and its position is described by $\mathbf{AR} = \mu\mathbf{AB}$ or $\mathbf{BR} = \lambda\mathbf{BA}$, then

$$\mathbf{r} = \lambda\mathbf{a}+\mu\mathbf{b} \quad \text{and} \quad \lambda+\mu = 1.$$

In this case, R divides AB in the ratio $\mu:\lambda$.

Now consider points that lie on AB but not between A and B. In Figure 4, $\mathbf{SA} = \frac{1}{2}\mathbf{AB}$ and $\mathbf{UB} = \frac{1}{3}\mathbf{BA}$; find the position vectors of S and U in terms of $\mathbf{a}$ and $\mathbf{b}$. Do your answers satisfy the ratio theorem? Notice that $\mathbf{AS} = -\frac{1}{2}\mathbf{AB}$. We say that S divides AB in the ratio $-\frac{1}{2}: 1\frac{1}{2}$ or $-1:3$.

3.1 Proof of the ratio theorem. First we shall consider a point P between A and B (see Figure 5), and suppose that $\mathbf{AP} = \mu\mathbf{AB}$ where $\mu < 1$.

The position vector of P is given by

$$\mathbf{p} = \mathbf{a}+\mathbf{AP} \quad \text{(from triangle } OAP\text{),}$$

$$= \mathbf{a}+\mu\mathbf{AB}.$$

But $\mathbf{AB} = \mathbf{b}-\mathbf{a}$ (from triangle OAB),

so $\mathbf{p} = \mathbf{a}+\mu(\mathbf{b}-\mathbf{a})$

$$= (1-\mu)\mathbf{a}+\mu\mathbf{b}.$$

This result is of the required form $\mathbf{r} = \lambda\mathbf{a}+\mu\mathbf{b}$ where $\lambda+\mu = 1$, and it only remains to show that $\mathbf{BP} = (1-\mu)\mathbf{BA}$.

Now $\mathbf{AP} = \mu\mathbf{AB} \Rightarrow \mathbf{AB}-\mathbf{PB} = \mu\mathbf{AB}$

$$\Rightarrow \qquad \mathbf{PB} = (1-\mu)\mathbf{AB}$$

$$\Rightarrow \qquad \mathbf{BP} = (1-\mu)\mathbf{BA}.$$

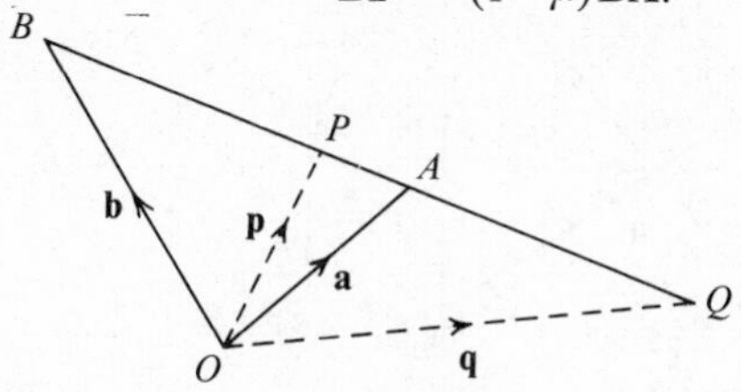

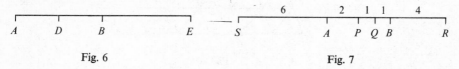

Fig. 5

The proof applies equally well to a point such as Q, but in that case μ will be negative and $1-\mu$ will be greater than 1.

Note that the ratio theorem is not dependent upon the position of the origin. The full meaning of this statement is brought out in Exercise C. The converse of the ratio theorem is:

If $\mathbf{r} = \lambda\mathbf{a}+\mu\mathbf{b}$ and $\lambda+\mu = 1$,

then R is a point on the line AB and it divides AB so that

$$\mathbf{AR} = \mu\mathbf{AB} \quad \text{and} \quad \mathbf{BR} = \lambda\mathbf{BA}.$$

Prove this converse theorem.

Exercise C

1. Write down (in terms of $\mathbf{c}$ and $\mathbf{d}$) the position vector of the point on CD two fifths of the way from C towards D.

2. Use the ratio theorem to find the position vectors of the following points in terms of $\mathbf{a}$ and $\mathbf{b}$:
  (i) the midpoint D of A and B, then the midpoint of B and D;
  (ii) the point E dividing AB in the ratio $2:-1$ (see Figure 6);
  (iii) the midpoint of E and D.

Fig. 6   Fig. 7

3. Figure 7 shows 6 collinear points with the distances between neighbouring points marked. Write down the vectors AP, AQ, AR and AS as multiples of $\mathbf{AB}$, and hence the position vectors of P, Q, R, and S in terms of $\mathbf{a}$ and $\mathbf{b}$, using the ratio theorem.

4. Draw a diagram like Figure 8 and construct the points with position vectors $\mathbf{a}+\frac{1}{3}\mathbf{b}$, $\frac{2}{3}\mathbf{a}+\frac{1}{3}\mathbf{b}$ relative to the origin O. Construct also the points with position vectors $\mathbf{a}'+\frac{1}{2}\mathbf{b}'$, $\frac{2}{3}\mathbf{a}'+\frac{1}{3}\mathbf{b}'$ relative to the origin O'. Comment on the results.

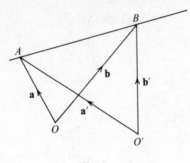
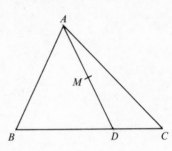

Fig. 8   Fig. 9

5. Draw a triangle ABC, and choose any point as the origin. Show on your diagram the points D and E, given $\mathbf{d} = \frac{1}{3}\mathbf{a}+\frac{2}{3}\mathbf{b}$ and $\mathbf{e} = \frac{3}{4}(\frac{1}{3}\mathbf{a}+\frac{2}{3}\mathbf{b})+\frac{1}{4}\mathbf{c}$. Does the position of E depend upon your choice of origin?

Show also the points F and G, given $\mathbf{f} = \frac{1}{2}\mathbf{a}+\frac{1}{2}\mathbf{c}$ and $\mathbf{g} = \frac{1}{2}(\frac{1}{2}\mathbf{a}+\frac{1}{2}\mathbf{c})+\frac{1}{2}\mathbf{b}$. Comment on the results.

6. In Figure 9, $\mathbf{BD} = 2\mathbf{DC}$ and $\mathbf{AM} = \mathbf{MD}$.

    (a) Write down the position vectors of D and M in terms of $\mathbf{a}$, $\mathbf{b}$ and $\mathbf{c}$.

    (b) If $\mathbf{CN} = \frac{3}{2}\mathbf{CM}$, find the position vector of N and so show that N lies on AB.

7. In Figure 10, write down in terms of $\mathbf{a}$, $\mathbf{b}$, $\mathbf{c}$ the position vectors of:

    (a) L;   (b) M;   (c) N;   (d) P.

8. Locate in Figure 10 the point with position vector $\frac{1}{6}\mathbf{a}+\frac{2}{3}\mathbf{b}+\frac{1}{6}\mathbf{c}$.

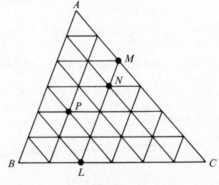

Fig. 10

9. ABC is a triangle. Show on a figure the points whose position vectors are:

    (a) $\frac{1}{2}\mathbf{b}+\frac{1}{2}\mathbf{c}$;   ($b$) $\frac{1}{3}\mathbf{a}+\frac{2}{3}(\frac{1}{2}\mathbf{b}+\frac{1}{2}\mathbf{c})$;   ($c$) $\frac{1}{3}\mathbf{b}+\frac{2}{3}(\frac{1}{2}\mathbf{c}+\frac{1}{2}\mathbf{a})$.

What geometrical result do you deduce?

334

10. If $2\mathbf{a} + \mathbf{b} - 3\mathbf{c} = \mathbf{0}$, what can you say about A, B and C?

11. Given that $\lambda\mathbf{a} + \mu\mathbf{b} + \nu\mathbf{c} = \mathbf{0}$, what is the condition on λ, μ and ν for A, B and C to be collinear?

12. Decide whether P, Q, R below are collinear—if so state the ratio in which Q divides PR:

   (i) $\mathbf{p} = \mathbf{a} + \mathbf{b}$, $\mathbf{q} = 2\mathbf{a} - \mathbf{b}$, $\mathbf{r} = 3\mathbf{b}$;

   (ii) $\mathbf{p} = -\mathbf{a} + \mathbf{b}$, $\mathbf{q} = 3\mathbf{a} + \mathbf{b}$, $\mathbf{r} = 4\mathbf{a} - 2\mathbf{b}$.

3.2   Centroids. Cut a triangle out of cardboard and try to balance it on a pencil point; mark the point of balance on the triangle. Is it special in any way? Is it equidistant from the vertices or from the sides?

Draw the three lines from the vertices to the midpoints of the opposite sides. These *medians* intersect in a point, called the *centroid* of the triangle, and this is the balance point for the triangle. Can we work out its position vector? We want the position vector of the intersection of two of the medians, say AD and BE in Figure 11. Start by writing down the position vectors of D and E.

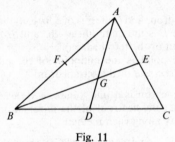

Fig. 11

Any point on AD has a position vector given by

$$\mathbf{r}_1 = s\mathbf{a} + (1-s)\mathbf{d} = s\mathbf{a} + \tfrac{1}{2}(1-s)\mathbf{b} + \tfrac{1}{2}(1-s)\mathbf{c}.$$

Similarly, any point on BE has a position vector given by

$$\mathbf{r}_2 = t\mathbf{b} + \tfrac{1}{2}(1-t)\mathbf{a} + \tfrac{1}{2}(1-t)\mathbf{c}.$$

If values for s and t can be found for which these two expressions are identically equal, then $\mathbf{r}_1$ and $\mathbf{r}_2$ will represent the same point, and this will be the point of intersection. The expressions are identically equal if

$$s = \tfrac{1}{2}(1-t),$$

$$\tfrac{1}{2}(1-s) = t,$$

and
$$\tfrac{1}{2}(1-s) = \tfrac{1}{2}(1-t).$$

All these relations are in fact satisfied by $s = \tfrac{1}{3}$ and $t = \tfrac{1}{3}$.

With these values, both $\mathbf{r}_1$ and $\mathbf{r}_2$ equal

$$\tfrac{1}{3}\mathbf{a} + \tfrac{1}{3}\mathbf{b} + \tfrac{1}{3}\mathbf{c};$$

this must be the position vector of the centroid G. Show that the third median also passes through this point.

Notice that
$$\mathbf{g} = s\mathbf{a} + (1-s)\mathbf{d} \quad \text{with} \quad s = \tfrac{1}{3},$$
$$= \tfrac{1}{3}\mathbf{a} + \tfrac{2}{3}\mathbf{d}.$$

G therefore lies two thirds of the way down the median AD from the vertex A. Similarly G divides each of the other medians in the ratio $2:1$.

Exercise D

1. Draw a triangle ABC and take a point O in the plane of the triangle to be the origin. Construct a vector $(\tfrac{1}{3}\mathbf{a} + \tfrac{1}{3}\mathbf{b}) + \tfrac{1}{3}\mathbf{c}$, and demonstrate that this is the position vector of the centroid of the triangle.

2. If G is the centroid of the triangle ABC, show that $\mathbf{GA} + \mathbf{GB} + \mathbf{GC} = \mathbf{0}$. Check by drawing.

3. If $ABCD$ is a tetrahedron, find (in terms of $\mathbf{a}, \mathbf{b}, \mathbf{c}, \mathbf{d}$) the position vector of the midpoint of EH, where E is the midpoint of BC and H is the midpoint of AD (EH is called a bimedian of the tetrahedron).

Show that this same point is the midpoint of the other two bimedians of $ABCD$. It is called the *centroid* of the tetrahedron.

4. A median of a tetrahedron is a line joining a vertex to the centroid of the opposite face. Show that the centroid of the tetrahedron (see Question 3) lies three quarters of the way along each median.

5. If P is the centroid of the tetrahedron $ABCD$, show that

$$\mathbf{PA} + \mathbf{PB} + \mathbf{PC} + \mathbf{PD} = \mathbf{0}.$$

6. If ABC is a triangle, and X, Y, Z are taken on the lines BC, CA, AB so that $\mathbf{BX} = -\tfrac{2}{3}\mathbf{XC}$, $\mathbf{CY} = \tfrac{3}{5}\mathbf{YA}$ and $\mathbf{AZ} = \tfrac{5}{2}\mathbf{ZB}$, express $\mathbf{x}, \mathbf{y}, \mathbf{z}$ in terms of $\mathbf{a}, \mathbf{b}, \mathbf{c}$ and show that $5\mathbf{x} + 16\mathbf{y} - 21\mathbf{z} = \mathbf{0}$. Are X, Y, Z collinear?

7. Repeat Question 6 taking the ratios to be λ, μ, ν, respectively instead of $-\tfrac{2}{3}, \tfrac{3}{5}, \tfrac{5}{2}$. Prove that

$$\mu\nu(1+\lambda)\mathbf{x} + (\mu+1)\mathbf{y} - \mu(\nu+1)\mathbf{z} = (\lambda\mu\nu+1)\mathbf{c}$$

and hence that if $\lambda\mu\nu = -1$ then X, Y, Z are collinear. This result is known as *Menelaus's Theorem*.

4. THREE DIMENSIONS

In the earlier sections leading up to the ratio theorem, we limited the discussion to two dimensions. Repeated application of the ratio theorem has taken us back into three dimensions. Let us now reconsider some of the

336

ideas of Section 2 in a wider context. All vectors in the plane OAB can be written in the form $\lambda\mathbf{a}+\mu\mathbf{b}$. Suppose we take a vector $\mathbf{c}$ not in the plane OAB. What can you say about all points with position vectors of the form $\lambda\mathbf{a}+\mu\mathbf{b}+\nu\mathbf{c}$? Explain why the position vector of any point in three dimensional space can be written in this form in a unique way.

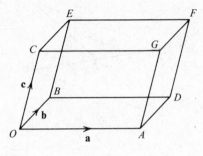

Fig. 12

What happens if we now impose restrictions on the parameters? Which points of the parallelepiped of Figure 12 have position vectors

$$\mathbf{r} = \lambda\mathbf{a}+\mu\mathbf{b}+\nu\mathbf{c}$$

with (i) $\lambda = 1$, (ii) $\lambda+\mu+\nu = 1$? What is the complete locus in each case? What type of locus is given by $\lambda+2\mu+3\nu = 1$?

4.1 Uniqueness. In Section 2, we saw that the position vector of any point in a plane can be expressed uniquely in terms of two general vectors $\mathbf{a}$ and $\mathbf{b}$. The argument extends to three dimensions; so if we discover two descriptions for the same vector in terms of three general vectors $\mathbf{a}$, $\mathbf{b}$ and $\mathbf{c}$, for example $\lambda\mathbf{a}+\mu\mathbf{b}+\nu\mathbf{c}$ and $\alpha\mathbf{a}+\beta\mathbf{b}+\gamma\mathbf{c}$, then we know that $\lambda = \alpha, \mu = \beta, \nu = \gamma$.

For an illustration of this idea, let us return to the discussion of the centroid of a triangle. The result $\mathbf{g} = \frac{1}{3}\mathbf{a}+\frac{1}{3}\mathbf{b}+\frac{1}{3}\mathbf{c}$ is independent of the position of the origin. First suppose that O is not in the plane of the triangle ABC. Then the position vector of each point in the plane can be expressed in the form $\lambda\mathbf{a}+\mu\mathbf{b}+\nu\mathbf{c}$ in one way only (and $\lambda+\mu+\nu = 1$). Consequently, when in Section 3.2 we showed that

$$\mathbf{g} = s\mathbf{a}+\tfrac{1}{2}(1-s)\mathbf{b}+\tfrac{1}{2}(1-s)\mathbf{c}$$

and $\mathbf{g} = t\mathbf{b}+\tfrac{1}{2}(1-t)\mathbf{a}+\tfrac{1}{2}(1-t)\mathbf{c}$,

we could have deduced that $s = \frac{1}{2}(1-t)$, these being the coefficients of $\mathbf{a}$ in the two expressions, and also $\frac{1}{2}(1-s) = t$ and $\frac{1}{2}(1-s) = \frac{1}{2}(1-t)$. Solving these equations gives $s = t = \frac{1}{3}$, as expected.

Notice the difference from the work in Section 3.2. There we said 'If the coefficients in the two expressions are the same, then we have found the position vector of the point of intersection.' Now we are saying 'For the point of intersection of the lines, the coefficients *must* be the same.'

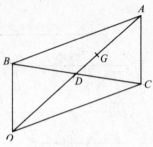

Fig. 13

Suppose now that O lies in the plane ABC. Then **g** can be expressed in terms of **a**, **b**, **c** in an infinite number of alternative ways. In Figure 13, we have the special case where $OBAC$ is a parallelogram. Then $\mathbf{a} = \mathbf{b} + \mathbf{c}$, and

$$\mathbf{g} = \tfrac{1}{3}\mathbf{a} + \tfrac{1}{3}\mathbf{b} + \tfrac{1}{3}\mathbf{c} = \tfrac{2}{3}\mathbf{b} + \tfrac{2}{3}\mathbf{c} = \tfrac{2}{3}\mathbf{a} = \tfrac{1}{2}\mathbf{a} + \tfrac{1}{6}\mathbf{b} + \tfrac{1}{6}\mathbf{c}, \quad \text{etc.}$$

In this case, **a**, **b** and **c** are not independent; there is a linear relation connecting them.

5. INDEPENDENT VECTORS

We understand that the position vector of a general point R in three dimensional space can only be written in the form $\mathbf{r} = \lambda\mathbf{a} + \mu\mathbf{b} + \nu\mathbf{c}$ if **a**, **b**, **c** are independent. To clarify the idea of independence of vectors, let us return first to two dimensions.

Write down in terms of the vectors **a** and **b** the position vectors of the points C, D, E and F in Figure 14.

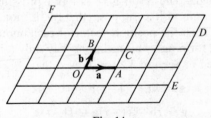

Fig. 14

Suppose we now choose two other vectors in the plane, **OE** and **OC** say, as our 'base' vectors. What are the position vectors of A, B, D and F in terms of **e** and **c**? Note that we can reach any other points of the plane using **e** and **c**, just as we did with **a** and **b**. Can we then choose *any* two vectors in the plane of OAB and use these to reach all points of the plane?

Given the vectors **a** and **b** as in Figure 14 suppose we choose combinations of them to give vectors **u** and **v** where $\mathbf{u} = \mathbf{a} - 3\mathbf{b}$ and $\mathbf{v} = 6\mathbf{b} - 2\mathbf{a}$. Is it possible to get to all points of the plane by taking multiples of **u** and **v**? Try to get to the point C. Why is this not possible?

You should find that taking multiples of **u** and **v** will only give us a line of points in the plane and not the whole plane. This is because we chose **u** and **v** so that they happened to be multiples of each other ($\mathbf{v} = -2\mathbf{u}$), and so in adding multiples of **u** and **v** we were in fact only taking multiples of the same vector. Vectors that are multiples of each other are said to be dependent. Two vectors, **c** and **d** are *dependent* if there exists a scalar λ so that $\mathbf{c} = \lambda\mathbf{d}$. When two vectors are not multiples of each other, they are said to be *independent*.

Example 2

a and **b** are independent vectors defining a plane through O. The point D has position vector $\mathbf{d} = 3\mathbf{a} + 2\mathbf{b}$ and C has position vector $\mathbf{c} = -\mathbf{a} + \mathbf{b}$. Are **c** and **d** dependent vectors?

It is immediately apparent that **c** and **d** are not dependent as they are not multiples of each other.

With 3 vectors, the situation is more complicated. Intuitively we wish to say that 3 vectors are independent if they are not coplanar. Then none of the vectors can be expressed as the sum of multiples of the other two vectors. If on the other hand, O, A, B and C lie in a plane, there will be a linear relation connecting **a**, **b** and **c**. What form does this take when (i) B is the midpoint of AC, (ii) O is the centroid of triangle ABC, (iii) O is the midpoint of AB, (iv) $\mathbf{OB} = \mathbf{BC}$?

The simplest formal definition is as follows:

a, b, c are linearly dependent if λ, μ, ν exist (not all zero) such that

$$\lambda\mathbf{a} + \mu\mathbf{b} + \nu\mathbf{c} = \mathbf{0}.$$

a, b, c are linearly independent if they are not linearly dependent.

This allows for the case where one of the scalars is zero, and the definition is easily extended to 4 or more vectors.

Exercise E

1. $ABCD$ is a parallelogram. Express **BD** in terms of (*a*) **AB** and **BC**, (*b*) **AB** and **AC**. Can it be expressed in terms of **AB** and **CD**?

2. Three coplanar vectors must be linearly dependent. Find the relation connecting **p**, **q**, **r** in each of the following:

   (i) $\mathbf{p} = 2\mathbf{a}+5\mathbf{b}, \quad \mathbf{q} = \mathbf{a}-\mathbf{b}, \quad \mathbf{r} = 3\mathbf{b};$

   (ii) $\mathbf{p} = 4\mathbf{a}-\mathbf{b}, \quad \mathbf{q} = 2\mathbf{a}+3\mathbf{b}, \quad \mathbf{r} = 8\mathbf{a}-4\mathbf{b};$

   (iii) $\mathbf{p} = \mathbf{a}+5\mathbf{b}, \quad \mathbf{q} = 2\mathbf{a}+\mathbf{b}, \quad \mathbf{r} = \mathbf{a}-6\mathbf{b}.$

3. Are three vectors **a**, **b** and **c** independent if **a** and **b** are independent, and **b** and **c** are independent?

4. Are the vectors $\mathbf{d} = \mathbf{a}-\mathbf{b}+\mathbf{c}$, $\mathbf{e} = \mathbf{a}+\mathbf{b}-\mathbf{c}$ and $\mathbf{f} = 2\mathbf{a}+\mathbf{b}-\mathbf{c}$ independent, given that **a**, **b**, and **c** are independent?

5. O is any point within triangle ABC (see Figure 15). With O as origin, the position vectors of A, B, C are coplanar and hence linearly dependent. If the relation connecting them is $\alpha\mathbf{a}+\beta\mathbf{b}+\gamma\mathbf{c} = 0$, show that $BU:UC = \gamma:\beta$.

   Show also that $\dfrac{BU}{UC} \times \dfrac{CV}{VA} \times \dfrac{AW}{WB} = 1$. This result is known as Ceva's Theorem.

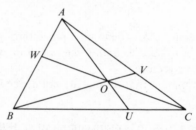

Fig. 15

6. Draw a diagram like Figure 1 to represent three independent vectors from an origin O and, by considering a few particular points, describe the locus of the point with position vector $\mathbf{r} = \lambda\mathbf{a}+\mu\mathbf{b}+\nu\mathbf{c}$ when

   (i) $\lambda = 1$ and μ and ν are unrestricted;

   (ii) $\lambda = \mu = \nu;$ (iii) $\lambda = \mu = 4;$

   (iv) $\lambda+\mu+\nu = 1;$ (v) $\lambda+\mu+\nu = 2;$

   (vi) $3\lambda+\mu+2\nu = 4;$ (vii) $2\lambda+\mu+\nu = 0.$

6. LINES AND PLANES

In Section 2.1 we found that, in two dimensions, the locus of a point with position vector $\lambda\mathbf{a}+\mu\mathbf{b}$ is a straight line if λ and μ are connected by a linear relation such as $3\lambda+\mu = 5$ or $\lambda+\mu = 1$. Now we find that, in three dimensions, the locus of a point with position vector $\lambda\mathbf{a}+\mu\mathbf{b}+\nu\mathbf{c}$ is a plane if the scalars are connected by a linear relation such as $3\lambda+2\mu+\nu = 7$. Can you demonstrate these results conclusively and show how to describe the positions of the lines and planes?

6.1   Vector equations of lines. In Exercises A and B we saw that all lines through the origin have an equation of the form $\mathbf{r} = \lambda\mathbf{d}$ where $\mathbf{d}$ is a vector in the direction of the line and λ is a scalar parameter (see Figure 16). This simply means that if we want to reach any point R on the line we must move so many multiples of $\mathbf{d}$ along the line from O. If t, s and μ are scalar parameters, show that $\mathbf{r} = \mu(2\mathbf{d})$, $\mathbf{r} = t(-\mathbf{d})$ and $\mathbf{r} = s(\frac{1}{4}\mathbf{d})$ all represent the same line. Find the values of t and s corresponding to $\mu = 4$.

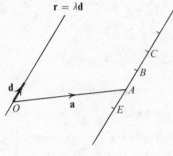

Fig. 16

The line AB does not pass through the origin. If $\mathbf{AB} = \mathbf{d}$, this vector gives the direction of the line. Write down the position vectors of A, B, C, E. Note that they are all of the form $\mathbf{a}+(\text{some multiple of } \mathbf{d})$. In other words to get to any point on the line we first move *to* the line by going to A and then *along* the line by taking multiples of $\mathbf{d}$. So the equation of the line is

$$\mathbf{r} = \mathbf{a}+\lambda\mathbf{d}.$$

Is this the same line as $\mathbf{r} = \mathbf{a}+\lambda(-51\mathbf{d})$?

Example 1 (again)

In this example, we had

$$\mathbf{r} = \lambda\mathbf{a}+\mu\mathbf{b} \quad \text{and} \quad 2\lambda+\mu = 1.$$

Eliminating μ gave $\mathbf{r} = \lambda\mathbf{a}+(1-2\lambda)\mathbf{b}.$

This is equivalent to $\mathbf{r} = \mathbf{b}+\lambda(\mathbf{a}-2\mathbf{b}).$

This is the vector equation of the line through the point with position vector $\mathbf{b}$ in the direction of the vector $\mathbf{a}-2\mathbf{b}$. In Figure 17, the vector $\mathbf{OZ} = \mathbf{a}-2\mathbf{b}$ has been constructed. We can reach a general point of the locus from the origin by making the displacement $\mathbf{b}$ followed by some multiple of $\mathbf{a}-2\mathbf{b}$. B is the point given by $\lambda = 0$. Show that P, Q, S, T correspond to $\lambda = -\frac{1}{2}, \frac{1}{2}, 1, 1\frac{1}{2}$.

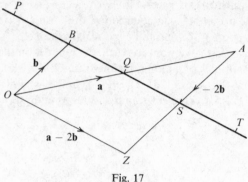

Fig. 17

Show also that if we eliminate λ instead of μ, we obtain

$$\mathbf{r} = \tfrac{1}{2}\mathbf{a} + \mu(\mathbf{b} - \tfrac{1}{2}\mathbf{a}).$$

Demonstrate that this equation gives the same straight line. What values of the parameter μ give the points P, B, Q, S, T?

Example 3

Find the position vector of the point of intersection of the lines

$$\mathbf{r} = \mathbf{a} + \lambda(\mathbf{a} - \mathbf{b}) \quad \text{and} \quad \mathbf{r} = 2\mathbf{b} + s(3\mathbf{a} + 2\mathbf{b}).$$

Here we have written the scalar parameters differently (λ and s) as we are looking for the particular value of λ and the particular value of s for which the expressions $\mathbf{a} + \lambda(\mathbf{a} - \mathbf{b})$ and $2\mathbf{b} + s(3\mathbf{a} + 2\mathbf{b})$ represent the same point,

i.e.
$$\mathbf{a} + \lambda(\mathbf{a} - \mathbf{b}) = 2\mathbf{b} + s(3\mathbf{a} + 2\mathbf{b}),$$

$$(1 + \lambda)\mathbf{a} - \lambda\mathbf{b} = 3s\mathbf{a} + (2 + 2s)\mathbf{b}.$$

If $\mathbf{a}$ and $\mathbf{b}$ are independent vectors we can equate coefficients so that

$$(1 + \lambda) = 3s$$

and
$$-\lambda = (2 + 2s).$$

Check that these are solved for $\lambda = -\tfrac{8}{5}$ and $s = -\tfrac{1}{5}$. Substituting these values in the original expressions gives the position vector of the common point as $\tfrac{8}{5}\mathbf{b} - \tfrac{3}{5}\mathbf{a}$.

6.2   Vector equations of planes. Discussion of the vector equation of a plane requires only a small extension of the ideas of the last section.

In Figure 18, OAB is a plane through the origin containing the vectors $\mathbf{a}$ and $\mathbf{b}$. Earlier in the chapter we found its equation to be $\mathbf{r} = \lambda\mathbf{a} + \mu\mathbf{b}$.

342

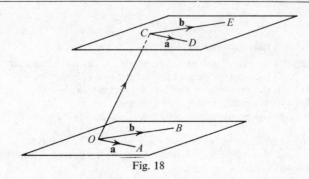

Fig. 18

What is the equation of the parallel plane CDE that does not pass through the origin? In order to get to any point of this plane we first move *to* the plane (for instance moving along OC) and then we move *in* the plane by taking multiples of **a** and **b**. Hence the equation of the plane is

$$\mathbf{r} = \mathbf{c} + \lambda\mathbf{a} + \mu\mathbf{b}.$$

Example 4

Given that **a**, **b** and **c** are independent vectors, what is the locus given by

$$\mathbf{r} = \lambda\mathbf{a} + \mu\mathbf{b} + \nu\mathbf{c} \quad \text{where} \quad \lambda + 2\mu + 3\nu = 4?$$

As there is a linear relationship between λ, μ, ν, we expect the locus to be a plane. We can make this fact clearer by eliminating one of the scalars:

$$\mathbf{r} = \lambda\mathbf{a} + \mu\mathbf{b} + \nu\mathbf{c},$$

$$\mathbf{r} = (4 - 2\mu - 3\nu)\mathbf{a} + \mu\mathbf{b} + \nu\mathbf{c},$$

$$\mathbf{r} = 4\mathbf{a} + \mu(\mathbf{b} - 2\mathbf{a}) + \nu(\mathbf{c} - 3\mathbf{a}).$$

Now this expression reveals that the locus of **r** is the plane through the point with position vector $4\mathbf{a}$, parallel to the two vectors $(\mathbf{b} - 2\mathbf{a})$ and $(\mathbf{c} - 3\mathbf{a})$ (see Figure 19).

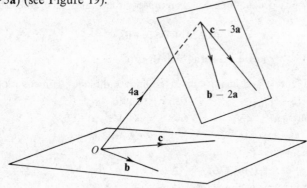

Fig. 19

Exercise F

1. Write down the equations of the lines

(i)   through the point with position vector $2\mathbf{a}-\mathbf{b}$, and having direction $-2\mathbf{b}$;

(ii) through the point with position vector $-\mathbf{a}+2\mathbf{b}$, having direction $\mathbf{a}-\mathbf{b}$;

(iii) through the points with position vectors $\mathbf{a}-2\mathbf{b}$, $3\mathbf{a}+4\mathbf{b}$;

(iv) through the points with position vectors $\mathbf{a}+\mathbf{b}$, $\mathbf{a}-2\mathbf{b}$;

(v)   through the points with position vectors $\mathbf{a}+2\mathbf{b}$, $3\mathbf{a}+6\mathbf{b}$.

2. Are any of the lines in Question 1 parallel? Find the points (*a*) where the first two lines meet, (*b*) where the second and third lines meet. Check by sketching the lines on a diagram.

3. What happens in Question 2 if **a** and **b** are not independent?

4. Do any of these equations represent the same line (check the direction first and then see if they have a common point)?

(i) $\mathbf{r} = 2\mathbf{a}+\mathbf{b}+\lambda(\mathbf{a}-5\mathbf{b})$;   (ii) $\mathbf{r} = 3\mathbf{a}-4\mathbf{b}+\lambda(\mathbf{a}-5\mathbf{b})$;

(iii) $\mathbf{r} = \mathbf{a}+\mathbf{b}+\lambda(5\mathbf{b}-\mathbf{a})$;   (iv) $\mathbf{r} = 3\mathbf{a}-\mathbf{b}+\lambda(-5\mathbf{b}-\mathbf{a})$.

5. Find the intersection of the line joining the points with position vectors $\mathbf{a}+\mathbf{c}$, and $4\mathbf{a}$ with the line $\mathbf{r} = \mathbf{a}+t(\mathbf{a}+2\mathbf{c})$.

6. Show that the plane with equation $\mathbf{r} = \mathbf{u}+\lambda\mathbf{v}+\mu\mathbf{w}$ passes through the points with position vectors $\mathbf{u}$, $\mathbf{v}+\mathbf{u}$ and $\mathbf{w}+\mathbf{u}$. Hence or otherwise write down an equation for the plane passing through the points with position vectors $\mathbf{a}$, $\mathbf{b}$ and $\mathbf{c}$.

7. Identify the loci represented by the equations below. If the locus is a plane, obtain its equation in the form $\mathbf{r} = \mathbf{u}+\lambda\mathbf{v}+\mu\mathbf{w}$ where $\mathbf{u}$ is the position vector of a point on the plane and $\mathbf{v}$ and $\mathbf{w}$ are vectors parallel to the plane.

$\mathbf{r} = \lambda\mathbf{a}+\mu\mathbf{b}+\nu\mathbf{c}$ (**a**, **b**, **c** independent) and

(i) $\lambda = \mu-1$;   (ii) $\lambda = \sin\mu$;

(iii) $\lambda+\mu+4\nu = 1$;   (iv) $1-\lambda = \mu-\nu$.

8. Show that the two equations below represent the same plane and explain why this is so:

$$\mathbf{r} = \mathbf{d}+\lambda(\mathbf{a}-2\mathbf{d})+3\mu(4\mathbf{c}+\mathbf{d}),$$

$$\mathbf{r} = \mathbf{a}-\mathbf{d}+s(\mathbf{a}+4\mathbf{c}-\mathbf{d})+t(\mathbf{a}+8\mathbf{c}).$$

9. Reproduce Figure 1 and identify on it the lines and planes with equations

(i) $\mathbf{r} = \mathbf{a}+\lambda(\mathbf{b}+\mathbf{c})$,   (ii) $\mathbf{r} = \mathbf{b}+\lambda\mathbf{a}+\mu\mathbf{c}$,

(iii) $\mathbf{r} = \mathbf{a}+\lambda(\mathbf{c}-\mathbf{a})$,   (iv) $\mathbf{r} = \mathbf{a}+\lambda(\mathbf{c}-\mathbf{a})+\mu\mathbf{b}$,

(v) $\mathbf{r} = \lambda\mathbf{a}+\mu\mathbf{b}+(1-\lambda)\mathbf{c}$,   (vi) $\mathbf{r} = \mathbf{c}+\lambda(\mathbf{a}+\mathbf{b}-\mathbf{c})$.

Obtain vector equations of the lines

(vii) *EF*,   (viii) *OG*,   (ix) *AE*.

Obtain vector equations of the planes

(x) *OBFG*,   (xi) *CEFG*,   (xii) *DEG*.

10. Is the line $\mathbf{r} = \mathbf{a}+\mathbf{b}+t(2\mathbf{a}+\mathbf{b})$ parallel to the plane

$$\mathbf{r} = \mathbf{c}+\lambda(\mathbf{a}+\mathbf{c})+\mu(2\mathbf{a}+\mathbf{b})\,?$$

If so, does the line lie in the plane? If not, find the point of intersection of the line and plane.

11. Repeat Question 5 for the line $\mathbf{r} = \mathbf{a}+t(\mathbf{a}-\mathbf{c})$ and the plane $\mathbf{r} = \lambda(\mathbf{a}+\mathbf{b})+\mu\mathbf{c}$.

12. Where does the line $\mathbf{r} = \mathbf{a}+t(\mathbf{a}+2\mathbf{b})$ meet the plane

$$\mathbf{r} = 2\mathbf{a}+\lambda(\mathbf{a}-2\mathbf{b})+\mu(3\mathbf{a}-\mathbf{c})\,?$$

13. Find the equation of the line of intersection of the two planes:

$$\mathbf{r} = \mathbf{a}+\lambda(2\mathbf{a}+\mathbf{b}+\mathbf{c})+\mu\mathbf{c},$$

$$\mathbf{r} = \mathbf{c}+\mathbf{a}+\lambda\mathbf{b}+\mu(\mathbf{c}+\mathbf{b}).$$

7. RECTANGULAR AXES AND CARTESIAN COORDINATES

All the results we have established in this chapter hold generally for any vectors $\mathbf{a}$, $\mathbf{b}$ and $\mathbf{c}$. Notice that we have never mentioned the *length* of the vectors nor the angles between them. The results we have established are part of what is called *affine* geometry, which is simply the study of vectors which can be added and subtracted and multiplied by a scalar. When we are concerned with lengths and angles, as we are with most everyday problems, instead of the more general geometry with vectors $\mathbf{a}$, $\mathbf{b}$, $\mathbf{c}$ and parameters λ, μ, ν, we usually use the geometry with unit vectors $\mathbf{i}$, $\mathbf{j}$, $\mathbf{k}$ and coordinates x, y, z. As the latter is a special case of the former geometry, we can use all the results we have established in this chapter.

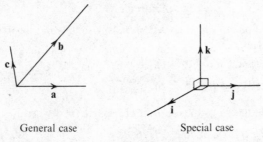

General case   Special case

Fig. 20

We shall use the usual right-handed mutually perpendicular system (Figure 20). As before, we shall write the position vector of $(2, 5, 3)$ either as

$$2\mathbf{i}+5\mathbf{j}+3\mathbf{k} \quad \text{or} \quad \begin{pmatrix} 2 \\ 5 \\ 3 \end{pmatrix}.$$

Example 5

Write down the equation of the line joining (1, 0, 2) and (3, 1, 0). Find where this line meets the plane $x+y-z = 1$.

The point with coordinates (1, 0, 2) has position vector $\mathbf{i}+2\mathbf{k}$. The line has the direction of the vector

$$(3\mathbf{i}+\mathbf{j})-(\mathbf{i}+2\mathbf{k}) = 2\mathbf{i}+\mathbf{j}-2\mathbf{k}.$$

The vector equation of the line is

$$\mathbf{r} = (\mathbf{i}+2\mathbf{k})+\lambda(2\mathbf{i}+\mathbf{j}-2\mathbf{k}),$$

i.e. $$\mathbf{r} = (1+2\lambda)\mathbf{i}+\lambda\mathbf{j}+(2-2\lambda)\mathbf{k}.$$

The plane has equation

$$\mathbf{r} = x\mathbf{i}+y\mathbf{j}+z\mathbf{k}, \quad \text{where} \quad x+y-z = 1,$$

i.e. $$\mathbf{r} = x\mathbf{i}+y\mathbf{j}+(x+y-1)\mathbf{k}.$$

The line meets the plane where

$$1+2\lambda = x,$$

$$\lambda = y,$$

$$2-2\lambda = x+y-1.$$

Solving these equations, we obtain the point of intersection as $(\tfrac{9}{5}, \tfrac{2}{5}, \tfrac{6}{5})$.

Exercise G

1. C is the point on AB such that $\mathbf{AC} = 3\mathbf{CB}$. Use the ratio theorem to find the coordinates of C if

(i) A is (2, 11) and B is (10, -1),

(ii) A is (1, 8, 4) and B is (5, 2, 6).

2. Find the coordinates of the centroid of triangle ABC when

(i) A is (0, 7), B is (3, 8), and C is (6, 3),

(ii) A is (3, 2, 3), B is (1, 5, 2) and C is (-1, -1, 4).

3. With the points of Question 2(i), express $\mathbf{c}$ as the sum of multiples of $\mathbf{a}$ and $\mathbf{b}$.

4. With the points of Question 2(ii), investigate whether $\mathbf{a}$, $\mathbf{b}$ and $\mathbf{c}$ are linearly dependent or independent.

5. Show that the points (4, 0, 7), (2, 6, 9) and (7, -9, 4) lie on a straight line.

6. Write down vector equations of

(i) the plane through $(0, 1, 1)$ parallel to $\begin{pmatrix} 1 \\ 2 \\ 1 \end{pmatrix}$ and $\begin{pmatrix} -1 \\ 0 \\ 1 \end{pmatrix}$;

(ii) the plane through the points $(1, 0, 1)$, $(1, 2, 1)$ and $(1, 1, 0)$;

(iii) the line through $(1, 7, 6)$ in the direction $\begin{pmatrix} 1 \\ -2 \\ 1 \end{pmatrix}$;

(iv) the line through the points $(1, 0, -1)$ and $(0, -1, 1)$.

7. Find where the two lines of Question 6 meet (i) the xy-plane, (ii) the yz-plane, (iii) the plane $\mathbf{r} = \mathbf{i} + \lambda(\mathbf{i}+\mathbf{j}) + \mu(\mathbf{i}+\mathbf{k})$.

8. Find a vector equation of the plane through the points $(1, 0, 2)$ and $(2, 1, 6)$, parallel to the line $\mathbf{r} = \mathbf{i} + t(\mathbf{j}+\mathbf{k})$.

9. Find an equation of the plane containing the two lines:

$$\mathbf{r} = \mathbf{i}+\mathbf{j}+t\mathbf{j}, \quad \mathbf{r} = \mathbf{i}+5\mathbf{j}+s(\mathbf{k}+\mathbf{j}).$$

Miscellaneous Exercise

1. Find the centroid of the tetrahedron $ABCD$ (see Exercise D, Question 3) where A is $(5, 3, 7)$, B is $(4, 1, 5)$, C is $(2, 8, 3)$ and D is $(-3, 0, 1)$. Verify that it lies on the median from A to the centroid of triangle BCD.

2. If $\mathbf{a}$, $\mathbf{b}$ and $\mathbf{c}$ are not independent, what is the locus of the point with position vector $\mathbf{r} = \lambda\mathbf{a} + \mu\mathbf{b} + \nu\mathbf{c}$? Consider all cases.

3. Find whether the origin lies in the plane containing $(-2, 1, 0)$, $(2, 1, 1)$ and $(2, -3, -1)$, i.e. whether the position vectors of these points are linearly dependent.

4. If a and b denote the lengths of the vectors $\mathbf{a}$ and $\mathbf{b}$, explain why

$$\mathbf{r} = \lambda\left(\frac{\mathbf{a}}{a}+\frac{\mathbf{b}}{b}\right)$$

is the equation of OX, the bisector of angle AOB (see Figure 21).

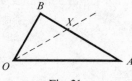

Fig. 21

Show that $\lambda = ab/(a+b)$ gives the point X and deduce that $AX:XB = AO:OB$.

5. If **b** and **c** are vectors of equal length, explain why **b**+**c** is perpendicular to **b**−**c**.

Take the centre of the circle ABC as the origin O, and let **a**+**b**+**c** = **h**. Show from **h**−**a** = **b**+**c** that AH is perpendicular to BC. Deduce that the altitudes of the triangle ABC meet at H. If G is the centroid of the triangle, what is the connection between **g** and **h**, and between O, G and H?

Calculate the coordinates of H if the vertices are $(7, 4)$, $(-4, 7)$ and $(-1, -8)$. Draw an accurate diagram as a check.

SUMMARY

Linear dependence

a, **b**, **c** are linearly dependent if scalars λ, μ, ν (not all zero) exist such that

$$\lambda\mathbf{a}+\mu\mathbf{b}+\nu\mathbf{c} = \mathbf{0}.$$

(There are similar definitions for more or less than three vectors.) Vectors are said to be linearly independent if they are not linearly dependent.

Vectors in a plane

Any three or more vectors in a plane are linearly dependent. If **a**, **b** are independent, then any other vector can be expressed in the form $\lambda\mathbf{a}+\mu\mathbf{b}$.

Ratio theorem

If C lies on AB and $AC:CB = \mu:\lambda$ with $\lambda+\mu = 1$, then **c** = $\lambda\mathbf{a}+\mu\mathbf{b}$. The converse is also true. These results are independent of the position of the origin.

Vectors in three dimensions

If **a**, **b**, **c** are linearly independent, then any other vector can be expressed in the form $\lambda\mathbf{a}+\mu\mathbf{b}+\nu\mathbf{c}$.

Vector equations of lines and planes

The equation **r** = **a**+λ**d** represents a line through A with direction vector **d**.

The equation **r** = **a**+λ**d**+μ**e** represents a plane through A parallel to the vectors **d** and **e**, provided that **d** and **e** are independent.

REVISION EXERCISES

11. POSITION AND SPREAD

1. Calculate the standard deviation of the numbers 3, 6, 9, 12, 15. What will be the standard deviation of the numbers 130, 160, 190, 220, 250?

2. In a class of 10 children the marks in an examination are 14, 18, 21, 25, 29, 29, 30, 31, 35, 38. Find the mean and the standard deviation, giving your answers to the nearest integer.

3. The masses (in kg) of the boys in each of the fourth forms in a school were recorded.

Mass	44–47	47–50	50–53	53–56	56–59	59–62	62–65
No. of boys in 4A	2	5	3	2	1	2	0
No. of boys in 4B	1	3	4	4	2	3	1
No. of boys in 4C	0	0	5	3	4	2	0
No. of boys in 4D	0	2	3	1	4	5	4

Find the mean and standard deviation of the masses of the boys in each form, and of the combined masses of all the boys in the fourth forms. Use a data zero and the two-standard-deviation check with each calculation.

4. A random sample of 100 skirts was measured at Ascot in 1965. Their lengths (to the nearest 5 cm) were as follows:

Length in cm	35	40	45	50	55	60	65
Number of skirts	3	15	9	17	30	20	6

(a) Work out the mean length (m) and standard deviation (s).

(b) Any skirt longer than $m+s$ was regarded as old-fashioned. Approximately how many old-fashioned skirts were there in the sample?

(c) Any skirt shorter than $m-1\frac{1}{2}s$ was considered outrageous. How many of these were there?

(d) Draw a histogram and show on it your answers to (b) and (c).

5. Marks out of 100 for a test taken by 100 boys were:

Range	0–9	10–19	20–29	30–39	40–49
Frequency	2	4	6	18	24

Range	50–59	60–69	70–79	80–89	90–100
Frequency	19	8	10	7	2

Calculate the mean and standard deviation.

Check that roughly $\frac{2}{3}$ of the marks were within one standard deviation of the mean.

6. Economy packs of frozen peas are marked 'Net weight 700 grams'. They are filled by a machine known to give a standard deviation of 25 grams. To give what average weight would you set the machine? List the factors you must consider in choosing your answer.

7. A small factory manufactures high quality tape recorders. The record of output over a period of 100 consecutive days is as follows:

Output	83–85	86–88	89–91	92–94	95–97	98–100	101–103
No. of days	8	18	20	24	18	10	2

Calculate the mean output m and the standard deviation s, and find on how many days the output exceeded $m+s$.

The management estimates that by introducing a bonus scheme they can raise the mean daily output to 96 tape recorders and reduce the standard deviation to 4. The proposal is to give each of the 25 employees engaged in production an extra £2 for each day on which the output reaches 100 tape recorders or more. If the selling price of each tape recorder exceeds the cost of the raw materials by £10, how much would the firm expect to gain on average by introducing the bonus scheme?

8.

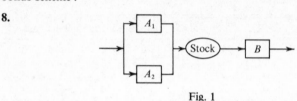

Fig. 1

Manufacture of a particular article requires two processes A and B. A small firm has two machines for A and one for B. Work study provided the following information.

Time for process A (in minutes)	6	7	8	9	10	11
Number of articles	4	11	21	29	23	12

Time for process B (in minutes)	3	4	5	6	7
Number of articles	15	34	30	16	5

(a) Basing your calculations on the above data, find the total weekly output of this article in a 40 hour week.

(b) Explain why there must be a stock of semi-manufactured articles ready for process B. What factors determine the optimum average stock level?

(c) Describe how you would use a simulation method to investigate the fluctuation in the level of this stock, assuming full production.

12. MECHANICS OF A PARTICLE

1. An electron of mass 9×10^{-30} kg in a magnetic field has a momentary acceleration of 6×10^{20} m/s². What is the force on it?

2. A man whose mass is 100 kg is travelling in a lift. If the thrust on the floor is 1200 N at a certain instant, what is the lift's acceleration? Later, the lift is going down and accelerating at 2 m/s². What is then the total force acting on the soles of the man's shoes?

3. A mass of 2 kg is swung round in a vertical circle. If the string attaching it to a fixed point is $\frac{3}{4}$ metre long, find the tension in it when the mass is at its lowest point and moving with speed 10 m/s.

4. After t seconds, the position vector of a particle of mass 10 kg is

$$\mathbf{r} = t^{\frac{3}{2}}\mathbf{i} + \sin t\mathbf{j}.$$

Find the force acting on it when $t = 4$.

5. A man weighs 700 N on Earth. How much would he weigh on a planet with one tenth the radius of the Earth? Assume the planets have the same density.

6. Find the magnitude and direction of the resultant of forces 80 N in direction 010°, 100 N in direction 070°, and 50 N in direction 150°. Obtain answers (i) by drawing a vector polygon, and also (ii) by using components.

7. A crane is hauling a crashed car of mass 1000 kg at 0·2 m/s straight up an embankment inclined at 15° to the horizontal. Find the tension required if the resistance to motion is 500 N and the wire from the crane to the car is approximately parallel to the ground.

8. A 2 tonne truck on smooth rails is pulled with a force of 600 N at an angle of 60° to the rails. Find its acceleration and the reaction between the wheel flanges and the rails caused by this force.

9. A particle of mass 10 kg starts from rest at the origin, and is acted on by a force $\mathbf{F} = 6t\mathbf{i} + (2t+3)\mathbf{j}$. Find the velocity and position at time t, and sketch the path of the particle during the first 2 seconds.

13. THE CHAIN RULE AND INTEGRATION BY SUBSTITUTION

1. Differentiate:

(a) $(2x+5)^9$;

(b) $(x^2+3)^2$;

(c) $\sqrt{(3-2x)}$;

(d) $\dfrac{1}{\sqrt{(x^3-1)}}$;

(e) $1-\cos 3x$;

(f) $\dfrac{1}{\cos^3 2x}$;

(g) $\dfrac{1}{2x^2+5x+1}$;

(h) $\cos^2 x - \sin^2 x$.

2. Sketch graphs for these functions showing all maximum and minimum points:

(a) $x \to \dfrac{5}{1+x^2}$;

(b) $x \to \cos^2 x$, $\quad -2\pi \leqslant x \leqslant 2\pi$;

(c) $x \to \left(x-\dfrac{1}{x}\right)^3$;

(d) $x \to (x^3-1)^2$.

3. The position vector of a particle at time t seconds is

$$\begin{pmatrix} t^2 \\ t^2-5t \end{pmatrix}.$$

Sketch the path of the particle for $0 \leqslant t \leqslant 6$ and show the velocity vectors when $t = 0, 1, 2, 3, 4, 5$.

What is the minimum speed of the particle?

4. The radius of a disc of metal is found to be expanding at a constant rate of 0·002 cm/s. What is the rate at which the area is changing when the radius is 15 cm?

5.

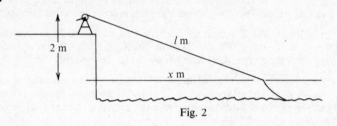

Fig. 2

A small boat is being winched towards a quay. The winch is 2 m above the level of the boat and is bringing in the rope at $\frac{1}{2}$ m/s. Express the distance x m from the quay in terms of the length l m of the rope and hence find dx/dt in terms of l and dl/dt. At what speed is the boat moving when it is 10 m from the quay?

6. Find the inverse function g of

$$f: x \to \frac{x^3 + 5}{2},$$

and the derived functions f' and g'. If $f(a) = b$, check that $f'(a) \times g'(b) = 1$.

7. Try to integrate the following, using your experience of chain-rule differentiation. Alternatively, use a substitution.

(a) $\displaystyle\int 2x(a - x^2)^3 \, dx$;

(b) $\displaystyle\int \frac{x}{(x^2 + 4)^2} \, dx$;

(c) $\displaystyle\int x^2 \sqrt{(1 - x^3)} \, dx$;

(d) $\displaystyle\int \frac{x^3}{\sqrt{(1 - x^4)}} \, dx$;

(e) $\displaystyle\int \sin^5 x \cos x \, dx$;

(f) $\displaystyle\int \frac{\sin x}{\cos^2 x} \, dx$;

(g) $\displaystyle\int 4x \cos (x^2) \sin (x^2) \, dx$;

(h) $\displaystyle\int (x - 1)(x^2 - 2x)^3 \, dx$.

8. Using the suggested substitutions, integrate the following:

(a) $\displaystyle\int_1^3 x(x - 1)^4 \, dx$, $u = x - 1$;

(b) $\displaystyle\int_0^2 2x \sqrt{(1 + x)} \, dx$, $u = 1 + x$;

(c) $\displaystyle\int_0^4 (1 + x) \sqrt{(3x + 1)} \, dx$, $u = 3x + 1$;

(d) $\displaystyle\int_0^2 \frac{1 - x}{(1 + x)^4} \, dx$, $u = 1 + x$.

9. Using the suggested substitutions, integrate the following:

(a) $\displaystyle\int_0^1 \sqrt{(4-x^2)}\,dx, \quad x = 2\sin u;$

(b) $\displaystyle\int_0^2 \frac{1}{\sqrt{(9-x^2)}}\,dx, \quad x = 3\sin u;$

(c) $\displaystyle\int_0^2 \frac{1}{\sqrt{(9-x^2)}}\,dx, \quad x = 3\cos u;$

(d) $\displaystyle\int_0^1 \sqrt{\left(\frac{x}{4-x}\right)}\,dx, \quad x = 4\sin^2 u.$

10. Integrate the following:

(a) $\displaystyle\int 5x(x^2+1)^{-2}\,dx;$ (b) $\displaystyle\int (x^2+1)^2\,dx;$

(c) $\displaystyle\int \frac{x}{\sqrt{(5x+1)}}\,dx;$ (d) $\displaystyle\int \frac{1}{\sqrt{(5x+1)}}\,dx;$

(e) $\displaystyle\int \frac{\cos 5x}{(1+\sin 5x)^3}\,dx;$ (f) $\displaystyle\int \frac{1}{\sqrt{(1-4x^2)}}\,dx.$

14. VECTOR GEOMETRY

1. Express the position vectors of the points P, Q, R, S and T in Figure 3 in terms of **a** and **b**.

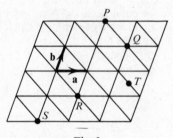

Fig. 3

2. A, B, C, D are four points with position vectors **a**, **b**, **c**, **d**. P, Q, R, S are the midpoints of the segments AB, CD, BC and DA. G is the centroid of ABC. H is the midpoint of PQ. Express the following vectors in terms of **a**, **b**, **c** and **d**: **p**, **q**, **r**, **s**, **g**, **h**.

What can you say about AC, PR, SQ? How is H related to the points R and S? How is H related to the points D and G?

3. If the magnitude of the vector **a** is given by a, what are the directions of the following relative to **a** and **b**?

(i) $\mathbf{c} = \dfrac{\mathbf{a}}{a} + \dfrac{\mathbf{b}}{b};$ (ii) $\mathbf{d} = \dfrac{\mathbf{a}}{a} - \dfrac{\mathbf{b}}{b}.$

4. Draw a line AB and mark on it the points with the following position vectors in those cases where the points lie on the line.

(a) $\mathbf{p} = 2\mathbf{a} - \mathbf{b}$;   (b) $\mathbf{q} = \frac{1}{4}\mathbf{a} + \frac{1}{2}\mathbf{b}$;   (c) $\mathbf{r} = \frac{1}{5}(2\mathbf{a} + 3\mathbf{b})$;

(d) $\mathbf{s} = \frac{1}{3}(3\mathbf{a} + \mathbf{b})$;   (e) $\mathbf{t} = 4\mathbf{a} - 5\mathbf{b}$.

5. Sketch the locus given by $\mathbf{r} = \lambda\mathbf{a} + \mu\mathbf{b}$ in the following cases:

(a) $\lambda - \mu = 1$;   (b) $\mu^2 = \lambda$;   (c) $\frac{1}{3}\lambda + \frac{2}{3}\mu = 1$.

6. Write down a vector equation (i) of the line AB and (ii) of the plane ABC where A is $(1, 2, 3)$, B is $(4, -5, 6)$ and C is $(7, 8, -9)$.

Does the point $(12, -8, -6)$ lie in the plane ABC?

7. With the usual notation, are the vectors $\mathbf{i}$, $\mathbf{j}$ and $\mathbf{k}$ linearly independent vectors?

Which three of the following four vectors are linearly dependent?

$$\mathbf{a} = \begin{pmatrix} 1 \\ 2 \\ 3 \end{pmatrix}, \quad \mathbf{b} = \begin{pmatrix} 3 \\ -2 \\ 1 \end{pmatrix}, \quad \mathbf{c} = \begin{pmatrix} 5 \\ 6 \\ 7 \end{pmatrix}, \quad \mathbf{d} = \begin{pmatrix} 5 \\ 2 \\ 7 \end{pmatrix}.$$

State the relation between the dependent vectors.

8. The vertices of a triangle are at $P(2, 2, 2)$, $Q(4, 0, 2)$ and $R(4, 2, 0)$. What is the position of the centroid of the triangle? What is the distance between the centroid and each of the vertices? What can be inferred about the shape of the triangle? Check your answer by calculating the lengths of the sides.

9. Write down a vector equation of the plane q which passes through the points $(1, 0, 0)$, $(0, 1, 0)$ and $(0, 0, 1)$. In what ratio does this plane divide the line segment joining the origin to the point $(1, 1, 1)$? What is the equation of the plane s which is parallel to plane q and which contains the point $(1, 1, 0)$? What is the distance between these two planes?

PROBLEM PAPERS

1

1. Sketch the graphs of

    (a) $y = 2^x$;   (b) $y = 2^{1/x}$;   (c) $y = x + 2^{1/x}$.

Show clearly how (b) and (c) behave for very small x and for very large x, and explain your reasoning.

2. If $f(x) = \tan x$, use the formula for $\tan(a+h)$ to find $f'(a)$ directly from the definition.

3. If $g(x) = \log_{10} x$, find $g'(a)$ for $a = 2, 3, 4, 5, 6$ as accurately as your four figure tables allow. What can you deduce from your results?

4. Sketch the graphs of

    (a) $|x+y| = 1$;   (b) $|x| + |y| = 1$;   (c) $|x| = |1-y|$.

5. The sum of the reciprocals of a set of n different positive integers is equal to 1. If $n = 3$, show that there is only one such set. Find also a set for $n = 4$, one for $n = 5$, and one for $n = 10$.

6. The integral

$$F(a) = \int_0^a \frac{1}{\sqrt{(1-x^4)}}\,dx$$

cannot be found analytically, but there are extensive $F(a)$ tables.
    In a particular problem, you need

$$\int_0^1 \frac{1}{\sqrt{(16-x^4)}}\,dx.$$

What do you look up? In another problem you need

$$\int_{\frac{1}{4}\pi}^{\frac{1}{2}\pi} \frac{1}{\sqrt{(\sin\theta)}}\,d\theta.$$

Can you find this with the help of the tables?
    Can you find limits between which the following must lie: $F(\frac{1}{2})$, $F(1)$, $F(2)$?

7. If $\mathbf{A} = \begin{pmatrix} 6 & 2 \\ 3 & 7 \end{pmatrix}$, show that $\mathbf{A}^2 - 13\mathbf{A} + 36\mathbf{I} = \mathbf{0}$ and hence that $\mathbf{A} = (\mathbf{A} - 6\mathbf{I})^2$.
Deduce two square roots of $\mathbf{A}$ and find two more in a similar way. Check your answers.
    Use this or any other method to find a square root of $\begin{pmatrix} 23 & 4 \\ 11 & 3 \end{pmatrix}$.

8. Prove that if n is any natural number, the last two digits of n^{20} are 00, 01, 25 or 76.

9. A shear S is described as $(MN: P \to Q)$, in which MN is the invariant line, so that $S(M) = M$ and $S(P) = Q$. What conditions must the vector $\mathbf{PQ}$ satisfy? Could the shear be described more briefly?

Given a point X not on MN or PQ, show how to construct $S(X)$. You may assume that a shear preserves straightness, parallelism, area and ratios along a line, and may use geoliner and ruler to draw parallel lines.

Prove that if G is the centroid of ABC, then $S(G)$ is the centroid of $S(ABC)$.

Draw a parallelogram $ABDE$ with centre C. Describe the shear S_1 which maps ABC onto CBD, and shears S_2 etc. such that $S_4 S_3 S_2 S_1(ABC) = CAB$.

By positioning first A and then AB, find shears S_5 etc. such that $S_7 S_6 S_5(ABC) = CAB$. Find also two more shears such that $S_9 S_8(ABC) = CAB$.

[*Hint.* Use a median as the first invariant line.]

10. 'The number of representations of a positive integer n as the sum of 4 squares of integers, representations which differ only in order or sign being counted as distinct, is 8 times the sum of the divisors of n which are not multiples of 4.' (Hardy and Wright, *Theory of Numbers.* O.U.P., Theorem 386).

Verify this result for $n = 12$, 13, and any two numbers greater than 50.

2

1. Show that, if n is an integer, $n^4 + 2n^3 + 5n^2 + 4n$ is divisible by 12.

2. A parabola has equation $y = kx^2$. Light is incident on the parabola from the positive y-direction, parallel to the y-axis. Show that all such light is reflected by the curve through a point F, and find F's coordinates.

3. The six runners in a race run in lanes numbered 1 to 6. I write down the lane numbers in order of finishing; a friend writes down the places in order of lanes. Thus, if I write 143625, he writes 153264. If I write 436215, what does he write? If he writes 436215, what do I write? Give three examples of races where we write the same. How many possible orders are there, and in how many of them do we write the same?

4. In the diagram, ABC is any triangle, and P, Q, R are points of trisection of the sides. Find the position vectors of A', B', C' in terms of the position vectors of A, B, C.

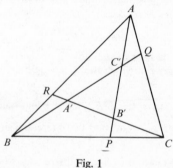

Fig. 1

Points of trisection of $B'C'$, etc. are now taken, and a triangle $A''B''C''$ formed inside $A'B'C'$ in the same way as before. This process is continued to give a sequence of nested triangles. Identify the point interior to every triangle of this set, and justify your answer.

5. Sketch the graph of $y = x^{\sin x}$ for positive x. Do not attempt to differentiate.

6. Prove that if the product of the gradients of two lines in the plane is -1, then the lines are perpendicular. State the converse theorem, and say whether it is true.

Draw the graphs of $xy = A$ for several values of A, both positive and negative. Sketch in some curves which always cut the original hyperbolae at right angles. Show that the general equation is $x^2 - y^2 = B$, and that if $B \neq 0$, they are also hyperbolae.

7. A 6×6 squared board is covered with 18 dominoes in the obvious way, each domino covering exactly two adjacent squares. Show that it is necessarily possible to draw a line, either across or down the board, which has dominoes on either side of it but does not pass through any domino.

Consider the similar problem with 32 dominoes on an 8×8 board.

8. A geometry is defined on the set of points

$$\{(x, y): 0 \leqslant x \leqslant 4, \quad 0 \leqslant y \leqslant 4, \quad x, y \in \mathbb{Z}\}.$$

All arithmetic operations are performed in arithmetic modulo 5.

A line is defined to be a set of points which satisfy some linear relation.
(*a*) What points are on the line $2x + 3y = 1$?
(*b*) What is the equation of the line on which lie $(1, 2)$ and $(4, 4)$?
(*c*) On which lines is the point $(3, 2)$?
(*d*) How many different lines are there altogether?

9. Unlimited supplies of straight rods (of negligible thickness) are available, all of whose lengths are integral multiples of one metre. They are used on the ground to form right-angled triangles and we denote by $N(i)$ the number of different right-angled triangles whose shortest side is i metres.
(*a*) Find $N(i)$ for $i = 12, 13, 14, 15$.
(*b*) Prove that for any given positive integer M, there exists a value of i such that $N(i) > M$.

10 S is a set of n positive integers whose sum is not divisible by n. Prove that it is possible to choose a subset of S, the sum of whose members is divisible by n.

PROJECT EXERCISES AND INVESTIGATIONS

1. BILINEAR FUNCTIONS AND MATRICES

1. Given $\qquad \mathbf{M} = \begin{pmatrix} 2 & -7 \\ 1 & -3 \end{pmatrix}$ and $\mathbf{r} = \begin{pmatrix} 5 \\ 1 \end{pmatrix}$,

find $\mathbf{Mr}$, $\mathbf{M(Mr)}$ and $\mathbf{M(M^2r)}$.
Given
$$f(x) = \frac{2x-7}{x-3},$$
find $f(5)$, $ff(5)$ and $fff(5)$.
Calculate $\mathbf{M}^2$ and find $ff(x)$.

2. Given $\qquad \mathbf{N} = \begin{pmatrix} 3 & -5 \\ 1 & -3 \end{pmatrix}$, $\mathbf{s} = \begin{pmatrix} 8 \\ 1 \end{pmatrix}$,

find $\mathbf{Ns}$, $\mathbf{N^2s}$ and $\mathbf{N^3s}$.
Given
$$g(x) = \frac{3x-5}{x-3},$$
find $g(8)$, $gg(8)$ and $ggg(8)$.

3. If $\qquad f(x) = \frac{ax+b}{cx+d}$ and $g(x) = \frac{px+q}{rx+s},$

find $fg(x)$ in its simplest form. Comment.

4. What are the inverses of
$$x \to \frac{ax+b}{cx+d} \quad \text{and} \quad \begin{pmatrix} a & b \\ c & d \end{pmatrix}?$$

5. In what ways are results for functions of the form $x \to \dfrac{ax+b}{cx+d}$ similar to those for the corresponding matrices, and in what ways are they different?

2. TRANSFORMATIONS OF GRAPHS

1. Show that the graphs of
$$y = (x-1)(x-2)(x-4) \quad \text{and} \quad y = (5-x)(6-x)(8-x)$$
are congruent. Give the equation of the image of the first graph under a half turn about $(5, 0)$.

2. Sketch the graphs of
$$y = \frac{x-3}{(x-1)(x-4)} \quad \text{and} \quad y = \frac{x-2}{(x-1)(x-4)}$$
and show that they are congruent.
What transformation maps the one graph onto the other?

3. Show that $\begin{pmatrix} \dfrac{1}{\sqrt5} & \dfrac{-2}{\sqrt5} \\[2mm] \dfrac{2}{\sqrt5} & \dfrac{1}{\sqrt5} \end{pmatrix}$ is the matrix of a rotation and that under this

rotation the graph of $13x^2 + 8xy + 7y^2 = 50$ maps onto the graph of $x^2 + 3y^2 = 10$. Sketch the two graphs.

4. Show that the graph of $x^2 - xy + y^2 = 5$ is congruent to each of the graphs in Question 3.

5. Under a rotation through $\theta°$ about the origin, the image of $x^2 + 3y^2 = 10$ has equation $ax^2 + bxy + cy^2 = 10$. Find $a + c$ and $b^2 - 4ac$. Generalize, and prove the results suggested.

3. DERIVATIVES OF b^x AND $\log_b x$

1. Investigate the derived function of $f: x \to 2^x$ by drawing its graph for the domain $-3 \leqslant x \leqslant 3$. Draw tangents, estimate their gradients and so complete this table.

x	-2	-1	0	1	2
$f'(x)$					
2^x					

Can you spot a connection between $f'(x)$ and $f(x)$?

2. Find approximate values of the derivatives of $g: x \to 10^x$ at $x = 1, 2, 3, 4$ by calculating average scale factors over small intervals as shown in the table. Complete the table by using logarithm tables in reverse to find the values of 10^x.

x	10^x	Increase in 10^x	Approximate value of $g'(x)$
1	10	0·23	23
1·01	10·23		
2			
2·01			
3			
3·01			
4			
4·01			

What does this suggest about the derived function?

3. For the function of Question 1, simplify $\dfrac{f(a+h) - f(a)}{h}$.

Show that $\displaystyle\lim_{h \to 0} \dfrac{f(a+h) - f(a)}{h}$ is proportional to 2^a.

4. Show that $g'(a) \propto g(a)$, and calculate the constant of proportionality as accurately as you can.

5. Your answers so far should show that for an exponential function $x \to b^x$ the derived function is $x \to kb^x$. Find approximate values for k when $b = 2, 4, 5, 10$. Comment.

6. Find the average scale factors for $x \to \log_{10} x$ over several small intervals such as $[1, 1\cdot01]$, and so guess the form of the derived function. Repeat for logarithm functions with other bases.

7. Simplify $\dfrac{\log_b ap - \log_b a}{ap - a}$. Does this confirm the result you guessed in Question 6?

4. POLAR COORDINATES AND GRAPHS

For this exercise, polar graph paper is useful but not essential.

1. Complete the table of values below for $r = 10 \cos 2\theta$.

θ	0	$\frac{1}{6}\pi$	$\frac{1}{4}\pi$	$\frac{1}{3}\pi$	$\frac{1}{2}\pi$	$\frac{2}{3}\pi$	$\frac{3}{4}\pi$	$\frac{5}{6}\pi$	π
r	10	5			-10				

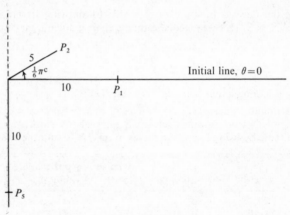

Fig. 1

The three points plotted in Figure 1 correspond to the three values of r given. To plot P_5, 'face in the $\frac{1}{2}\pi$ radians direction and move backwards a distance of 10 units'.

Plot all the points from the table and join them up. Then extend the domain and complete the curve.

2. Draw (or sketch) several other graphs of the family $r = 10 \cos a\theta$, taking, for example, $a = 1, 3, 4, 5$ and $a = \frac{1}{2}, \frac{1}{3}, \frac{1}{4}, \frac{2}{3}$.

How many loops does the complete graph have if a is an integer? Comment on the graphs obtained when a is a fraction.

3. Draw (or sketch) several graphs of the family $r = a + b \sin \theta$, and comment on the result of taking

　(i) $a > b$;　　　　　(ii) $a = b$;　　　　　(iii) $a < b$.

4. Draw the graphs of the family $r = \dfrac{3}{1 + e \cos \theta}$ for which $e = \frac{1}{2}, 1, 2$. Do you recognize the shapes of these graphs?

360

5. Show that with a suitable choice of Cartesian axes,

$$r = \sqrt{(x^2+y^2)}, \quad \cos\theta = x/r \quad \text{and} \quad \sin\theta = y/r.$$

Then obtain Cartesian equations for

$$r = 10\cos\theta, \quad r = 10\cos 2\theta, \quad r = 1+\sin\theta, \quad r = \frac{3}{1+\cos\theta}.$$

6. The position of a point is given in *bi-polar coordinates* by its distances r, r' from two fixed points O and O'. Investigate the graphs given by various simple equations in bi-polar coordinates, such as $r = 3r'$, $r+r' = 10$, $r+2r' = 15$, $rr' = 24$.

5. REGRESSION LINES

Figure 2 illustrates a situation that often arises in experimental science. An experiment that was expected to lead to a straight line graph has been carried out. Because of experimental errors, however, the observed values of the variables give non-collinear points. In practice the next step is generally to draw the 'best straight line through the points'. Can you define the 'best' line, and devise a statistic to represent the 'average error'?

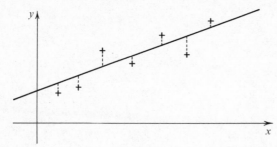

Fig. 2

1. Suppose we define the average error associated with the line $y = kx+l$ as the root mean square of the displacements parallel to the y-axis of the points from the line.

Show that this is
$$z = \sqrt{\left[\frac{1}{N}\sum_{i=1}^{N}(kx_i+l-y_i)^2\right]},$$

where the points are (x_1, y_1), (x_2, y_2), ..., (x_N, y_N).

2. (*a*) On a graph, plot the nine points whose coordinates are given in the following table.

x	-4	-3	-2	-1	0	1	2	3	4
y	$-6\cdot1$	-6	$-3\cdot3$	-2	$0\cdot4$	$1\cdot7$	$3\cdot9$	$4\cdot4$	$7\cdot0$

(*b*) Work out Σx_i, Σy_i, Σx_i^2, Σy_i^2, $\Sigma x_i y_i$, and so write $\Sigma(kx_i+l-y_i)^2$ in as simple a form as possible.

(*c*) Find the values of k and l which minimize this expression. With these values, draw the graph of $y = kx+l$. Would you agree that this is the 'best straight line' through the nine points?

3. A general formula for a line such as that in Question 2 (called a regression line) is found most easily by changing the origin to the point $(\bar{x}, \bar{y})$, i.e. using the transformation $x = X + \bar{x}$, $y = Y + \bar{y}$. The coefficients of the regression line $Y = aX + b$ result then from minimizing $(1/N)\Sigma(aX_i + b - Y_i)^2$, where $\Sigma X_i = 0$, $\Sigma Y_i = 0$. Find these values of a and b, and hence show that the equation of the line is

$$(y - \bar{y}) = \frac{v_{xy}}{v_x}(x - \bar{x}),$$

where v_x is the variance of the x_i's, and v_{xy} (the covariance of x and y) is defined as $(1/N)\Sigma(x_i - \bar{x})(y_i - \bar{y})$.

4. Suggest other definitions of 'best straight line' and 'average error' and find what results they give with the data of Question 2.

ANSWERS

CHAPTER 1

Ex. A **1.** (a) 7, 11, 15, 19, 23, 27; 43; 83; (b) 7, 1, -5, -11, -17, -23; -47; -107. **3.** 7118·9, 7122·4, 7125·9, 7129·4, 7132·9. **5.** 7, 21, 63, 189; 7×3^{11}. **6.** (a) 1, 1·25, 1·50; $(0·25^{19})$; (c) 25, 36, 49, 20^2; (e) 12·5, 62·5, 312·5; $(0·02 \times 5^{19})$; (g) 0, 5, 0; 10.

Ex. B **1.** (a) 4, 7, 13, 25, 49, 97, 193, 385; (b) 1, $\frac{1}{2}$, $\frac{2}{3}$, $\frac{3}{5}$, $\frac{5}{8}$, $\frac{8}{13}$, $\frac{13}{21}$, $\frac{21}{34}$, $\frac{34}{55}$, $\frac{55}{89}$, $\frac{89}{144}$.

Ex. D **1.** (a) -3, -1, 1, 3, 5; A.P.; (c) 12, 48, 192, 762, 3048; G.P.; (e) 0, 4, 16, 48, 128; (g) 1, -2, 3, -4, 5. **2.** (a) $u_n = 4n-3$; (c) $u_n = 3(-2)^{n-1}$. **3.** (a) 1, 3, 7, 15, 31; (c) 1, 3, 7, 15, 31; (e) 1, 3, 6, 10, 15. **5.** (a) -26, -35, -44; A.P.; (c) $13\frac{1}{2}$, $40\frac{1}{2}$, $121\frac{1}{2}$; G.P.; (e) $2a+4$, $2a+5$, $2a+6$; A.P.; (g) $\frac{1}{30}$, $\frac{1}{42}$, $\frac{1}{56}$. **6.** (a) 14th; (c) 8th; (e) $(n+1)$th; (g) 12th. **7.** 8; $\frac{1}{8} \times 2^n$ mm. **9.** (a) 2, 4, 6, 8, 34; (b) $u_n = 2^{n-1} + \frac{1}{6}(n-1)(n-2)(n-3)(n-4)$. **10.** (a) 3, 5, 7, 9, 11; 201; (c) 2, 1, 2, 1, 2; 1; (e) 1, 0, 2, 0, 3; 0. **11.** $u_n = n^2$; $u_1 = 1$, $u_{k+1} = u_k + 2k + 1$. **13.** (a) 300, 3000; (c) 0·9, 1·0; (e), 0·009, 0·001; (g) 3, 3; (i) 100, 1000.

Ex. E **1.** (a) 3, $2\frac{1}{2}$, $2\frac{1}{3}$; $u_n \to 2$; (c) $\frac{2}{3}$, $\frac{4}{5}$, $\frac{6}{7}$, $\frac{8}{9}$; $u_n \to 1$; (e) 0, $\frac{2}{3}$, $\frac{6}{4}$, $\frac{12}{5}$, $\frac{20}{6}$; $u_n \to \infty$. **2.** (a) $u_n = 120/n \to 0$; (c) $u_n = (n-1)/(2n-1) \to \frac{1}{2}$. **3.** (a) No; (c) No. **5.** $u_4 = 66$; $u_2 = 48$, $u_6 = 72$; $u_n \to 84$. **7.** 3·5, 3·18, 3·16, 3·16; $u_n^2 \to 10$.

Misc. **1.** 2, 4, 10 28, 82, 244; $u_n = 3^{n-1} + 1$. **3.** 1, 2, 1·75, 1·73, 1·73. **5.** $u_1 = 0$, $u_{k+1} = u_k + f_k/f_{k+1}$.

CHAPTER 2

Ex. A **1.** No. **3.** 5·6 kg/ha. **5.** 80p/ha, 2 kg/ha.

Ex. B **1.** About 1930; 50 %. **3.** 3700.

Ex. C **1.** 11·25 m, 5 m/s. **5.** £168; $c = 3d^2 + 3d$. **7.** $PV = 3155$; $V = 126$ when $P = 25$.

Ex. D **1.** $6\frac{1}{4}$, 10, $11\frac{1}{4}$, 0. $\{x: 0 \leqslant x \leqslant 11\frac{1}{4}\}$. **3.** 270, 280. $\{x: 0 < x < 300\}$. **5.** $\{H: -2 \leqslant H \leqslant 2\}$. **7.** (a) Reflection in 0; (b) translation -4; (c) enlargement, scale factor $\frac{1}{2}$, centre 0; (d) enlargement, scale factor 3, centre 1. **9.** $\{y: 0 \leqslant y \leqslant 9\}$.

Ex. E **1.** -30, 160, 190. $13\frac{1}{3}$ °C. **3.** $\frac{1}{2}$, 3, $\frac{1}{3}$, 2, 4. $1/a$, $1+a$, $1/(1+a)$, a, $2+a$. $gf: x \to 1 + 1/x$, $fg: x \to 1/(1+x)$, $ff: x \to x$, $gg: x \to 2+x$. -1, 0. **5.** $\mathbb{R} \times \mathbb{R}$. $fg: \begin{pmatrix} x \\ y \end{pmatrix} \to \begin{pmatrix} ap+br & aq+bs \\ cp+dr & cq+ds \end{pmatrix} \begin{pmatrix} x \\ y \end{pmatrix}$. **7.** $fg = gf = h$, $fh = hf = g$, $gh = hg = f$.

Ex. F **1.** 0·6 amp; 22 ohm. $R \to R+2 = u \to 12/u = 12/(R+2) = I$. $I \to 12/I = v \to v-2 = 12/I - 2 = R$. **3.** (a) $x \to \frac{1}{2}(x+3)$; (c) $x \to 1/(x-3)$; (e) $x \to \frac{1}{7}(2 - 3/x)$. **5.** $ef = f = fe$.

Ex. G 1. (a) 250; (b) 200; (c) 50; (d) 200; (e) 0 or 300.

Misc. 1. a, c, e. **3.** $\frac{1}{36}, \frac{2}{36}, \frac{3}{36}, \frac{4}{36}, \frac{5}{36}, \frac{6}{36}, \frac{5}{36}, \frac{4}{36}, \frac{3}{36}, \frac{2}{36}, \frac{1}{36}$. Yes; no.
7. 9. If domain = $\{\frac{1}{2}, 1, 1\frac{1}{2}, 2, 2\frac{1}{2}, 3\}$ and codomain = {positive integers},
range = {3, 6, 9, 12, 14, 17}. **9.** Domain = {1, 2, 3, ..., 10}. 85; 595.

CHAPTER 3

Ex. A 3. Parallel. **9.** Symmetrical about Oy: 5a, b; 6b; 8a, b. Half turn
symmetry about O: 5c; 6a; 7b.

Ex. B 3. $x^2 = x^3$ when $x = 0$ or 1; $x^2 > x^3$ for $0 < x < 1$; $x^2 < x^3$ for
$x > 1$. **5.** (1, 1); (1, 1) and (−1, 1). **9.** (a) even; (b) odd.

11. (a) (1, 0); (c) (−1, 0) and (0, 0). **13.** (a) $y \to 2$, (i) less, (ii) greater;
(c) $y \to 1$, (i) less, (ii) greater.

Ex. C 7. Translations parallel to Ox.
15. $f(3) = f(-3); f(c) = f(-c)$. **17.** All powers of x are even powers.

Ex. D 1. (a) odd; (c) neither; (e) even; (g) odd. **3.** Reflection in
$x = 90$, $x = 270$ etc.; half turn about (0, 0), (180, 0) etc.; translation of $\binom{360}{0}$,
$\binom{720}{0}$ etc.

5. (a) $y = (x-1)^3$; (b) $y = x^3+2$; (c) $y = (x-2)^3+4$.
7. (a) $y = 6x-x^2$; (c) $y = (x+3)^2-6(x+3)+2$.
8. (a) $y = x^2-9$; (c) $y = \frac{1}{2}(9-x^2)$. **9.** f, g odd: (i) odd, (ii) even,
(iii) odd; f, g even: (i) even, (ii) even, (iii) even; f odd, g even: (i) —, (ii) odd,
(iii) even. **10.** (a) $f^{-1}: x \to 2x-6$; (c) $f^{-1}: x \to 1/x$; (e) $f^{-1}: x \to x/(x-1)$.

Misc. 6. (a) Translation $\binom{0}{a}$; (c) translation $\binom{a}{b}$; (e) stretch $\times 1/a$ in
x-direction. **9.** $g(x) = \frac{1}{2}(f(x)-f(-x))$, $h(x) = \frac{1}{2}(f(x)+f(-x))$.

CHAPTER 4

Ex. A 1. (i) all equal; (iii) $(c+d)^2 = c^2+2cd+d^2$; (v) $a(b+c) = ab+ac$;
(vii) $(c-b)^2 = (c-b)(c-b)$, $c^2-b^2 = (c-b)(c+b)$. **2.** (i) No; (iii) yes;
(v) no; (vii) no.

Ex. B 1. (i) 1; (iii) $45\frac{1}{2}$. **3.** (i) $15x^2-6x$; (iii) x^3-6x^2-2x; (v) $4x^2-9$.
7. (a) x^3-1; (b) $\mathbf{M}^3-\mathbf{I}$.

Ex. C 1. (i) $-4x^3+3x^2-2x-2$; (iii) $2x^4-7x^3+7x^2-3x-2$; (v) $2C$.
3. (i) $12x^5-20x^4-x^3+27x^2-26x+8$; (ii) $6x^6-19x^5+31x^4-29x^3+13x^2-2x$.
4. (i) $4x^2+4x+1$; (iii) $5x-1$; (v) $25x^2-10x+1$; (vii) $12x^2-2x-4$.
7. (i) (a) $-1+5x-4x^2+2x^3$; (b) $2x^3-4x^2+5x-1$; degree 3.
(iii) (a) $4-2x^2-x^3+x^5$; (b) $x^5-x^3-2x^2+4$; degree 5.
9. (a) $3x^3-2x^2+x+1$; (b) $-x^3-2x^2-x+7$;
(c) $2x^6-4x^5+x^4+3x^3+6x^2+4x-12$.
11. (i) $2x^2-x-1$; (iii) $4x^2+12x+9$; (v) $6+10x-4x^2$; (vii) $6x^2+13x-15$;

364

(ix) $400x^2-40x+1$.　　**13.** $11; -6$.　　**15.** $12+5x-2x^2$.　　**17.** x^4-16.
19. $1+2x+x^2$, $1+3x+3x^2+x^3$, $1+4x+6x^2+4x^3+x^4$,
$1+5x+10x^2+10x^3+5x^4+x^5$, $1+6x+15x^2+20x^3+15x^4+6x^5+x^6$.

Ex. D　1. $(x+1)(x+2)$.　　**3.** $(x-2)(x-3)$.　　**5.** $(x+4)(2x-3)$.
7. $(3x-4)(x+2)$.　　**9.** $(x-4)(x+6)$.

Ex. E　1. $(x+3)(x+2)$.　　**3.** $(x-5)(x-3)$.　　**5.** $(x-9)(x-2)$.
7. $(3+x)(2-x)$.　　**9.** $(2x-3)(x+1)$.　　**11.** $(2x+5)(x+3)$.
13. $(x^2+6)(x^2+4)$.　　**15.** $(x+2)(x-9)$.　　**17.** $x(2x+7)$.　　**19.** $(2x-3)^2$.
21. $(2x+3)(4x-3)$.　　**23.** $(x^2-1)(x^2-4)=(x+1)(x-1)(x+2)(x-2)$.

Ex. F　1. $(3x+2)(2x+5)$.　　**3.** $3(4x+1)(3x+2)$.　　**5.** $3(x^2+16)$.
7. $(x-3)(7x+2)$.　　**9.** $(3x+2)(4x-5)$.　　**11.** $2(x-2)(7x+1)$.
13. $\frac{7}{2}(x-1)(3x-1)$.　　**15.** $\frac{1}{6}x(x^2-30x+18)$.　　**17.** $-3x(2x-1)$.
19. $(x+1)(x-3)$.　　**21.** $(x-2)(x^2-3x-4)$.

Ex. G　1. Yes.　　**3.** Yes.　　**5.** Yes.　　**7.** 5.
9. Possible factors $(x\pm1)$, $(3x\pm1)$.　$P=(x+1)^2(3x-1)$.
11. Possible factors $(x\pm1)$, $(x\pm2)$, $(x\pm3)$, $(x\pm6)$, $(2x\pm1)$, $(2x\pm3)$.
$P=(x+1)(x+2)(2x-3)$.

Ex. H　1. $q=18, r=1$.　　**3.** $Q=x^2-4x+11, R=-27$.　　**5.** $Q=\frac{3}{2}$,
$R=\frac{11}{2}$.　　**7.** $Q=x+4, R=4x-8$.　　**9.** $Q=x-2, R=5x-5$.
11. $P=x+2$.　　**13.** (i) $(x-1)(x^2+x+1)$;　(ii) $(x-3)(x^2+3x+9)$;
(iii) $(x-c)(x^2+cx+c^2)$.　　**15.** (a) Possible factors $(x\pm1)$, $(x\pm2)$, $(x\pm4)$,
$(2x\pm1)$.　$P=(x+2)^2(2x-1)$.　(c) Possible factors $(x\pm1)$, $(x\pm3)$, $(2x\pm1)$,
$(2x\pm3)$. P cannot be factorized.

Ex. I　1. $3x^3+6x^2y^2$.　　**3.** $x^2y-5x+2xy^2-10y-3xyz+15z$.
5. $4x^2+12xy+9y^2$.　　**7.** (iii) and (v) are correct.　　**8.** (i) $26x^2+3xy-9y^2$;
(iii) $x^3+6x^2y+12xy^2+8y^3$;　(v) $2x^3$.
9. (a) $x^2-4xy+y^2$;　(b) $4x^2+2xy+y^2$;　(c) $3x^2-2xy+3y^2$.
11. (a) $(x-2y)(x-3y)$;　(c) —;　(e) $(x-2y)(x^2+2xy+4y^2)$.

Ex. J　1. $(x+5)(2x+1)$.　**3.** $27x^2+81x+61$.　**5.** $(x+1)(x+5)(x+2)(x+6)$.
7. $\frac{1}{4}x^2(x+1)^2$.

Ex. K　1. $\frac{7}{17}$.　　**3.** $\dfrac{x+1}{x-1}$.　　**5.** $\dfrac{x^2+x+1}{x+1}$.　　**7.** $\dfrac{x-7}{x+3}$.

9. $-\left(\dfrac{2x-1}{4y^2+2y+1}\right)$.

Ex. L　1. $\dfrac{11}{6x}$.　　**3.** $\dfrac{2x}{x^2-1}$.　　**5.** $\dfrac{7-3x}{(1-x)^2}$.　　**7.** $\dfrac{13x}{6}$.　　**9.** $\dfrac{5}{3}$.

11. $\dfrac{x^2+15}{3x}$.　**13.** $\dfrac{11}{x^2}$.　**15.** $\dfrac{3x+5}{(x+1)(x+2)}$, $\dfrac{-x-3}{(x+1)(x+2)}$, $\dfrac{2}{(x+1)(x+2)}$,
$\dfrac{x+1}{2(x+2)}$.　**17.** $\dfrac{1+2x-x^2}{(1+x)(1-x)^2}$, $\dfrac{-1-x^2}{(1+x)(1-x)^2}$, $\dfrac{x}{(1+x)(1-x)^3}$, $\dfrac{x(1-x)}{1+x}$.

19. $\dfrac{2x^2-2x+5}{(x-1)(x-2)(x+1)}$, $\dfrac{6x-3}{(x-1)(x-2)(x+1)}$, $\dfrac{1}{(x-1)^2}$, $\dfrac{(x+1)^2}{(x-2)^2}$.

21. $\dfrac{3}{(x-1)(x-3)}$.　　**23.** $\dfrac{4}{x+2}$.

25. $f^{-1}: x \to \dfrac{3x+4}{x-1}$, $g^{-1}: x \to \dfrac{x+3}{x-2}$, $h^{-1}: x \to \dfrac{3x-5}{x-3}$. h is self-inverse.

27. (i) $\dfrac{a-b}{ab}$, $-\dfrac{1}{ab}$;   (ii) $\dfrac{3a-3b}{(3b-2)(3a-2)}$, $\dfrac{-3}{(3b-2)(3a-2)}$;

(iii) $\dfrac{a^2-b^2}{a^2b^2}$, $-\left(\dfrac{a+b}{a^2b^2}\right)$.

Misc. 1. (i) $(5, -9, 1, 2)$ and $(6, -23, 22, -1, -10)$;
(ii) $(4, 6, 2, -4)$ and $(3, 6, 8, 6, -27, 4)$;   (iii) $(a_0+b_0, a_1+b_1, a_2+b_2, b_3)$ and
$(a_0b_0, a_0b_1+a_1b_0, a_0b_2+a_1b_1+a_2b_0, a_0b_3+a_1b_2+a_2b_1, a_1b_3+a_2b_2, a_2b_3)$.
3. $r = 23/14$, $s = -29/14$.   **5.** $q = 2x^5+x^4+2x^3+5x^2+6x+12$, $r = 29$.
7. $a_5 = 3$, $r_4 = 32$, $r_3 = 140$, $r_2 = 312$, $r_1 = 351$, $r_0 = 163$.

CHAPTER 5

Ex. A 1. $v = 3$ m/s, apparently.
3. 1935–45, 3 thou/year; 1940–50, 3·3 thou/year; 3·6, 4·1, 4·5, 4·9.
5. 10, 30, 50, 70 m/s. $d = 5t^2$.   25, 85 m/s.

Ex. B 1. [4, 7], [1, 13]. S.F. = 3.   **3.** 4, -4.   **5.** 17 m/s.
7. 12, 11, 10·5, 10·1;   8, 9, 9·5, 9·9; $b+5 \approx 10$ when $b \approx 5$.
8. (a) 36, 33, 31·5, 30·3;   24, 27, 28·5, 29·7; $3b+15 \approx 30$ when $b \approx 5$.
(c) answers as in (a) with 6 added.
9. $(b^2-3b-4)/(b-4) = b+1$;   7, 6, 5·5, 5·1, 5·001.

Ex. C 1. (a) [18, 50], [18, 32], [18, 19·22], [2, 18], [8, 18], [16·8, 18].   16,
14, 12·2, 8, 10, 11·8.   Derivative is 12.
(b) A.S.F.'s and derivative are 7.   (c) A.S.F.'s are 23, 21, 19·2, 15, 17, 18·8;
derivative is 19.   **3.** A.S.F.'s are $b^2+5b+25$, $\frac{1}{3}(b+5)$, $-b-4$, $-1/(5b)$;
derivatives are 75, 5, -9, $-\frac{1}{25}$.   **5.** $\frac{1}{6}$.   **6.** (a) 4;   (c) -2;   (e) $\frac{1}{3}$.
7. (a) 4, 6, 8, 10; $2a$.   (c) 4, 6, 8, 10; $2a$.   (e) 12, 27, 48, 75; $3a^2$.
8. (a) $b+a$;   (c) $b+a$;   (e) b^2+ba+a^2.
9. (a) $2a+h$;   (c) $2a+h$;   (e) $3a^2+3ah+h^2$.

Ex. D 1. (a) $x \to 10x+3$;   (c) $x \to 3x^2-2/x^2$;   (e) $x \to 6x^2+8$.
2. (a) 11, 6;   (c) $7\frac{3}{4}$, $2\frac{1}{16}$;   (e) 1, 2.
3. $f': t \to 30-8t$.   26, 22;   44, 14;   54, 6;   56, -2. $v = 0$ when $t = 3\frac{3}{4}$;
$f(3\frac{3}{4}) = 56\frac{1}{4}$.

Ex. E 1. (a) $2x$;   (c) 1;   (e) $-1/(x+2)^2$.   **3.** $f': x \to 1/(2\sqrt{x})$;
$g': x \to 1/(3\sqrt[3]{x^2})$.

Ex. F 1. $-4, 0, 4$.   **2.** (a) $2\frac{1}{4}$;   (c) -4;   (e) 0.
3. (a) $3x^2-20x$;   (b) $2-1/(2\sqrt{x})$.
5. (a) $(2, -8)$ min;   (b) $(0, 0)$ max, $(2, -8)$ min.
7. After 4 s;   40 m/s; $t = 3$.
9. 15, 5, 0, -5, -15 m/s; -10 m/s² throughout.   **11.** 4·49;   4·5;   4·8, 4·4.

Ex. G 1. 3.   **2.** (a) $(-5, -25)$ min;   (c) $(\sqrt{3}, -6\sqrt{3})$ min,
$(-\sqrt{3}, 6\sqrt{3})$ max;   (e) $(1, 2)$ min, $(-1, -2)$ max;   (g) $(-2, -4)$, $(2, -4)$ min;
$(0, 12)$ max.   **3.** $\sqrt{12} \approx 3.5$.   **5.** 32 m.   **7.** 6 cm.
9. $f': x \to 3x^2-12x$, $f'': x \to 6x-12$. When $x = 2$, graph of f'' crosses Ox, graph
of f' has a minimum, graph of f'' has a point of inflexion.

Ex. H **3.** (a) 6, 1, -2; (c) $6\frac{1}{2}$, $-1\frac{1}{4}$, $2\frac{1}{4}$. **4.** (a) $(0, 0)$; (c) $(0, 1)$; (e) $(0, -4)$. **6.** $(1, 1)$; 0. **7.** (a) $(0, 0)$ infl; $(-\frac{3}{8}, -\frac{27}{2048})$ min; (c) $(0, 0)$, $(6, 0)$ min; $(3, 81)$ max.

Misc. **1.** $0\cdot145, 0\cdot072, 0\cdot048$. $f'(a) \propto 1/a$. **3.** b, d. **5.** Integers; 0.
9. $x = 2$. **11.** (a) $\frac{1}{8}$; (b) 8; (c) $-\frac{1}{256}$; (d) $\frac{1}{64}$; (e) 2. (i) Yes; (ii) no; (iii) no.

REVISION EXERCISES

Rev. 1 **3.** (a) $u_1 = 8$, $u_{k+1} = u_k \times \frac{3}{2}$; $u_n = 8 \times (\frac{3}{2})^{n-1}$. (c) $u_1 = 20$, $u_{k+1} = u_k + 6$; $u_n = 14 + 6n$. (e) $u_1 = 3$, $u_{k+1} = 3u_k + 2$; $u_n = 4 \times 3^{n-1} - 1$.
5. (a) $100, 50, 25, 12\frac{1}{2}$; $u_1 = 100, u_{k+1} = \frac{1}{2}u_k$; $u_n = 100 \times (\frac{1}{2})^{n-1}$. (b) $1, 4, 9, 16$; $u_1 = 1, u_{k+1} = u_k + 2k + 1$; $u_n = n^2$. **7.** $u_1 = 0, u_2 = 1, u_{k+2} = 2(u_{k+1} + u_k)$.

Rev. 2 **1.** $7, -17, -25, 5 - 6x, 13 - 6x, 4, -\frac{1}{3}, \frac{1}{6}(5 - x), \frac{1}{2}(7 - 3x), \frac{1}{3}(7 - 2x)$.
2. (a) $\{x : 1\frac{1}{2} \leqslant x \leqslant 6\}$; (c) $\{x : 0 \leqslant x \leqslant 16\}$; (e) $\{0, 1, 2, 3, ..., 12\}$.
3. (a) fg; (c) fg^{-1}; (e) gff.
5. (a) $f(3) = 6, f^{-1}(6) = 3$; (b) $\{x : 0 \leqslant x \leqslant 14\}$; (c) $x \to 4x$ for $0 \leqslant x \leqslant 1$, $x \to x + 3$ for $1 \leqslant x \leqslant 5$, $x \to \frac{4}{9}x + 5\frac{7}{9}$ for $5 \leqslant x \leqslant 14$; (d) $10\cdot4$.

Rev. 3 **4.** (a) Odd; (c) odd; (e) neither; (g) neither.
6. (a) $y = \sqrt(x - 2)$; (c) $y = \sqrt(-x)$; (e) $x = \sqrt{y}$; (g) $x = -\sqrt{y}$.
7. (a) $f^{-1} : x \to (10 - 3x)/(x - 3)$; (b) $g^{-1} = g$.

Rev. 4 **1.** (a) $x^3 + 6x^2 + x - 5$, $x^4 + 11x^3 + 30x^2 - 10x - 50$; $q = x^2 + x - 5$; $r = 15$; (b) $x^3 + x^2 + 11x - 1$, $x^5 + 4x^4 + 4x^3 + 30x^2 - 13x - 6$; $q = x - 4$, $r = 26x - 10$; (c) $2x^3 - x^2 + 10x + 3$; $4x^4 + 15x^2 + 12x + 2$; $q = x^2 - x + 4\frac{1}{2}$, $r = -2\frac{1}{2}$. **2.** (a) $(x - 16)(x + 3)$; (c) $(2x - 3)(2x + 3)(4x^2 + 9)$; (e) $(3x - 10)(2x - 3)$. **3.** $q = x^2 - x + 2, r = -5$.
5. (a) $3x^2 + h^2$; (b) $-1/(x^2 - h^2)$; (c) $2x + 4$.
6. (a) $\dfrac{-2}{(x + 1)^2 (x - 1)}$; (c) $\dfrac{2}{3x - 4}$; (e) $\dfrac{4(x - 4)}{x^2 + 3x + 4}$.
7. (a) $\frac{1}{4}x(x - 2)(3x - 5)$; (b) $\frac{1}{6}n(n - 1)(n + 1)$.
9. $(x - 1)^2$; $\{x : x \leqslant -2$ or $x = 1\}$.

Rev. 5 **1.** (a) $f' : x \to 21x^6 - 16x^3 + 12x - 12$; (c) $f' : x \to 8x + 12$.
2. (a) $5, -2, -2$; (c) $0, -9, 0$, infl.
3. (a) -6; (b) $1 - 1/a^2$; (c) $g' : x \to -2x/(1 + x^2)^2$. **5.** $(4, 15)$. **7.** 5 cm.

CHAPTER 6

Ex. A **1.** (a) 30, 20, 10, 20, 30; (b) $29\cdot5, 28\cdot1, 25\cdot9, 23\cdot1$; (d) $-25, -30, 31, 18$; (e) $y = 10\cos(180t)° + 20$.
2. High 0300, 1500; low 0900, 2100; fastest rate $= 2\cdot6$ at 0600, 1200 etc.

Ex. B **3.** (a) $0\cdot0175, 0\cdot0175, 0\cdot0164, 0\cdot0151, 0\cdot0134, 0\cdot0112, 0\cdot0087, 0\cdot0060$, $0\cdot0030, 0$; (c) $x \to -0\cdot0175 \sin x°$.

Ex. C **1.** $K \approx 0\cdot035$. **3.** $t \to -31\cdot5\sin 180t°$, $t \to 2\cdot625\cos 30t°$.

Ex. D **1.** (c) 1, $0\cdot5$, 1; (d) $0\cdot2955, 0\cdot9553, 0\cdot8912, 0\cdot4536$; (e) $1, -1$.
4. (a) $-3\sin x$; (c) $2\cos x - 5\sin x$; (e) $2\cos 2x - 5\sin 5x$.
5. (a) 12, 2 m; (b) 5.14 p.m.; (c) $12\cdot57$ h; (d) $2\cdot5$, $1\cdot35$ m/h.
7. (a) $2\pi, \pi, 4\pi, \frac{1}{5}\pi$; (b) $x = 2\sin 2\pi t$, $x = 2\sin 20\pi t$, $x = 2\sin 400\pi t$.

9. (a) π; (b) $1 \cdot 5$; (c) $v = -1 \cdot 5\pi \sin \pi t$, $a = -1 \cdot 5\pi^2 \cos \pi t$; (d) $v = 0$ when $t = n$, where $n \in \mathbb{N}$; v is max when $t = 2n + 1 \cdot 5$. $a = 0$ when $t = n + 0 \cdot 5$; a is max when $t = 2n + 1$. **11.** $|h| < 0 \cdot 55$.

Ex. E 1. $\frac{3}{4}\pi$, $\frac{3}{2}\pi$, $\frac{5}{3}\pi$, $\frac{13}{6}\pi$, 4π, $\frac{17}{4}\pi$, $\frac{3}{8}\pi$, $\frac{1}{5}\pi$, $\frac{3}{5}\pi$, $\frac{11}{18}\pi$ radians.
3. $-1, 1, \frac{1}{2}\sqrt{3}, -\frac{1}{2}\sqrt{3}$. **5.** $\theta = 1\frac{1}{4}$ rad, $A = 126$ cm².
7. (a) $r^2\omega$; (b) $\frac{1}{3}r^3\omega$.

Ex. F 1. (a) B' is $(-\frac{3}{5}, \frac{4}{5})$, $\begin{pmatrix} \frac{4}{5} & -\frac{3}{5} \\ \frac{3}{5} & \frac{4}{5} \end{pmatrix}$; (c) $(-\frac{4}{5}, -\frac{3}{5})$, $\begin{pmatrix} -\frac{3}{5} & -\frac{4}{5} \\ \frac{4}{5} & -\frac{3}{5} \end{pmatrix}$.

3. $\mathbf{R}_a\mathbf{R}_b = \mathbf{R}_b\mathbf{R}_a = \begin{pmatrix} \frac{33}{65} & -\frac{56}{65} \\ \frac{56}{65} & \frac{33}{65} \end{pmatrix}$. A rotation.

5. $\cos(\theta - \phi) = \cos\theta\cos\phi + \sin\theta\sin\phi$, $\sin(\theta - \phi) = \sin\theta\cos\phi - \cos\theta\sin\phi$.

Ex. G 1. $\cos^2\theta + \sin^2\theta = 1$. **5.** $\cos\phi$; $\sin^2\theta + \cos^2\theta = 1$.
7. $\cos\theta = \frac{4}{5}$, $\sin\phi = \frac{15}{17}$; $\frac{84}{85}$, $-\frac{13}{85}$, $\frac{36}{85}$. **9.** $\sin 2\theta = 2\sin\theta\cos\theta$.
15. $\cos 3\theta = 4\cos^3\theta - 3\cos\theta$.
17. (a) $\sin A$; (c) $2\cos P\cos Q$; (e) $\cos x$; (g) $\pm\tan x$. **19.** $0 \cdot 8748$, $0 \cdot 5152$.

Misc. 1. $\sin x$. **3.** (b) $y = 0 \cdot 5\sin 800\pi t$; (c) 400π mm/s.
5. (ii) $\left(\dfrac{\tan h}{h}\right)\left(\dfrac{1 + \tan^2 a}{1 - \tan a \tan h}\right)$.

CHAPTER 7

Ex. A 3. (d) $5\mathbf{i} + \mathbf{j}$; $\sqrt{26}$ at $11 \cdot 3°$ to Ox. **5.** (d) $\mathbf{i} - \mathbf{j}$; $\sqrt{2}$, $-45°$.
7. (d) $\mathbf{j}$; $1, 90°$. **9.** (a) 72 km/h, 48 km/h; (b) 8 m/s, 0.
11. (a) $(0, 0)$, $(1, 0 \cdot 74)$, $(2, 1 \cdot 45)$; $37°$ to horizontal, 25 m/s.

Ex. B 1. (a) $\mathbf{0}$, $\mathbf{i} + 3\mathbf{j}$, $4\mathbf{i} + 6\mathbf{j}$, $9\mathbf{i} + 9\mathbf{j}$; (b) $2t\mathbf{i} + 3\mathbf{j}$; (c) $3\mathbf{j}$, 3, $90°$;
$2\mathbf{i} + 3\mathbf{j}$, $\sqrt{13}$, $56 \cdot 3°$; $4\mathbf{i} + 3\mathbf{j}$, 5, $36 \cdot 9°$; $6\mathbf{i} + 3\mathbf{j}$, $\sqrt{45}$, $26 \cdot 6°$.
3. (a) $2\mathbf{i} + 3\mathbf{j}$, $3\mathbf{i} + \mathbf{j}$, $4\mathbf{i} - \mathbf{j}$, $5\mathbf{i} - 3\mathbf{j}$; (b) $\mathbf{i} - 2\mathbf{j}$; (c) $\sqrt{5}$, $-63 \cdot 4°$ at all times.
5. (a) $\mathbf{0}$, $\mathbf{i}$, $2\mathbf{i}$, $3\mathbf{i}$; (b) $\mathbf{i} + \pi\cos\pi t\mathbf{j}$; (c) $\mathbf{i} + \pi\mathbf{j}$, $3 \cdot 32$, $72 \cdot 3°$ when $t = 0$ and 2;
$\mathbf{i} - \pi\mathbf{j}$, $3 \cdot 32$, $-72 \cdot 3°$ when $t = 1$ and 3.
7. 5, $2\mathbf{n} + (1 - 6\pi)\mathbf{e}$, $2\mathbf{n} + \mathbf{e}$; 0, $(2 - \frac{5}{2}\pi)\mathbf{n} + (1 + 6\pi)\mathbf{e}$.
9. (i) $16\mathbf{n} + 12\mathbf{e} + 48\mathbf{u}$; (ii) 112 m, $16\mathbf{n} + 12\mathbf{e} + 8\mathbf{u}$, 138 m; (iii) 115 m, 192 m.
11. $-10\mathbf{j}$ for each interval.

Ex. C 1. (a) $5\mathbf{i} + 10\mathbf{j}$, $5\mathbf{i} + 10\mathbf{j}$; (c) $-0 \cdot 12\mathbf{i} + 0 \cdot 48\mathbf{j}$, $-0 \cdot 24\mathbf{i} + 0 \cdot 96\mathbf{j}$.
2. (a) $\mathbf{0}$; (c) $\mathbf{j}$. **3.** (a) $-5\mathbf{i} + 3\mathbf{j}$; (b) $4\mathbf{i} + 2\mathbf{j}$; (c) $-2\mathbf{i} + 2\mathbf{j}$, $4\mathbf{i} + 2\mathbf{j}$, $10\mathbf{i} + 2\mathbf{j}$.
5. $25\mathbf{i} - 5\mathbf{j}$, $25\mathbf{i} - 10\mathbf{j}$, $25\mathbf{i} - 20\mathbf{j}$, $25\mathbf{i} - 100\mathbf{j}$. **7.** 10^7 m/s, $36 \cdot 9°$.
9. $2\mathbf{i} + 4\mathbf{j}$. **11.** $t = 2$; $\mathbf{r} = -27\mathbf{i} - 68\mathbf{j}$, $\mathbf{a} = 12\mathbf{i} + 42\mathbf{j}$.

Ex. D 1. Velocity: 10 at $36 \cdot 9°$, 8 at $0°$, 10 at $-36 \cdot 9°$; acceleration: 2 at $270°$ at all times. **5.** Velocity: 20 at $270°$, 3 at $0°$, $23 \cdot 3$ at $59°$, $48 \cdot 3$ at $56°$; acceleration: 20 at $90°$, $20 \cdot 9$ at $73 \cdot 3°$, $23 \cdot 3$ at $59°$, $26 \cdot 9$ at $48°$. Point of inflexion.
7. (a) $-\mathbf{i} + 4\mathbf{j}$; (b) $y = 2x^2 - 1$. **9.** $a = v^2/r$; towards the centre of the circle.
11. 3; $(1, 4)$; 15.

Ex. E 1. 10 rad/s; 95·5 rev/min. **3.** $18 \cdot 9$ m/s; $37 \cdot 7$ m.
7. $2 \cdot 5 \times 10^5$ km/h².
9. (a) 463 m/s, $3 \cdot 35 \times 10^{-2}$ m/s²; (b) 231 m/s, $1 \cdot 67 \times 10^{-2}$ m/s².
11. 10 m.

Misc. 1. (i) $x = t^{3k}$, $y = t^{2k}$ where k is odd; (ii) Yes, if t is restricted to non-negative values. **3.** Gradient $= 1/(4\pi)$. **7.** $27 \cdot 4$ m/s, $22 \cdot 6$ m/s.

CHAPTER 8

Ex. A **1.** (a) 128, 2^7; (c) 48; (e) 4, 2^2; (g) 24; (i) 6561, 3^8.
3. (a) 5^6; (c) 2^4. **4.** (a) 2; (c) 5; (e) a. **5.** (a) $2x^5$; (c) 3; (e) 1; (g) xy.
6. (a) F; (c) F; (e) T. **8.** (a) 2^4, 1; (c) 3^3, $\frac{1}{3}$; (e) 4^5, $\frac{1}{4}$.
9. (a) 2; (c) 10; (e) 2. **10.** (a) 2^{12}, 2^3; (c) 3^6, 3^3.

Ex. B **1.** (a) 5^2; (c) $7^{\frac{1}{3}}$; (e) $3^{\frac{3}{4}}$. **2.** 2^3, $4^{\frac{3}{2}}$; (c) 2^{-2}, 4^{-1}; (e) $2^{\frac{2}{3}}$, $4^{\frac{2}{3}}$.
3. (a) $\frac{1}{64}$; (c) $\frac{1}{2}$; (e) 3; (g) 1; (i) $\frac{1}{729}$. **5.** (a) 4; (c) 256; (e) 16807; (g) $\frac{1}{4}$.
6. (a) 0·45; (c) 1·8; (e) 0·15. **7.** (a) x^{-1}; (c) x. **8.** (a) 6; (c) 1.
9. (a) 6·9284; (c) 7·0710; (e) 4·2426; (g) 5·6568; (i) 22·361.

Ex. C **1.** (a) $-3x^{-4}$; (c) $-5x^{-6}$; (e) $-5x^{-2}$; (g) $\frac{1}{4}x^{-\frac{3}{4}}$; (i) $\frac{3}{2}x^{\frac{1}{2}}$; (k) $-\frac{1}{3}x^{-\frac{4}{3}}$.
2. (a) $2nx^{2n-1}$; (c) $2nx^{2n-1}$; (e) $-\frac{1}{2}nx^{-\frac{1}{2}n-1}$; (g) $\frac{3}{2}x^{\frac{1}{2}}$.
3. (a) $\frac{1}{16}$, $-\frac{1}{32}$; (c) $\frac{1}{2}$, $-\frac{1}{16}$.

Ex. D **1.** 1·6, 2, 2·4, 3, 3·7, 4·5, 5·5, 6·8 millions; 2·3, 3·9, 4·8 millions;
12.42 p.m. **3.** $m = 50 \times 0·8^t$. (a) 1·5 years ago; (b) in 1·6 years time.
5. 2·08, 5·19, 0·58. **7.** (a) 6·7; (c) 5·8; (e) 1·9. **9.** No.

Ex. E **1.** 0·68, 0·86, 1·54, 1·72, 1·86; $\log_5 12 = \log_5 3 + \log_5 4$,
$\log_5 16 = 2\log_5 4$, $\log_5 20 = 1 + \log_5 4$. **2.** (a) -1; (c) 6; (e) 3; (g) -1; (i) 2.
3. (a) 4; (c) 2; (e) $\dfrac{1}{\sqrt{10}}$. **4.** (a) $+$; (c) $-$.
5. (a) 1·79; (c) 0·41; (e) 2·89; (g) 0·345; (i) 0·46. **6.** (a) 7; (c) 6; (e) 2.
8. (a) 1·477; (c) 3·301; (e) $-0·398$; (g) 0·827. **9.** (a) 1, 2; (c) $b = a^2$;
(e) a; (g) -4.

Ex. F **1.** (a) 2·4972; (c) $\bar{1}$·4972. **2.** (a) 271·8; (c) 271 800.
3. (a) 0·2337; (c) $\bar{1}$·9594; (e) $\bar{1}$·7456. **4.** (a) 4038; (c) 0·001 387.
5. (a) 0·2576; (c) $\bar{2}$·8213; $\bar{1}$·0238.
6. (a) 4·4019, 0·4891; (c) $\bar{6}$·5298, $\bar{1}$·3922; (e) $\overline{10}$·4303, $\bar{2}$·9367.
7. (a) 1·0828; (c) $\bar{1}$·6020; (e) 2·6848; (g) 0·6712; (i) 2·7126.

Ex. G **1.** 39·6. **3.** 0·001 18. **5.** 0·949. **7.** 7900.
9. $3·01 \times 10^{14}$. **11.** 19·0. **13.** $4·08 \times 10^{-9}$. **15.** $2·53 \times 10^4$.
17. $9·46 \times 10^{12}$ km. **19.** 4·79.

Ex. H **1.** (a) 4·5; (c) 1·08; (e) 2·10. **2.** (a) 1·65; (c) 0·0996; (e) 0·578.
3. $1·99 = \log_9 80 > \log_4 7 > \log_6 7 > \log_{10} 9 > \log_3 2 = 0·631$. **9.** 13·1.
11. $b = 2$, $k = 1·5$; 8·5, 96.

Ex. I **1.** $z \propto d^3$.

Misc. **1.** (i) 0; (ii) 1; (iii) not defined. **3.** Stretch $\times \frac{1}{3}$ in x-direction or
translation of log 3 in y-direction; translation of 3 in x-direction; stretch $\times 3$ in
y-direction. **4.** (a) $1·29 \times 10^8$; (c) $4·76 \times 10^{-5}$; (e) 57·2.
5. $\log_3 10 \times \log_{10} 3 = 1$.
9. (a) Use $\log 3 = \log 2 + \log 1·5$ etc.; (b) $\sqrt{2} = 1·41$, $\sqrt{6} = 2·45$.

CHAPTER 9

Ex. B **1.** (a) $2+3+4 = 9$; (c) $1+4+9+16 = 30$; (e) $2+4+8+16 = 30$;
(g) $-1+8-27+64 = 44$.

3. (a) $(2+3)+(4+3)+(8+3)+(16+3)$; (b) $u_1 = 5$, $u_{k+1} = 2u_k - 3$.

4. (a) 86; (c) 86; (e) 37.   **5.** (a) $\sum_0^5 (7+5i)$; (c) $\sum_1^6 \frac{1}{i}$; (e) $\sum_1^4 \frac{i}{i+1}$.

Ex. C 1. (a) $\sum_0^9 (i+1)(i+3)$, $\sum_0^{10} i(i+2)$; $\sum_1^{10} i(i+2)$; (c) $\sum_0^5 64(\tfrac{3}{4})^i$, $\sum_1^6 64(\tfrac{3}{4})^{i-1}$;

(e) $\sum_0^n (-1)^i x^i$, $\sum_1^{n+1} (-1)^{i-1} x^{i-1}$; (g) $\sum_0^{n-p+1} ar^{p+i-1}$, $\sum_1^{n-p+2} ar^{p+i-2}$.

2. (a) $\sum_0^{20} (1+3i)$; (c) $\sum_0^4 2\times3^i$.   **5.** 1, 3, 6, 10, 15, 21, 28, 36, 45, 55, 66.

1, $1\frac{1}{2}$, 2, $2\frac{1}{2}$, 3, $3\frac{1}{2}$, 4, $4\frac{1}{2}$, 5, $5\frac{1}{2}$, 6. $s_n/n = \frac{1}{2}(n+1)$, $s_n = \frac{1}{2}n(n+1)$.

7. 27; $\sum_1^{27} (10+3i)$; $u_{14} = 52$; $s = 1404$.

9. Both sums are $11+19+27+35$; $\sum_6^9 (8i-37)$; $\sum_{-2}^1 (8i+27)$.

10. (a) T; (c) F; (e) T; (g) T; (i) T.   **11.** (a) 4; (c) 43; (e) 37, $e = d - 3c$.
13. (a) 54; (b) $61\frac{1}{2}$; (c) 11·985.

Ex. D 1. (a) 575; (b) 477.   **3.** (a) 195; (c) $nr + \frac{3}{2}n(n+1)$.

5. (a) $\sum_1^{32} (-2+3i)$, 1520; (c) $\sum_1^{39} (10+2i)$, 1950.

8. (a) $\sum_1^7 (i^2+3)$; (c) $\sum_1^n (i+1)^2$; (e) $6^2 = 36$.

9. (b) $u_n = 3n^2 - 3n + 1$; $\sum_1^n i^2 = \frac{1}{6}n(n+1)(2n+1)$.

Ex. E 1. (a) 385; (c) 1938; (e) $\frac{1}{6}n(2n^2+15n+37)$.
3. (a) 2124; (c) $n(n+1)(n^2-3n-2) = -24 = -8-16$ when $n = 2$.
5. $a = 1, b = -3, c = 1$.   **7.** $a = 1, b = 9, c = 6$; $\frac{1}{4}n(n+1)(n+3)(n+14)$.
9. $\frac{1}{4}(i-2)(i-1)i(i+1)$.

Ex. F 2. (a) $7(2^{10}-1)$; (c) $1+2^{19}$.   **3.** 12.   **5.** £529; £7 less.
7. £2950.   **9.** (a) $s_n = \frac{2}{3}(1-(-\frac{1}{2})^n) \to \frac{2}{3}$ as $n \to \infty$;
(b) $s_n = \frac{3}{2}(1-(\frac{2}{3})^n) \to \frac{3}{2}$ as $n \to \infty$.   **11.** $\frac{23}{99}(1-(0·01)^n)$; $\frac{23}{99}$.

Misc. 1. (a) 100; (b) 0; (c) 5740.   **3.** (a) 100; (c) 90; (e) 21.

5. $\sum_{p=1}^3 (a_{2p}b_{p3})$, $\sum_{p=1}^3 (a_{ip}b_{pj})$.   **7.** $a^2hn + ah^2(n-1)n + \frac{1}{6}h^3(n-1)n(2n-1)$, where
$hn = b-a$. Limit $= \frac{1}{3}(b^3-a^3) = $ area under the graph of g from $x = a$ to $x = b$.
9. $[\sin(n+\frac{1}{2})h - \sin\frac{1}{2}h]/(2\sin\frac{1}{2}h)$; $[\cos\frac{1}{2}h - \cos(n+\frac{1}{2})h]/(2\sin\frac{1}{2}h)$.   **11.** £429.
13. $(n+1)^3 - 1$.   **15.** $s - s_5 = 0·0625$; $s - s_{15} = 0·000061$.

CHAPTER 10

Ex. A 1. $d \approx 750$ m.   **3.** $v \approx 300$ m/s.   **5.** (a) Distance travelled;
(b) $200+$; (c) 232; (d) 280, 184; (e) the averages are 192, 224, 234; (g) 234.

Ex. C 1. $32(1+1/n)$.   **3.** 55, 91.   **5.** 66·7, 77·5; 68·4, 75·6.

Ex. D 1. (a) $16(1+1/n)$, $16(1-1/n)$; (b) $\frac{32}{3}(1+1/n)(2+1/n)$,
$\frac{32}{3}(1-1/n)(2-1/n)$.   **3.** $\frac{1}{4}b^4(1+1/n)^2$, $\frac{1}{4}b^4(1-1/n)^2$. Limit $= \frac{1}{4}b^4$.
5. (a) 63, 126; (b) 76, 107; (c) $63h/(2^h-1)$, $63h \times 2^h/(2^h-1)$.

Ex. E 1. (a) $\frac{1}{2}$; (b) $4\frac{1}{2}$; (c) $4 = \int_{1}^{3} x\,dx.$ **3.** $\int_{a}^{b} x^2\,dx = \frac{1}{3}b^3 - \frac{1}{3}a^3.$

Ex. F 1. (a) $3\frac{1}{2}$; (c) 3; (e) 7; (g) $\frac{1}{3}b^3 - \frac{1}{3}.$ **3.** $63 + 1664 = 1727.$
7. (a) 60 m; (b) 40 m.

Ex. G 1. $x \to \frac{1}{3}x^3 + k$, where $k = \frac{1}{3}, 0, -\frac{8}{3}, -\frac{125}{3}.$ **2.** (a) 6; (c) 1.
3. (a) 260; (c) $65\frac{1}{3}.$ **4.** (i) (a) $5x^4$; (c) $2x^7$; (e) $\cos x - \sin x.$ (ii) (a) $x \to x^5$;
(c) $x \to \frac{1}{8}x^8$; (e) $x \to \sin x + \cos x.$
5. (a) $x \to \frac{1}{6}x^6$; (c) $x \to \frac{1}{4}px^4 + \frac{1}{3}qx^3 + \frac{1}{2}rx^2 + sx$; (e) $x \to -\cos x.$
6. (a) $L = 0, F(2) = 10$; (c) $L = 1, F(2) = \frac{1}{2}.$
7. (a) 74; (c) $\frac{1}{2}$; (e) $\frac{3}{4}$; (g) $11\frac{1}{4}.$ **9.** $20/\pi$ m^2; $2000/\pi$ m^3.

Ex. H 1. (a) $\frac{2}{3}x^{\frac{3}{2}} + k$; (c) $\frac{1}{3}ax^3 + \frac{1}{2}bx^2 + cx + k.$
3. $f(x) = 2x^3 - 18x + k$, for any $k.$ **5.** $3\cdot47$ m/s; $3\cdot50$ m/s.
7. (a) $-5\frac{1}{2}$; (b) $-\frac{1}{6}.$

Ex. I 1. (a) $-\frac{1}{4}$; (c) 0; (e) $2\frac{1}{2}$; (g) $-6\frac{2}{3}.$ **3.** (a) $I_1 = -I_2$; (b) $I_3 = I_4.$
4. (a) $\frac{3}{2}(a^{\frac{2}{3}} - 1)$, no limit; (c) $\frac{3}{4}(a^{\frac{4}{3}} - 1)$, no limit; (e) $\frac{3}{7}(a^{\frac{7}{3}} - 1)$, no limit.
5. (a) Limit $= \frac{3}{2}$; (c) $\frac{3}{4}$; (e) $\frac{3}{7}.$

Misc. 1. (a) Both 39; (b) $\frac{3}{40}, \frac{14}{3}.$ **5.** (a) $-4\frac{1}{2}$; (c) $57\frac{1}{6}$; (e) 108.
7. (a) $0\cdot693$; (b) $1\cdot57$; (c) $1\cdot26.$

REVISION EXERCISES

Rev. 6 1. (a) $1/\sqrt{2}, -\sqrt{3}/2, -1, -\sqrt{3}/2, -1/\sqrt{3}$; (b) $-0\cdot259$;
(c) $\sin x, -\sin x, \cos x, \cos x.$ **3.** (a) $5\cos 5x$; (c) $-2\sin 2x$; (e) $6\cos x.$
5. (b) $0\cdot362$; (c) $0\cdot00738.$ **7.** $\frac{2}{3}, \frac{3}{4}, \frac{1}{12}(2\sqrt{7} + 3\sqrt{5}), \frac{1}{12}(\sqrt{35} - 6)$; greater.

Rev. 7 1. (a) $12\mathbf{i} + 8\mathbf{j}, 10\mathbf{i} - 4\mathbf{j}$; (b) $-2\mathbf{i} - 12\mathbf{j}$; (c) $-2\mathbf{i} - 8\mathbf{j}$;
(d) $14\mathbf{i} + 9\cdot8\mathbf{j}, 14\mathbf{i}, -9\cdot8\mathbf{j}, -9\cdot8\mathbf{j}.$
3. (a) $\sqrt{2}, 45°$ to horizontal; 2, vertically downwards; (b) $t = 1$, (c) $t = 1\frac{1}{2}$;
(d) yes. **5.** (a) never; $\pi + 2n\pi$; $\frac{1}{2}\pi + 2n\pi$; $\frac{3}{2}\pi + 2n\pi.$ **7.** 89 rad/s; 2000 m/s$^2.$

Rev. 8 1. (a) x^{11}; (b) x^8; (c) $1/x.$ **2.** (a) 4; (c) 32; (e) 100.
3. (a) $x^{-\frac{1}{2}}$; (c) $x^{\frac{4}{5}}$; (e) $\frac{1}{18}xy^{\frac{1}{2}}.$
5. (i) $\frac{1}{4}, \frac{1}{2}, 2, 8, 16$; (ii) $\frac{1}{9}, \frac{1}{3}, 3, 27, 81$; (iii) $25, 5, \frac{1}{5}, \frac{1}{125}, \frac{1}{625}.$
6. (a) $3\cdot303$; (c) 3; (e) $7\cdot409$; (g) $-2\cdot303.$ **7.** (a) 3; (c) $1\cdot16.$
9. (i) $y = bx^c$; (ii) $y = b10^{cx}$; (iii) $y^2 = 10^z$; $1\cdot92$; $70\cdot8.$
10. (a) $84\cdot4$; (c) $0\cdot952.$ **11.** (a) $3\cdot74$; (c) $5\cdot44.$
12. (a) $0\cdot632$; (c) $3\cdot62.$ **13.** (a) $4\cdot62 \times 10^8$; (c) $1\cdot91 \times 10^5.$
14. (a) $4\cdot43 \times 10^{-5}$; (c) $0\cdot360.$ **15.** (a) $11\cdot2$; (c) $1\cdot73.$

Rev. 9 1. Outputs are 147 and 39364.
3. (a) $\sum_{1}^{25}(15 + 5i)$; (c) $\sum_{0}^{14} 1\cdot1^i$; (e) $\sum_{1}^{20} i \times 3^i.$ **5.** (a) 45; (c) 30.
6. (a) $1 + 3\sum_{2}^{n} i$; (c) n^2; (e) $-\sum_{1}^{n}(2i - 1).$ **7.** (a) T; (c) F; (e) T.
8. (a) 75, 570; (c) $2^{-17}, \frac{8}{3}(1 - (\frac{1}{4})^{20}).$
9. (a) $7 + 5n, \frac{1}{2}n(19 + 5n)$; (c) (i) $74\cdot2, 116\cdot4, 158\cdot6, 200\cdot8$; (ii) 48, 72, 108, 162.

Rev. 10 1. $2\cdot75$ km. **3.** (a) $13\cdot5, 15\cdot3$; (b) $0, 5\frac{1}{3}$; (c) $-2\frac{17}{54}, 2\frac{17}{54}.$
4. (a) $x \to \frac{1}{4}x^4 + 3x^2 - 7x + k$; (c) $x \to 3\sin x - \cos x + k$; (e) $x \to \frac{2}{3}x^{\frac{3}{2}} + \frac{1}{2}x^{-2} + k.$
5. (a) $\frac{1}{3}$; (c) $1\frac{29}{32}.$ **7.** $t = \pm1$; decreasing; 8 m. **9.** $13\frac{1}{2}.$

CHAPTER 11

Ex. A **1.** (a) 12·0, 12·5, 13·1 %; (b) 22·6, 23·6, 23·7 %.

Ex. B **1.** (a) 30; (b) 38; (c) 4.   **5.** $d = 203$, the median.
7. (a) 392; (b) 340.   **9.** 191, 26·7, 26·7.

Ex. C **1.** 6 for the first process, 3 for the second.   **3.** Mean $= 29\frac{1}{2}$ mm.

Ex D **3.** (a) 103·3 g; (c) 200 g.   **5.** £19·10. An increase of about 90p per day.   **7.** 430.

Ex. E **7.** 149·5 s for A, 149 s for B.

Ex. F **1.** $m = 6$, $s = 2·45$.
3.

	Mean	S.D.	(a)	(b)
(i)	4	1·22	66	97
(iii)	4·4	1·56	62	96
(v)	3·75	1·58	61	97

Ex. G **3.** (a) $m = 27$, $s = 5·85$; (b) $m = 26·6$, $s = 5·91$.   **5.** 440 g.

Ex. H **3.** (a) 27·0, 5·86; (b) 26·6, 5·91.

Ex. I **1.** $k = -2\frac{2}{9}$; a and b are 2 and 5.
3. (b) 190, 180 cm; (c) 1025; (d) $a = 39$, corresponding to a height of 161 cm.

Misc. **3.** 22·4 g.

CHAPTER 12

Ex. A **5.** $4(\mathbf{i}+\mathbf{j})$, $12(\mathbf{i}+\mathbf{j})$, $-2(\mathbf{i}+\mathbf{j})$.

Ex. B **1.** (a) 0·1 m/s²; (b) 1 m/s².   **3.** (a) 400 N; (b) 350 N; (c) 0.
5. (a) **0, 0, 0**; (c) **0**, $30(\mathbf{i}+\mathbf{j})$, $15(\mathbf{i}+\mathbf{j})$.   **7.** 10·4 N.

Ex. C **1.** (i) 100 N; (ii) N 36·9° E (or W), N 53·1° W (or E).   **3.** 2 kg.
5. (a) 3·21 N; (b) 53·5° from **v**; (c) 8·07 N, 85°.
7. $4\mathbf{i}$, $-3\mathbf{i}+5·2\mathbf{j}$, $-0·87\mathbf{i}-0·5\mathbf{j}$; $0·13\mathbf{i}+4·70\mathbf{j}$, $0·013\mathbf{i}-0·470\mathbf{j}$.
9. $(\frac{1}{2}v^2 - 1000\cos 80°)$ N; 31·6 m/s; 867 N.

Ex. D **1.** 98 N. (a) 8·9 m/s²; (b) 4·4 m/s²; (c) 2·5 m/s².
3. 13 900 N; 1420 kg.   **7.** (a) 0·0139 m/s²; (b) 1 N.
9. 8·5 m/s².   **11.** 1·2 m/s².   **13.** $M^{-1}L^3T^{-2}$.
15. (a) FA^{-1}; (b) V^2A^{-1}; (c) VA^{-1}; (d) $FV^{-6}A^2$; (e) $FV^{-4}A^2$.
17. $(2V\sin\theta)/g$; $(V^2\sin 2\theta)/g$.

Ex. E **13.** 5 m/s².   **15.** 0·8 m/s²; 4·8 N, 2·2 m/s.
17. 0·38 m/s².   **19.** 5074 N; 5079 N.   **21.** 1·73 m/s².   **23.** 1·1 m/s².
25. 130 m/s; 33 800 N.

Ex. F **1.** 4·6 m/s²; 25 N.
3. (a) 12·2 N, 10·4° to OA; (b) 5·12 N, 15·1°; (c) 15·2 N, 218·5°.
5. (a) 1·4 N, 0·2 m/s²; (b) 23·4 N, 2·9 m/s²; (c) 31·4 N, 3·9 m/s².
7. (a) 92·1 N, 33·5 N; (b) 0·075 m/s²; (c) 92·8 N; (d) $98-87·2$ N, 31·7 N.

Ex G 1. 7·04 s.
3. $v = u-4+4\cos 2t$, $x = (u-4)t+2\sin 2t$; $u > 8$ or $u < 0$; $t = 0·64$.
5. 19·5 m/s at 48·8° below horizontal; 38·6 m, 1·4° above horizontal.
7. 5·6 km.   **9.** $(a, 2a)$.   **11.** 6×10^{-9} s; 2×10^6 m/s; $0·024\mathbf{i} - 0·016\mathbf{j}$.

Misc. **1.** (i) $9·1 \times 10^5$ N; (ii) $4·4 \times 10^5$ N; (iii) $2·8 \times 10^4$ N.
3. (a) 25·6 N, 13·6 N.   **5.** (ii) (a) 766 N, 643 N; (b) 500 N, 866 N.
7. 2·80 N at 26·6° to the radius.   **9.** (i) $W\sqrt{3}$; (ii) 30°; (iii) 75°.

CHAPTER 13

Ex. A 1. (a) $2(x-1)$; (c) $3(x-3)^2$; (e) $4x(x^2+3)$.
2. (a) $-1/(x+3)^2$; (c) $-2x/(x^2+1)^2$.   **3.** $f'(t) = \sin 2t$.
5. (a) $x \to 6(2x-1)^2$; (c) $x \to -2/(x+3)^3$; (e) $x \to 4\cos 4x$.

Ex. B 1. (a) $x \to 12(3x+4)^3$; (c) $x \to 2\sin x \cos x$; (e) $x \to -\tfrac{1}{2}\sin x(1+\cos x)^{-\frac{1}{2}}$.
3. a; $9/a^2$; a; $27/a^3$.

Ex. C 1. (a) $8(2a+3)^3$; (c) $-2/(2a+1)^2$; (e) $-(3-2a)^{-\frac{1}{2}}$; (g) $4\cos 4a$.
2. (a) $3(2x-2)(x^2-2x+4)^2$; (c) $-2x(1+x^2)^{-2}$; (e) $2x/(1-x^2)^2$;
(g) $-6\cos 3x \sin 3x$; (i) $3(\cos x - \sin x)(\cos x + \sin x)^2$.   **3.** $\tfrac{5}{12}$.
5. (a) $\sec x \tan x$; (b) $2\sec^2 x \tan x$; (c) $\sec^2 x \tan x/\sqrt{(\sec^2 x - 1)} = \pm \sec^2 x$.

Ex. D 1. (a) $9(3x+5)^2$; (c) $-\tfrac{1}{2}(1-x)^{-\frac{1}{2}}$; (e) $-3/(3x-2)^2$; (g) $24/(6-4x)^3$.
2. (a) $4\left(1+\dfrac{1}{x^2}\right)\left(x-\dfrac{1}{x}\right)^3$; (c) $x^2(x^3-1)^{-\frac{2}{3}}$.

3. $(0, 1)$, $(\tfrac{1}{2}\pi, 0)$, $(\pi, 1)$, $(\tfrac{3}{2}\pi, 0)$, etc.   **5.** 32π cm³/s.
7. No, since $dh/dt \propto h^{-2}$.   **9.** $h = \sqrt{(169-x^2)}$; $\tfrac{1}{6}$ m/s.

Ex. E 1. (a) $6(2x-1)^2$; (c) $60x^4(3x^5-4)^3$; (e) $-2x/(1+x^2)^2$;
(g) $-\cos x/(\sin^2 x)$. (a') $\tfrac{1}{6}(2x-1)^3+k$; (c') $\tfrac{1}{60}(3x^5-4)^4+k$;
(e') $-\tfrac{1}{2}/(1+x^2)+k$; (g') $1/\cos x+k$.
2. (a) $\displaystyle\int 60x(3x^2+1)^9\,dx = (3x^2+1)^{10}+k$; (c) $\displaystyle\int \frac{1}{x^2}\cos\frac{1}{x}\,dx = -\sin\frac{1}{x}+k$;

(e) $\displaystyle\int \cos x/\sqrt{\sin x}\,dx = 2\sqrt{\sin x}+k$.

3. (a) $\tfrac{1}{2}(x^3+2)^2+k$; (c) $\tfrac{3}{4}\sin^4 x+k$; (e) $-\tfrac{1}{2}/\sin^2 x+k$; (g) $\tfrac{1}{2}/(1-x^2)+k$.
5. (a) 3; (b) 0; (c) 34.   **6.** (a) $\tfrac{1}{15}(3x+5)^5+k$; (c) $\tfrac{1}{10}(1-5x)^{-2}+k$.
7. (a) $\tfrac{1}{3}\sin(x^3)+k$; (c) $\tfrac{1}{5}x^5+\tfrac{3}{2}x^4+4x^3+4x^2+k$; (e) $\tfrac{1}{3}\sqrt{(6x-5)}+k$.
8. (a) 4; (c) $20\tfrac{1}{3}$; (e) $\tfrac{15}{16}$; (g) 1·65.

Ex. F 1. $2\tfrac{1}{8}$.   **3.** $u = \tfrac{2}{3}x$; 6π; πab.   **5.** $u = 4-3x$; 1, 7, $\tfrac{1}{3}$; $\tfrac{6}{49}$.
6. (a) 0·16; (c) 0·49.

7. (a) $\displaystyle\int_1^2 (x-1)/x\,dx = 0·307$; (c) $\displaystyle\int_2^4 (u-2)/u\,du = 0·614$;

(e) $\displaystyle\int_0^1 (1-u)/(2-u)\,du = 0·307$.

Ex. G 1. (a) $\tfrac{1}{5}(x+4)^5-(x+4)^4+k$; (c) $-\tfrac{1}{8}(5-x^2)^4+k$;
(e) $-2\cos\sqrt{x}+k$; (g) $1/\cos x+k$.

Ex. H **1.** (a) $\frac{2}{45}(1+3x)^{\frac{5}{2}}-\frac{2}{27}(1+3x)^{\frac{3}{2}}+k$; (c) $\frac{1}{36}(4-3x)^4-\frac{7}{27}(4-3x)^3+k$;
(e) $\frac{4}{3}(x^3-2)^{\frac{3}{2}}+k$. **2.** (a) $\frac{1}{24}(5-2x)^6-\frac{11}{20}(5-2x)^5+k$; (c) $\frac{3}{16}(2x^2-1)^{\frac{4}{3}}+k$;
(e) $-\frac{1}{2}(b\cos x-a\sin x)^2+k$. **3.** $(a)\frac{3}{16}$; $(c)\frac{1}{90}$. **4.** $(a)\,4\frac{1}{3}$; $(c)\,0.35$; $(e)\frac{1}{6}$.
5. $\frac{1}{2}\sin^2 x+k$; $-\frac{1}{2}\cos^2 x+c$. **6.** $(a)\frac{1}{6}(2x+1)^{\frac{5}{2}}+\frac{5}{2}(2x+1)^{\frac{1}{2}}+k$; (c)—; (e)—.
7. $(a)\,\frac{16}{7}$; $(c)\,\frac{32}{15}$; (e) 0; $(g)\,(2\sqrt 2)/3$.

Ex. I **1.** $(a)\frac{1}{5}(x+1)^5-\frac{1}{4}(x+1)^4+k$; $(c)\frac{2}{5}(x+2)^{\frac{5}{2}}-\frac{2}{3}(x+2)^{\frac{3}{2}}+k$.
2. (a) 0.93; (c) 0.52. **3.** 0.17. **4.** $(a)\frac{1}{4}\pi$; (c) 0.66.
5. $(a)\frac{1}{6}\pi$; $(c)\,0.045$; $(e)\pi$. **7.** 0.58; $(a)\,0.68$; $(b)\,1.05$. **9.** (a) No; (c) no.

Misc. **1.** $(-1, 1)$ and $(-1, -1)$. **3.** (a) $\mathbf v = -a\sin 2t\mathbf i+a\sin 2t\mathbf j$; $\frac{3}{4}\pi$ or
$-\frac{1}{4}\pi$ radians from Ox; (b) $\mathbf v = -3a\sin t\cos^2 t\mathbf i+3a\sin^2 t\cos t\mathbf j$; $\pi-t$ radians
from Ox when $0 < t < \frac{1}{2}\pi$, $-t$ radians when $\frac{1}{2}\pi < t < \pi$, etc.
5. $\mathbf v = (1-\cos t)\mathbf i+2\sin t\mathbf j$, $\mathbf a = \sin t\mathbf i+2\cos t\mathbf j$; $(0.97, 2.67)$, $(5.32, 2.67)$.
9. (a) $-8\sin 8x$; (c) $p/\sqrt{(p^2+2)}$; (e) x/y. **11.** 0; 4π.

CHAPTER 14

Ex. A **1.** $\mathbf a+\mathbf b$, $\mathbf b+\mathbf c$, $\mathbf a+\mathbf b+\mathbf c$, $\mathbf a+\mathbf c$; $\frac{1}{2}\mathbf a$, $\frac{1}{2}(\mathbf a+\mathbf b)$, $\frac{1}{2}(\mathbf b+\mathbf c)$, $\mathbf a+\frac{1}{2}\mathbf b$,
$\mathbf c+\frac{1}{2}(\mathbf a+\mathbf b)$, $\mathbf c+\frac{1}{2}(\mathbf a+\mathbf b)$. **3.** $\mathbf r = \lambda\mathbf a$.
5. $\mathbf r = \lambda(\mathbf a+\mathbf b)$, $\mathbf r = \mathbf b+\lambda\mathbf c$, $\mathbf r = \mathbf a+\lambda(\mathbf c-\mathbf a)$.
7. $\mathbf r = \lambda\mathbf b+\mu\mathbf c$, $\mathbf r = \mathbf a+\lambda\mathbf b+\mu\mathbf c$.

Ex. B **1.** (a) Parallel; (b) (v) and (vii); (c) $\lambda = 3$ and $\lambda = -1$, $\lambda+4\mu = 1$
and $2\lambda+8\mu = 21$.
3. (i) $\mathbf r = 5\mathbf a+4\lambda\mathbf b$; (ii) $\mathbf r = 5\mathbf a+\lambda(2\mathbf a+\mathbf b)$; (iii) $\mathbf r = 5\mathbf a+\lambda(\mathbf a+\mathbf b)$.
7. (ii) Midpoint of AB; on BA produced so that $\mathbf{BA} = \mathbf{AQ}$.

Ex. C **1.** $\frac{3}{5}\mathbf c+\frac{2}{5}\mathbf d$. **3.** $\frac{1}{2}, \frac{3}{4}, 2, -\frac{3}{2}$; $\mathbf p = \frac{1}{2}\mathbf a+\frac{1}{2}\mathbf b$, $\mathbf q = \frac{1}{4}\mathbf a+\frac{3}{4}\mathbf b$, $\mathbf r = -\mathbf a+2\mathbf b$,
$\mathbf s = \frac{5}{2}\mathbf a-\frac{3}{2}\mathbf b$. **5.** E and G coincide. **7.** $\mathbf l = \frac{2}{3}\mathbf b+\frac{1}{3}\mathbf c$, $\mathbf m = \frac{2}{3}\mathbf a+\frac{1}{3}\mathbf c$,
$\mathbf n = \frac{1}{2}\mathbf a+\frac{1}{6}\mathbf b+\frac{1}{3}\mathbf c$, $\mathbf p = \frac{1}{3}\mathbf a+\frac{1}{2}\mathbf b+\frac{1}{6}\mathbf c$. **11.** $\lambda+\mu+\nu = 0$, with λ, μ, ν not
all zero.

Ex. D **3.** $\frac{1}{4}(\mathbf a+\mathbf b+\mathbf c+\mathbf d)$. **7.** $\mathbf x = (\mathbf b+\lambda\mathbf c)/(1+\lambda)$, $\mathbf y = (\mathbf c+\mu\mathbf a)/(1+\mu)$,
$\mathbf z = (\mathbf a+\nu\mathbf b)/(1+\nu)$.

Ex. E **1.** (a) $\mathbf{BC}-\mathbf{AB}$; (b) $\mathbf{AC}-2\mathbf{AB}$. No. **3.** Not necessarily.
6. (i) $ADFG$; (iii) a line parallel to OC through a point on OD produced;
(v) DEG.

Ex. F **1.** (i) $\mathbf r = (2\mathbf a-\mathbf b)+\lambda(-2\mathbf b)$; (iii) $\mathbf r = (\mathbf a-2\mathbf b)+\lambda(\mathbf a+3\mathbf b)$;
(v) $\mathbf r = \lambda(\mathbf a+2\mathbf b)$. **3.** All the lines coincide. **5.** $\frac{10}{7}\mathbf a+\frac{6}{7}\mathbf c$.
7. (i) $\mathbf r = -\mathbf a+\mu(\mathbf a+\mathbf b)+\nu\mathbf c$; (iii) $\mathbf r = \mathbf a+\mu(\mathbf b-\mathbf a)+\nu(\mathbf c-4\mathbf a)$.
9. (i) AF; (iii) AC; (v) $ADEC$; (vii) $\mathbf r = \mathbf b+\mathbf c+\lambda\mathbf a$; (ix) $\mathbf r = \mathbf a+\lambda(\mathbf b+\mathbf c-\mathbf a)$;
(xi) $\mathbf r = \mathbf c+\lambda\mathbf a+\mu\mathbf b$. **11.** Not parallel. **13.** $\mathbf r = \mathbf a+t\mathbf c$.

Ex. G **1.** (i) $(8, 2)$; (ii) $(4, 3\frac{1}{2}, 5\frac{1}{2})$. **3.** $\mathbf c = -\frac{13}{7}\mathbf a+2\mathbf b$.
7. (i) $(-5, 19, 0)$, $(\frac{1}{2}, -\frac{1}{2}, 0)$; (ii) $(0, 9, 5)$, $(0, -1, 1)$; (iii) $(7\frac{1}{2}, -6, 12\frac{1}{2})$,
$(\frac{1}{2}, -\frac{1}{2}, 0)$. **9.** $\mathbf r = (\mathbf i+5\mathbf j)+\lambda\mathbf j+\mu(\mathbf k+\mathbf j)$.

Misc. **1.** $(2, 3, 4)$. **3.** No. **5.** $\mathbf g = \frac{1}{3}\mathbf h$; O, G, H are collinear, with
$OG = \frac{1}{3}OH$; H is $(2, 3)$.

REVISION EXERCISES

Rev. 11   **1.** $3\sqrt{2}$; $30\sqrt{2}$.   **3.** $(4A)$ 51·7, 4·73; $(4C)$ 55·1, 3·24; (Total) 54·8, 5·03.   **5.** 49·8, 19·6.   **7.** 91·9, 4·52; 18 days. £33.

Rev. 12   **1.** $5\cdot4\times10^{-9}$ N.   **3.** 287 N.   **5.** 70 N.   **7.** 3040 N.
9. $v = \frac{3}{10}t^2\mathbf{i} + \frac{1}{10}(t^2+3t)\mathbf{j}$, $\mathbf{r} = \frac{1}{10}t^3\mathbf{i} + (\frac{1}{30}t^3 + \frac{3}{20}t^2)\mathbf{j}$.

Rev. 13   **1.** (a) $18(2x+5)^8$; (c) $-(3-2x)^{-\frac{1}{2}}$; (e) $3\sin 3x$;
(g) $-(4x+5)(2x^2+5x+1)^{-2}$.   **2.** (a) $(0, 5)$, max; (c) no max or min.
3. 3·54 m/s.   **5.** $x = \sqrt{(l^2-4)}$; $dx/dt = (l/\sqrt{(l^2-4)})\,dl/dt$.   0·51 m/s.
7. (a) $-\frac{1}{4}(a-x^2)^4 + k$; (c) $-\frac{2}{9}(1-x^3)^{\frac{3}{2}} + k$; (e) $\frac{1}{6}\sin^6 x + k$; (g) $\sin^2(x^2) + k$.
8. (a) 17·1; (c) 33·8.   **9.** (a) 1·91; (c) 0·73.
10. (a) $-\frac{5}{2}(x^2+1)^{-1} + k$; (c) $\frac{2}{75}(5x+1)^{\frac{3}{2}} - \frac{2}{25}(5x+1)^{\frac{1}{2}} + k$;
(e) $-\frac{1}{10}(1+\sin 5x)^{-2} + k$.

Rev. 14   **1.** $\mathbf{a}+2\mathbf{b}$, $2\mathbf{a}+\mathbf{b}$, $\mathbf{a}-\mathbf{b}$, $-2\mathbf{b}$, $2\frac{1}{2}\mathbf{a}-\frac{1}{2}\mathbf{b}$.
3. (i) Bisector of angle between $\mathbf{a}$ and $\mathbf{b}$;   (ii) bisector of exterior angle.
7. Yes; $2\mathbf{a}+\mathbf{b}-\mathbf{d} = 0$.   **9.** $\mathbf{r} = \mathbf{i}+\lambda(\mathbf{j}-\mathbf{i})+\mu(\mathbf{k}-\mathbf{i})$; $1:2$;
$\mathbf{r} = 2\mathbf{i}+\lambda(\mathbf{j}-\mathbf{i})+\mu(\mathbf{k}-\mathbf{i})$; $1/\sqrt{3}$.

INDEX

acceleration, 100, 105–7, 146–9, 151–7, 273–81
  angular, 155
  average, 146, 147, 148
  instantaneous, 147
addition
  of algebraic fractions, 83
  of polynomials, 68
addition formulae, 132, 135
affine geometry, 345
algebraic factors, testing for, 75
algebraic fractions, 65, 81–4
  applications to functions, 83
algebraic models, 24, 26, 267, 283
angular acceleration, 155
angular velocity, 153–5
arc length, 129
Archimedes, 207
area of sector, 129
  on histogram, 258–9
  transformation of, 312
  under graph, 200–10, 219, 221–2
  with variable scale factor, transformation of, 323
arithmetic progression, 7–8, 12, 18
  sum of, 189, 199
asymptote, 39, 46
  parallel to y-axis, 47
average scale factors, 89–101
  for general function, 90

bilinear functions, 358
Brahe, Tycho, 279

centroid, 335, 336, 337
chain rule, 303–10, 321
  alternative statement of, 305
  application to rates of change, 307
  deductions from, 315
  for differentiation of composite function, 326
  integration by, 310
  reversal, 312, 315, 320
change, rates of, 88, 120, 125
characteristic of logarithm, 169
Chebyshev, 260
circle, motion in, 153–5, 158
circular functions, 119–36, 304
  connection between, 135
  derived functions, 131–2

circular measure, 136
codomain, 26, 27, 32, 35, 37
components, 287–90
composite functions, 28, 38, 298–303
  differentiation of, 299–303
  integrals of, 312
  mapping diagrams, 29–30, 300
compound interest, 12, 173
computer conventions, 66
computers, 3–9
  sequence generation, 3
  stores, 3, 4

data lists, 7–9
definite integrals, 208–11, 216–18, 315, 327
  substitution in, 318
derivatives, 92, 120, 135, 162, 181
  alternative form, 98, 130
  graphical method, 120
  notation, 101–2, 111
  numerical method, 120
  of b^x and $\log_b x$, 359
  second, 105–8, 111
derived functions, 95–7, 98, 103, 111, 120, 162, 212, 301, 302, 305
  circular functions, 131–2
  graphical method, 120
  numerical method, 120
  trigonometric, 120, 121
detached coefficients, method of, 69
difference method, 191, 193, 195
differentiation, 119, 212
  definition, 97
  from first principles, 98, 130
  of composite functions, 299–303:
    chain rule for, 326
discontinuity, 40, 47–8
displacement, 100, 101, 144, 212
displacement diagram, 292
displacement – time graphs, 100, 105
displacement vector, 138, 140
division, of algebraic fractions, 82
  of polynomials, 75–8
domain, 26, 27, 32, 35, 36, 37, 45
'dot' notation, 148
dry runs, 4

equations, solution where unknown is index, 174

377